GRUNGE IS DEAD

THE ORAL HISTORY OF SEATTLE ROCK MUSIC

Published by ECW Press, 665 Gerrard Street East
Toronto, Ontario, Canada M4M 1Y2
416.694.3348 / info@ecwpress.com

LIBRARY AND ARCHIVES CANADA CATALOGUING IN PUBLICATION

Prato, Greg
Grunge is dead : the oral history of Seattle rock music / Greg Prato.

ISBN 978-1-55022-877-9
ALSO ISSUED AS:
978-1-55490-877-6 (PDF); 978-1-55490-347-4 (EPUB)

1. Grunge groups—Washington (State)—Seattle. 2. Grunge music.
3. Rock musicians—Interviews. I. Title.

ML3534.3.P912 2009 782.42166097977 2 C2008-907553-6

Editor for the press: Michael Holmes
Cover design: Bill Douglas at The Bang
Type: Melissa Kaita
Photo section: Rachel Ironstone

CONTENTS

This book is dedicated to Kurt Cobain, Tomata du Plenty, Ben McMillan, Kristen Pfaff, Stephanie Sargent, John Baker Saunders, Layne Staley, Andy Wood, Mia Zapata, and all other Washington-based musicians who are no longer with us.

ACKNOWLEDGMENTS

Thanks to Jack Endino, Mark Arm, Susan Silver, Matt Vaughan, Rebecca Roybal, Dave Dederer, Drew Church, Carrie Stamper, and all the photographers who submitted great pix — your help with this book was much appreciated. But wait, there's more! I'd also like to thank my wife Mary and all my family — Lucille and Robert Prato Jr., Lorraine and the Raz, Little Adam and Baby Aiden, Kris Fleischmann, James Fleischmann, Mikey and Erin Fleischmann, Little Elle, Sylvia and Bob "The Voice of Reason" Fleischmann, Ellen Fleischmann, the Stanleys, Dennis and Cheryl Sullivan, Steven and Jen Castro, Baby Lily, Megan Sullivan, Mellow Michael Sullivan, Grandma and Grandpa Conrad, Grandma and Grandpa Prato, Uncle Eddie, Giacomo and Angela DiMaggio, Angie and Big Michael Prisciandaro, the three little dwarves (Little Michael, Antonia, and Daniela Prisciandaro), Phyllis Basso, Giacomo Caesar Basso, Alan and Beth Tagliamonti, Amy Tagliamonti, Betty Tagliamonti, Tony Clifton, Brendon Cohen, Matt and Martha Baumbach, Adam Krieg, Stefan and Allison Farkas, Orson and Sariah Joseph, Stephen Gross and Karen, Folly, Dirty David Britt, Dave "Dice" Kay, Shawn "The Bear" Bearor, Jack Castronova, Louis "Flossi" Rossi, Mr. Flugz, Mr. Magoo, Greg Hampton, Chip Ruggieri, Clint Weiler, Carol Kaye, Dan Weiss, Lloyd Jassin, Joel McIver, Martin Popoff, Michael Holmes and the folks at ECW, my friends at the Wantagh Post Office, the staff at Pietro's Pizza . . . and you, too!

FOREWORD

As my high school days were drawing to a close, there was certainly something bubbling in the hard rock world. Bands like Faith No More, Jane's Addiction, Living Colour, and the Red Hot Chili Peppers were showing that not all rock bands had to sing about "fast cars and fast women" or dress like goofball spandex cowboys. Having only attended strictly big arena rock shows up to this point, I didn't know quite what to expect when I agreed to attend a show on Saturday, March 17, 1990, at a club called L'Amour in Brooklyn, New York. The two main reasons I purchased a ticket for this three-band bill were to see the aforementioned Faith No More, as well as sci-fi metal headliners Voivod. After FNM's fantastic set, the next band, which I was least familiar with, came onstage.

The singer didn't wait long — upon the first notes of the opening number, he was climbing over the crowd on pipes attached to the ceiling (if my memory serves me correctly — already shirtless, and wearing shorts that were completely covered in silver electrical tape), before dropping himself into the sea of "moshers" below. The guitarist looked like something out of Cheech and Chong, with a full-on beard, and his eyes seemingly constantly closed — as if he were reaching a state of nirvana playing monstrous Sabbathy riffs. The bassist's large mop of curly hair bobbed in time to the music, while the drummer bashed out some impressively complex yet primal beats. This, my friends, was my introduction to the mighty Soundgarden.

Needless to say, soon after, I was a major convert, buying just about every

Soundgarden recording that I could get my hands on, and reading all the interviews on the band that I could gather. And in most of the articles, it was mentioned that there were other similarly styled bands from Soundgarden's hometown — Seattle — that were on their way up the ladder as well. Over the next year or so, it appeared as though each month, there was a new band from the Seattle area to discover — Mother Love Bone, Alice in Chains, Tad, Temple of the Dog, Mudhoney, the Melvins, the Screaming Trees, etc. And of course, when Nirvana and Pearl Jam hit, the rock world had thankfully shifted towards music that was both honest and real. And along with it came the word that would forever be associated with the movement: grunge.

While the movement didn't turn out to be as long lasting as many figured it would, what it packed into a four-year period (1990–1994) was pretty darn extraordinary. How many songs from this period are still being played on the radio? How many of these albums sound as great today as when they first came out, continue to sell, and are still being discovered by younger generations? I rest my case. It may have only lasted a few years, but for a few brief and shining moments, grunge certainly shifted the direction of culture (and even fashion), and brought in an unmistakable feeling of change — just as the '60s hippie and '70s punk movements had.

The original idea for doing this book came about when I was doing a Soundgarden article for *Classic Rock* magazine back in 2004. While interviewing the group's early producer, Jack Endino, he mentioned that almost every single article being written about grunge bands nowadays were by writers who were not from the Seattle area, yet were giving their "revisionist take" on what happened. Which got me thinking . . . what if a book was comprised of nothing but quotes from the actual people that experienced the movement firsthand, tracing it from its very beginning to its end? In other words, letting them tell the entire story as it unfolded (with only chapter intro paragraphs from yours truly). Nearly 130 interviews later, here we are.

Enjoy!

Greg Prato
New York, July 2008

p.s. Want to let me know what you thought of the book? Email me at: gregprato@yahoo.com, or see what I'm up to at: myspace.com/gregpratopage.

1960s–1970s

CHAPTER 1

"It was mainly isolation": 1960s–1970s

Think that grunge began with Soundgarden, Nirvana, and Pearl Jam? Think again. Grunge's roots stretch back to the '60s and '70s, as evidenced by such garage-punk bands as the Sonics, the Wailers, the Telepaths, and the Lewd, among others.

KENT MORRILL: [The Wailers] started in '58. We played teen dances mainly — there were no such thing as clubs. High school dances, armories, a famous place here called the Spanish Castle. We were all from different schools; so all the schools followed us. When we played dances, we drew like 2,000 or 3,000 kids — we were very popular, especially in the Northwest. We were influential on a lot of groups — we have quotes from the Beatles, that they got some of their original ideas from [the Wailers], because our records were bootlegged over in England. "Tall Cool One" was a Top 30 hit. Twice.

BUCK ORMSBY: [Jimi Hendrix] used to come to our dances at the Spanish Castle. He wanted to jam with us, but we didn't know him that well. He really liked our guitar player — our guitar player was an innovator. Jimi used to say to Rich [Dangel], "If your amp goes out, I've got mine in the car." But it never did happen. He was a big Wailers fan. One of his songs, "Spanish

COURTESY OF ART CHANTRY

Seattle native Jimi Hendrix comes home, 1968

Castle Magic," was written about that place we played.

I joined the Wailers in '60, after they came back from their East Coast tour. Their label was Golden Crest Records in New York. Golden Crest wanted them to stay there and make records. They decided they were going to come back — their parents wanted them to finish high school. When they returned, they asked me if I wanted to join the band. They said Golden Crest was not happy with them, and they decided, "Well, maybe that's the end of the story." I said, "I don't think this is the end of the game. The Wailers could be a great, great band. If the label is not going to do anything with you anymore, let's start our own label." Three of the guys said, "No, we're too young and we don't know anything about it." We worked that weekend. I took money out of my pocket, put it on the table, and said, "Who's in?" And Kent Morrill and Rockin' Robin did the same thing.

KENT MORRILL: [Etiquette Records'] first release was "Louie Louie," which became number one all over the Northwest — actually two times. Then the Kingsmen picked up on it and got the big hit. We had groups like the Galaxies, the Bootmen — probably close to a dozen acts we produced. We had about ten albums that [the Wailers] did. Some of our best-known songs were "Tall Cool One," "Roadrunner," "Dirty Robber." ["Out of Our Tree"] was pretty close to being a national hit. We opened for the Stones and just about every group.

BUCK ORMSBY: We opened an office in Tacoma, Washington, on Sixth Avenue. We started getting tapes from all over the Northwest. This one lady called and said, "You've got to go hear [the Sonics]." So I went over to this garage. They played this real raucous rock 'n' roll song that Gerry Roslie wrote. Remember all the dance songs like "Do the Chicken"? I said, "That was the best thing I heard all day. I don't want to date anything here by having it a dance song that's going to come and go. Rewrite the lyrics, and I'll come back." I went back and it was the song "The Witch." I said, "That's it — we're going to record *that*."

So we took them into the studio, recorded that, but they didn't have any other songs — that was the only original song they had. So we put "Keep A-Knockin'" — the Little Richard song — on the other side. I took that record up to the radio stations, and nobody would play it, because it was so outrageous and different. I talked to Pat O'Day [a DJ at KJR], and he said, "This is a little outside of what we're doing here. Get some charts — see if somebody else will play this record." So we kept pounding this thing — it took us about six months to get the charts. We got it played on independent radio in the Northwest into Canada and down into Oregon. There was this one station in Seattle that was a small AM station — I think it was KEW — they gave us a chart and some of the other cities in the Northwest. I took those charts in. Pat said, "I'll go see the group." He was knocked out, came back, played the record. In about a week, it went up to number two on the major station.

ART CHANTRY: The Sonics were astonishing — they were, like, the best rock band. There was always this jealousy between the Wailers and the Sonics, because the Wailers wanted to be big stars, and the Sonics were becoming big stars — even though they couldn't play their instruments. Now, the Wailers are a great band, but the bulk of their output was pretty drecky — they had a lot of bad records and bad songs. But the Sonics were much more consistently great. It was the difference between musicianship, the Wailers, and passion, the Sonics.

KENT MORRILL: Basically, it was geography. In those days, people thought the Northwest still had covered wagons and Indians. So if something was popular in the Northwest, they didn't look at it the same as if it were number one in New York or Hollywood. It was mainly isolation. But that isolation was the reason why we could come up with such an original sound.

BUCK ORMSBY: We released several singles from the Sonics and two albums — [1965's] *Here Are the Sonics* and [1966's] *Sonics Boom.* I was always in the studio; Kent was always in the studio. Sometimes background singing on the Sonics was the Wailers. We basically ruled the roost here for a while — until '69.

KENT MORRILL: They had a little dissension amongst [the Sonics]. The Parypa brothers didn't get along. Gerry is a very shy person, so he had all these reservations before he would perform — he wouldn't go on an airplane, he wouldn't go on a boat. He's still that way. In 1969, [the Wailers] decided that "if we want to make it, we have to move to Hollywood." We moved and got nowhere. We wound up having to commute to San Francisco to even work. The guys wanted to go back — I decided to stay in L.A. and do production work. We took a sabbatical for about ten years.

BUCK ORMSBY: The one thing that slowed us down was the British invasion. Everybody — even American bands — started talking with an English accent. The label was dormant for a while, and then I started it back up again. We started reunions with the Wailers in the '70s. Kent dropped out of the label, Rockin' Robin was killed in a car wreck in San Francisco.

ART CHANTRY: I'm a little older than a lot of the guys. The first concert I went to was Jimi Hendrix — I was of that generation that was too young to be a hippie and too old to be a punk. I was an outsider no matter where I stood.

BRAD SINSEL: It was basically tavern-based — club scene cover tunes. *Hideous.* By the time I got there, we found one band that was able to combine their original tunes with a lot of "butt rock" stuff — Mojo Hand. Some of us from my hometown of Yakima glommed onto that, and took that band over. But before we got there is where it gets confusing. Our lead guitarist, Rick Pierce, joined up with Ze Whiz Kidz. I remember in '73 hearing tales of him doing some festival with Aerosmith — with Ze Whiz Kidz at the bottom of the rung — in Eastern Washington. Next thing I know, we start our own band, Ze Fabulous Pickle Sisters — glam rock/Bowie stuff. We sucked. But we got absorbed with Ze Whiz Kidz — we opened for the New York Dolls at the Moore Theatre.

ART CHANTRY: Ze Whiz Kidz are extremely important. They were a musically glam gay theater troupe that lived in the Northwest, and most of the guys in the band were at one point or another part of the Cockettes, in San Francisco. A lot of really interesting people came out of Ze Whiz Kidz. For instance, Satz from the Lewd, and Tomata [DuPlenty], who was in the Screamers and the Tupperwares. Tomata is a fascinating character, because he was the one who pioneered Northwest punk. He was producing honest-to-God DIY punk posters in 1972 for Ze Whiz Kidz. And he put on the earliest punk shows in the Northwest.

Three Whiz Kidz, early '70s

RICK PIERCE: There was no mistaking who was in Ze Whiz Kidz or who were our hangers-on, because we didn't leave the house unless we were wearing five pounds of makeup and had our hair ratted a foot high. There was a club called Shelly's Leg, where the bands coming through town would go. That's where I got to meet Robert Plant and Jimmy Page. The Seattle crowds then had a provincial attitude — they liked anything if it was from somewhere other than Seattle. In Seattle, the opening was, "You're from here, so you can't be any good." We were starving — living on the glamour of it, and drinking for free at Shelly's Leg. Brad and I knew what we wanted to do — a more conventional type of rock band.

ART CHANTRY: I was in that crew of the mid '70s that cruised around in cars and listened to Led Zeppelin and Rolling Stones — desperately channel surfing for anything. There wasn't even any fucking oldies stations in the Northwest back then.

MARK ARM: I'm from Kirkland, a suburb northeast of Seattle. Growing up in the '70s, I listened to Top 40 radio. By junior high, I discovered album-oriented FM radio. Rock 'n' roll was verboten in my house — my mother is a former opera singer who grew up in Hitler's Germany. I used to sneak into our Volkswagen Beetle because I could listen to the radio without turning on the ignition. I'd sit alone listening, hoping for "Green Eyed Lady" instead of "We've Only Just Begun." So when I heard FM radio for the first time, I was drawn to the harder, louder stuff — the Nuge, KISS, and Aerosmith.

JOHN BIGLEY: I was born here in Seattle. The music thing happened right off the bat. Backwards though — Beethoven, then the Black Sabbath single, "Iron Man." That was it.

BILL RIEFLIN: '75, I was fifteen years old — there was no music scene. I was in a band called the Telepaths, and as far as I know, we were really the first, so-called underground, punk-inspired group. Fairly nihilistic in outlook — inspired by the Stooges and the Velvets. When we discovered the Sonics, the world became even more exciting. A very interesting combination of people, mostly teenagers, although the rhythm guitar player was a thirty-five-year-old marketing professor, from the University of Washington — Homer Spence. We were the first band of that ethos that started putting on our shows — we weren't a bar band, we played a couple of covers, things like "I Wanna Be Your Dog." Mostly we wrote our own songs and made a lot of noise.

KURT BLOCH: I was born here. Started wanting to be in a band in high school, in the mid '70s. There's no textbook for starting a band — you listened to records and saw bands on TV. It seemed so un-doable — you get together with your friends in the basement, and it's like, "How do you do this? I know how to play some chords, but then when everybody plays together, it just doesn't sound right" [laughs].

DAVID KINCAID: [Heart] were *the* Seattle band, and they were huge. This is back when they were still a real rock 'n' roll band, before they turned into that "pop '80s cleavage band." They were really a great band, and [Ann Wilson] could sing her ass off.

RICK PIERCE: TKO got signed in '77 to MCA. We didn't release [an album] until '79 — our first tour was with the Kinks. Right after eight weeks of getting booed offstage, we started opening for Cheap Trick — their first U.S. tour off of [1979's] *At Budokan*. We were doing 20,000 seats a night — we went on to do the Japan Jam. But shortly after, MCA folds Infinity because Ron Alexenburg had cut a deal with the pope for a $6 million non-recoupable advance. It's when [Pope John Paul II] was touring the United States, and the logic was you look at [the pope] filling stadiums, and [the pope] is a singer. So side A of the LP is his speeches, and then you flip it over, and it's Polish folk songs. The thing tanked. Alexenburg got shit-canned.

ART CHANTRY: Essentially, you're an island and it has this "island mentality" — this isolated mentality. The people that didn't leave stewed and festered in their own juices. And that's why you saw this incredibly incestuous band scene — these people had been playing music and partying with each other for ten or fifteen years before anybody took notice. It was a highly charged and fascinating time to be here. Some of the most amazing shows, people, creative acts were done by these totally obscure people in the Northwest — just trying to live.

BILL RIEFLIN: It was very "do it yourself." If you wanted to put on a show, you had to find a hall, get a PA. God knows how any of it actually happened. But it did. In 1977, there was a guy named Roger Husbands, and he was the manager of the Enemy. Roger opened a club, initially in the Odd Fellows Building on Capitol Hill — the Bird. There were bands doing any number of things — pop tunes, maybe weirdly Beach Boys–inspired, hardcore punk, singer-songwritery guys, experimental guys, older guys, younger guys.

KURT BLOCH: There was this one store in Seattle that sold import records — Campus Music. There was definitely a "Campus Music scene" in the University District in Seattle. When we were fourteen or fifteen, me and my brother would take the bus down and spend our lunch money buying 45s. We really liked the hard bands — Blue Öyster Cult, UFO, the Scorpions, the first Montrose record [1973's *Montrose*]. We always thought, "Why can't they make records that are loud guitars — start to finish?"

CALVIN JOHNSON: I'm from Olympia, Washington. Here it was 1977, and you're reading about the Stooges. But you couldn't get their records — they were out of print. If you were lucky, you'd find one at the cutout bins. If bands went on tour, they often didn't bother going to Seattle.

MARK ARM: I went to this private high school, Bellevue Christian. My friends and I were really into music, and we found this cool record store in Bellevue — Rubato Records. It was the only used record store on the east side. The people who worked there were cool and would point us in different directions. After graduating high school, I went to college in a small town in Oregon. Remarkably, the small record store in McMinnville had one copy of each of the first two Stooges records on Canadian import.

KEVIN WOOD: We were totally into Elton John and KISS — the theatrical aspect. Andy [Kevin's youngest brother] was doing his own thing, I was doing my own thing, and Brian [Kevin's middle brother] was doing his own thing. Andy and I were into the same stuff — anything hard-edged. We saw KISS in '77. I was fifteen, which would have made him eleven. We found some seats as close as we could get, but at this time, they were pretty far back. The show started — Cheap Trick came on and just rocked. After that set, we turned to each other — he said, "That's what I want to do." And I said, "Me too."

CALVIN JOHNSON: Punk rock came along, and I was like, "We're going to have that teenage revolution we were waiting for." But I always say, "Punk rock is the teenage revolution that never happened."

KURDT VANDERHOOF: Grew up in Aberdeen, Washington. In the '70s, it was great — it was a logging town. Lots of money — people worked and partied really hard. Then in the early '80s, the timber industry took a dump.

TIM HAYES: I really don't like talking about Aberdeen. If you had a funny haircut — even if you wore a pair of Converse All Stars or Vans — they'd sit there like, "What's the deal with this?" Or if you had a little color in your hair — "Faggot!" You'd end up getting in fights, people talking a lot of shit behind you, the cops would pull you over. I ended up working at Wishkah Mall with a huge ass pompadour, and people would walk by and "see the freak."

CHARLES PETERSON: I grew up in Bothell, Washington. Took about an hour by bus to get to downtown Seattle. At about sixteen, I discovered punk rock. I went to the nearest mall, which would have been Northgate Mall — to the Budget Tapes and Records. I bought the first Clash album [1977's *The Clash*] based on the cover — and songs like "White Riot" and "I'm So Bored with the U.S.A." I went home, put that on, and sold all my hard rock records.

CALVIN JOHNSON: I went to Europe with my German class in '77, and I was like, "I'm going to buy some of these punk rock records" — I couldn't find them anywhere in Olympia. This is July of '77 — right when the Sex Pistols' "God Save the Queen" is number one, and punk rock is really happening. When I got back from Europe a few months later, I got involved with the local radio station, KAOS. That's when this whole world of music opened up to me.

KURT BLOCH: I don't think we heard any punk records until the second Ramones record [1977's *Leave Home*]. No one said, "This is punk rock," we thought this was just another cool, loud band. We heard about it on TV, there was a thing about English punk bands on one of those nighttime news shows. We went to the record store the next week — they were out of "God Save the Queen," but they had "Pretty Vacant," and got the Saints' first twelve-inch. Over the course of a month, all these records were coming out, and we were like, "This is the way to be." So we started peg-legging our Levi's and trying to find leather jackets. My first band, the Cheaters . . . we could get through a Saints song! In early '78 I suppose, we tried getting some shows. Never looked back after that.

TOM PRICE: I'm from North Seattle, as are Kurt Bloch, Duff McKagan. I went to Roosevelt High School, and there was a band there called the Mentors. They would play at rental halls. Us younger kids, who still had long hair and bell-bottoms, we'd see a couple of older punk rock dudes — they would throw folding chairs, smash light bulbs. Me and my buddies were all, "How cool!" Me and my buddies really liked the Lewd — the original lineup. We'd go see them at a place called the Golden Crown downtown. I must have been a freshmen or a sophomore, and I walked into school with short hair, jeans, Converse, a plain white T-shirt. With the reaction I got, I could have been naked and painted blue.

COURTESY OF ART CHANTRY

Spiky haired punkers the Lewd, late '70s

KURDT VANDERHOOF: The Lewd had already formed by the time I joined — I was a junior in high school. The Ramones came to town, and [the Lewd] opened. I met the lead singer, Satz, [he] said they were looking for a new bass player. I came up for an audition and got the gig. So I quit high school, moved to Seattle, and joined a punk rock band. Made a single, "Kill Yourself." Then we relocated to San Francisco.

JOE KEITHLEY: Pretty sure it was June or July 1979 [the first time DOA played Seattle] — we had just put out the seven-inch single, "Disco Sucks." We went down to San Francisco and did shows at the Mabuhay Gardens. [Brad Kent, guitar] decided to stay there. So we arrived in [Seattle], it was just the three of us. We played a miserable set — I hadn't played guitar in a couple of months and forgot everything. I would qualify that show as the shittiest show DOA ever did. But the next time was far more interesting — we played at the Washington Hall, up in the U District. We had a really solid following in Seattle after that.

KIM WARNICK: Late '70s, it was pretty much just getting going. You had to look beneath the surface. As far as the scene or community, it was super small.

STEVE MACK: They were these super cheap shows at the Paramount Theater — it ranged as far and wide as Patti Smith to the Kinks. And the Clash — that was the first honest-to-God punk rock group that I got to see live. After that, it was all over. You saw the Clash onstage and just realized, "I never want to see another boring rock enormo-dome band again — I want more punk rock." That's when gigs started popping up at the Showbox, the Gorilla Room, and places like that. That's just when the whole explosion happened.

CHAPTER 2

"Seattle was the closest city": Transplants

Although Seattle and its surrounding towns can be pinpointed as the birthplace of grunge music, many of the genre's most renowned contributors hailed from other parts of the U.S., before settling down in the rainy city.

MATT DENTINO: Kim [Thayil], myself, Hiro [Yamamoto], and [Bruce] Pavitt grew up in Park Forest, Illinois — a suburb of Chicago. I first met Kim in Little League about '72, and we became friends when we enrolled in an experimental alternative high school there [the Active Learning Process School]. I subsequently got kicked out for being *too* alternative — Bruce and Hiro also attended. I still believe that grunge was birthed in Park Forest.

KIM THAYIL: Tom Zutaut — who signed Mötley Crüe and Guns N' Roses — he's Bruce Pavitt's age, they were a grade above me. Our high school had a radio station, and I briefly worked there. Zutaut was the station manager.

BRUCE PAVITT: When I was a kid, my favorite toy was an AM radio — I spent a lot of my days listening to music, spent all my money on 45s. A real shift for me happened when I was seventeen — I started dating a girl and all four of her brothers were into music. They wound up moving to Chicago — around '77 — and they got tapped into the punk scene. So I was able to go to shows and listen to British imports right as they were coming out.

STU HALLERMAN: I went to ALPS — Kim Thayil was a year older than me. One of my old friends growing up was Hiro Yamamoto.

HIRO YAMAMOTO: Kim Thayil and I met in high school — he was a year ahead of me. Back then he even seemed argumentative [laughs]. He liked to talk and was introspective. He's really into philosophy. You could tell he was thinking about where he fit in the world and what it all meant, all the time.

KIM THAYIL: When I was in Chicago, there was a handful of us who were punk rock fans. My first band formed in '77 — Bozo and the Pinheads. We played the school sock hop talent show at the end of the year. We did a bunch of Ramones, Pistols, Devo, and originals I wrote.

BEN SHEPHERD: I was born in Japan, then we moved to Texas. When I was three, we moved up here — I've lived across the water from Seattle my whole life. Never really lived in Seattle until [recently]. My dad used to play guitar — the first song I ever heard was "Big River" by Johnny Cash. Then when I was eight, I heard [Iggy and the Stooges' 1973 release] *Raw Power*. That was it — I was doomed. I had older brothers and sisters, so I'd go all the way from Earth Wind & Fire and Eartha Kitt to Syd Barrett and Captain Beefheart. Even though we were poorer than hell, they always had music going.

CHAD CHANNING: I was born in Santa Rosa. I moved around a lot — my dad was a disc jockey in radio. We moved to Washington in '78. Shortly after, I met Ben Shepherd, in the fourth grade. When I met Ben, he was getting into punk rock, so I was being introduced to the Dead Kennedys, the Clash, the Sex Pistols, the Circle Jerks. I was all about soccer when I was a kid — until I got [in] this accident. It messed my legs up pretty bad. I got into music after that.

MATT CAMERON: I was born in San Diego, California. I started playing in bands when I was thirteen — I played in a KISS cover band with some neighborhood kids. By the time I was sixteen or seventeen, I had been in a bunch of different bands, and [was] playing professional gigs. I think the career chose me. I moved up to Seattle in '83.

JOHN LEIGHTON BEEZER: Everyone who was serious about their career left Seattle for L.A. Jeff [Ament] was probably the first person in the world to leave Montana for Seattle.

JEFF AMENT: I went to college in Missoula for two years. About halfway through my sophomore year, a group of us went to see the Clash and the Who [in Seattle]. And I think X was playing the Showbox the night before. We heard that the following spring, there was going to be a punk rock club opening up, which turned out to be the Metropolis. I went to school to get a graphic design degree, and halfway through my sophomore year, they decided that they were going to focus more on the fine arts program. The fact that they were opening up this club in Seattle, I had a couple of friends out there, and a couple of people I'd met on that trip — I just decided that I would go to Seattle for a year and get my residency before I go back to school. I never went back to school — I worked in a restaurant for six or seven years.

BRUCE FAIRWEATHER: I grew up in Hawaii. I left in 1981 and went to the University of Montana. I met [Jeff] the first day of school, skateboarding — he had shorts on that said "Sex Pistols" and "999." We ended up hanging out and skateboarding a lot — he didn't play anything and I was playing. I think it was Christmas or Easter, Jeff saw Who Killed Society in Missoula. He totally dug this band, so the next Monday, he's like, "We've got to start a band!" He bought a bass, found a drummer, and started Deranged Diction. We played a bunch of shows out there, put a tape out, went through a couple of singers and drummers. [Bruce played guitar.] By 1983, three of us — me, Jeff, and Sergio Avenia, our drummer — decided to pursue it more. Seattle was the closest city.

JEFF AMENT: The spring of '82 is the first recording we did, and then we recorded a couple more times in '83 and '84. I made a compilation tape that I sold, and traded tapes through *Flipside* and *Maximumrocknroll.* When I decided to go to Seattle, nobody else was going to go with me. And then at the last minute, Sergio decided to go. We loaded up my car with his drums, my amp and bass, and I think we each had a suitcase. We didn't have any money — I had maybe 200 bucks, and it probably cost $100 in gas to get to Seattle. My friend, Randy Pepprock, who I'd met in Missoula, was working out there, and he said I could sleep on his floor for a couple of weeks. Right about that same time, the Metropolis opened up. Maybe a month after I'd been there [in the spring of '83], Bruce Fairweather — who was still in Missoula — his girlfriend broke up with him, so he was looking to move out. Before he moved out, I started to look for somebody that could sing, or play guitar and sing. That's when I met Rod Moody.

ROD MOODY: By that time, I was singing and playing along to the Dead Kennedys and Black Flag, and writing punk songs myself, so I was able to keep up with the ultra-speedy thrash that [Deranged Diction] had going on. They had a tape called *No Art, No Cowboys, No Rules*. Hearing it now, it was pretty generic hardcore, but at the time — "Wow, I'm in a hardcore band!" Jeff was really into D.C. hardcore at the time — SS Decontrol, Void, Faith, etc. Even then he was really motivated. He started a zine — only one issue actually went out — booked all the shows, became friends with all the players and club bookers, made posters, and was making plans to put out a full-length. We ended up playing with Hüsker Dü, Butthole Surfers, and a couple other national bands. We played the Met mostly, but also Munro's Dance Palace, and maybe the Lincoln Arts Center. We also played an extremely redneck bar in Tacoma, and it marked the first and last time I have ever seen people swing dancing to hardcore.

Our drummer was a misfit to say the least. When Grant Hart, drummer for Hüsker Dü, who had long shaggy hair, complimented us after our opening set, Sergio, not knowing who he was, said, "Shut up, you fucking hippie!" Then there was the time we played in Vancouver, B.C., and the border guard asked us if we had any firearms in the car. Sergio, who had a Mohawk, said "No, but we have plenty of heroin and cocaine under the spare tire!" Jeff was the musical director of the band, and once he started getting into KISS and Bad Company, we slowed down a bit. Mark Arm said that we went from being the fastest band in Seattle to the slowest. Maybe the combination of the punk dude that was getting more into rock and the rock dude who got into punk was taking over a bit. For the life of me, I cannot remember why Diction broke up, but I am pretty sure it was in '84.

TAD DOYLE: I grew up in Boise, Idaho, for the first twenty-six years of my life — a town of about 250,000 people. When I left, the growth rate was *negative* — people were leaving. I went to college there, graduated high school, became a journeyman butcher, and moved to Seattle to do music. I used to go to Seattle a lot to see shows. For me, that was worth driving 500 miles for. Then I moved to Seattle and spent a lot of time looking for a job. I did quite a few things, including landscaping, a butcher again, then worked at Kinko's for a few years.

STEVE FISK: I'm from California. Somewhere along the way, I got interested in synthesizers. Synthesizers were very limited at that time — you needed a tape deck to do anything with a synthesizer — so I learned how to run tape decks. By the time I was twenty-seven, I was recording bands — very badly. I came at it backwards — all my friends learned about microphones and shit in college. I picked that up without any formal training, just by making my own mistakes. I moved to eastern Washington in the '70s. From there, to Olympia in the early '80s.

STEVE TURNER: I'm from Texas — Houston. But I ended up in Seattle when I was two. Moved out to the suburbs — Mercer Island. Didn't really have any interest in rock 'n' roll. I was a skateboarder, and in '79, all the skateboarders were into punk rock. Suddenly, instead of Ted Nugent blasting at the skate park, it was Devo and the Clash. Devo was actually my first concert. The next night, Black Flag played, and I went to see that too. That was pretty much it for me.

JONATHAN PONEMAN: I was born in Toledo, Ohio. I grew up there, and moved to Washington when I was seventeen — with my then-girlfriend. I did what I did best at the time — pump gas. We lived [in Bellingham] for a couple of years. Then she turned twenty-one and was able to go into the bars, and said, "I love you and I wish you a lot of luck, but I think it's time for us to break up." So I moved to Seattle, and over the course of several years, played in a bunch of bands, started working at the Paramount Theater. All this time, I had been going in and out of college.

STEVE TURNER: I almost flunked out of Mercer Island High — I was a little *too much* into the punk rock thing [laughs]. I was the only even marginally punk rock kid on Mercer Island at the time. The only other people that were into it had already graduated from high school, so I was left alone there. I was pretty miserable. So my parents helped me get into a private school

— Northwest School for the Arts. I went there for my senior year, and I met Stone [Gossard].

BRUCE PAVITT: I moved to Olympia in '79, to go to Evergreen State College. The Evergreen scene was interesting because they had a radio station, KAOS, that specialized in independent releases. So their entire library had a deep collection of punk, new wave, independent releases. And there was a magazine called *Op*, that reviewed indie records.

KIM THAYIL: *Op* split into two magazines — *Sound Choice* and *Option.* There's KAOS radio, and a bunch of bands — the Beakers, the Blackouts. So Bruce is sending us these singles, tapes, and copies of the magazines. And that was certainly a reason why we'd want to move out to the Seattle area. It seemed like a romantic, accessible scene for a high school or early college teenager/musician. Eventually, I think Hiro was twenty and I was twenty-one. We packed up Hiro's Datsun B210 — with clothes, amps, and whatever money we had, and drove out on I-90. Hiro and I at the time simultaneously had our bands break up and our girlfriends leave us [laughs]. We moved out in '81. That's a big move when you're broke, a college dropout, and have nothing going on [laughs].

CHARLES PETERSON: I met Kim Thayil in college — I was introduced by Bruce Pavitt. We'd go to this $2.99 special Chinese restaurant all the time, and talk philosophy for *hours.*

BEN SHEPHERD: My older brother, Henry, had moved away from Kingston and was living in Seattle, and met this guy, Kim. They were friends, and he brought Kim over to our house. I was about fourteen.

KIM THAYIL: [We came to Seattle for a] number of reasons — getting out on your own, getting out of Chicago, adventure, education. Music was another goal.

Early–Mid '80s

CHAPTER 3

"It was so easy to freak people out in those days": Early–Mid '80s

The beginning of the '80s saw the local Seattle music scene shift from bar bands that specialized in covers to original do-it-yourself punk bands, that built the Seattle punk scene up from scratch. And with unforgettable local performances by up-and-coming punk acts from outside of the area (Black Flag, DOA, etc.), the grunge fuse was officially lit.

TOM PRICE: Something I don't see mentioned much — the violent reaction people had to you, just for being mildly punk rock. Every day, you'd be walking down the street, and people would yell "Faggot!" and throw beer bottles at you. You'd get jumped by frat boys or stoners. Everywhere you went, it was a daily occurrence. I'm forty-three now, I have a couple of kids, and it just seems so weird to me, to think how inured to violence I was. I'm not a real big guy — I was never a big fighter — but I was very good at putting on the stone face and ignoring them. And if they decided they were going to beat me up anyhow, I got good at running fast. I got good at appearing to be beaten up, but knowing how to protect myself, so I wasn't really injured at all. For me, the exciting part was the music and all the great bands. But the daily tension and violence maybe added to it.

REGAN HAGAR: The cop stuff would all happen on Bainbridge. The Seattle stuff was more, "Big city cops — try to avoid them." But on Bainbridge there were three cops. Everyone knew everyone's names, so they'd see Andy and I in Winslow, pull over — "What are you guys doing? Let me see the bottom of your shoes, we just had some crimes." It was just a chance to hassle us. A couple of times they would separate and handcuff us, and then let us go.

MARK ARM: I went to Linfield, a small college in McMinnville, Oregon, from '80 to '82. There were maybe four people who listened to punk rock and then there were maybe eight more sympathetic to new wave. Largely populated by cowboy jocks. One time, my friend and I cut our hair down to half an inch and dyed it. My bleach job turned out spotty, so it looked like I had leopard spots. We went into the cafeteria — this is a school with a population of 2,000 or less. The whole place fell completely silent and everybody just stared at us. I was at the Coke machine filling up my glass, and this football player who I lived down the hall from earlier in the year comes up to me and goes, "Devo, *I'm going to kill you.*" That's all they knew at that point, was Devo, so of course, I got called "Devo" by all these people. It was so easy to freak people out in those days.

CHARLES PETERSON: Ended up going to college at the University of Washington, and met Mark Arm in the dormitories there. [Mark] turned me on to underground American punk rock/post punk. At that point, it seemed what I really wanted to study was photography. Throughout junior high and high school, I'd been on the newspaper taking photos. My mother for my birthday and Christmas would always buy me these nice photo books. So it just seemed like something to do — go out, and photograph bands at the local clubs. And then quickly [it] turned out my friends had bands as well, and that they needed photographs.

BLAINE COOK: Lots of hall shows, lots of drugged and intoxicated people. Always violence, always senseless. Always senseless vandalism, and that's why [with] the hall shows, you could only do one or two at a certain hall — you'd get booted out.

DUFF McKAGAN: Punk rock was a refuge for people that didn't fit in at school or on sports teams — punk rockers were the guys getting beat up by the jocks. By early '82, it was all the jocks from out in the suburbs shaving their heads, coming to gigs, and fighting.

TOM PRICE: Black Flag became popular, hardcore became popular. And all of sudden, people would show up — you'd see them around the University District one day, and then the next day, they'd be full-on Mohawk and leather jacket. We'd call them "overnight punks" or "insta-punks." In the '80s, it became really divided — you were art, new wave, hardcore, or rockabilly.

ED FOTHERINGHAM: It rains a lot in Seattle — people played loud guitars in their basements, and when they were old enough, they played shows.

PAUL BARKER: I remember it being fairly frustrating. Promoters just couldn't put on shows in all-ages places. It seemed easier to play in bars or taverns — as far as a place to play that serves alcohol. Also, the concept of "big fish, small pond" — there were only so many shows you could play. If you played once a month, would people still care about the band? At what point do you oversaturate it?

JOHN BIGLEY: There was no place to play — it was playing in gallery storefronts, warehouses. Once in a while, sucker some tavern into putting on a show, that would inevitably turn into a one-off calamity. "Short-haired weirdoes showed up the other night — you should have seen it!"

JOHN CONTE: [University Avenue] — the place to be. If you had something to say, if you were trying to promote your band, that was the place to hang out. It was the place to get seen, and the place to start rumors.

JIM TILLMAN: The audience was pretty much every kid that was a weirdo. There weren't too many people from the suburbs. You'd see the same people at every show, and half the people in the crowd were in bands. It was a lot more rambunctious — a lot of jumping around, hollering, and drinking. But the difference between what I see then and now is that then, there weren't any of these "New York, stand there with your arms folded" audiences. *Everybody* was jumping around.

WHITING TENNIS: One show would lead to another, and then you'd meet a friend. The next thing you know — "I can put a band together." You see kids that are younger than you — it's so inspiring.

ROD MOODY: I used to see shows all the time, and met a gay, goth Fartz fanatic named Wilum Pugmyr, who ran a great zine called *Punk Lust*, which largely served as his outlet to gush about the Fartz.

TIM HAYES: When I'd go to Seattle I'd pick up a copy of *Desperate Times* — a great local punk zine that would have show reviews and write-ups on new bands and records. If there was a show in Seattle we wanted to see, I'd drive the vw bus or Ghia to Oly, pick up Greg and Swervo or whoever, buy a fifth of whiskey, a half rack of cheap beer, and head to the show. We'd get as far as Fife — twenty miles from Olympia — and have to pick up another half rack. By the time we parked at the garage across from the Showbox, Greg would be passed out and Swervo puking his guts. After shows I wouldn't get back to Aberdeen until five in the morning — and have to work a few hours later.

CHUCK DUKOWSKI: The first Black Flag shows in Seattle must have been in 1979 or 1980. The first tour took us north to Vancouver by way of San Francisco, Portland, and Seattle. The first show was at a kind of fancy club beneath a restaurant in the waterfront entertainment district of Seattle. Ron Reyes [aka Chavo Pederast] was the singer at the time. We did two sets and opened for Chinas Comidas on at least one. When we went on, the crowd was small but grew. We extended it by repeating a few songs and playing a long and wild version of "Louie Louie." We met Kyle [Nixon] and his friends standing in the stairs outside that led to the backstage area. They invited us to their house afterward to spend the night. I remember using my baseball style slide to take down some tables in the middle of the dance floor while we were playing. There were these people in the middle of the dancing mass insisting on sitting at a table and getting all 'tudinal about it.

KYLE NIXON: February '80 [I saw] Black Flag, and then by May, I met Paul [Solger], and we formed Solger. I was raised in Bellevue, which is across the lake from Seattle — the east side. By the time I was in the band though, I had left home, moved to Seattle, and lived with some girls. We only played seven shows. None of us knew each other and we never got along really. It came out in our music and our stage shows, but it also helped us break up quicker too.

STEVE MACK: We were suburban kids, and Kyle decided, "Let's invite Black Flag to play." We didn't know what we were going to do and how we

PIC BY BLAINE COOK

Seattle punks, early '80s

were going to pay them. And Kyle said, "I've talked to these guys, and what they need is a copy machine to make flyers." He'll probably kill me for saying this, but what he did was swipe the copy machine from his mom's office, and promised Black Flag that if they came up and played, they could have it! So we had a gig in this hall down on the Central District of Seattle. At that point, the Central District was pretty rough. He asked me to be security, which is laughable, because I'm not a big, threatening guy at all. So there we are. All of a sudden, all these punk rock people started showing up at the venue — we were way out of our depth at that point. These are like city kids with honest-to-God leather jackets, purple hair.

The promoter decided to pull the gig. "You didn't tell me this was a punk rock gig — I'm not letting punk rockers play through my PA!" We spent hours trying to convince this guy, "*Please,* you got to understand — we've got people driving up from Los Angeles." We convinced the guy to leave his PA there. The second band was Pointed Sticks [from Vancouver] — they started playing, people started slam dancing, and somebody called the police. The police came and shut the place down. I had a big slash mark across my face where some girl grabbed me. I went back across the water to Bellevue that night, feeling like it had been a rite of passage.

CHUCK DUKOWSKI: I remember wishing they hadn't stolen that Xerox machine. They were so earnest and excited about it, you couldn't say no. And it never worked — we tried to have it repaired and everything!

DUFF McKAGAN: Black Flag really started to hit its stride when Henry [Rollins] first got in the band. *It was godlike.*

DERRICK BOSTROM: You've got to keep in mind that when you're in Seattle — especially if you're the Meat Puppets — you're really focused on the next day, which is when you hit that Canadian border. You get up early and vacuum the shit out of your van. Most of my memories of Seattle is doing just that.

SLIM MOON: I went to a DOA show that turned into a riot. All I knew about punk rock were the clichés I learned from reading *Newsweek* articles. For my first punk rock show to turn into a riot . . . I saw a skateboarder walk down the street and smash out the window of every car parked on the street with his skateboard. Set all the dumpsters on fire nearby, and somebody sprayed an anarchy sign on the side of a police car. I was like, "Oh my God, punk rock really is everything they say it is!" I jumped right into it after that.

JOE KEITHLEY: I think this was '83 or '84 — at the Lincoln Arts Center. People around the country always think of Seattle as the bastion of liberalism and progressive thinking, but for some reason, the city counselors thought it would be a wise idea for kids to hang around malls, 7-Elevens, and plan petty thefts — rather than going to listen to music. So there were never any all-ages shows in Seattle. Four hundred kids showed up, and the place held 300, so it was jam-packed. I don't think we played at all — the fire marshall came and declared the place was over-full and they didn't have a proper license. Then the fire marshall made everyone clear out of the building — at which point the Seattle police showed up. I wouldn't call it a full-scale riot, but *half* a riot happened, with bottle throwing and smashing. I remember seeing three Seattle police cars that had "DOA" spray painted on the back end of the car. I thought, "If I ever get pulled over down here and the guy figures out I'm in DOA, they're going to haul us down to the station and make us work it off in the body shop."

PIC BY BEV DAVIES — BEVDAVIES.COM

Canada's wild and wooly DOA (Joey Keithley is second from left)

SCOTTY CRANE: The same with the GBH/Accüsed show and the ferryboat — a bunch of punkers destroyed a ferryboat with axes and fire extinguishers.

TOM NIEMEYER: It was the first gig by the Accüsed in Seattle that my mother decided to come out to. Beer bottles were flying around the cabin of the boat, and skateboarders were trying to bust their friend out from a broom closet that the ferry workers made into an impromptu jail cell. GBH wrote a song about it called "Pass the Axe." My mom asked if this was how all our shows ended.

JOE KEITHLEY: Vancouver and Seattle are pretty close — there's only the stupid border in the way that stops people from going to see shows back and forth. People would go, "DOA was the first or second punk band I ever saw." Between us and Black Flag, we probably did more shows, played in more towns, went back and forth, and crisscrossed more times than anybody else. I couldn't say there was anything wildly different about [Seattle crowds] — other than the fact that we could not figure why you guys were drinking this shit beer all the time. Import some Canadian stuff!

LARRY REID: Seattle got to be a high profile stop on the punk rock circuit — the audience was really enthusiastic, fairly sophisticated, and large. I think on a national level too, punk rock started to come into its own — SST, Chuck Dukowski was touring his bands to death. There were a lot of bands that were influential in Seattle that I think had impact here beyond.

KIM THAYIL: Touch and Go was influential — all these Seattle bands loved the Butthole Surfers, Big Black, and Scratch Acid.

KEN STRINGFELLOW: The Wipers played in Bellingham — I got to see them at an all-ages show. That left a pretty strong impression on me.

JACK ENDINO: There was a big influence from Joy Division on quite a few people. A big influence from the Birthday Party. Both of them were weird, angular, dissonant, strange, non-commercial bands.

MATT VAUGHAN: The Replacements had a lot to do with influencing the Seattle scene. Their off-or-on performances, ripped up jeans and no care adolescent, backyard keggers, sittin' on the roof behavior was an attitude we all related to. But they were also smart and wrote great songs.

LIBBY KNUDSON: I always tell my "alternative" niece who's sixteen, "There used to be *characters*. We used to see bands and you'd be scared." Bands like Tales of Terror from San Francisco were an awesome band — I know they affected everyone. We'd never seen stuff like that before. Tex and the Horseheads — hairy-scary, fall-out-of-the-van. We would listen to Aerosmith's *Rocks*, the Stooges, the MC5, Blue Cheer, the Dead Kennedys, Black Flag — it was like the revolving jukebox. My niece always asks me, "What do you think?" And

I'm like, "Well, go buy the Scratch Acid record [1991's *The Greatest Gift*]." It was just the community thing — somebody would get a new record and go, "Oh, you've got to listen to this."

DUFF McKAGAN: Every band was just kind of ripping off ideas, or writing ideas/songs together. It was very paternal. Every band had every other band's back — it was like nothing I've ever seen since.

CHAD CHANNING: We wouldn't have a whole lot of money. We'd have enough — three or four bucks — to get across the ferry, and then we'd try to figure out how to get into the shows. There was one occasion, where a couple of my friends had managed to sneak on the ferryboat, sneak into the show — I think they went to see Fang — and then ended up sneaking back on the ferryboat again.

KEVIN WOOD: There was nothing going on in Bainbridge. It was more of a hippie community. It was just easy — jump on a ferry and you're right downtown, in the middle of the thick of it all. The music scene — right there pretty much at the end of a ferry ride.

JONATHAN EVISON: My chief contribution to the history of Seattle music is that I introduced Stoney Gossard and Andy Wood on Bainbridge Island in 1983. Stoney used to spend the night on the island now and then and go to school with me. Andy and I had home ec class together at the time. That's where they met. I was thirteen when I started March of Crimes. I was called Munkeyseeker back in the day — don't ask me why. Ben Shepherd joined the band in 1982. Ben was excellent — as long as he ate his lithium. His Twin Reverb was the sweetest sounding amp ever. Stone Gossard joined the band in 1984 — he brought some Van Halen licks with him. To Stone's credit, the first song he ever wrote had two guitar parts — one of them consisted of a single note that was bent up and down to dizzying effect, the other part had two chords. I sometimes call March of Crimes "the Art Blakey and the Jazz Messengers of the Seattle punk scene,"

PIC BY DAMON ROMERO

A young, pre-Soundgarden Ben Shepherd

because of the number of distinguished talents that worked their way through our ranks. We gave Jello Biafra the master tape of what was supposed to be our record, and he lost it. We were too stupid to make a copy.

SLIM MOON: March of Crimes was one of the greatest hardcore bands I'd ever seen. It's crazy how many people from all these bands came from Port Orchard or Gig Harbor. There was a whole scene over there, and Ben was one of those. You could make an argument that the story of the Seattle scene is really the story of just one or two graduation classes in Gig Harbor [laughs]. The people that invented grunge.

KRISHA AUGEROT: We would regularly hang out at Nordstrom's café — Stone and Regan picking out the ladies [laughs]. It was kind of the glam time — Stone had long hair and lots of hairspray, scarves. And Regan as well — a little bit of lipstick or eyeliner.

STEVE TURNER: It was so alien to me. I remember friends trying to convince me that KISS was cool. I was like, "God, that stuff is *so* stupid" [laughs]. [My first band] was the Ducky Boys, and that was just Jeff Covell and Stone. We never even played a show — we just played in Jeff's basement. They were kind of metal kids, and I was a punk rocker. They actually turned me on to some stuff I liked, like Motörhead and early Alice Cooper. And I turned them on to more of the punk rock stuff — I remember Stone liking the more melodic/L.A. kind of hardcore stuff, like Agent Orange and Social Distortion. Before that, he'd hated all punk rock [laughs]. We cross-pollinated a bit, tried to play some songs, and never really got anywhere.

CHAD CHANNING: We were mischief-makers. In Kingston, when we lived there, there was no "cop shop." If someone called the police, it would take the police twenty minutes to show up — because the closest cop shop was in Poulsbo. We used to go out at night, and never stay at anybody's place. I would say, "I'm going to stay at Andy's house," Andy would tell his dad, "I'm going to stay at Ben's," and Ben would say, "I'm going to stay at Chad's." And we ended up not staying *anywhere* — just camp out in the woods for the evening. Hang out, spray paint the town — cans at the ready. We did a fair share of getting things by "sticky fingers."

A lot of times, we'd stay out at Jefferson Beach, during the summer time. What we would do is me and Ben would stay at Andy's place. We'd chop wood for Andy's dad, and he'd give us five bucks apiece. We'd go buy eggs and bacon, steal packs of smokes, and we'd be set for the day [laughs]. We hitch-hiked everywhere we went — we didn't have cars. One time, we were heading up to Jefferson Beach — which we called JB — and we had this case of beer on us. We just broke the whole thing up and stuck it in our jackets and hitch-hiked. One time, we decided we were going to jam. We got our gear — the drum set, amps, guitars — carrying all this heavy stuff down the road. We'd go about fifty feet and then take a break. All the while we're trying to hitch-hike! We finally wound up getting a ride from a guy with a van or a truck or something. Only when you're young . . .

MARK ARM: I lived close to University Way, which, for some unknown reason, has been called "The Ave" since the dawn of time. The black leather punks hung out on the Ave, usually in front of the Post Office or Roxy Music, which was a record store. Most of the people I hung out with didn't own black leather jackets. We thought the guys who dressed like Sid Vicious or the Exploited were "punk rock Fonzies." I drew a Flipper fish on the back of a black and white checked trench coat and wore brown boots. Stupid little things like the color and style of your footwear seemed like important signifiers at that age.

BEN REW: I hung out on Broadway and on the Ave. They had a Baskin-Robbins and a 7-Eleven up on Broadway — that's where everybody would hang out. Everyone — the skinheads, punk rockers, rockers — all hung out together. The only group that was really mutually exclusive was the Bopos, a bunch of mod guys that would ride around on their scooters. Half of them were from rich families and half of them were dirt poor. They'd go pick fights all the time.

JOE TOUTONGHI: Jak's Team and Bopo Boys were founded on skateboards and punk rock, and just being free — living life on your own terms. Doing exactly what you wanted to do when you wanted to do it. The Bopo Boys, three of them are brothers of mine. Rob Alexander was this kid that we called "Bopo," because he bounced around when he walked. It became a nickname for him, and they just took it from there and ran with it. Our gang had a club, the Grey Door. We got pretty notorious. I'm a Jak, I was never really a Bopo Boy, but since they were my little brothers, I was with them all the time.

MARK ARM: There was a group of punk rock dorks called the Bopo Boys, who would go around in a little pack carrying their skateboards. They would get the smallest guy in the group to try and pick a fight with someone, and then they would all gang up and beat the shit out of whoever took the bait.

LIBBY KNUDSON: They were a loosely organized gang, I guess. They all looked like they were brothers — they were all skate hooligans. They were all very sweet for the most part. They were cute and dangerous.

JOE TOUTONGHI: I wouldn't call it a gang — it was more *a brotherhood.* Just a bunch of guys that really looked out for each other. We didn't go fight other gangs, we didn't sell drugs — on an organized level. There was no organization to it — just a bunch of guys from different walks of life that loved skateboards, punk rock, and travel around. We caused a lot of havoc — we did a lot of shitty things to people. We got in fights all the time — we didn't fight alone. We'd go to parties and just pilfer the liquor cabinet and medicine chest. It got to the point where we would be kicked out of shows and parties before we even got there, by people that didn't know us. A lot of what you've heard about the Bopo Boys is true.

TIM HAYES: It was just like one massive party back in the day.

JOHN LEIGHTON BEEZER: I used to call it "the small world effect" — "How do I know you? Oh yeah, your sister went to school with my drummer's brother. And also, we both work at Starbucks."

MARK ARM: That's what was cool about the Seattle punk scene, as opposed to what went on in the L.A., Boston, and New York hardcore scenes. We didn't have a bunch of bald ex-jocks beating the shit out of hippies or each other. In Seattle, the punk, hardcore — or whatever you want to call it — scene of the early '80s was pretty open. Anyone could come.

CHAPTER 4

"'79 through '84 was *hopping*": Power Pop, New Wave, Heavy Metal

Right around the time that the seeds were planted for grunge, Seattle experienced an explosion of power pop, new wave, and heavy metal–based bands around the region. Some were forgotten (the Allies, the Beakers), some thrived locally (Shadow, TKO), while some would go global (Queensrÿche, Metal Church).

DAVID KINCAID: Part of the early '80s was a revival of the '60s. The early Beatle thing became huge again — the Kinks, Creedence. Sixties stuff played with a modern edge. It became part of the downtown club scene. That early period — '79 through '84 — was *hopping*.

DAVE DEDERER: In '79/'80, there were a couple of really good bands in town, that almost broke out. The Heaters, who became the Heats, had a big regional single called "I Don't Like Your Face." They were skinny tie power pop, like the Shoes or 20/20. And there was another band called the Cowboys. They weren't really punk rock — either one of them could have been rock stars. They were just great rock 'n' roll bands. They played at bars mostly, but they would play at the U Dub Ballroom or outdoors at Seattle Center at the Mural Amphitheater.

MARK SMITH: The Visible Targets were predominantly a girl group — we always laughed about their name because the girls wore tight spandex pants and they had big asses. "Visible Targets," get it? The Beat Pagodas were very good live. Really interesting music — lots of percussion, no guitar — a fun dance band. We played with the Neo Boys from Portland, we played with 54-40, there were other bands like Rally Go! and Little Bears from Bangkok.

KIM THAYIL: The Beakers were pretty cool — sounded like Gang of Four, Talking Heads, Pere Ubu. Quirky, herky-jerky — that chaotic, edgy element of new wave.

MARK SMITH: For [the Beakers'] first show, it was just really a noisy amateur trio. Oddly enough, after that show, the guys that ran Modern Productions were like, "Do you want to play at the Showbox?" We were like, "OK, we're going to get a bass player." We had met the guys in the Blackouts, and the singer in the Blackouts' girlfriend, Frankie [Sundsten], played the bass pretty well — she joined us. We were on a compilation from Mr. Brown Records, which was K Records early, then a seven-inch single also from Mr. Brown Records, and then Engram Records put us on the first *Seattle Syndrome*. That was it. And we recorded some other stuff, but we didn't last long enough to release it. A lot of that's on [2004's *Four Steps Towards A Cultural Revolution*].

PIC BY KRISTINE LARSEN — KRISTINELARSEN.COM

The Beakers

KURT BLOCH: The Young Fresh Fellows' first record came out [1984's *The Fabulous Sounds of the Pacific Northwest*]. Got in a van, and started playing around the country.

DAVID KINCAID: [The Allies] wrote this tune, "Emma Peel," and ended up getting lots of local play, which was unheard of back then. We were on the air for ten years with that tune — it kept us working. By the time I left Seattle in '85, we were pretty much the top-drawing club band. The Heats had national interest from labels — they had toured with Heart. At one point, we had a producer come up, who had produced the Bangles. At another point, another label came — the choice was between us and Queensrÿche. They signed Queensrÿche. The woman had the nerve to say to me, "Does the world need another band like the Allies?" I shot back, "Well, they sure as hell don't need another Queensrÿche!"

KURT BLOCH: There was a metal scene, a regional bar band scene — that was going fairly strong then. Bands playing mostly original music.

TIM BRANOM: In 1981, when I first started playing out live, there was a pretty big scene going on, with Lake Hills and Bellevue. That's where Myth would play a lot — with Geoff Tate — and a bunch of other bands. Geoff Tate would always put glitter in his hair. They were really good — they were actually better than Queensrÿche, but they didn't get the record deal [laughs].

MATT VAUGHAN: Geoff Tate was in Myth and his vocals were untouchable — he had that Euro metal thing about him. The guy was essentially an opera singer with a five-octave range. At the same time, there was a band called the Mob — named after the Black Sabbath *Mob Rules* record. Those two bands knew of each other, and Geoff secretly slipped in for a few days and cut a demo. My mom, Diana Vaughan, had been an independent label promoter in the '70s. [She] heard it, got 'em a deal to EMI before they even did a show. It was kinda tricky though because Geoff never quit Myth and the demo had no band name attached to it, so he had to be lured over. As the name might suggest, Geoff was a bit of "a myth" himself — nobody saw him around much. He lived in Tacoma, was reclusive, went to Skinny Puppy shows, and took opera lessons. A month later, they received a feature story in *Kerrang!* That was that — they sold millions of records, toured the world. They had to come up with a name quick. The first song on the demo was "Queen of the Reich" — [Queensrÿche] was cut from that. Great band for its time and I'm sure guys like Mike McCready and other metalheads pricked up their ears. It was also a motivator for a Seattle band to make it big. This was a metal city, no matter how you slice it.

KURDT VANDERHOOF: I left the Lewd, and stayed in San Francisco for almost a year, trying to put together Metal Church. There was a small group of us in San Francisco — we would get Iron Maiden imports, Motörhead, Saxon. All that stuff from England. I couldn't find any good musicians that wanted to do a metal band. I wound up coming back home and starting it with people that I had grown up with.

EMILY RIEMAN: Over there in the metal scene, the girls all flocked after guys who were in bands. It was definitely the boys were in the bands and the girls were not. Remember, we're talking about eighteen-, nineteen-year-olds, and they're all setting up this pseudo rock star environment, where there's a backstage, and who's in and who's out. And I was like, "What the fuck is this all about?" [Laughs.] It was the antithesis of what the punk scene was in Seattle.

MARK ARM: I remember seeing Overlord, and the singer had really long hair, an all-red jumpsuit, and Capezio dance shoes. One guitarist looked like Johnny Ramone, the other kept throwing kisses out into the audience and shaking everyone's hands in the front row — at one point he may have thrown flowers into the crowd. The scope widened, and there was more co-mingling — not so much in terms of music, but at least in terms of parties. The parties weren't all punk rock people anymore — there would be punks *and* people who were in Shadow and Overlord, and their friends who were not afraid to hang out with the punks [laughs]. But I think that's an important thing — especially in the Green River to Pearl Jam trajectory — which includes Mike McCready from Shadow. The kids in Shadow were really into Def Leppard, Hanoi Rocks, and KISS. I remember their goal was to sign to a major label at a younger age than Def Leppard.

EMILY RIEMAN: I went to high school with [McCready] at Roosevelt. When I was in high school, my friends were basically the Fastbacks and the Silly Killers — all these people in that crowd, who were a bit older than I was. One night, Shadow was playing with Overlord somewhere in Seattle, and almost on a lark, everybody was like, "Let's go see what these bands sound like, these metal bands — it'll be funny." And I said, "No! It'll *not* be funny! You don't understand, I go to high school with these people — they're fools man! They walk around the halls of Roosevelt High School like they're fucking rock stars, and they're *sixteen years old!*" All wearing their spandex and stupid hair. I just loathed that shit — I hated Roosevelt, I hated high school.

PIC BY PATRICIA COLE

Evidence of rampant eyeliner and Aqua Net abuse in Seattle, early '80s

I said, "You're not going to make me go see these people play on my own free time on the weekend." Of course, everyone was like, "No, let's do it — it'll be fun." So we all got into the car and went. I remember Lulu [Gargiulo] was standing too close to the stage — there was a line between the band and the audience — and they actually had some security person pull her off, and that created a lot of havoc. At one point, this girl was yelling at Lulu to "Get the fuck out of the club!" I ended up grabbing her around the neck, and Lulu punched her straight in the face. It was a total clash between punk rock and metal. I remember getting in the car with everybody and going, "I told you they were stupid!"

DAVE DEDERER: That scene was much more influential than it gets credit for. They'd have shows at Lake Hills and hundreds of people would show up. As opposed to the shows downtown at the time, where sixty-two people would show up.

MATT VAUGHAN: A lot of that was coming out of the east side — prior to the Microsoft boom. It was very much like an *Over the Edge* suburb — where kids wanted to blow up their school. I guess you could call it "the Lake

Hills scene" — there was a skate rink called Skate King, and on certain nights, they would have heavy metal shows. Battle of the bands — Shadow was one of those bands. So there was a huge metal influence going on.

TIM BRANOM: The scene just kept on moving. I remember it started off in Bellevue, and it worked its way into Ballard, this little Norwegian town. A lot of really talented bands like TKO, Rail, SATO, and a lot of bands from the Lake Hills era were huge.

JOE SHIKANY: [Rail] entered the basement tape contest [for MTV] and won a record deal. But before they had done any of that — they got on a tour with Van Halen. They toured the country with them and were totally unsigned.

JERRY CANTRELL: TKO was another band that I thought was really cool. I loved Brad's voice.

PIC BY PATRICIA COLE

Proof that Seattle punkers weren't safe from mullets

BRAD SINSEL: The second TKO album [1984's *In Your Face*] led to a big part of the tragic metal scene in Seattle. We tested it out in a lot of all-ages clubs — Mr. Bill's and the Lake Hills Roller Rink. Queensrÿche used to open for TKO, Jerry and all those guys from Alice [in Chains] were kids when we were doing that Lake Hills stuff. It was good for us, because we had a little pull, so we could headline — we could do whatever we wanted there. If you rocked and it was heavy, you were accepted.

TIM BRANOM: My girlfriend and all the girls looked almost exactly the same — really slutty, spiky blond hair with hairspray. Everyone had a leather coat and jeans.

ED FOTHERINGHAM: They were probably all listening to KISS, and I was listening to Devo. There's actually not that much difference.

JEFF GILBERT: I was so entrenched in the metal scene. Metal at that point [was] more into getting out of that big "doom and gloom" crap. We had tough, lean, mean, punk rock–inspired metal bands like Metal Church, Forced Entry, Panic, Bitter End, Coven, Sanctuary. Stripped down, street machine metal.

JACK ENDINO: The Accüsed was another one that mutated from a punk rock band into a thrash metal band. The Accüsed started in '82, and are a fairly crucial part of the scene, because they're still around today.

SLIM MOON: The Accüsed was always a riot. They had that whole Martha Splatterhead thing — an iconic cartoon image that would be on all their records. They called themselves "splatter core." If somebody started out punk and then got a metal influence, that was really respected. But if they were metal, and then got a punk influence, they were suspect. So the Accüsed — because it started out as a hardcore band — was taken seriously. But their shows were just crazy. I got an elbow in my face that gave me a scar on my eyebrow. The last time I ever did a stage dive was at an Accüsed show.

TIM BRANOM: The Accüsed seemed like the most powerful band I'd ever seen in my life. I would be standing right next to the singer as he was singing, and you felt like the place was going to explode. Like a volcano was going off.

BLAINE COOK: There was a point, for a year or so, the Accüsed had really garnered a lot of popularity locally. But right after I joined, things dropped out. A lot of the all-ages clubs that were in Seattle — the downtown area — closed down. So after the first show we did in Seattle, there was nobody there, literally. It actually took us quite a few years to get a good reception in Seattle.

TIM BRANOM: About this being a huge Seattle scene — it wasn't. At all.

CHAPTER 5

"A floodgate of creativity in the Northwest": Blackouts, Fastbacks, U-Men, Mr. Epp and the Calculations, Duff McKagan

Five artists/figures figured prominently in grunge's formation — the Blackouts, the Fastbacks, the U-Men, Mr. Epp and the Calculations, and Seattle native Duff McKagan — the latter of which would move to Los Angeles and go on to fame as a co-founding member of Guns N' Roses. A small and tight-knit Seattle music community created a local buzz.

JIM TILLMAN: The Blackouts were probably the best band to ever come out of Seattle. *Amazing.*

LARRY REID: The Blackouts were probably the forerunners to what was later known as "the Seattle sound." They weren't your standard punk rock band — they had a pretty sophisticated sound and instrumentation. Really influential band.

BILL RIEFLIN: I have a specific memory where Eric Werner, after the Telepaths broke up, asked if I wanted to be in a band with him and the bass player from the Telepaths. I hated that idea — being in "a rock trio." So I said I wouldn't do it, unless there was a fourth element in there. Roland Barker, with whom I lived, was an interesting character — played keyboards and saxophone. He was a little shy at first, and we kept at him until he agreed. So then the Blackouts formed. I remember our first show — the Cultural Center at the University of Washington, a little theater — we played with

Red Dress. [Bassist] Paul Barker got involved in 1981 — he'd been living in Germany. Then the next significant thing that happened in the Blackouts is all the band's gear was stolen. That left us as a three-piece, playing bass, saxophone, and drums. That one incident radically reconfigured and redirected the Blackouts.

PAUL BARKER: We played a show at this horrible club at Pioneer Square — Baby-O's. This was unfortunately one of those circumstances where the club was a bar . . . at the time, the liquor laws were such that if you were going to serve hard liquor, then fifty or sixty percent of your income had to come from food. So you'd play at a place that was a fucking restaurant — or the owner would separate the restaurant from the bar area — but they would still be connected. I don't remember the name of the band that we were opening for — it was one of the more popular bar bands. We felt that we were not connected to that bar bands scene, we were [part of the] punk rock scene. So we thought, "If we're going to open for this horrible band, then let's do something really great." Our manager managed to get a gallon of pig's blood from a butcher, and we decided that we were going to cover ourselves in ash and pig's blood, wear loincloths, and perform that way. So we did, and it was incredibly nasty [laughs]. I don't remember how well that show was attended, but it was pretty gross. In hindsight, did anybody really care at the time?

BILL RIEFLIN: There was another time that the Blackouts — for Halloween — dressed up as Hasidic Jews.

DAVE DEDERER: They're one of the better bands I've seen anywhere. I first saw them in maybe 1982 — I remember going to see Killing Joke and they opened. I had heard their EP, [1981's] *Men in Motion*. Bill Rieflin had this unbelievable snare drum sound — the rumor was that he had a timbale with a snare mounted underneath it. They were just unbelievable. And Eric, the singer, was an amazing front man. They blew Killing Joke away.

BILL RIEFLIN: Our manager at the time worked at the Showbox Theater, and they brought in a bunch of national and international acts. So we got the pick of shows to open for. In one way, it made us unpopular with people. We played a lot and we were a really good live band — we just didn't do a lot of recording.

DANIEL HOUSE: Their music had this sharp, angular angst — almost like shattered glass.

JOE NEWTON: It was fully realized and full-formed — not just people scratching away at the surface. And that's part of the reflection of the real early Seattle scene — it was just people scratching around.

LARRY REID: Unfortunately, right around the time they peaked artistically, they left town. That left a void, that was filled almost immediately by bands that would become more closely associated with grunge.

PAUL BARKER: We lived in Boston for a couple of years, played a bunch of shows there. Unfortunately, the daily grind really started wearing on everybody, and the concerns were more towards, "You have to pay your fucking rent." We thought, "If this is the way it's going to be, then why don't we move somewhere we actually want to live?" So we moved to San Francisco. Everybody managed to get jobs and we played shows. Eventually, there was a point where nothing was happening. Although everybody loved the idea of the band, the band just didn't have any energy anymore. A fair degree of apathy set in — it just dissolved. When we were living in Boston, we met Al Jourgensen — he produced an EP for the band. I stayed in touch with Al, and after his *Twitch* record, he wanted to get a band together. So I asked Bill Rieflin and Roland Barker — the three of us then went on tour with Ministry in '86.

BEN SHEPHERD: One of my favorite bands was the Blackouts. That's a record you should find [2004's *History in Reverse*].

PAUL BARKER: I was hanging out with [Kim Thayil] one time. He goes, "I remember the Blackouts played a final show in Seattle at the Lincoln Hall — it was really sad. I was there with my friends and everybody was really upset." I said, "Really? I didn't think anybody really cared."

LARRY REID: The Fastbacks were around — the Fastbacks were more of a punk-pop synthesis. This is really proto-grunge era — the basis of the sound started to emerge at that point.

KURT BLOCH: After the Cheaters split up, my parents' basement had our gear there, so, "Let's play some music — I'll play drums." We played like that for a little while. "I'm not very good on drums, let me get somebody else." And we never stopped. [The Fastbacks'] first show was in early '80. The only thing we could do was rent a hall and put on our own shows. We weren't twenty-one yet, and certainly none of our drummers were even close to being twenty-one. I think one of the times we tried to play in a bar, the drummer wasn't even eighteen — he wasn't old enough to fill out a Minor Musician's Permit, to go in and play in a bar.

KIM WARNICK: That Fastbacks formed when we were just out of high school. We were just the worst band in the world. Lulu could hardly stand and sing and play guitar, I wasn't even singing at that point, and Kurt was the worst drummer. It probably wasn't until our friend decided to join — Duff McKagan. He actually could play the drums, so Kurt got to move to his actual instrument — the guitar. Somewhere around that time, I started singing. And then the drummer problems started, as we had many through the years.

EMILY RIEMAN: I remember [Kim] once saying it seemed ludicrous when the Fastbacks were playing — she was onstage, she'd look out, and everybody she knows or hangs out with was standing there watching the band. It was just this moment of absurdity to her.

KIM WARNICK: We were never the most popular band. We weren't hardcore, but we were fast. We weren't punk . . . I guess we kind of were — but we didn't really fit in anywhere. We were just floundering around, trying to put out records, and playing shows. We did a couple of good shows — we opened for PiL and for the Ramones.

KURT BLOCH: We couldn't get anything done. We didn't have any money, and we barely had jobs. We put out a couple of EPs and a 45, wrapped them up and sent them to people. Other than Vancouver and San Francisco, I don't think anybody seemed to like us at all — almost least of all Seattle [laughs]. We'd play very infrequently around here — we'd play Vancouver often enough, because there was a good scene up there in the early '80s, that you kind of felt part of. For some reason, DOA liked us — I think the first tour we did was open a bunch of shows for DOA.

The Fastback's Kim Warnick (Kurt Bloch in background)

JOE KEITHLEY: They were just a great band — a real pop band that had cool songs and played well. Pioneering punk-pop.

CHARLES PETERSON: I remember seeing the Fastbacks, and [saying], "Wow, those are the *real* punk rockers."

KIM WARNICK: The records started sounding better — Kurt was producing and it got better. People started to like it — we could actually go on tour and make enough to stay afloat out there. Stuff that never happened for us before.

EMILY RIEMAN: What was so great about the Fastbacks — there were girls in the band. That totally shaped my entire view that there was never for a minute anything weird to me about a girl being in a band. To this day, when they make "the women in rock issue" in *Rolling Stone*, it always seems bizarre that it's even an issue that people talk about. Because it was just ingrained in my brain — it was perfectly normal — because Kim and Lulu were my friends.

[Kurt Bloch] was an amazing guitarist. It wasn't just a bunch of punk rock and barre chords — he could play *anything*. That's what was so great about seeing the Fastbacks too — they would whip these weird covers out of the closet. They would play "Everybody Wants Some!!" by Van Halen — you'd be standing there like, "What the fuck? Is this really what I think it is?" Kurt Bloch could play it exactly like Van Halen. It was just so funny to see Lulu sing these David Lee Roth lyrics! They were totally marching to their own drummer.

The Fastbacks' Lulu Gargiulo

KURT BLOCH: We played "Highway to Hell" once opening for DOA in 1981, and people started spitting and throwing their shoes at us. It's like, "Wow, what's the matter — don't you guys like AC/DC?" It didn't even occur to us that people would be pissed off.

EMILY RIEMAN: I remember "the Fastback House" — Kim and Lulu lived there, and all the bands practiced in the basement. The Living — that was Duff McKagan's band — the Silly Killers, and the Fastbacks. I'm lucky that I was surrounded by people where even though it was a rough and gritty punk scene, we would listen to Alice Cooper, Cheap Trick, and Parliament. So I always felt I can listen to anything I want freely and openly. I don't think I realized how special that was until later when I met a guy from Charlotte, who was talking about how there was a line drawn between people that were new wave, hardcore, and metal. They did not mix. I thought, "God, what a sucky way to be."

XANA LA FUENTE: I've seen all this stuff about Seattle bands, and no one ever talks about them. I don't understand why. All I know is that Kim is a really solid, stand-up chick, who was nothing but supportive of every musician.

KURT BLOCH: Certainly, the Fastbacks and the U-Men had nothing in common musically, except that we loved each other and were great friends.

CHARLES PETERSON: The U-Men were definitely the godfathers of the Seattle music scene. John Bigley is just this giant of a man — kind of like "a Quasimodo Nick Cave." They were so cool — they drove around in this crazy old school bus, dressed all in black, and just rocked.

BRUCE PAVITT: The U-Men pretty much dominated the scene. They were about the only thing going for a couple of years.

TOM PRICE: Me and Charlie Ryan started it — me on guitar — and we were both seventeen or eighteen, living in a rental house in the U District. Working as dishwashers and being unemployed a lot of the time. We were so poor, and we had no equipment. If Charlie broke a drumstick, we wouldn't be able to practice for a week, until somebody got paid, and we were able to buy another pair of drumsticks. Just total cobbled together equipment. Our original bass player was a girl named Robbie Buchan, who was a runaway from Alaska, and we met John Bigley, who was more from the hardcore end of the scene. We'd see him at parties, and he was this amazing character. One of the first times I saw him, he tripped and fell through a window. Broke the window, landed in a pile of glass on the ground — four or five feet below. Charlie and I went, "Man, we should get this guy to be our singer!" We had no idea if he could sing or anything.

JOHN BIGLEY: At a Johnny Thunders show, Robbie came up and asked me. Apparently, they thought I was crazy — they were intimidated.

TOM PRICE: We had all these songs with no lyrics. He didn't, at that time, write lyrics — we were practicing in a basement, and there was all kinds of cleansers and paint cans. He would pick up a paint can, and start singing whatever was written — all the technical information. He was always high or drunk — just out of control. We started out playing parties, and you never knew if he would actually sing or not. Sometimes he'd not feel like singing — he would just attack somebody or fall.

JOE TOUTONGHI: Bigley was an intense screamer — really intense eyes, almost a stalker-looking kind of guy onstage.

JOHN BIGLEY: Early, we made it thirteen shows that were raided by the cops or called off — or noise complaints. We got a bit infamy for that. I don't think that any of our first shows were at an organized club or even with a PA. It was pretty crude stuff. Keg of beer, people running around on acid.

TOM PRICE: In 1982, Robbie quit the band, and we got Jim Tillman on bass. That changed everything. He was an amazing bass player — just a really great musician. He had some resources, some equipment, and he knew how to fix amplifiers. The whole level of technical proficiency went up.

JIM TILLMAN: I was blown away. There'd be a song that was total balls-to-the-wall punk rock, and then weirdo chords. Tom really liked seventh chords, so he had this signature sound with his Mustang.

LARRY REID: John Bigley came to me — I remember this phone call like it was yesterday — "We need some help." I'd gone to see their band a couple of times, and I was just fascinated. It was this strange concoction of hardcore punk, traditional Northwest garage, rockabilly, and psychedelia — even though they didn't know how to play their instruments [laughs]. You'd go to their shows, and didn't know what was going to happen. So I took [the U-Men] under my wing. I guess I was managing them — they were fairly unmanageable by 1983.

TOM PRICE: Larry Reid really knows how to promote stuff — take a regular show, and turn it into an event. A lot of the shows we did, we'd have ridiculous costumes or a gimmick. I remember doing a Halloween show, and we all performed wearing Speedos and swim goggles. It made people think, "What are they going to do next?"

TIM HAYES: I remember seeing a show with a wrestling match in a loft. They had a ring set up and before the U-Men played, they had a group of local amateurs wrestling.

TRACY MARANDER: They had a gal come out in a bikini between songs, and she would hold up a card with a number. Like between boxing rounds.

SUSAN SILVER: One show at the Rainbow, they wrapped themselves in sheets and dusted themselves in ashes.

JOHN BIGLEY: Then the reputation grew — slaughtering of animals [laughs]. If you were cool, you'd make it to the show. Maybe we'd actually play, and you'd have something to talk about.

TOM PRICE: Sometimes, we wouldn't really even play — we'd do some weird sketch or something.

DAVE DEDERER: The only band that I care about from that era was the U-Men, who in my opinion, were maybe the greatest rock 'n' roll band of all time — *anywhere, period.* I'll never forget the first song of the first show at the Grey Door. Their first five-song EP [1984's *The U-Men*] is one of the greatest records ever, and it opens with this song, "Shoot 'Em Down," which starts with this guitar, and that *"WOW WOW WOW"* scream that John Bigley does. They come to that part where he yells, and the songs kicks in — I remember literally feeling as if I'd been lifted off my feet and slammed against the back wall. It was one of the greatest live music moments I've ever experienced.

JOHN BIGLEY: Another one of the bands rented the Laurelhurst Community Center — Laurelhurst is an affluent suburb out by the University of Washington. We loaded our gear in, and word got out that "the weirdos had taken over the community center!" A "vigilante group" of teenagers from the neighborhood got together, and started breaking out car windows and beating people up in the parking lot. Somehow, got the Bat-Signal out, and some of our toughest, craziest, doing-that-punk-rock-thing-'cause-they-had-to people showed up, and equalized the whole thing. Lots of people running around bleeding, screaming, and crying. The police showed up, and started throwing our shit into the parking lot — *just chaos.*

CHARLES PETERSON: Every year, Seattle has this festival at the Seattle Center called Bumbershoot. [The U-Men] played at the Mural Amphitheater, which is outdoors — there used to be a little water moat around the stage.

I think it was a Friday afternoon at four. Back then, for someone like the U-Men to play was pretty daring. Unbeknownst to anybody, Larry decided to set the moat on fire during their show! [Laughs.] So he dumps bottles of gasoline or kerosene into this moat, and set it on fire. The whole audience went fucking ballistic — in the middle of this field, there were about 100 people slam dancing madly. And all the other people — the families with strollers — [their] jaws dropped! A couple of lame security guards thinking that we were all fighting or something, and trying to pull us all apart. They just got trampled. Of course, the U-Men were banned from ever playing the Seattle Center again.

TOM PRICE: It was cool being onstage and having this solid twenty-foot wall of flame right in front of you.

DAWN ANDERSON: I saw an acoustic U-Men show that was incredible. I remember being mostly impressed by Bigley's voice — he was this great blues singer.

LARRY REID: When the U-Men got on Homestead, that really kicked open a lot of doors, and opened a floodgate of creativity in the Northwest. The U-Men's sound didn't have much in common with grunge, but their attitude did. A lot of the bands that became well-known opened for the U-Men. Other venues would begin to book some of these edgy bands, because the U-Men proved that they could make money.

JIM TILLMAN: We were one of the first underground/weirdo bands to go on tour. This was in 1984, and it wasn't a nationwide network of venues that you just hop from night to night and play. We would rely on friends and network the people we knew. I saved up a bunch of money, and bought a school bus, and we drove around the country at fifty miles per hour. Going from Los Angeles to Texas to Minneapolis. Played some amazing shows with amazing bands — the Butthole Surfers, Tex and the Horseheads, Scratch Acid, Tales of Terror. One of the destinations for those tours was "Woodshock," which was taking place in Austin at this crazy ranch, with a river running through it. It was a two or three day festival. I heard this story once I got there — a couple of guys were driving along in their pickup truck on their way to Woodshock, and they saw a lone cow close to the road. They shot and killed it, stuck it in the back of their pickup truck, brought it to the show, skinned it, made fajitas out of it, and sold them [laughs]. A little entrepreneurial spirit.

MARK ARM: The U-Men went to Texas and stayed in Austin for a month, and basically just starved. Tom Price will tell you he was eating raw potatoes because he didn't have any money.

JIM TILLMAN: I found one of our notebooks, and we had [tour cost] breakdowns. It was really hilarious — at one point it says, "$60. Beer: $20. Net: $40. Alternator: $60. Net: negative $20." I was very skinny — I had a gallon of peanut butter I had brought from home and lived off of that. And I discovered when you're really hungry, if you drink a couple of root beers really fast and jump up and down, it'll fill you up.

JOHN BIGLEY: Lots of trouble with the law — we got messed with a lot. There was a very low level of respect back then for us and what we did.

TOM PRICE: To describe what the U-Men did as "touring" is kind of a misnomer. I think our first tour we were gone for three months and we did maybe five or six shows. It was more like we'd migrate down to L.A. for a month, then we'd migrate over to Texas. Eventually over the years, it got to be a little more like a regular tour.

JOHN BIGLEY: This fellow [producer John Nelson] mainly did bluegrass, children's music, and gospel. We wound up sticking with him for the majority of the recordings we did. Another standout was he was booked, and we needed to get this single recorded. We got recommended to this studio — kind of heavy metal, north end, up in the suburbs. None of us had a car, so we had five cabs full of stuff. A fellow answers the door with [a] crazy ass metal black T-shirt, big beard, and long hair — Rick Rubin–looking guy, without the cool part [laughs]. He's pretty nervous. Just the way we looked, and we used old equipment — old Fenders and beat-up amps. We get set up, we did this instrumental — I was looking in the glass, and the guy is rolling his head around. The guy is speechless — staring at the console. Tom goes, "Is there something wrong?" And that guy looks up, and goes, "Nothing's wrong, unless you consider the fact that you go against every musical recording principle.

This is the most asinine garbage I've ever heard. *We're done.*" Takes off his headphones, turns off the light, goes out in the hallway, and gets on the phone. The next morning — we actually recorded in the daylight, in the a.m. — at Crow, where we had gone all the time before. Banged out this seven-inch — "Dig It a Hole" and "Solid Action."

LARRY REID: In 1985, I left and turned the band over to Susan [Silver].

JIM TILLMAN: Susan was great — a true music fan. Susan stepped in and tried to help us get some gigs — but it was all sort of informal. Her interest in music led her to start managing other bands, and eventually, managing Soundgarden. She helped us as much as she could — she did wire us some money for [an] alternator. We probably still owe her that.

TOM PRICE: Eventually, the band fell apart — around '88. One day, we were all kind of drunk, and I went on about, "Man, we've got to get going, we've got to start touring — it's time to shit or get off the pot." And everybody kind of nodded, "OK, OK." The next time I went to band practice, nobody else showed up [laughs]. I hadn't quite realized that I presented an ultimatum. Even after that, it took a while to get it through my thick skull that everybody quit the band.

DAVE DEDERER: They drove so many things — even though they didn't sound like what grunge became. The U-Men's level of musicianship was fantastic. They had a real rhythm section that swung. "The grunge guitar" became a Fender Mustang with the racing stripe on it — as played by Steve Turner, and copied by Kurt Cobain. That was Tom Price in 1983 or '84 — he had a red Fender Mustang, which *nobody* in the world played at that time. Seriously — it was like a junk guitar.

NILS BERNSTEIN: John Bigley was way sexier than Chris Cornell.

LARRY REID: The success of the U-Men really started to make a lot of these younger musicians consider punk rock as almost a viable vocation. I would see them at almost all the gigs — Stoney Gossard, [Steve] Turner, Mark Arm.

MARK ARM: A couple of the kids I hung out with in high school had this imaginary band named after a math teacher, Mr. Epp. We would find whatever was at hand, and just record it. We'd record stuff into a cassette player, mess with it, scream into another cassette player, and turn on a vacuum cleaner, and stuff like that. We didn't have any idea what we were doing — just entertaining ourselves. This AM radio station started up, KZAM — it was the only radio station that embraced new wave. One DJ there, Stephen Rabow, at one point decided, "If you're in a band, send in your tape, and I'll play it." He devoted two of his whole shows, which I think were three hours apiece, to playing *whatever* came in. We sent in something, and he dubbed it "By far the worst, and hence, the best thing that came in" [laughs]. We were super jazzed. We went on a flyering campaign around Seattle — it was all about Mr. Epp. We didn't have instruments, but we would stick up posters around downtown Seattle. After [Mr. Epp's drummer] Darren's sixteen-year-old brother joined on bass, he would take a bus downtown to the Free Zone. Most of the buses in King County would come through the Free Zone downtown. And he would go from bus to bus and write "Mr. Epp" on the back of the seats. It got to the point where if you got on almost any bus, there would be Mr. Epp graffiti on it.

EMILY RIEMAN: I was walking down University Avenue with Satz around '82 — there was a poster for Mr. Epp stapled up. I said to Satz, "Who the hell is that?" And he said, "Eh, some geeks from the east side" [laughs].

MARK ARM: We figured out that we could rent halls and put on shows ourselves. We would ask other local punk bands to play, many of whom had *no* idea who we were. They probably thought we were geeks, and that we were bullshit. We opened for Savage Republic at Ground Zero Art Gallery. Darren wanted to cover that Velvet Underground song "The Gift." We switched instruments, and Darren pulled out this reading lamp, and read the story. That really pissed off some of the punks. This idiot Walter and some of the Bopos created havoc, and broke windows at that show because neither Mr. Epp or Savage Republic were "punk" enough. In the process of playing in this band, we picked up a few principles about playing music, or at least rock 'n' roll. Like, we learned about the barre chord and how to tune a guitar [laughs]. We never made any money — we'd lose the damage deposit because the toilets got trashed. One time we lost our damage deposit at the Polish Hall, because the Bopos stole meat from the freezer.

DAVE DEDERER: They were coming down the Pere Ubu spectrum to me — or Flipper, early Butthole Surfers. Openly trying to be aggravatingly, annoyingly weird.

STEVE TURNER: [Mark] wanted to make the band more "rock 'n' roll," and he convinced them to let me join on second guitar. That lasted six months — we practiced a lot, played two shows, the other guys didn't like the more rock 'n' roll leanings, and broke up the band [laughs].

MARK ARM: I first met Steve . . . I think it was at a TSOL show. He had just started playing guitar shortly before [joining Mr. Epp]. We worked on new stuff for six months before playing another show. Then Darren and Smitty decided that they didn't want to do it anymore. So we played a farewell show at the Metropolis. Darren and Todd's dad ran a hair salon. One of them filled up a garbage bag with hair clippings swept off the floor. We threw that out over the audience during our last song — nearly choking the crowd and ourselves.

JOHN LEIGHTON BEEZER: I was going to school in California, and would read *Maximumrocknroll* to see what was going on back in Seattle. And nothing sounded interesting at all except for Mr. Epp — "Mohawk Man" was a great track.

SUSAN SILVER: It was a real sense of community and enthusiasm. You'd have to ask yourself, "Has Mark Arm cloned himself? Because he's everywhere!"

JOE TOUTONGHI: [Duff McKagan] was part of the punk scene. That was before he hocked everything and moved to L.A.

DUFF McKAGAN: I was in a lot of bands, man. I'm the last of eight kids — a lot of my brothers, sisters, and kids in the neighborhood were hippies. So around my house there were a lot of acoustic guitars, drums. Hendrix and the Stones playing on the stereo. But it seemed like it was too old for me . . . although I dug it. I started seeing punk rock flyers for gigs at the Bird, with the Lewd, the Mentors, the Enemy, DOA, Subhumans. It was scary and exciting at the same time. And I was already playing guitar at this point — one of my older brothers had taught me a few chords.

PIC BY LIBBY KNUDSON

Duff McKagan goes the way of the beret

This guy came walking down our street — he would walk home from school — and he had a pink Mohawk. I was like, "*That's one of those dudes!*" One day I went out there, and was like, "Hey man, what's going on?" His name was Chris Utting. He said he was starting a band, and Andy — this kid I came up with — and I had been playing at our junior high school, up in this sort of "jam room" at Eckstein Middle School, where they had some amps. Chris Utting was starting a band, with this guy from the Refuzors — one of these band's names I'd seen on these flyers. This is like '78 — I was fourteen. We'd take three buses down, and we started writing songs with Mike Refuzor. It was the first incarnation of this band that became the Vains.

DAVE DEDERER: The first time I met [Duff] was at a friend's house at a party in seventh grade. He had a silk shirt on opened to his navel, stood next to the stereo, and played DJ and air guitar the whole night. He was already known to be a talented musician in seventh and eighth grade.

DUFF McKAGAN: Playing with Mike Refuzor was fucking cool — that guy is awesome. There were junkies down at his apartment — very eye-opening for me. There was a girl down there — she was dying from cancer and she was strung out on dope. It was *so real.* I was still living with my mom, but they welcomed me and Andy into this really punk rock, hard environment. They took us for what we were — a couple of kids. You were accepted for whatever you were, which was cool, because I didn't really know where I was accepted at school. I got kicked out of school, and got expelled a couple of times. So it was a place for me to fit in. Then Mike Refuzor went back to the Refuzors, so we kept going.

JOHN LEIGHTON BEEZER: He was *so freaking cool.* He was the baby in this family of older brothers who had all perfected the art of being cool ahead of him, and handed it down. He was a leather jacket punk rocker in '79 — I definitely studied him. I remember running into him later. He said, "Hey, I haven't seen you in a while. What are you listening to?" And I listed three bands — Motörhead, Agent Orange, and something else. He looks down at his jacket, and he's wearing three pins — Motörhead, Agent Orange, and . . . I'm like, "He must think I'm the biggest idiot!"

JOE TOUTONGHI: Duff and I were really good friends. I met him playing pinball at a used record store on University Avenue — Cellophane Square — that had pinball machines in the back. Drink beer and playing pinball for hours — they were open 'til midnight. They'd always have punk rock playing.

DUFF McKAGAN: I was asked to join the Fastbacks — they wanted me to play drums. Kim Warnick was really important to me — she had a car and all the coolest music on cassette. She had *everything.* She'd come pick me up — I was already listening to the Ramones, the Sex Pistols, and the Clash — but she turned me onto the Sweet, Slade, and T. Rex.

KIM WARNICK: He was so young — like fifteen. We were in Vancouver, Canada — we did some radio interview up there. They asked us, "What do you hope to get out of playing music?" And Duff said, "I just want someone to move my equipment for me!" You have to be careful for what you wish for.

KURT BLOCH: He played with us until late 1980, after we recorded our first single ["It's Your Birthday"/"You Can't Be Happy"]. We probably argued too much for him — sat there fighting and throwing shit at each other, instead of getting anything done.

DUFF McKAGAN: I was always playing in at least two bands. I started playing drums in the Fartz — right around when I turned seventeen. That was pretty kick-ass.

BLAINE COOK: He was a member of the Fartz for a short period of time. We did the single, "Because This Fuckin' World Stinks," and then Jello Biafra wanted to do something with us. This buddy gave us $500 to record [1982's] *World Full of Hate* twelve-inch EP. Back then, you didn't have gear — you just had whatever you could cobble together. We were all stuffed in Tommy Hanson's VW Beetle, making our way to the studio. You had to rent tapes, because tapes were $200. We were able to get all the recording and mixing in one evening. And there was enough money afterwards to get beer and burgers at Dick's.

MARK ARM: The Fartz were the fastest band that I'd seen — I saw them open for the Dead Kennedys. I decided that as long as the drummer keeps a beat, it doesn't really matter what the rest of the band is playing. Of course, listening back to their seven-inch a few months later, I realized they were actually playing riffs.

JOE TOUTONGHI: I painted his mom's deck and front porch with him. We brewed our own beer, Duff's Brewskies — that was long before *The Simpsons* had Duff Beer. Ed Huletz — the Silly Killers' singer — his mom bought an investment house, and Duff, Ed, and I lived there. Had insane parties every night — pretty much went crazy at that house.

BLAINE COOK: I called him "Duffski" at that point in time.

JOHN CONTE: We're both Catholics. Catholics have a tendency to notice one another — just by our mannerisms, habits, or how we speak. As a musician, he reminds me of the stories of Brian Jones — being able to lock him into a room with an instrument that he had never played, and come out fifteen minutes later, having learned how to play it. Good Lord, you'd go to a party, and the girls were all over him within fifteen seconds.

DUFF McKAGAN: Paul Solger and I started playing guitars together, and decided to explore that — we morphed Ten Minute Warning into this really heavy, experimental band. Our singer, Steve Verwolf, was this guy with long hair and tattoos, and he'd pour silver paint over himself when we played. Greg Gilmore was the drummer, and he would play with his back facing the crowd. It was a really fucking cool band. Really heavy, really slowed down. Born in this damp basement of this girl's house — that's where we stayed and rehearsed.

LIBBY KNUDSON: Steve Verwolf was a little "hairy-scary" — you never knew what he was going to do.

JEFF AMENT: We were in such awe of that band. They seemed a little less approachable.

BLAINE COOK: Them kicking me out of the band one Sunday morning, and not paying me for the last shows we did — that was the last memory with Duff [laughs]. Wanting to get my $15 so I could go see the Damned play. I ran into Duff, and I was like, "What the fuck? Where's my fifteen bucks from that show?" "Oh, that got used for something else." Luckily, I ran into some other clown I knew — he had just won tickets off the radio.

DUFF McKAGAN: I didn't plan on leaving [Seattle]. What happened in Seattle in the early '80s . . . recession hit Seattle especially hard. There was no Microsoft — there was just Boeing. Boeing was going through some problems in the '70s, they were threatening closing down, and there were billboards around Seattle — "Would the last person who leaves Seattle please turn out the light?" Basically, Seattle was going to *shut down*. And it almost did in the early '80s. You'd go downtown, and I swear, it would be, like, newspapers blowing down the street. Pretty desolate. And heroin started to creep its way into the scene. It became epidemic by '83. There was pretty much no place to play — except for rented rehearsal places. If you were twenty-one and over I guess there was, but it wasn't supported by the punk rock scene — because everybody was underage. That's when I bailed — in August of '84.

JOE TOUTONGHI: He was going to give himself a year to become a rock star. He had an old black '72 Maverick or something, that the brakes went out on, and he crashed into a BMW dealership down there. But he did it.

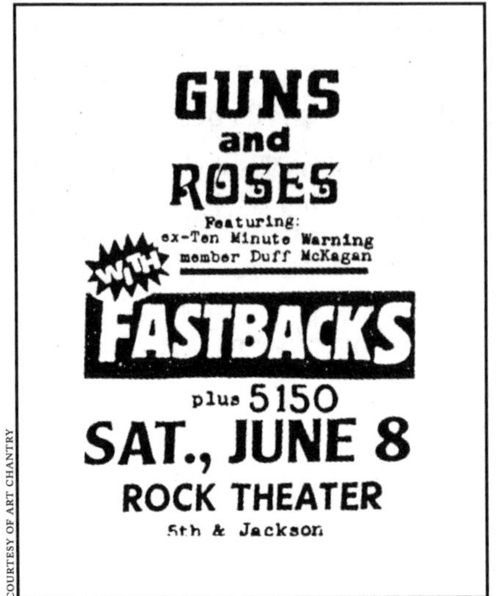

Whatever became of the Fastbacks' bill-mates?

JOHN LEIGHTON BEEZER: I have no idea what happened in Los Angeles, but based on what I do know about Guns N' Roses, he went down there, was looking for a band, found some reasonably talented musicians, and kicked them into shape. Axl Rose was quoted in interviews as saying, "I was really influenced by Elton John." OK, well, whatever happened with Guns N' Roses, it wasn't coming from him [laughs]. I see Duff as basically the guy who went down there and preached the gospel to the savages. Guns N' Roses making it was the first indication that whatever we were onto was for real.

BLAINE COOK: I remember when Guns N' Roses first came to play in Seattle. That was maybe 1985 — he showed up wearing some long, black and red leather trench coat.

MARK ARM: Guns N' Roses played one of their first shows at the Gorilla Gardens. There was a packed hardcore show in the other room, but only a few people — mostly Duff's friends — watched Guns N' Roses. I went 'cause I saw a flyer that said "DUFF'S NEW BAND FROM L.A.," and I was a huge Ten Minute Warning fan. I don't remember much except that they butchered a couple of Stones songs. I couldn't believe that Duff quit Ten Minute Warning and moved to L.A. for this. They did get way better — I watched them destroy the Cult a couple of years later.

DUFF McKAGAN: [Guns N' Roses] opened for the Fastbacks up there. That year I was down in L.A., we formed this band, and we wanted to tour right away — we didn't have a record out or anything. I booked us a punk rock tour — down the West Coast, starting in Seattle. We had to hitchhike to Seattle — our car broke down not even 150 miles outside of L.A. — and use the Fastbacks' gear. So we were pretty dead tired. It took us three days to make it up there. We played the gig, and we *sucked*. But it was fun for me to be up there — hanging out with all my old compadres.

JOHN CONTE: Duff was going to make it. I don't even think it was on his to-do list. It was just going to happen.

TOM PRICE: I remember running into him when the U-Men were down there. He had clearly lost weight — hadn't eaten in quite a while. A few months later, "Welcome to the Jungle" hits, and Duffski is a super rock star.

CHAPTER 6

"Church was really in session": Venues, *The Rocket*, Record Stores, Radio

In addition to bands, other factors figured prominently into the creation of grunge and the Seattle music scene of the '80s, including punk venues where up-and-coming bands could play, *The Rocket* newspaper, select record stores, and local radio.

EMILY RIEMAN: In the early '80s, there were a lot of all-ages clubs. Someone would rent the room at UCT, IOOF, the Polish Hall, or St. Joe's. It was real do-it-yourself punk rock.

TIM HAYES: There seemed to be a lot of alternative venues: the Golden Crown, Danceland, Rosco Louie, Washington Hall, Gorilla Room, Bahamas Underground, Wrex — which turned into the Vogue — Astor Park, the Meatlocker, the Funhole, the Mountaineers, Rainbow Tavern, Grey Door, Graven Image, Metropolis, the Ditto, and of course the Showbox.

LARRY REID: There were sporadic attempts at creating venues — the Bird comes to mind.

NICK SCOTT: The Bird was basically an Odd Fellows Hall, I believe, with the shows on the second floor, and a big staircase that I would periodically stumble down completely wasted after getting peanut butter thrown all over me by the Weirdos. The Talmud Torah would become the venue for out of town bands. The Talmud Torah — like all the punk clubs — was filthy, in a questionable area, and smelled like old beer and punk rockers' sweat. It got hotter than hell in there with the 650 BTUs coming out of each person, and would just shake when some of the louder bands would play there. I think it had become the Showbox by this time.

JOHN BIGLEY: Back then, [the Showbox] was more of a rental hall. No drinks — just $5 in, goons at the door, bad PA, and that was it. They had some really killer shows — church was really in session.

KIM WARNICK: It's a pretty big place. I think its capacity is 1,000 or so.

REGAN HAGAR: The Showbox was a little oasis. Right in the downtown area, by the public market. If you go there now, it is so cleaned up — it's hard to imagine it was ever that way. I went in with another friend, Rob Alexander, from Bainbridge High School — this guy approached us, and said, "Do you guys want to come to the show next week? Hang these flyers — I'll let you in for free." So we hung flyers, and then that following week, a guy who worked for Modern Enterprises — which was a couple of guys who were bringing bands to the city — were renting out the Showbox. I basically didn't leave. I was one of the youngest there — we ranged from fourteen- to nineteen-year-old kids. We did everything — cleaned it, hung posters for the week's shows, tore tickets, ran security. They basically paid us in cheap beer for the longest time — we were just happy to be there. We also had a room that had a lot of records, and we hung out there during the day — like a club fort.

BLAINE COOK: Regan Hagar and I had a "black market thing" there — we were taking people's money and letting them in at shows that were sold out. We had quite a little bank account set aside.

KYLE NIXON: The floor — during the shows — would bounce up and down, because it was spring-loaded.

ROD MOODY: It was always an adventure, due to the presence of a donut shop next door, which attracted the creepiest drug-pimping lowlife imaginable. As well as a bunch of brainless heavy metal kids. So when punks with two-foot-tall pink Mohawks ran into these people, it got pretty sketchy. Fights and stabbings were commonplace on the sidewalk and in the parking lot.

REGAN HAGAR: It lasted for a few years, and then those guys tried to get bigger and branch out into renting bigger venues, and it all fell apart. The Showbox shut down for a few years, and then later reopened. I think for a while it turned into a showgirl place.

BILL RIEFLIN: Rosco Louie was a really great place — it was an underground art gallery down in Pioneer Square.

LARRY REID: I graduated from art school and opened up a gallery in 1978 — Rosco Louie. It was heavily influenced by punk rock. I started incorporating punk shows into visual art aspects of my gallery. Fairly small, but we had a remarkable run of interesting national and local bands. One hundred people would really pack the place. We had a lot of groups that otherwise wouldn't have come to Seattle — Arto Lindsay's DNA, the Bush Tetras. I closed the gallery at the end of 1982. I went to a show in 1983 in San Francisco at a place called Tool and Die. I just fell in love with this dingy little place, and in 1983, I opened Graven Image Gallery. The focus of that was less on visual arts — it was a club and a practice space.

ALICE WHEELER: The Graven Image was a really small art gallery down in Pioneer Square. They had a basement where bands would play — it was really claustrophobic, especially when you got like twenty-five people in there. I remember seeing the U-Men play there.

DYLAN CARLSON: The Graven Image had a sister club that was even smaller and dingier — the Grey Door.

ROD MOODY: The Grey Door hosted some amazing shows. One of the more memorable involved a group of skaters who built a bonfire in the middle of the street at a Suicidal Tendencies show, and skated through or over the flames.

JONATHAN EVISON: The Grey Door used to pay us in pot.

BRUCE FAIRWEATHER: It was like a Bopo Boys' club. They had quarter pipe in there, so people could skateboard around, and the Bopo Boys would basically stand around and act tough. They tried to steal your beer.

BILL RIEFLIN: The Gorilla Room I remember didn't last very long. Places were always being opened up and closed down — by the liquor board, or the police. Anything that smacked of wildness — like a bunch of kids renting halls and playing music — was really suspect, and watched very carefully.

DUFF McKAGAN: The owner who ran [the Gorilla Room] was pretty shady, and that was good for us — because we could go in there, drink, and play. The Liquor Board came in there, busted me, and arrested me. That place actually closed down not too long after that.

MARK ARM: In 1983, a Frenchman named Hugo — who had saved up a bunch of money fishing in Alaska — came down to Seattle and decided that he wanted to start a youth center. He got a space in Pioneer Square and opened up the Metropolis. I don't think his dreams of a youth center materialized, but it became an all-ages place, where punk bands could play. It was a place for touring bands and local bands alike. Mr. Epp played there — Hugo paid us $100 the first time. We were like, "Oh my God, I can't believe we made *$100!*" The Metropolis was a musical incubator for the kids who were on the cusp of becoming twenty-one. Several of those kids would end up in Soundgarden, Green River, Girl Trouble, Skin Yard, Feast, the Melvins, and Nirvana. Buzz Osborne and Matt Lukin from the Melvins would drive out from Aberdeen almost every weekend to hang out at the Metropolis. They would crash on somebody's floor, and then go back to Aberdeen on Sunday. Sometimes they'd bring friends, like this really tall guy, who turned out to be Krist Novoselic. I'm sure Kurt [Cobain] came with them sometimes, but I didn't meet him then. They would have assorted people — ranging from total stoner freaks to future lumberjacks. Dale Crover was one of these stoner dudes with the sheepskin-lined denim jacket and a scrub moustache [laughs].

JEFF AMENT: The Metropolis really allowed us to grow. It was easy to get a show, no matter how crappy your band was. They had shows three, four, or five nights a week. I went up and asked Hugo, "I can't afford to go to all these shows. Is there some work I can do?" He said I could sweep up after

PIC BY PATRICIA COLE

Crowd chaos at the Metropolis, 1984

every show and get in for free. A really great, communal vibe there — almost hippie-like, in some regards.

TRACY MARANDER: I remember the Metropolis being dark and black inside — it was pretty small and very sweaty. The smell of clove cigarettes.

ROD MOODY: Susan Silver — later to become Mrs. Chris Cornell — worked the door and helped book the shows.

SUSAN SILVER: Metropolis was physically a beautiful space. It had been an old bar — probably in the turn of the century — so it had a gorgeous wood carved bar. An old one-story brick building in the area of Seattle known as Pioneer Square — where Seattle was really built, and then built again once it burned down. This was the early 1900s. [Hugo] and my boyfriend Gordon [Doucette] put a lot of energy into the inside. It had been empty for years, and they did a lot of really creative things with color and galvanized steel, and built a stage. There was a parachute for a stage backdrop. Our posters every week said, "All ages, anyone." It was really a place for people to come and enjoy music, but also to be creative. It was a space for people to come work on art projects, or have community meetings. We'd rent these 16mm films from the library and show foreign art films on the wall without sound during the show. I ran the Juice Bar, helped with the atmosphere, and mediating between the partners if necessary. That segued into booking shows on my own after it closed.

ROD MOODY: It was all pretty remarkable considering the place only lasted a year — before "the man" shut it down.

MATT DENTINO: [In the] fall of '84 a friend had me work on an old Chinese movie theater — Gorilla Gardens. Opening night, I tended bar and all the alcohol disappeared quickly — cheap drinks to my friends. That proved to be my payment for all the backbreaking work I had done. They had rows of discarded Boeing airplanes seats used in the theater which I had to move myself after cleaning, then de-trashing that rat infested gig near Chinatown. Someone said Bruce Lee had visited there when they showed his movies in the early '70s. He is buried in Seattle and went to UW [University of Washington] too.

CHRIS HANZSEK: It was all red velvet chairs — red velvet carpet.

CHARLES PETERSON: That was a rank place if there ever was one [laughs]. But a really vital venue.

KIM THAYIL: There were two venues — Rock Theater and the Gorilla Gardens. The whole thing was called "Gorilla Gardens/Rock Theater." Sometimes you'd have one set of acts in one hall — two different admission fees. Sometimes you'd have one admission fee and have seven bands alternating stages. That did well for a few years — they got a lot of national, international, and local bands. It was an opportunity for local bands to open up for touring acts.

MARK ARM: Sometimes, there would be two different shows going on at once. And sometimes, there would be a pop metal show in one room and a punk rock show in the other. These two audiences would meet in the lobby and

PIC BY PATRICIA COLE

The March of Crimes plot their next move (note a slightly afroed Buzz Osborne in the crowd)

toilets. It was so funny, you'd see these punk rock dirt bags mixing with kids in pink spandex and teased hair. I'm sure everyone from each side was looking at each other saying, "You look retarded!" [Laughs.] I remember watching a security guy stop a David Lee Roth emulator at the door because he had a bottle of Jack Daniels. And the fake David Lee pleading, "You've got to let me in; I'm supposed to be onstage! I need this bottle! It's not really booze — *it's filled with Coke.*" The security guard sniffed it, and let him in.

MICHELLE AHERN-CRANE: Andy [Wood] took me to my first punk rock show — it was his eighteenth birthday — at the Gorilla Gardens. It was a sort of infamous night — where the rockers got into a fight with the punk rockers. Andy, at the time, was a rocker, and I remember seeing somebody pick him up by his white fur coat and hurl him into a chain link fence. It is a notorious show, because it was on the news. I don't know what caused it — it was really obvious what camp you were in back then.

SCOTTY CRANE: The two crowds got in a fight that spilled into the streets and Molotov cocktails were being thrown — vandalism through the area. News helicopters captured it for the evening news. I remember watching it on TV with my mom — who was horrified — and said that I would not be able to go there anymore. As if either of us had a choice — the club was closed for good.

KIM WARNICK: The Crocodile Café is another great one — smaller, but it's been here since the early '80s. I know the Fastbacks played when it was a Greek restaurant — I think we may be one of the few bands that can attest to that. It was like playing your living room.

DUFF McKAGAN: The Vogue was the Wrex before it was the Vogue — it was twenty-one and over. You had to sign your minor's musician form to play there. In the Fastbacks, we played there opening for Joan Jett, but I would have to go in, go straight to the stage, play the gig, and leave. It wasn't any fun for me.

GARRETT SHAVLIK: The Vogue shows were always Tuesday and Wednesday nights — that's not your typical party night. And there was this guy, Monty, who was the bartender, and he owns the Vogue. He dressed in drag, but was this burly guy. And Monty was super sweet, he was like, "Anything you guys need, just let me know."

BEN REW: You'd go up to places like the Frontier Room, and people were fucking nodded out of their skulls. That was right down the street from the Vogue.

KRISHA AUGEROT: The Monastery was a gay disco, that for some reason or other, they started marketing to regular kids. On the weekends we would go there with Stone and Regan, and some of my friends — I hung out with a group of girls that were all very young. Fourteen years old and going out all night long — doing drugs and staying there from nine to nine in the morning.

DAVID MEINERT: [The Monastery] was targeted by the more social conservatives. There were all sorts of rumors of drugs, teen prostitution — although I think really, it was a gay dance club. They eventually passed this law, called the Teen Dance Ordinance — if you had anyone under eighteen, you couldn't have anyone under fifteen or over twenty-one. It basically shut down that scene.

DYLAN CARLSON: In Tacoma, there was a place called Community World Theater, that had a lot of shows.

ALLISON WOLFE: [The Community World Theater] is a great place — an old theater that was scraped out, and Nirvana played there all the time. Neko Case worked the door.

KIM THAYIL: There was the Golden Crown, that we played at a couple of times our first year. The Bad Brains played there once for five bucks. And then they started booking more local acts. It was upstairs from this Chinese restaurant. The Golden Crown was more downtown.

JEFF AMENT: When I think about when it really happened, I think about the Ditto Tavern. There were basically ten or twelve bands playing two or three nights a week. A bunch of great bands came out of that — Feast, Bundle of Hiss. It was really small — fifty to 100 people. It was a real friendly, competitive vibe. It was like, "Show us what you've got." I remember being at those shows and being psyched, like, "Wow, our little bands are getting *good*."

CONRAD UNO: I tended bar at [the Rainbow Tavern], and [Jonathan] Poneman and KCMU started having Tuesday nights there. It was a tavern — your typical beer and wine pub — but they had music there for twenty years. The main indication for me was that they started having these Tuesday nights, and they started being big nights.

LIBBY KNUDSON: The Central in Pioneer Square was always kinda walking the gauntlet, because that was "Fratville" down there.

MATT FOX: The Motor Sports Garage was this old shell of a garage. It was really cavernous — probably built in the '20s or '30s. By then, it was almost semi-destroyed. It was an odd place — there was a big, expansive parking

PIC BY PATRICIA COLE

The Accüsed rock the Metropolis, January 6, 1984 (note Ben Shepherd in the crowd on left)

lot. It was in the part of town by the Re-bar and RKCNDY, where there wasn't much else in service around there.

BEN REW: I worked at the Paramount and the Moore Theatre. The Paramount didn't look like it does now. They would have showcases, and it would be half full. It was pretty rundown — they kind of modernized it when they redid it.

JEFF GILBERT: Some of the better ones were some of the worst ones — i.e., Squid Row. If you looked under "shit hole dive" in the dictionary, it would have their picture there. But that was the thing — the metal guys were always smarter. They found ways to do bigger and better shows — they would rent halls. Throw their own kegger parties outdoors on hand-built stages. The grunge guys never did that. They would just pack themselves in insanely small corners, and the feedback was horrendous. And nobody knew to turn it down — to play less than ten would mean you're not serious. These places stunk so bad — from the bathrooms that never got cleaned, to the beer that spilled and never got mopped up. The grunge crowd, I've got to tell you, these people *did not bathe.* And you put them in a room that gets sweaty and hot — ugh. I swear, it would bring tears to your eyes. It was like moshing with rancid onion people. The metal guys all just smelled of beer and leather.

MARK SMITH: Early on, nobody cared. I mean, *The Rocket* cared.

GRANT ALDEN: I worked at *The Rocket* — I was there for seven years and two weeks. Charlie Cross and I had gone to college together, and I had written for Charlie in college. When we were both getting out of college, *The Rocket* was briefly for sale — but it really wasn't, it was just sold to the people who were working on it. Charlie and I talked about buying it, and then six years later I think, it went on the market again. It had been owned by a sort of consortium of people, who had taken equity in lieu of salary. And many of them no longer lived in Seattle, so it was agreed to sell it. Charlie was in a position to buy it, and I wasn't, so I went to work for him. A couple of years after I started, Charlie got a contract to do a Springsteen book, and gave me the magazine to run while he was doing that book. Then he got another deal to do a Led Zeppelin book. So it ended up being four or five years that he was doing books and I was managing editor. He came back and I left. I worked from February of '87 to March of '94 — I was managing editor from March of '89 to March of '94. I got to know my way around the music industry. I got to have a career by having that job at that time that I would not otherwise have had.

ART CHANTRY: Everybody hated *The Rocket* because it always had a snotty attitude towards everybody. It's been kind of erased from the history, but the truth is *The Rocket* was the kiosk/information-point/gathering-point for the Seattle underground. Without *The Rocket*, half these bands would have never formed, because that's where they met each other — through the free musician classified in the back. Even Nirvana formed out of that. And Sub Pop Records began as a column in *The Rocket*. Art directors for *Newsweek, Village Voice, Metropolis, Vibe, Vanity Fair,* and many others started out at *The Rocket.* So I ended up becoming the art director [at *The Rocket*], and I was probably the most notorious of all the art directors — I was art director four times over ten years. Through that, I started to meet more and more of these people. You might walk in, and Kim Thayil would be hanging out, or maybe even Robert Crumb would be there for some reason. It was this amazing flow of people.

GRANT ALDEN: When Charlie bought *The Rocket*, he thought that the way to make it more viable was to put bigger name national acts on the cover. As it happened, about the time Charlie got those book contracts, there started to be local music that was compelling. Now, there were staff arguments about direction — constantly — to the extent that I rose to power as the voice of those who argued we should cover local music. I got to work with incredibly gifted designers. I got to work with a couple of the best photographers in the country — notably Charles Peterson.

CHARLES PETERSON: I shot in black-and-white for two reasons. One was economic, and it's kind of all I knew really — from my experience with the high school newspaper and yearbook — as well as by photographers like Robert Frank, Garry Winogrand. It has a certain resonance to it that color doesn't. But beyond that, you can develop it yourself in your bathroom. From my friend's bands' purposes, what they usually needed was black-and-white versus color at that point. As far as "the flash and drag shutter effect" goes, I took that one from Garry Winogrand — the classic street photographer from the '60s and '70s — I saw a series that he did at the Fort Worth Rodeo, and he used that effect. I started playing around with that, and for a while, took it to the extreme.

ART CHANTRY: Charles Peterson was like a "photographer's photographer." He is by far the best photographer — the guy is brilliant. [Sub Pop] exploited the shit out of him — I don't think they ever paid him a dime for anything. They traded letting him use their bathroom as a darkroom in exchange for free photos.

TOM HAZELMYER: I think one factor overlooked in the development of Seattle musically was the fact that the city had more good record stores than any city its size should normally be able to support. Places like Fallout were as vital if not more so than any club at the time. I remember meeting more folks that way than in any club setting.

MATT VAUGHAN: Fallout is essentially where Sub Pop was born. I think their office was there, behind the store for the first year or two. Those [Sub Pop] tapes were coming out of there — and all those early singles — right out the back of the record store. So that gives you an idea of how influential a record store can be to what became the scene — Sub Pop essentially renting space from a record store that was only about 500 square feet. Cellophane Square was *the spot* in the U District. It was more of a garagey scene. The Replacements probably broke right out of that store — as far as turning people on to that band.

KATHY FENNESSY: I worked at Cellophane Square in the U District. Sometimes [Nirvana] would come in, and Mark Lanegan, Matt Cameron, Kim Thayil. I would find out what they were into. I remember Kurt [Cobain] bought a Bats album — [1990's] *The Law of Things. Very un-grungy.*

JOHNNY RUBATO: At [Rubato Records] we were a music/cultural connection for many suburban kids who were looking for something a little more rock 'n' roll than their malls were giving them.

MATT VAUGHAN: On the west side of town, you had Penny Lane, which is where I was working. It closed and I opened Easy Street in '88 while still a freshman at Seattle U.

SCOTT VANDERPOOL: The fun part was a fair amount of the Sub Pop roster was working at Muzak. There was this big tape duplication room, and they would all call me at the radio station when I was on, and make requests. Everybody's music influences would come together on this radio station. KCMU was all volunteer at the time. For example, Friday afternoons were me and then Mark Arm.

MARK IVERSON: KCMU was totally listener-sponsored, listener-powered — just like WFMU. [Playing local bands] was highly encouraged, and we were lucky, because we had really good local music. Bruce Pavitt used to be at KCMU, as was Kim Thayil — there was a bit of a legacy at the station. And Mark Arm used to be there — it was always fun to read his comments on the records. He'd used his real initials — his name is Mark McLaughlin — so if he liked an album, he'd write, "MM . . . good!" Quite a lot different from what it's evolved into — KEXP. There was a local show called "Audio Oasis," which was really good.

SCOTT VANDERPOOL: In the late '80s, because I made enough of a stink at KCMU, I got offered a job at a commercial station — KXRX. There wasn't really what they would call an "alternative station" now, at that time. There had been KZAM, "the rock of the '80s" — they folded.

DAVID KINCAID: We had a great radio station, AM sort of modern rock that was alternative — KJET. Jim Keller was the program director — he would play everything — anything that wasn't commercial. And he would play a lot of local stuff.

JOE NEWTON: There was a station called KRAB that was really eclectic — more eclectic than KCMU at that time.

CATHY FAULKNER: KISW had two specialty shows — one was called "Seattle Zone." Damon Stewart introduced the community to a lot of bands before anybody knew who they were. Almost to a point where it was like we were beyond our "Seattle quota," and it was hard to balance it with a lot of the other national bands. The shows ended up becoming completely local and almost incestuous.

CHAPTER 7

"The punk rock David Lee Roth": Malfunkshun

To many, grunge music is associated with flannel shirts and Doc Martens boots. However, one of the first-ever grunge acts was glam-based — Malfunkshun. The group featured flamboyant singer/bassist Andy Wood, and despite their glitzy attire and makeup, proved to be a major influence and favorite of future renowned grunge bands.

DALE CROVER: We were at the Gorilla Gardens, and Buzz [Osborne] is telling me, "There's this band that's going to play, Malfunkshun, and their bass player dresses like a chick. He's really pretty looking. He says he'll walk down the street and dudes will whistle at him — then they realize he's a guy!" As he's telling me this, I'm listening, but also watching this really cute girl in a fur coat with white pancake makeup walking to the stage. I'm watching this girl take her bass up onstage, plug in, and then go to the mic, and say something, and I'm like, *"OH!"* They had really funny stage banter — them being from "Olympus" and playing "love rock," with "Landrew," and "Thundarr" on drums. They were really wild — they had this guitar player who constantly played crazy leads. Almost Eddie Van Halen–style, but sometimes no rhyme or reason at all — it didn't matter if it was in key.

SLIM MOON: Landrew took the whole glam thing to its ultimate/most ridiculous conclusion. He was on a complete separate track from the '80s glam thing — the post–Van Halen, hair metal, L.A. thing. He took the original '70s influences as far as you could — Marc Bolan, Elton John, and KISS. This character, Landrew the Love God from Mount Olympus. But the songs were good.

The incomparable Landrew the Love God

DAVE REES: I moved to Bainbridge Island in 1974, meeting Andy Wood shortly after that. I was in seventh grade, he was in fourth. I was home sick from school — Andy came to our house with my younger brother to listen to records. What could fourth graders be listening to? Andy put on "Paranoid" by Black Sabbath. When he was in sixth grade, Andy won a contest to go on KZOK and have his own radio show for three hours. He had a couple of bits worked out, did a Mister Rogers impression, played a lot of KISS and Alice Cooper. He was brilliant. Later, he called it "depressing." He realized his dream of being a disc jockey was over — there was no immediate feedback from the audience. Andy said, "Now I'm going to have to be a rock star."

REGAN HAGAR: I liked him right away. We were both outsiders to the scene. And he accepted me being a punk rocker. He had long hair at the time — I was a little confused why he was so open to everything. They just made a movie about him [2005's *Malfunkshun: The Andrew Wood Story*], and they didn't necessarily talk about what a comedian he was. He used to tell me if he didn't make it in rock 'n' roll, he was going to be a stand-up comedian, and I think he would have been successful at either. We discovered a lot of things together — drugs and whatever else.

KEVIN WOOD: He brought home his first bag of weed when he was in seventh grade. Me and my brothers were always partying. The only drug problem we had was when we ran out of drugs — otherwise, we were OK. Brian and Andy fought a lot, but I think it was mostly lighthearted. Brian would tease Andy — Andy was younger. Andy would blow up and Brian would laugh — it was kind of a game for Brian to see how he could push Andy's buttons. It was 1980 or 1981; Andy and I decided we were going to skip out on Easter dinner at my grandma's house. We stayed home and made a tape — we called it *Malfunkshun*. Later, we hooked up with a drummer and bass player. After a while, we got together with Regan, who became *the* drummer, and we formed as a three-piece.

SCOTTY CRANE: In 1980, my family moved to Bainbridge Island. One of the first people I met — because they lived two doors down — was the Wood family. I met Andy on the school bus. We got off at the same stop, walked down to his house. Regan and Kevin were there — they were about to practice. There was always craziness with Kevin and Brian. Kevin was really sweet and the oldest — kind of Andy's caretaker. Brian was insane and somewhat dangerous. There was one story I remember with Brian that his mother had told him to cut his hair or quit drinking. So he came home drunk with a bald head! And his mom moved out — I think disappeared for a month or something. There was a lot of stress in that house.

DAVE REES: I got my chance to perform with Andy in 1981. Malfunkshun was just forming and didn't have a bass player. I borrowed a bass from a friend and joined Malfunkshun, despite the fact that I had never played before. Our first show [was] near a strawberry field — Andy called it "the Strawberry Jam." On the way to the show, my 1970 Buick Estate Wagon was filled with equipment, so Andy and Regan rode on the roof. When we got to the gig, Andy's hair was gone — Regan had cut it off. Andy went on stage with a T-shirt that had a crossed out swastika — he was anti-hate, but had not come up with "love rock" yet. I later moved to Seattle and did the world a favor — gave my bass to Andy.

REGAN HAGAR: We would [wear makeup in public]. One time we each did half of our faces — he would do the left side and I would do the right side. I remember going to a basketball game one time like that — people just *freaking out*.

SCOTTY CRANE: Andy was so likeable as a person — onstage and off. He was so welcoming into his world that he could get away with *anything*. Even though he had a heart of gold, he did some really awful things that other people would not get away with. And with Andy, it becomes part of his folklore and part of his legend. One of the things — in high school, there was this guy — I'm guessing he made up this rumor, that he walked into this guy's room, and found [him] fucking a bag of marshmallows and smelling a can of tuna fish. And everyone believed it! The guy was just tortured by it. There was this other guy; he graduated in the early '80s. He lived on a goat farm and Andy made up a rumor that this guy was fucking his goats. In 1995, a friend of mine was going to Evergreen State College, and said that there was this older student there that everyone called "The Goat Man." I asked him what his name was, and I'm like, "Oh my fucking God — this poor guy!" It followed him all the way to Evergreen — for twenty years! Those are really mean, horrible things to say about people, but yet Andy got away with it.

There was a band in Seattle that played the high school dance that Malfunkshun had wanted to play. I wasn't at this dance, but the story that I heard is that Andy and Regan went, were mad about not playing, and maced the band. And got away with it! But that might be a myth.

REGAN HAGAR: Malfunkshun wasn't trying to play at the high school dance. We were at a dance, held in the cafeteria. There's a place called the Commons, that are outside, and we were hanging out there. The band was on break, and came walking out to the same area. Andy and I had our hair up, or some kind of eye makeup on, and the guys made some wisecracks. We made some smart-ass comments back about their band. One of the guys did not like that *at all* — they must have been considerably older than us. [He] came over and tried to grab Andy, and Andy and I had just figured out mace at that time — because Andy in particular was getting beat up quite a bit. He pulled it out and warned the guy, the guy laughed it off and came at Andy, Andy sprayed him, the guy recoiled, and his buddies started coming our way. Andy and I just took off running. The cops pulled us over — it ended up being nothing more than hassled, handcuffed, being put in the cop car. Never had to go deal with the band.

DUFF McKAGAN: Malfunkshun were playing some gigs on the island, and started to come over to Seattle to play at the Grey Door. There was Andy with his Steinberger bass with no headstock, dressed in KISS makeup. The Grey Door, the biggest gig there was maybe fifty people, and whenever Malfunkshun played, there were probably five or ten. But he would be onstage and point to the left — "*I want all of you out there!*" — like he was playing an arena. It instantly endeared you to the guy.

PIC BY BLAINE COOK

Kevin Wood, pre-metallic makeover

DAVE REES: Malfunkshun was the loudest and most entertaining three-piece band I've ever seen. Yes, they were louder than Motörhead.

KEVIN WOOD: Everyone had a good time at a Malfunkshun show. It was an open-minded sort of feeling. I was afraid first, of offending the sensibilities of the punk rockers. But they welcomed us with open arms. I think we opened up doors for bands to just come out, be themselves, and play. It's kind of what started the whole evolution of the punk turns into the rock.

MARK ARM: I first saw Malfunkshun in '82, when they opened for Discharge at the Showbox. Andy tossed grapes in the air and caught them in his mouth between songs, when he wasn't giving some bizarre high-speed rap about how they came down from Mount Olympus. You never knew what you were going to get at a Malfunkshun show. Sometimes, they didn't seem like they could keep it together. And sometimes, they were the best band ever.

REGAN HAGAR: Having guitar solos in our music was totally taboo for punk rock. We were mixing styles, where other people weren't. People were into the 666 stuff, and we were 333 — good fighting evil. We had this whole imaginary world going on — it was Andy who was really generating that.

CHAD CHANNING: These guys were like glam rock, but their music wasn't at all. They were playing this total noise. The first recordings I'd heard before I ever saw them — I did *not* picture them to look like what they played.

BRUCE FAIRWEATHER: Andy would sometimes wear this hideous little quilted rabbit fur jacket, that would barely fit him — with his little cherub belly hanging out, and white makeup on his face.

SCOTTY CRANE: In between songs, he would tell jokes like a stand-up comedian. Jack [Endino] has a story about him stopping in the middle of a set to make a sandwich.

SUSAN SILVER: I put on a lot of shows at the Central Tavern. I would have him emcee as Landrew the Love Child, and he may sing a song or two, tell jokes, or be his effervescent, charming little self.

TRACY MARANDER: I remember we went to one [Malfunkshun] show in Olympia, where Kurt was really tired. Got a chair, sat, and fell asleep during the show.

STEVE TURNER: Malfunkshun — I'd seen them around at shows causing trouble and stuff. They were kind of a bad group of people [laughs]. They were always fucking things up at punk shows. They were part of the University Ave./Bopo Boys gang of punks that liked to wreck stuff. But they were really sarcastic and funny while they did it.

SCOTT VANDERPOOL: The guy was just born to be a rock star. And of course, being "rock starlike" at that point was really uncool. It was very un-punk.

MATT FOX: Andy was very quiet . . . and turned into Freddie Mercury onstage.

KRISHA AUGEROT: He reminded me of John Belushi — constantly made everyone laugh, he was a total showman. He wanted to be as over-the-top as he possibly could. And I think in his real life, he was insecure, but in his stage performances, he was like from another planet, [where] he ruled the world. Unfortunately, like most of these kind of artists like that, they have that dark side, and he was an addict.

SCOTTY CRANE: In probably '86, Andy's drug problem started to get bad. I had gone to Andy, to see if he knew where to get acid. He told me he could sell me a couple of hits. He said, "Come to the show tonight." I went to the show, and had taken this acid with a friend. It was totally fake. The next day, I went to his house, and was like, "Dude, you fucking sold me paper!" And he broke down and started crying. This is one of the rare times you got to see the heart of Andy. He told me how he was a drug addict and that he needed the money for cocaine. He said he would pay me back, and he did.

TRACY MARANDER: One time, we were at the Central Tavern. [Andy] was there, he was going to come into the girls' bathroom, and they were like, "You're a boy, you can't come in!" He's like, *"But I'm so much prettier than you girls!"*

DAVE REES: Andy was a promotional genius — his ideas were big. He wanted to compete with Van Halen and Aerosmith, not the local bands. As people walked off the ferryboat from Bainbridge in Seattle, [there] was a cattle walk — large metal walls on either side. Andy wrote a story on each panel of the wall. In the end it paid off with "Rock 'n' roll's only chance, Malfunkshun." Every person who rode the boat from Bainbridge to Seattle knew who Malfunkshun was — they couldn't escape Andy's marketing.

BLAINE COOK: Total self-promotion. They made a lot tapes and did a lot of Xeroxing — flyers all over town.

ROBIN TAYLOR: He was a DHL delivery kid during the day, rock star via night.

LIBBY KNUDSON: He was "the punk rock David Lee Roth."

SCOTTY CRANE: You would go over to his house in the morning and he would offer you breakfast. You would ask him what he was going to make, and he would say, *"Pancake surprise."* You'd ask him what the surprise was, and he would never tell you.

KIM THAYIL: If you were to have a conversation with him, he'd usually end up singing part of the conversation.

BLAINE COOK: We had gone to see those David Bowie movies, *The Man Who Fell to Earth*, and maybe one other one. I'm there with Regan and Andy, and this theater is just packed. His girlfriend at the time is completely, 100 percent sucking his dick [laughs].

CHRIS HANZSEK: Every time he would show up and record vocals for the *Deep Six* compilation, he'd be in full costume. Some brand new pair of sunglasses, a funky hat, a giant scarf, and a funny coat. I remember thinking, "This is a studio, you don't have to dress up." But he did — I think that's what got him into character.

HIRO YAMAMOTO: [Andy] lived with Chris [Cornell] for a while. [Soundgarden] practiced in that place. Andy would be there a lot hanging out. The two juxtaposed against each other — just seemed like two complete opposites. Chris was this real quiet, introspective guy, who barely even said a word, and Andy was this guy with a huge flair. It just seemed really funny that they were roommates.

REGAN HAGAR: That was a good time — we didn't like Andy being alone. He had already announced to us that he was a little scared of drugs. We would go to his apartment prior to that and bang on the door — we'd know he was in there, and that kind of freaked us out. He wasn't a junkie, but he was slipping around the recreational use that most of the people in town were doing. So when he moved in with Chris — and Chris is really straight — I was excited. I thought it was really good for both bands, because they pressured each other, and there was a writing frenzy between Chris and Andy. Andy got a girlfriend that started living there.

XANA LA FUENTE: A vintage clothing store is where I worked with this girl, Chrissy. Now they call them Goths, but back then, we used to call the people that dressed like that Bat-Cavers. She was a Bat-Caver, but with a slick, vintage touch. She always drove vintage cars — she was a big influence on me fashion-wise. We always dressed in '40s suits — every other girl in the '80s was doing feathered hair and black short skirts. Fantasy was downstairs at the time, and this vintage store I worked at was upstairs. Andrew and Regan walked upstairs into this little antique mall; Andrew was looking at a guitar that he ended up buying. Regan walked into this store I was working at. I remember him staring at me, and he said, "Just a minute." The story is that he went and told Andrew, "Your future wife is in the next room." Andrew walked in, we talked for a while — he was totally goofy. Wearing light brown corduroys. Capricorn men have no taste, OK? Really tacky. He was living in Bainbridge, and he would come into town every single day on the ferry, and sit, and talk with me for about an hour or two — hang out with me at work. We would have dates where we would hold hands in the park. We didn't sleep together until we were living together with Chris [Cornell]. I think that's a really important thing in a relationship. There's a lot of magic in that.

KRISHA AUGEROT: She was the love of his life. They were great together — both like rock stars. She was over-the-top, and she commanded a lot of attention. And so did he. I think they were really happy together. I just think that becoming a star in real life — moving to the next level — was a lot of pressure. So he turned to drugs a little bit more than usual. And Xana was . . . she sought attention from other places, when she wasn't getting it from him. That tore him up a lot. She had a lot of other male friends that she would hang out with — whether or not she had relationships with them, I can't say. But it seemed that way. I think Andy was extremely jealous, and probably in the back of his mind thought he wasn't worthy. That probably brought the dark side out of him more — the depressed side. That was a vicious cycle — that was the poison in the relationship. They got in physical fights a lot, but I think that he would go inward, and that would be a big problem for drug use.

XANA LA FUENTE: Me and Andrew lived with Chris for a long time. Chris had heard that Andrew was looking for a room to rent, and invited him to move in. And then I came along, and he asked him, "Can she live here too?" I remember telling Chris, "You won't ever have to wash any dishes or cook a

PIC BY BLAINE COOK

Regan Hagar, attempting his best Gene Simmons impersonation

single meal." And the day I was moving out, I was washing some dishes, and I'm like, "You fucking asshole, you never washed a single dish!" And he said, "Well, you said you wanted to be Mom!"

Next to the kitchen, there was this water heater room — no bigger than a closet. That was [Chris's] studio. He recorded a lot of really great stuff in there — original stuff for Temple of the Dog like "Wooden Jesus." I remember him throwing lyrics away — I used to take them out of the trash and un-crumble them. He'd be sitting on the couch drinking black coffee, looking at the ocean. He'd gotten laid off of Ray's Boathouse, and was really down. I said, "Don't worry — you're going to be a huge rock star."

KEVIN WOOD: We were thinking if [Malfunkshun] kicked ass long enough, somebody would take notice and sign us. We did a couple of demos, but we didn't do much about shopping it around. We had a manager, but it just fell apart. We recorded our demos in '87, and then broke up a year after that. We didn't really give ourselves a chance.

REGAN HAGAR: We always felt like we were influencing everybody, and we weren't getting what we deserved. For instance, we'd been a band for three or four years, and out comes Green River, and they were immediately drawing tons of people to their shows. They were doing really well — nothing ever went wrong for those guys. They were good friends of ours, but we were always confused how we got missed. *The Rocket* wasn't writing about us — the Fartz were on the cover. We didn't get a lot of the national acts spots — Green River or Soundgarden would. It was frustrating.

KEVIN WOOD: The main reason why we didn't get our just desserts is because the Mother Love Bone guys pulled Andy out of Malfunkshun. I mean, Andy of course decided to go along. His vision was clouded and he didn't see the end result. We were a more powerful band and had a lot more potential, because Mother Love Bone was conforming to the Guns N' Roses formula, and we were still a very unique, big-sounding band. We definitely could have gone a lot farther than Mother Love Bone, and Andy I think in the end would have been a lot happier. Malfunkshun was about freedom, and we had the formula down. We struggled for years — mainly with our own musical abilities — but finally fell into a groove towards the end. You could feel it was going to take off. And then all of the hype that came around with Mother Love Bone and Soundgarden — we were completely overshadowed.

REGAN HAGAR: We never said, "The band is over." We thought Andy was going to do Love Bone, and it was going to open doors for Malfunkshun — then we were going to be able to make Malfunkshun or Andy records, aside from Love Bone. But Love Bone — within months — had major labels looking at them. Within a year's time, they were signed and off to California recording and touring.

Now people respect Malfunkshun on a level that didn't happen then. But our egos were full-blown — we thought we were the loudest band in the city, and we prided ourselves on that. Which sounds ridiculous now. But you know . . . *teenagers.* It was still when the dream was perfect in a sense. Where you would get into a band, take over the world, become incredibly wealthy, and live in a very decadent lifestyle. It sounds trite, but that's really where we were at.

CHAPTER 8

"Godzilla knocking over buildings": The Shemps, Soundgarden

The roots of one of grunge's most renowned bands, Soundgarden, lay in the Shemps, an obscure group that specialized in the exact style that local punkers/proto-grungers looked to eradicate — cover bar bands.

KIM THAYIL: There's some book that said, "In the mid '80s, the only heavy bands going at the time [in Seattle] were Green River and the Shemps." I'm like, *"What?!"* The Shemps had nothing to do with that scene. *At all.* This weird bar band experience that lasted a handful of months — that's all it should be referred to.

HIRO YAMAMOTO: A friend of ours was in a cover band. This guy, Matt Dentino, was from Park Forest like we were. When he was in high school, he was a great guitarist — he played better than any of us. He was playing rock 'n' roll and put an ad in *The Rocket* looking for a singer.

KIM THAYIL: When we moved out to Seattle, Hiro did not play bass — he played mandolin. He learned bass because I was showing him all the scales. Matt Dentino was a fan of *The Three Stooges*, and nobody else was a fucking *Three Stooges* fan, or gave a shit about it. But Matt called it the Shemps because he thought it was funny. Hiro had no interest in the music, other than it was a learning experience for him — he would learn how to play bass in a working situation. So he did that for a couple of months, got sick of it, and quit. When

Hiro quit, Matt had his hands tied because he had booked a few gigs in advance. I never played bass in any situation other than jamming — I'm a guitarist. So he was crashing on our couch, and says, "Kim, if I get you a bass, would you learn these songs?" I was like, "Eh, I don't know man." As much as I love Hendrix, I just had no fucking interest in Hendrix, Stones, or Doors songs at that point in my life. But, he needed the help. Somehow, I ended up with a bass for a period of time.

MATT DENTINO: We played eight or ten times.

HIRO YAMAMOTO: Chris [Cornell] answered an ad as a singer, and he needed a place to stay. So he ended up moving into our house.

MATT DENTINO: When I first met Chris, he was a punk and, like, eighteen. He had short hair and was a cook. When he came in that little apartment — I was living in Kim's three by six closet for a year — he just knocked it out of the ballpark. I think the first tune we tried was "White Wedding," and that was it. He also did a scary Jim Morrison — his timing and phrasing on everything was just powerful and raw, the way it's supposed to be sung.

KIM THAYIL: Chris had been a drummer in bands, and wanted to try singing. Chris at some point knew it was a waste of time, but he also knew it was an opportunity to not play drums and practice singing in front of twenty or thirty people. Chris had a really good voice — but I had no interest in doing anything musical with the guy, because it seemed to me that Chris really wanted to be in a fucking bar band. If I pictured my "dream Stooges or MC5 band," none of these guys fit in this picture.

MATT DENTINO: The first Shemps gig was inside the Morning Star Cafe on Eleventh Avenue Northeast, which literally was a ten by fifteen foot cement room, complete with tables for patrons to sit. Matt Cameron was there.

MATT CAMERON: They were playing Morning Town Pizza — it was hippie pizza place in the University District of Seattle. I was playing with another band at the time — Feedback — that played before the Shemps. I remember Chris being a really strong presence — Chris's singing back then was still incredible.

KIM THAYIL: I was friends with Mark Arm, and I did talk Mark into coming to see us. It was pretty hilarious — a bunch of drunk blues-rock losers . . . and then Mark and me.

MARK ARM: Kim is an old friend of mine. We took philosophy classes together at the University of Washington. I met him at a TSOL show at the Showbox. This also might have been the show I met Steve at, but I clearly remember Kim at that show. Kim would always show up to class ten minutes late and proceed to monopolize the conversation — which irritated the professor to no end [laughs]. Kim ended up getting a degree in philosophy from the same institution. This guy with long hair and a moustache came up to me and said, "Hey, aren't you in my philosophy class?"

MATT DENTINO: Like any musician, I had a dream to have this killer world-changing band, and worked every day of my life to do so — especially all of '84. Right when it was just beginning to happen, I started to think that in all these dreams of everything I wanted, that maybe [I] really should not be there. It wasn't the best for me in a health kind of way — doing drugs, raising hell, and chasing women, *mostly unsuccessfully*, 24/7. I was raised with a patriotic moral basis, and I said, "Man, I've got to get out of here, because this sinning is really not good for me." Then I had an experience with God and I became a Christian. I knew they were going to make it. It was very painful, but I left to become a Christian, and minister music in churches, or wherever I play.

HIRO YAMAMOTO: Chris was living at my house and we started jamming. We used to go upstairs — I'd play bass, he'd play drums, and we'd just jam out for hours at a time. So that's kind of how it started. Chris was younger than us — he was just a kid. He might have dropped out of high school. He was young and quiet — he really liked to keep to himself. Me and Kim would sit around, drink beer, and watch *David Letterman*. He was more private — he liked to disappear in his room and think. Kim didn't live at that house; he lived in a different place. It was Eightieth and Roosevelt. That's when Soundgarden started — in that house.

KIM THAYIL: I was not their first thought. I was probably not even their second thought — I think I was their eighth or ninth [laughs]. The other guitarists either couldn't play very well, or didn't have the same interests or vision as Chris or Hiro. And that had gone on for a number of months, apparently. Hiro would bring me up, because Chris only knew me as the bass player in that band — he didn't know I played guitar. So Hiro said, "Kim's a good friend of mine. He's a really good guitar player and he likes a lot of the same things I like. Maybe we should have him jam? But y'know, Kim has a girlfriend, he's going to college, he's got a job — he's really busy."

Eventually, I went by and jammed. And *immediately* everything clicked — the first day we jammed, we wrote two songs. Stylistically, it didn't sound like anything any of us had heard — it wasn't the heavy stuff we ended up doing. Everybody was interested in their contribution — everyone liked the material we came up with and how it supported their interest in their instrument. And Chris — at this time — we didn't realize yet that he had lyrical ideas. So we had these songs that were entirely arranged instrumentally that were very interesting. So we said, "Let's do it again tomorrow." We were very happy, very satisfied — we were all smiling, it was so much fun. The next day, we wrote three songs. So in two days and a case of beer, we wrote five songs. They're all songs that we ended up playing live and recorded, but none of them we released on vinyl. But that's where it ended — those two days and those five songs. I still had to finish my last quarter at the University of Washington, I still had this new relationship, and I was still working full-time at this Native American Cultural Center. I was also working at the radio station, at the University of Washington.

Hiro and Chris started calling me over the next couple of weeks — "Dude, let's go jam again next week." "I can't, I've got to work." And they would call again the next day. It was weird, because they seemed really eager — Hiro was calling a lot, and even Chris called a couple of times. Then I started feeling pressured — "Well, man, I've got all this stuff going on. I think maybe in a couple of days I can come by." And Hiro started getting mad — I guess he told Chris, "Y'know, *fuck Kim*. He's kind of flakey, it's hard to motivate him to do shit." Eventually, he confronted me. I thought it was weird, he was acting like a jealous girlfriend — "*Are you my boyfriend or not?*" I was like, "Yeah, I liked what we did, I liked it a lot — I'm really fucking busy, man! I've got shit to do!" So I came by and jammed again, and this time, maybe came up with one song idea. They wanted me to commit. I was able to practice with them three nights a week eventually. I lost my fucking job because I was spread too thin. Now I had no money, but I was able to go rehearse with these jerks [laughs].

HIRO YAMAMOTO: It just started us three playing instrumentals mostly. And then we were like, "We got to start to write some lyrics." We had about six or eight songs — half of them I sung and the other half Chris sang. Of course, I didn't have much of a voice — Chris was a great singer. [Kim] would come over, we'd play for a while, and then we'd end up drinking beer for the rest of the night [laughs]. We lived in a great house where we could practice until two or three in the morning. We lived on a busy street corner, so nobody even cared that we played.

KIM THAYIL: By two months, we had four-tracked a cassette of fifteen songs — we called it *The First 15*. Our first gig was two and half, three months later — opening up for Three Teens Kill Four, a New York band.

MATT DENTINO: I saw their first show. [They opened] for some band, and I thought they blew them away. Their first show was upstairs . . . I don't even know the place. There was Astroturf — it was like a club, but the rest of the building was for golfing or baseball. I played hooky that night from church.

KIM THAYIL: On the strength of that and throwing the tape around, we got our second gig, which was two months later, in February [1985] — opening for Hüsker Dü and the Melvins.

JEFF AMENT: I remember seeing them open up for Hüsker Dü at the Gorilla Gardens. They were a three-piece at the time. Chris was playing drums and singing. Kim's amp was way louder than anybody else's onstage — he played through a phaser the whole time, and a chorus pedal. That was their predominant sound. But I thought they were pretty frickin' cool.

CHAD CHANNING: I went to their second show — I put a tape in the board and recorded it. Unfortunately, that recording is long since gone.

BEN SHEPHERD: The very first show I saw they blew some national act away. I have the set list from that show somewhere. They sounded huge, and their riffs weren't stupid or anything — something more to them. Something disturbing and huge.

BRUCE PAVITT: One thing that I noticed about Soundgarden that I thought was interesting was the racial makeup of the group — it was very unusual. The bass player was Japanese, the guitar player was Indian. You have to reflect back on that time — a lot of the metal scene was very white, very homogenous. So to see any other cultures in there was interesting.

HIRO YAMAMOTO: Those were great times. We were more new wave–ish at that time. We weren't a grunge band, necessarily. Those were just exciting shows. I was amazed that Chris could do that — he was playing his heart out on drums and screaming and singing.

JACK ENDINO: He was very into Neil Peart. He was a pretty good drummer.

DALE CROVER: Too bad he didn't stick on drums as a front man, because I think there should be more drummer front men.

DYLAN CARLSON: Not quite as metal as they became. They were still heavy, but more that Keith Levene–ish type sound — a cleaner guitar sound. A lot of harmonics, and not necessarily real straightforward rhythms. A little more "post punk."

MARK PICKEREL: There was this girl that worked at a record shop here in Seattle, who kept telling me about her friends [who] play in this band, Soundgarden. I think she described them as being Bauhaus meets Aerosmith.

SLIM MOON: We actually made fun of them, because of their obvious influences. We also made fun of their name — we thought their name was terrible — we called them "Noise Cabbage." But then they really evolved.

SUSAN SILVER: It was in the area of town called Belltown, where there were a lot of old, one-story brick buildings. And there was an artist named Carl Smool, who was having a Halloween party. I went there with a friend of mine who was a performance artist and singer, Chuck Gerra, who went under the moniker Upchuck. He dressed in wild costumes — Kabuki outfits or military outfits. That Halloween, he dressed me up as him — in a long blond fright wig and platforms — and that was the first time I saw Soundgarden. They were a three-piece. It was mind-blowing — they were amazing.

JEFF AMENT: The pieces were already there. Hiro was a super-interesting bass player, Kim had that heavy psychedelic quality to his guitar playing, and Chris had the voice. Chris had an *incredible* voice. That was apparent even at that first show. I was like, "Wow, that's a really different kind of a voice for a hardcore band." It's just different — whenever the drummer sings. It just isn't heavy — if they're not out front, it just doesn't seem . . . the only thing I had to compare it to at that point was Don Henley. It just didn't make sense to me. There weren't too many rules in the hardcore world, but having a singer who acted crazy and ran around was probably one of most important things — in terms of getting the energy across. The energy changed a lot when Chris just had a mic.

KIM THAYIL: We had to make a decision — whether we wanted him to be our drummer or our singer, because it was taxing for him to do both. Believe it or not, Hiro and I actually thought he was more valuable to us *as a drummer*. Because of his songwriting ability, we would work out arrangements on the drums. Hiro had really established his musical relationship with Chris as a rhythm section. We didn't want to lose that — the instrumental part was what we felt was strong. So we thought, "Let's get a guy to sing," some guy who has some dynamic personality and voice. Somebody with some theatrical skills, charisma . . . *a monkey*, y'know? [Laughs.] We knew he could sing, but I guess we didn't actually think, "Well, here's this great-looking, statuesque front man." We just thought he was more reserved — he didn't seem like "a presence." But we knew he could sing. We did that for a good half-year to a year, before we got Scott [Sundquist] as our drummer. Scott worked with Chris at the restaurant, Ray's Boathouse.

REGAN HAGAR: Andy always called him the Sun King.

JACK ENDINO: The first time I saw them live; they were introducing their new drummer, Scott Sundquist. They played half the set with Chris on drums, then he came out, and said, "We want to introduce our new drummer — I'm just going to sing now." Scott came out, finished the set, and Chris just stood there and sang. After that, they played for about a year and a half with Scott

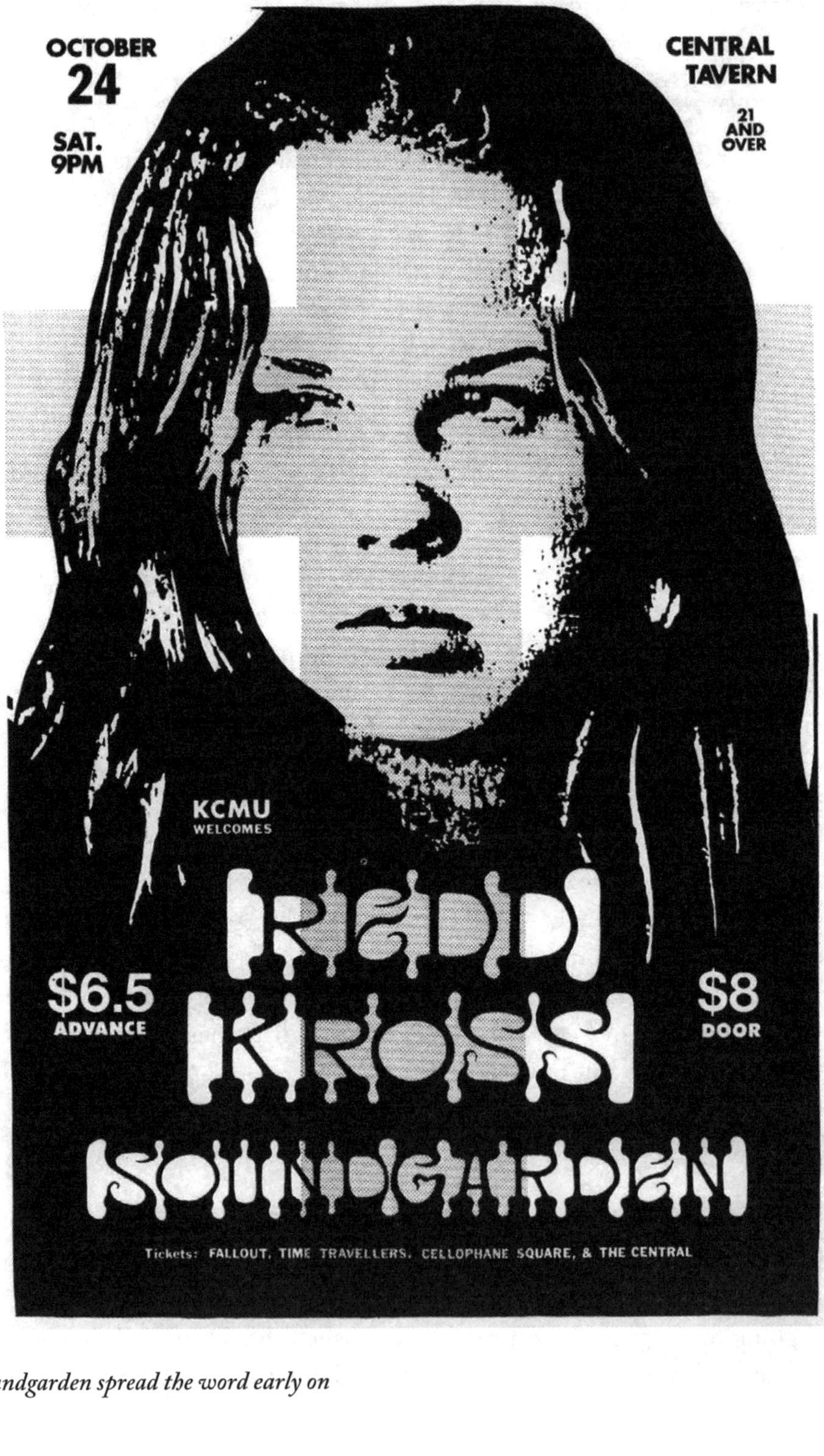

OCTOBER
24
SAT.
9PM

CENTRAL
TAVERN
21
AND
OVER

KCMU
WELCOMES

REDD
KROSS

$6.5
ADVANCE

$8
DOOR

SOUNDGARDEN

Tickets: FALLOUT, TIME TRAVELLERS, CELLOPHANE SQUARE, & THE CENTRAL

FLYER BY JIM BLANCHARD — JIMBLANCHARD.COM

Soundgarden spread the word early on

on drums — some amazing shows. Scott was an older guy; he had a Ginger Baker touch on the drums. A rolling, jazzy feel, that was really dynamic, and very fluid. It wasn't so "conventional heavy rock" as they became later. It was a slightly psychedelic kind of vibe. And at times, pretty amazing.

KEN STRINGFELLOW: When I first saw them, Chris Cornell dressed and acted like Jim Morrison. Leather pants, staying by the mic, writhing around it a little bit.

JIM TILLMAN: He was the first person in the scene who really had control over his voice. He knew what notes he wanted to hit and could hit them. Nobody else could.

MARK ARM: They were pretty cool, but Chris's antics got a little annoying. I'm all for somebody flailing around onstage and engaging the audience — but he would wear a tearaway shirt. It's one thing to take off your shirt, but it's another thing to pre-rip the seams. He'd grab the front of his shirt and pull straight off in a forward motion. It was a preplanned part of the act designed to show off his good body. Y'know, maybe there was some jealousy there, because my body was not nearly as hot [laughs]. But it just seemed so contrived — it didn't seem like a genuine reaction to the music. To be fair, I did some fairly contrived things in Green River. I played most of one show with a fish down my pants, the joke being that my huge bulge was actually a perch, which I pulled out and split open — spilling fish guts on the crowd. This was a punk rock gross-out act — not an act of narcissism.

KRISHA AUGEROT: I was fifteen and Chris Cornell was shirtless and twenty — it was an awesome band to watch. So full of energy and really raw. They were the ultimate garage, dirge, sexy, heavy rock.

CHARLES PETERSON: I met Chris [Cornell] at a party one night. God, he seemed just like a little boy at the time. We all started wrestling, we were all fucked-up. Wrestling and tripping down the street to another party. He looked younger than all of us, and I remember all the girls at the party just fawning all over him. Me and the other guys pretty much packed it in for the evening at that point.

ALICE WHEELER: They were the first local band that I ever saw that had groupies. They had a lot of these really sexy girls that would come sit in the front, and would throw themselves at Chris Cornell.

LIBBY KNUDSON: His throat, man, and being a girl too, I always thought [in] punk rock, the level of the playing field was all the same. And then to see him get there and take off his shirt, it was like, "Oh Lord — *you're not like my other friends!*" I remember thinking this could fly with the other peeps, especially at that point in the '80s, when Ratt and Mötley Crüe were going on there. I was like, "Those people should love this" — in theory.

MARK PICKEREL: It was hard to figure out at what point did they cross the line from rock 'n' roll parody with actual inspired rock 'n' roll.

SUSAN SILVER: One show at the Ditto, [Cornell] had written all over himself, and was just all over the club. I remember there was a fish involved and a lot of writhing around [laughs]. He'd go into a trance practically, in those early days. He covered every square inch of some of those places on some nights.

JACK ENDINO: I remember them playing the Ditto Tavern, and I think the only people in the audience were five people! I have a poster from those days, it says "Soundgarden/Skin Yard — $2" [laughs]. It's from, like, a Tuesday. *Those were the days.*

GARRETT SHAVLIK: I never really got it. They were like a prog-metal band, and we were sloppy punks. Great fucking people — just a different walk of life.

KIM THAYIL: Besides our own four-tracking for practice, Stuart was the first guy to record us outside of the band, I believe.

STU HALLERMAN: Some good memories there. Just a basement recording in their house by Green Lake in Seattle. When it was time to get guitar sounds for Kim, I started by asking him, "How would you like it to sound?" He said, "Hmm . . . I want it to sound like Godzilla knocking over buildings!" So I thought about it, I moved the mic a little bit, dialed in a little bit, a couple of little knob turns, and there was that sound he was looking for.

I was coming from Olympia, that had some punk rock going on, but I was hanging out with hippies. I came home with this really cool cassette of my buddies playing this music that was really great. But I knew if I play this for my friends, they'll shrug and go, "Eh, too aggressive for me — not Grateful Dead–like enough." And everyone I played it for was like, "I didn't think that was my cup of tea, but this is really good!" There was something just really musical and interesting — anyone could get in one listen.

HIRO YAMAMOTO: That's basically the only [recording] that has Scott on drums. The thing about Scott — he was ten years older than me. Scott was really cohesive — he made sure we were all getting together. So those times with the band were really fun, because Scott was more of a fatherly figure — he made sure as a band we were a band. To me, those were the best days of Soundgarden. After Scott left, we were more of "individuals" that played in a band. When we played with Scott, we were all kind of a family. We wanted to go on tour, and Scott had a young kid. So he wasn't up for it. It was the saddest times of Soundgarden.

MATT CAMERON: I was playing [in] Feedback, and we eventually became Skin Yard. Kim came to some of our shows — we started talking. We figured out that we lived pretty close to each other. Then he told me to check out his band at the Rainbow Tavern — I did, and I was completely blown away. I loved it instantly — they were my favorite band in Seattle. I heard that Scott left, and I called Kim. I said, "I'd like to try out." I knew a few of their songs — "Heretic," "Incessant Mace," and a few of their other earlier songs. I remember Chris really liked the way I played. They had a gig in a week's time at the Central Tavern — it was baptism by fire. I just threw myself in there and never looked back. We strictly kept to [playing] the Northwest when I first joined — around '87.

KIM THAYIL: It got a lot crisper, tighter. We were looking for something in terms of more minimalism — trying to hold down a beat, and a strong repetitiveness in the beat. But at the same time, Matt was obviously a great improv drummer. We certainly jammed a lot, and a number of songs had an extended solo section — not necessarily guitar solos, it might be drums, bass, or just feedback. And Matt had that ability — Matt could play a minimal, tight jazz kit. He was also available to tour, as well as contributing to the songwriting.

SCOTT VANDERPOOL: The early Soundgarden stuff . . . *eh.* They were pretty spotty. They had some great songs early on, but they got better. A big reason for that was when they got Matt Cameron. I'm a drummer, and I'm not worthy to stand in the same room with that guy. He's phenomenal.

JACK ENDINO: After they got Matt in the band, they became more focused, and narrowed down to, "We're just going to play these big rock riffs." They zeroed in on the sound they became known for later. When he joined Soundgarden, they became something to be reckoned with.

KIM THAYIL: It took a few years for it to evolve into this "Sabbath-influenced punk" that it became. It was more of a "punk-influenced Sabbath." The roots of everything we were listening to really were things like the Birthday Party, Killing Joke, Wire, and Joy Division, as well as the Meat Puppets, Black Flag, Minor Threat, and the Butthole Surfers. The people that fit into that scene were definitely the U-Men, Malfunkshun, Green River, Soundgarden, and the Melvins. It all kind of came together — we all liked each other. We were all influencing each other, and listening to each other's record collections.

JEFF GILBERT: Kim's mind works very mathematically, so when you listen to their time signatures, you have all these polyrhythms going on. That's because that guy is a goddamn human calculator. Him and Matt together — Matt will be playing in one time signature and Kim in another, and it will create this weird push-pull thing, that gives it that tension. In fact, some people tried to mimic Soundgarden, and couldn't. When Kim did solos, they weren't really solos as much as going back to that garage thing — playing as fast as you can for however how many beats you have to fill up.

I walked out of [the Vogue] pretty much changed. It took all of my preconceived notions about heavy music and turned them inside out. There were all these chords that didn't seem to make sense together, and these riffs that were in the weirdest time signatures. Very dissonant-sounding chords. But man, Matt Cameron would come in, and the whole thing would just detonate. I've seen Soundgarden fifty, sixty times, and there are those nights where it's not just a show — *it's a biblical experience.* Where you come out and your whole body's buzzing. That's what it was the first time I saw them. I thought, "Oh dear God, how do these four guys make this sound?" It was like a newer version of Led Zeppelin. Just this insanely powerful sound, but they were doing something so different and dark — but not evil [laughs].

STU HALLERMAN: Kim did not like bands like Led Zeppelin, and Hiro didn't like rock 'n' roll at all as a teenager. So everyone at the time was like, "Oh, obviously these guys are a Led Zeppelin rip-off," when whatever resemblance they had was really natural — that's just the way they hit their guitars and screamed. It was a coincidence more than anything. I think we all came to like Led Zeppelin at some point in our lives, but it was not a direct influence for them.

ROD MOODY: I saw one of Soundgarden's early shows at a place called Scoundrel's Lair. Chris Cornell later claimed that Led Zeppelin had no effect on him, but they played at least *three* Zep songs back to back.

JOHN LEIGHTON BEEZER: They came out with a song, "Incessant Mace," which was flat-out stolen from "Dazed and Confused" by Led Zeppelin. Not even a little bit. But it was twelve minutes long, heavier than shit — Led Zeppelin didn't play small clubs [laughs]. It was like, "God, this is a rip, but . . . y'know, they're really good!"

SCOTTY CRANE: When I listen back to those early recordings of Soundgarden, I'm still in awe. Such an amazing band. They're one of those things where it's like . . . I get so sick of Led Zeppelin because I heard them so much on the radio. But if I stay away from Led Zeppelin for five years and then I listen to it, I'm like, "Oh my God! That's such an amazing group of four people to get together." It seems like a frickin' miracle — the odds of getting that chemistry between four people in Led Zeppelin. And when I think of certain Soundgarden songs, I get the same feeling. The whole is greater than the sum of the parts.

KIM THAYIL: We were generating interest. We knew we needed someone for no other reason than this — to answer the phone and make phone calls while we were at our jobs. We needed someone to help us get the gigs — especially when some bigger band was coming to play at the Paramount or Moore Theatre. We wanted to be able to get those shows, and Susan was a local promoter we thought could help us out in getting these gigs, maybe booking tours. And we were starting to get interest from labels. We were about to make a record with Sub Pop — we knew we might have lawyers get involved, we anticipated somewhere down the road we night need an accountant. These were decisions that were going to take up a lot of our time, and we needed someone to do that with us — so that was going to be Susan.

HIRO YAMAMOTO: But then her and Chris were dating at that time — that was the other part of it.

SUSAN SILVER: I'd met Chris at a vintage clothing store that I'd worked in, and we started going out. They'd been a band already for about a year. A friend, Faith Henschell, who worked at KCMU, was sending these compilation tapes out to people. And someone from a record company heard it and called. In the meantime, Bruce Pavitt had been introduced to Jonathan Poneman through Kim. I had no intention of managing Soundgarden — I'd been managing the U-Men and a pop group, the First Thought. One thing led to another, and I started doing their business — just to help them out.

I can't remember how they felt [about Chris and I dating]. I didn't want to manage Soundgarden in the beginning — it was by default. It was just too *Spinal Tap* at that point. But nobody else was there to help them — no regrets about that whatsoever. The thing that I really tried to keep conscious of at all times was their feelings — I tried to keep a field of neutrality, and let everyone know that I was there for all of them, and not just as "the singer's girlfriend" [laughs]. I guess the fact that I'm still really close to the other three guys says how that worked out.

ART CHANTRY: [Susan] was into control — she controlled everything. And because she was such a kingmaker, she was given the ultimate power in the Seattle scene. Very few people have that amount of power. I mean, *she was even more powerful than Sub Pop.* Oh my God. She knew how to work it because she had est [Erhard Seminars Training] training, essentially. She was afraid of nothing. She used to be a stringer at *The Rocket* — I remember her showing up at *Rocket* parties. I remember when she first showed up with her new boyfriend, Chris. He's like the only guy in [Soundgarden] that didn't go to college. Keep in mind, Kim had some kind of degree in philosophy, Matt had serious jazz training, and Hiro [earned] his pharmacology degree. These guys were serious scholars — they were pretty heavy-duty guys. And they had this lead singer who was this beautiful guy who dropped out of high school, and he was [later] married to the manager. Talk about your difficult power structure.

She was awesome — just like Courtney Love was awesome. Whenever these little musical subcultural scenes develop — power, control, participation, and thought is pretty much evenly divided among everybody. Women and men are equal, and they're all equally working the system and working the power. And then as soon as money enters the picture, the men push their way to the front and start grabbing, and the women get shoved out. And to see women who actually survive in these systems and remain powerful — the overcompensation joke you hear about with women in corporate environments, well, it's times a thousand in rock circles. The women who survived in these scenes in the Northwest were very special people. Susan, Courtney Love, people like that — wow. Kathleen Hanna — *oh my fucking God.* These people are astonishing — they're like superhuman. And they're a little on the scary side too. Anybody who survives this kind of a scene and prospers, they really have to have this edge that is lethal. It's really weird to watch this whole process work. Endlessly fascinating.

JOHN BIGLEY: [The U-Men] came back from this tour — it turned into four months — and ran into Hiro. Hiro goes, "You guys should tour more, because we've been getting these kick-ass shows — the shit's *on!*" [Laughs.] They had more impact earlier than Nirvana — Soundgarden had a little jump on them as far as the local buzz deal. I laugh my ass off — they used to open for us and we'd pay them fifty bucks. Fast-forward a few years, I'm in the basketball arena, and I'm backstage sitting in their dressing room — bumming beers off 'em [laughs].

CHAPTER 9

"Just because you can, doesn't mean you should": The Melvins, Green River, Screaming Trees

Along with Malfunkshun and Soundgarden, three other bands are considered to be important "proto-grunge" contributors — the Melvins, Green River, and the Screaming Trees. While all three create their own unique spin on classic hard rock sounds, all have roots in punk rock, as well.

DALE CROVER: I'm from the now-famous Aberdeen, Washington — famous for not much besides unemployment and a failing logging industry. There wasn't much to do there, and there wasn't that many bands. I had older friends that played in local cover bands — one that ended up becoming Metal Church. Through one of the guys in that band, I discovered all kinds of heavy metal — Judas Priest, Iron Maiden. When I was thirteen or fourteen, I played in some really bad cover bands. That's really all there was — if you wanted to be in a band, [you'd] play with people that wanted to do high school dances. To do these shows, it was covers of the day. I liked a lot heavier stuff — that's all I could get my hands on. I did play with another guy — this wild guitar player. He tried to play Randy Rhoads–type stuff, but he couldn't really do it, so it would come out being this crazy, noisy thing. We were this weird two-piece instrumental band. He was the first guy to do drop-D tuning, which later inspired the Melvins to do the same thing, which in turn inspired a ton of other bands to do the same thing. It all came from that guy.

PIC BY LIBBY KNUDSON

The Melvins' Dale Crover, mammoth drums, and a whole bunch of graffiti

TIM HAYES: In '79–'80, I worked at DJ's Sound City at the Wishkah Mall, in Aberdeen. I would try to convince the manager to order Saints records — he'd get promos of Saints, Richard Hell, Stranglers, Dead Boys. He'd go, "Tim, take them. I don't want them played in the store." That was my introduction to my record collection, basically. Buzz [Osborne] and Matt [Lukin] would come in — I'd pitch them on a Black Flag or Adverts record. They started jamming together. I remember they'd come in and go, "Hey Tim, we started a band. We're doing some Clash covers and stuff." The early part of the Melvins was just a ripping, fast, punk rock/hardcore band. Then all of a sudden it seemed to shift into this "how slow can you go" type band. People at the time were *secret* Black Sabbath fans. Whereas the Melvins turned that all upside down, like, "This shit's really cool, and we can add a punk edge to it." Now they're like the forefathers of the whole thing.

KURDT VANDERHOOF: I became friends with Buzz — we were in junior college together. He started borrowing all my first generation punk records. Apparently, that was influential in the formation of the Melvins.

DALE CROVER: There was this one cover band I played in — we had this show that was on the radio. It was for an organization called the Sunshine

Kids — they got volunteers to take mentally disabled people to their jobs, or grocery shopping. So they're having this Christmas program — it was at the Elks Hall in Aberdeen. My band showed up, and there were these other guys there — the Melvins. They were from the neighboring town, Montesano. They played, and it was totally crazy. I'd seen [the 1979 Ramones film] *Rock 'n' Roll High School* and I knew Motörhead, and these guys were a cross between those two bands. They would play all these really fast songs. And the radio station that this was on was in Aberdeen — their playlist was Kenny Loggins and light country stuff. For these guys to be on the radio was pretty crazy. There's a record out that has part of that performance on it [2005's *Mangled Demos from 1983*]. Watching this guy in a cowboy hat trying to introduce them and talk to them between songs — which, there weren't any spaces between songs — was pretty funny. That was my first introduction to punk rock.

TRACY MARANDER: They didn't really look punk rock — all of the other bands looked punk rock or new wave–ish. But they played very fast and did KISS covers.

CHARLES PETERSON: I just remember them as these crazy, weird fucking guys from the hicks. I have a picture of the Butthole Surfers playing at the Gorilla Gardens, and Buzz in the audience.

DALE CROVER: Then I saw those guys open up for Metal Church in Aberdeen — Metal Church's first show. Everybody was really confused when they played. But everybody was into it at the end, because Krist Novoselic — who was a popular guy at high school — came out and played "Sunshine of Your Love" with them. It was way before Krist was in any other band — it wasn't too long later that Krist brought both of those guys over my house, Matt and Buzz, because they were looking for a new drummer. He's the guy who introduced us, and I've been in the band ever since.

There wasn't any place to play in Aberdeen. You'd maybe play a kegger party, high school dances — that was it. If you could play anywhere else, that was amazing. So when those guys came over and asked me to join, I knew they played gigs out of town. I was like, "That's great, we could play in Olympia!" That's like a big city compared to Aberdeen. I thought [Buzz] was Chinese — I couldn't tell. There weren't too many Chinese people in Aberdeen, I guess it was my vision of what a Chinese person would look like. Then I thought he might be gay — he was kind of fucking around with Krist Novoselic, wrestling or something, and I thought that was kind of odd. Then I realized that's just his way of fucking around. We would have "van fights" — where it would be like one person sleeping and then you punch him in the balls. That stuff still goes on, believe it or not — we're still stuck in the eighth grade. [His hair] wasn't as big and crazy, but it was definitely a fro. Other people when they see Buzz ask if he's Middle Eastern or where he's from. He's got some kind of roots traced back to West Virginia. One time we broke down by where his family is from, and it's just real hicks-ville.

JEFF GILBERT: Buzz looks like something out of Sideshow Bob.

TOM HAZELMYER: One of the first shows I saw [at Gorilla Gardens] was Hüsker Dü — they were friends from back home. One of the opening bands was the Melvins. I expected some generic, second generation hardcore, but when they started playing, I remember standing there with my mouth open, and turning to Bob Mould, who had the same expression as me. All he could say was "Holy fuck!" Imagine the Melvins playing their trademark intense riffing and strange changeups and time signatures — but at hardcore speed.

DAWN ANDERSON: I saw them really early on — this show they did with Soundgarden. Matt Lukin was insane at that show — doing all this posturing, and acting like a lead guitarist, even though he was a bass player. I remember overhearing some of the art rock people saying, "Do these guys know that this is a joke?"

DALE CROVER: Buzz was inspired by Black Flag's *My War* — side two — that everybody hated. A lot of people like it now, but at the time, all the punkers were like, "This isn't fast, we can't slam to this."

STU HALLERMAN: A few years later I did sound for them, in Olympia. The first band for me was almost the sound check — I struggled to get a decent mix on them. Here come the Melvins — Dale in his underwear, setting up these huge, huge drums. Just giant, empty cavernous drums, with no pillows or padding in them. We do the set change, get everyone miked up, go back to the mixing board, the drum sticks come down, and the guitar is hit, and my jaw dropped. OH MY GOD! An enormous, giant, godlike sound coming offstage. *The Melvins had changed.* I still get bands coming into my studio now that claim lineage to the Melvins' sound — Earth, Sunn O))) — very much emulating what the Melvins carved out back in those days.

DALE CROVER: There's one show where we played with [Green River] — our van was screwed up, so we borrowed their gear. Playing on the drummer's set, he had a really huge bass drum. He was going for a Jerry Nolan/New York Dolls–type thing — I think a 26-inch bass drum. And I was like, "Wow, this is awesome!" And he's like, "Good luck finding one. I had to order this and it took six months to get." I went to this music store in Olympia maybe a week later, and I'm like, "You guys have a 26-inch bass drum?" And they're like, "Well, not a single drum — *a whole set* that has a 26-inch bass drum, a 20-inch floor tom." I was like "*Eeeeee!* OK — here's a down payment of 25 cents, can I buy it?" That's how I got into big drums.

I remember when we went to record, it was either our first seven-inch or the first *Deep Six* comp. Recorded that with Chris Hanzsek — at this studio, Ironwood. The owner came out, I had my drums set up and they're miking them. He's like, "Ugh, these things sound disgusting!" The heads were all caved in — you could eat cereal off them. *Soup bowls.* I would fool the sound guy at whatever place we were playing. I would have a pillow in it while we were setting up, and then right before we'd play, I'd have the guys hand me the pillows out of the bass drum.

[The shows were] always fun — they weren't real well attended. In Olympia and Seattle people liked the Melvins. Then when we did play out of state, people didn't like it at all. The one thing that the Seattle music scene had going for it — all these bands had their own unique style. Like, "There's this band, Malfunkshun, that's 'punk rock KISS,' Soundgarden is this weird blues band, almost Zeppelin-esque." And then our band, those guys were into all kinds of different music. It wasn't just like, "We only like listening to Black Flag." It's like, "We listen to classic rock *and* Black Flag. And weird new wave stuff like Blondie and Devo, and we *still* listen to KISS, Queen, and Lynyrd Skynyrd." They didn't have any musical prejudice at all.

STEVE TURNER: They ended up sounding like the Swans, and they never even heard of the Swans! Then they bought a Swans record, thought it sucked, and continued to listen to KISS [laughs].

BLAINE COOK: It was too *slooow* and *dragging* for me at that point in time.

JOHN LEIGHTON BEEZER: I used to listen about five minutes and go, "Got it. Heavy. I will now go home and shoot myself." It's almost like eating a fistful of sugar — I like sugar, it generally makes everything better, but it's just way too much.

JOE NEWTON: Here was a band that seemed to be coming from outer space.

HIRO YAMAMOTO: They all came out in *Star Trek* costumes one time. The Melvins were so scary [laughs].

JEFF AMENT: Green River played maybe our third show with the Melvins, at the Grey Door. I remember seeing Krist Novoselic — I think he was driving the van and helping out with their guitars. I'd never seen somebody helping out a punk rock band, sort of teching. I remember playing Buzz's Les Paul, and it hardly had any frets on it — the frets were super-low. I was like, "Wow, this guitar is the easiest guitar I've ever played." A frickin' killer band.

MARK IVERSON: I was watching the Melvins, and Buzz was so into it. At the end of the show, he just collapsed. He passed out right in front of me — someone grabbed a pitcher of water and threw it on him.

JEFF GILBERT: Their fan base was *insanely loyal* — would follow them anywhere. Kurt Cobain in particular — almost at every show.

VAN CONNER: I remember the Melvins being super loud. They played all the time — that was their life.

NILS BERNSTEIN: What struck me about the Melvins early on was that their Black Sabbath thing wasn't at all ironic or comic — which is a given with bands now, but wasn't then. The other band then that was so blatant with the '70s metal influence was Green River, but they played it a little bit for laughs — at least in their outfits, if not musically.

The Melvins' Buzz Osborne and Matt Lukin

DAWN ANDERSON: In the early days of it, say the mid-to-late '80s when Green River started, there was a big element of humor in it that just didn't really translate to the rest of the world. A lot of it was they were posturing and saying, "Isn't this funny, we're so heavy metal, ha ha." Eventually, as time went on, it became OK for it to not be a joke, and for them to say, "We're going to rock — we're going to be real extreme about rocking. And if you don't like it, fuck you."

BRUCE FAIRWEATHER: After a while, [Deranged Diction was] fed up — it wasn't going anywhere and we were burned out. Steve and Mark had been doing stuff together, so Steve, Jeff, Mark, and Alex formed Green River.

JEFF AMENT: I saw all those guys at shows. I think the first time I talked to Mark, it was a non-band night [at the Metropolis] and Hugo asked if I wanted to play records. I was still into some '70s hard rock, so I was mixing Minor Threat, SSD, Black Flag, the Dead Kennedys, and Poison Idea with Aerosmith, maybe a Ted Nugent track. I remember I played a song off Aerosmith *Rocks* — "Sick as a Dog" or something — and Mark came up and said, "That's a great song, but the *really* great song is 'Nobody's Fault.'" That broke the barrier. Around that time, he said, "You should come check out my band, Mr. Epp." I don't know if it was that night or the next week, but he asked me what I thought. I told him, "You and Steve are cool, but I didn't really like the rest of it" [laughs]. What they were doing was pretty arty — I was into more structured hardcore stuff.

STEVE TURNER: [I was] talking to Jeff Ament. We somehow convinced him to be in a band with us. We formed Green River in the spring of '84. Stone joined after the first show — for more guitar muscle. They were getting more into the metal side of things — they were turned on by Venom. *I was not.*

JEFF AMENT: I was kind of a straight edge guy. Between my work and trying to get the band going, I was pretty focused — I didn't really have a lot of time to screw around and party. Mark, Steve, Alex, and I had been playing together for a couple of months at that point. At some show, Mark and I were standing with some folks, and Stone came up with his friend, Chris Peppard, and just started talking a mile a minute. He and Chris were kind of like Laurel and Hardy — going back and forth. Super high-energy. He goes, "Who are you?" I go, "I'm Jeff." He goes, "Oh, Jeff Diction — I've heard about you. *Cool name, man.*" Being a smart-ass. I was a Montana kid — if somebody said something smart-ass, you'd hit them. I had no sense of humor and fighting was kind of the way you got to know people. I think Mark sensed that I was about to punch him — "Oh no, he's cool!" Mark mentioned Stone might be a great second guitarist. I wasn't so sure because I didn't know him, but Mark said, "He has a Les Paul and a Marshall half stack," so that won me over. We both wanted the band to be heavier.

MARK ARM: Stone went to high school with Alex and Steve. Steve had been playing with Stoney and two other guys in a band called the Ducky Boys, but they never got far because their singer was too shy to sing at practice. So Stone joined Green River, which was good, because we got to practice at his parents' house. We had been practicing over at Steve's parents' place on Mercer Island, which was a bus trip out of town. Stone's parents lived up on Capitol Hill, which was much easier for everyone to get to. I'm sure all these parents just *loved it* [laughs].

JEFF AMENT: I was excited about being in a band with those guys, because I saw in their respective bands, they were the guys putting up the flyers and doing the networking. We got big shows right off the bat — I think we played with Black Flag and the Dead Kennedys [within] the first four or five months we were a band. It was killer — we rehearsed all the time and wrote a ton of songs right off the bat.

DAVE DEDERER: I had a funny moment — it was my sophomore year of undergraduate school. I was going to U Dub, it would have been '84–'85, and Stone Gossard — who's a family friend, our dads had been good friends since they were young men — was going to the U. I think he was just a freshman — two years behind me. I'll never forget hanging out with him one lunchtime, and he was basically getting ready to drop out of school. He had his full-on

PIC BY LIBBY KNUDSON

Green River's Mark Arm and Steve Turner see God!

Johnny Thunders look going on. That whole thing was starting then — people wanted to have bands that were the New York Dolls meets Pere Ubu meets Def Leppard [laughs]. Stone was listening to *Pyromania*, KISS, and the New York Dolls. They started to put it all together, and it didn't work very well [laughs]. Green River is an example of that — "Hey, let's mash all this stuff together and see if it works!" People figured out how to make it work [later]. Alice in Chains and Soundgarden figured out how to make it be something that was new that sounded good.

JOHN LEIGHTON BEEZER: It was like a lab experiment that went horribly wrong. "What happens if we mix this with this? Oh shit!" They were the band that galvanized everybody.

LIBBY KNUDSON: Green River — the name itself, they always joked, "It's a drink." But at the time, it was kind of heavy because what was going on with the Green River killer. That was kind of punk.

JOHN LEIGHTON BEEZER: Everyone in Seattle knew they were talking about a serial killer. That right there really sets the tone for a lot of things — the whole thing was easily misunderstood by outsiders. And that's probably one of the reasons why [when] Green River toured nobody was enthusiastic. It was like, "What, a Creedence cover band?" I remember going to their first show — August of 1984 — there were probably forty people there. I later told people I was blown to the back of the room — I really could not believe what I was seeing. Steve was quoted at the time as saying, "We were trying to get the sound of a jet aircraft taking off," and it was the same sort of effect. It wasn't a wall of noise; it was a *barrage* of noise. When I saw [Jeff], he was dressed like a combination of Steven Tyler and KISS. He had these chiffon scarves tied to his belt, had face paint on, and his hair was all teased up. And he was playing a Destroyer guitar. He might have even had spandex — I don't know if he went that far. The other part of them — Mark, Steven, and Alex — all looked like delinquent preppies. They had Oxford shirts with the collars out, and their hair just a little bit too long.

DALE CROVER: A couple of guys in the band had Mötley Crüe haircuts.

MARK ARM: Jeff was on a really big KISS kick, so at this first show, Jeff shows up with white makeup. I remember Steve and I going, "That's weird — where did that come from?" [Laughs.] I vaguely recalled Jeff talking about the possibility of makeup, but I thought he was joking. I'm sure the fact that Landrew from Malfunkshun wore white face paint played into Jeff's decision.

The first batch of Green River songs were pretty simple, but our music became increasingly complex. "Tunnel of Love" probably has twelve parts and nothing repeats. We were trying to stretch our abilities, to try things out, and push ourselves. And to tell you the truth, it wasn't very good. Steve could see that at the time, whereas the rest of us were caught up in the fact that we were *doing this.* Which brings up one of my favorite adages when it comes to music — "Just because you can, doesn't mean you should." Just because Yngwie Malmsteen can play as fast as he can, doesn't mean he should. It turns music into a totally soulless exercise of technique.

CHRIS HANZSEK: Mark Arm was what I liked to see in a singer — somebody wild, playful, sometimes serious, sometimes not. But all the time, very "stretch it to the limit." He would stage dive with the minimum number of people.

TOM PRICE: Every time I saw them, they would have some sort of accident, and somebody would be bleeding. They bled a lot. Once, I went to see them — I'd gotten off work late, and Mark was always fucking with the audience. They were playing and I was pushing my way through the crowd at the Central Tavern. Right as I got up to the front of the stage, the crowd parted like the Red Sea — Mark had a pitcher of beer, and launched it directly into my face. I didn't see what was coming — he just douched me from head to toe.

ED FOTHERINGHAM: Metal crept in from other places, and I think Mark liked it. Steve certainly did not. He was like, *"Fuck this."* I'll never forget, they had a photo shoot, he had pretty long hair, and they were begging him not to cut his hair for the photo shoot, and he cut it very preppie short. It's a great photo — he's in his Brooks Brothers shirt, little prep jacket, and clean, short hair, when everyone else is wearing eye shadow. It's very wrong and cool.

STEVE TURNER: It was a great experiment at first, because we had such diverse tastes. Then as we got better, the songs had gotten just too complex. I couldn't remember them, I couldn't play them [laughs]. And I slowly really didn't want to — they were just not my thing. I had discovered the Milkshakes and Billy Childish, on top of already really liking the '60s garage stuff. And things like the Replacements were one of my favorite bands at the time — Meat Puppets had just done [1984's] *Meat Puppets II.* And they were heading [into] the other direction of post-hardcore, into the more hard rock/metal thing.

JEFF AMENT: We made the first record at Crow. Crow had a sixteen-track; we thought that was going to be better. We saved a couple hundred dollars and knocked that record out in three or four days. I remember we went in, set up, and I don't think there was a lot of overdubbing. We started sending tapes around and there was a little bit of interest — which was kind of shocking. This guy, Steve Pross, who worked at Enigma, wanted to put the record out. I think Enigma and Homestead were the first two letters that we got back. Enigma sent us, like, a sixty-page contract and Homestead sent us a two-page contract — so we went with Homestead.

CHRIS HANZSEK: Green River were spending their parents' money when they were making [1985's] *Come on Down*, so there was a little bit more leisure time. By the time we got to the *Deep Six* compilation, you could hear them starting to bicker a little bit about what direction the band was supposed to go. Jeff seemed to be the spokesperson for the contingent that said, "Let's get organized, let's make this slightly more commercial, let's put this in a widely accepted arena rock thing." Whereas Mark was like, "Let's be Iggy Pop, light ourselves on fire, and run around." So there was a strain between "Let's consciously *try* to sell records" or "Let's consciously try *not* to sell records."

STEVE TURNER: The first record had a couple of good songs on it, and also some pretty bad stuff. I decided I had to quit, and they got better after I quit. The replacement was more fitting, when they got Bruce. Made much more sense. I figured I was done in a certain way — I was kind of over it. I scared some of my friends, because I re-enrolled in college and gave away all my clothes. They really worried about me for a few months.

BRUCE FAIRWEATHER: A lot of guitar players play the exact same thing — punk rock bands especially. We worked at trying to be different. We tried to play off of each other and tried to be dynamic, although it was loud and fast. Some of it sounds dated now, but it's definitely some intricate shit we worked out.

MARK ARM: Our first tour — which was supposed to coincide with the first Green River record — ended up being a seven-show tour across the United States. Seattle to New York and back. We drove out to Boston, called up Gerard Cosloy at Homestead, and he's like, "Oh yeah, I forgot to tell you, there's no show in Boston" [laughs]. This was in '85. We played two shows with Big Black — one in Lexington, Kentucky, and that was really weird. Big Black had two EPs by then and I figured there'd be tons of people there. There were less than thirty. We played with them again in Columbus, Ohio, and there were maybe seventy-five. We stayed in Columbus for a couple of days, and played a pickup show with Decry. We saw the Necros and the Minutemen, which was fantastic. I'm so glad we did, because [Minutemen singer/guitarist] D. Boon died a few months later.

We played Detroit a couple of days before Halloween — it was the big Halloween punk rock show starring Samhain, which was Glenn Danzig's band right after the Misfits. I remember driving into Detroit, and we're like, "This is going to fucking rule — home of the Stooges, the MC5!" We popped a Stooges tape in, and we're ready for a real cool time. As we drove into

Detroit, we realized that there's *really* no place for us to pull over. It was a bombed out, burned out, shell of a town, with these shadowy figures huddled in corners. We ended up finding a hotel that looked safe enough to us milk toasty Seattle kids. We went to breakfast the next morning and the waitress asked us in a thick Michigan accent, "Are you guys gay? You guys talk gay" [laughs]. This was an indication of how the show was going to go for us that night. Jeff had poofed up his hair, and was wearing this pink tank top that said *San Francisco* in cursive, purple lettering. And all these people in their black leather were fucking *livid*. I thought we were rocking hard — rolling around on the ground and playing the shit out of our songs — but people just couldn't get past the way we looked; Jeff in particular. There was this one girl who kept spitting, yelling, *"Faggot, faggot!"*

JEFF AMENT: At one point, I put my foot in front of her face, and her boyfriend reached around, grabbed my foot, and pulled me into the crowd. At least three guys jumped on my back and started pounding me. All I remember is having my bass on, facedown — I could hear my bass making this growling noise. When the security guy finally came over and pulled the guys off me, everybody in the band was just standing onstage watching me get my ass kicked [laughs]. I remember being a tad disappointed by that. Like, "Hmmm, my crew just watched me get my ass kicked."

BRUCE FAIRWEATHER: Mark jumped into the crowd, and I think Alex went running to the front. Stone and I just looked at each other and backed up, like, "Fuck that!" [Laughs.]

MARK ARM: I'd gotten pulled into angry crowds before, like when we opened for Black Flag and Saccharine Trust in Seattle. Jeff would always be the first to jump in the crowd to help me out. So I'm like, "Oh great, *I've got to go help Jeff now*." So I jump into the crowd, and the next thing I know, we're surrounded by the biggest, fucking scariest dudes — ready to kill us. The only thing that saved us was that the security guy was a cop with a gun. He saved our asses. We were packing our stuff up in the alley afterwards, and some guy is walking around with a skinned goat head [laughs]. A couple of kids came up to us and said, "I totally get what you're doing — you're doing the Stooges and Alice Cooper. Right on, that's great!" But to most people in Detroit in '85, we were not punk enough. Gerard Cosloy got us two shows in the New

York area. We played clean up at CBGB's in front of the staff and a couple of Japanese tourists. I still had a blast. I was stoked just to be at CB's. We also opened a CMJ Homestead showcase at Maxwell's. I had saved up $700 from my shitty job to go on this tour. Basically, it was my summer vacation.

BRUCE FAIRWEATHER: It was hit or miss, but we were generally pretty tight — unless we were really drunk. Mark was pretty entertaining. We would always do something crazy. We had this guy, Mike Larson, who was our manager — we did this one show opening for Agent Orange in Seattle, and Mike's like, "You guys got to do something crazy this time. I think you need a fish, Mark . . . [put it] down your pants! But not like a fresh fish — a really *old* fish." So he went down to the market and all the fish vendors, asking them for old fish. He finally found some old stinky fish and put it out in the sun. Mark put it down his silver lamé pants. Alex had borrowed Agent Orange's drum rug. Halfway through the set, Mark reaches down into his pants, pulls out this fish, spins it over his head, and throws it out into the crowd. Immediately, it comes onstage, and gets mashed all over the place. Agent Orange is on the side of the stage, and it's all over the drum riser — they're not happy at all. I think one of the guys grabbed the fish, went up to Stone, and scraped it down his arm — cut him open with the scales. When I was in Love Battery years later, we played with those guys, and I'm like, "Hey, I used to play in this band Green River, we had this stinky fish onstage." The guy just glared at me.

SCOTT VANDERPOOL: Onstage at Bumbershoot, Green River had this cooler filled with green Jell-O, that they threw out into the crowd. Made a god-awful mess.

ED FOTHERINGHAM: [Mark] was definitely more active than he is now onstage. Plus, he wasn't saddled to a guitar. It was a different experience — he'd jump around a lot. He was younger and more spry [laughs]. He's still fairly spry, but it hurts when you hit the ground.

KURT BLOCH: It was Mark Arm at his most unhinged.

BRUCE PAVITT: Mark Arm, I remember one show in particular — him climbing up the PA stack and leaping on some lights there. Basically, endangering himself physically.

JEFF AMENT: The first record that we put out through Sub Pop, [1987's] *Dry as a Bone*, was kind of a weird deal. It came out through Sub Pop, but we ended up paying for most of it. We paid for the recording of it, some of the pressing of it, and some ads. Which is fucking crazy — we were giving Bruce Pavitt money to put out records! I'm happy to say that when I finally got paid back for all that stuff about seven years ago, I got it all in ten-dollar bills, and every single thing I bought, I thought about it. "Oh yeah, this is from Bruce Pavitt — a slice of pizza" [laughs]. I relished every bite of that $200 I got paid back.

JONATHAN PONEMAN: Even though they were doing a completely original revisionist take on it, it made me uncomfortable, until I saw them do their *Dry as a Bone* record release show. To this day, one of the greatest shows I'd ever seen in my life — completely blew me away. For a long time, I felt like, "I love Green River . . . but I love Soundgarden." But after I saw that record release party, Green River was indisputably the coolest band in Seattle. That show — it was a hot July day in 1987 — blew my mind apart.

REGAN HAGAR: They drew so many people — it was a scene that was more than just what the Showbox scene used to be — a lot of old punks. Green River drew in a lot of college kids — people that came from the suburbs.

BRUCE PAVITT: I think the records did a pretty good job, but it was a better live show.

MARK ARM: We made two more attempts at touring, both down the West Coast. Our plan for our '86 tour was to go down to L.A., and then cut over and go to Texas — we were supposed to play with Scratch Acid and Poison 13. So we bought this broken down, dilapidated school bus from Jeff's dad. It didn't take us as far as we wanted to go — we ended up ditching it in L.A. [Earlier] Jeff and Stone went out to Montana to pick it up, and it barely made it to Seattle. This should have set off alarm bells. Our first show was in Portland. Portland had a really gnarly group of skinhead Nazis then. A couple of them went to prison for killing an Ethiopian man — they were just retarded assholes.

We played at the Satyricon, and there were a couple of skinheads, just hating us, giving us all kinds of grief — yelling at us and throwing shit. I guess our hair was too long. The last song of the set was a cover of the Dead Boys' "Ain't Nothin' to Do," I remember doing this really quick forward bend, and at the same time, Jeff was going in the opposite direction with his bass — so my forehead hit one of his tuning pegs and split open. I ran into the bathroom right after the song to wash the blood off my face, and this skinhead comes in, and goes, "Oh, I guess they already got to you," turned, and walked away. It seemed to me that this guy was new and his initiation was to go beat up one of those "hippies" from that band.

We played a killer house party in Medford, Oregon, and maybe two shows in San Francisco. We had two shows in L.A. that were two weeks apart. The second was for our return trip from Texas, but the bus went tits up in L.A., so we never made it to Texas. We had to call our parents, at least I did — "Hey, uh, I need a plane ticket home" [laughs]. Because we didn't make any money on these tours. That tour was cursed. Come to think of it, all our tours were cursed. Most of the band stayed in Hollywood, but I went down to Laguna Beach with Bruce to ride those two weeks out at his folks' house. They were super nice, but two weeks is a long time to stay at someone else's parents' place.

JEFF AMENT: We had a show with Jane's Addiction — that was the last show — at the Scream, in downtown L.A. The thing that I remember the most is when Jane's Addiction played, being blown away that this band that didn't have a record out was playing in front of 2,000 people — who knew all the words to the songs. They were a really weird band. They weren't conventional in any way. I remember thinking how much I loved the rhythm section — Stephen Perkins and Eric Avery were doing some shit at that point that I don't think I'd ever seen done on a punk rock level. Stone and I were standing on the side of the stage — just fuckin' blown away. At some point, Mark and Bruce said how much they thought that they sucked. That pretty much was it — I think Stone and I knew at that point.

We didn't know what we wanted to do, but whatever it was, it was different than what Mark wanted to do. I remember reading that Mark thought the end happened when I wouldn't let his friends on the guest list, because I had filled it with record company people — which is partially true. They were all the people that helped us get most of the shows down the West Coast, and I felt it was the least we could do. Of course, only a few of them showed up — so he was ticked off. I think if we had been better communicators and talked about our differences better, we would have turned into an incredible band. We could probably have been as good as Jane's Addiction. But shit, we were twenty-one, twenty-two, twenty-three at the time. I didn't want to work in a restaurant the rest of my life — that's for sure. I don't think any of the guys had to work to pay their rent, so I don't think it was as hard a decision for them. For seven years, I got up at five in the morning and went to work — I couldn't wait to not do that. I guess that made me a careerist. I do like how my career turned out.

MARK ARM: On or near Halloween, we got together at the practice place. Jeff, Stone, and Bruce announced that the band was breaking up. I actually felt relieved at that point — I didn't know what I was going to do, but a weight was definitely lifted off my shoulders. I think the difference of musical opinion worked well for a while — it worked on *Dry as a Bone*, which is the best thing that Green River did. But it just became too big of a strain after a while. And fair enough — not everyone is going to be into the same thing. I vaguely remember going out that night and just getting hammered. I ran into Dan Peters at the OK Hotel and exclaimed, "Green River broke up." And then I puked! [Laughs.]

KURT BLOCH: By the end, it had occurred to me that that band was not going to last. The "pro rock" faction versus the "anti rock" faction. The world is probably better that Green River broke up into two factions [laughs].

JOHN LEIGHTON BEEZER: I think they were all getting laid for the first time in their lives. Girls would go to the shows and go, "Oh, these are rock stars — I want a rock star!" And it's like, "*No, no, no* — these are fake rock stars, they're joking!" So they were forced to face this moral issue — "We were kind of doing a put-on, but hey, it's working. Should we be what people think we are and milk it? Or should we recoil in horror and go, 'No, this is the exact opposite — this is terrible'?" That's what split the band apart.

MARK PICKEREL: I remember being intimidated by Green River's reputation, because by their description, it sounded like they had a lot in common with the Screaming Trees. I always felt like they were the band we'd really have to prove ourselves against — if we were going to build a following in Seattle. But that didn't prove to be an issue at all. Before we moved to Seattle, all the bands that performed in Ellensburg were so competitive, and talked so much shit behind each other's backs. Before we became accepted in the Seattle music community, I remember thinking that all these bands were going to be our enemies. We were so surprised to be warmly accepted by not just the audiences in the Northwest, but by the bands themselves. It seemed like the bands worked closely together to make things work for each other — to serve a common goal.

We formed the early incarnation of the Screaming Trees — which hosted several names — [in] about 1982. We started a group called Him and Those Guys, which was me, Van Conner, Lee Conner, and a guy named Dan Harper on bass. Van met [Mark] Lanegan at drama class — I believe Lanegan was a senior at the time. It was around my sophomore year in high school. Van approached Lanegan — just from having a mutual appreciation of everybody from Motörhead to Black Flag to more obscure '60s artists. I was already a drummer — I could play pretty well considering my age. We decided to start this new band, that would just be me, Van, and Lanegan. It was just going to be a three-piece punk band.

But Van's mom, Kathy, got really pissed off, because we were using equipment that Lee had part ownership of, and that his mom had also. She stormed into our rehearsal, and demanded that we let Lee back into our new band. So we reluctantly agreed, since our only other option was to find another practice space, which we couldn't afford to do. [At] this particular point, Van and Lee were having a bit of a rivalry. Really competitive. Plus, Lee was going through this phase where he was jealous of Van's and my own social life. Our social life had blossomed into something where we were continually doing fun things that Lee wasn't included in. Lee was kind of a social outcast. He was older than us, and we were really his only friends. So that made his mom even more angry, that we were excluding him from our new lineup.

VAN CONNER: Our first practice was just me, Lanegan, and Pickerel. Lanegan was playing drums, I was playing guitar, and Pickerel was going to sing. But we only lasted one practice like that — we kind of sucked [laughs]. We shoveled it around — my brother played guitar — and we ended up being the lineup that we were in the second practice.

MARK PICKEREL: By my junior year, Lee had become more serious about songwriting — had bought a home recorder, and started making four-track demos that were really cool and really psychedelic. Really strong songwriting, that was on par with the kinds of songwriting you'd hear from Love, the Byrds, Bob Dylan, the Seeds, the 13th Floor Elevators. The songs were so developed — they didn't sound like copies of other artists' songs.

STEVE FISK: I was working at this recording studio in eastern Washington — a guy I went to college with built a recording studio. I knew Mark, just because he was a fan of one of the records I put out in the early '80s — my band Anonymous, on [1981's] *Let Them Eat Jellybeans*. They decided to come in one day; it was totally their decision. We ended up putting out what they recorded, on a little tiny label we started over there. They were playing like a live show — jumping around and everything. They set up in a line, like they were onstage. Because there were brothers in the band, there was a lot of spirited debate — but really nice people. I worked on four records with the Screaming Trees, I haven't done that with hardly anybody. And I did all that before I knew anybody from Seattle — so I didn't even have any comparisons.

MARK PICKEREL: None of us really knew what we were doing — we all had pretty specific ideas about how we wanted to be presented to the world, and how we saw ourselves. On the other hand, there was a lot of confusion within the band. I mean, I was still a junior in high school when I was recording [1985's *Other Worlds*]. So my influences varied from everything to current David Bowie hits to early Cream, 13th Floor Elevators. I was still very impressionable.

We knew that we were outcasts, so we had that working against us — so we thought. Although coming to find out later that that ended up appealing to people — because we were so sheltered, it really helped us create our own little culture in Ellensburg. I watched that Ramones documentary recently [2003's *End of the Century*], and I immediately felt a kinship with those guys. It reminded me so much of our story — four absolute misfits who had a common vision. At the same time, there were a lot of personalities within the band that didn't really work together, but somehow, managed to figure out a way to continue to move forward every day.

CHAPTER 10

"The next logical step is to start a label": K Records, Sub Pop Records, C/Z Records

Sub Pop Records was the most renowned Seattle-area independent record company to form in the '80s, and figured prominently in putting grunge on the map. But there are also two lesser-known labels, K and C/Z, which gave a home to future renowned bands. Add to it the emergence of Jack Endino as the "go to" producer of local bands, and grunge now had a launching pad that put it on a global scale.

CALVIN JOHNSON: I was involved with [radio station] KAOS, which had developed within the context of being a community radio station. The listeners are the programmers too — serving the disenfranchised elements of the community. Out of that grew *Op* — a magazine dedicated solely to independent produced music. And it wasn't concentrating on any one genre — it was any genre that had artist-owned voices and labels. I was involved in that as a writer and various capacities. If you looked at music magazines at the time, even *Slash* or *New York Rocker* is going to give lip service to major label bands. Which would never get covered in *Op*. Not only was *Op* about independent music, but it was concentrating on American music.

Bruce Pavitt moved to Olympia in '79, and was involved with KAOS and *Op Magazine*. He did his radio show, *Subterranean Pop*, which was all independent, and decided to do a fanzine — like *Op*, but it was only about local punk rock and new wave bands. But he was focusing on the Northwest and Midwest — two areas that were completely ignored. From the second issue on, I was working with Bruce pretty closely. It just seemed like the next logical step is to start a label that would work with our local scene. It wasn't a label until years later — it was a fanzine from 1980 until '83. And then after that, he moved to Seattle, and it was a column in *The Rocket*, called Sub Pop. It was also a radio show on KCMU, but it wasn't a label until the late '80s. When Bruce went on tour for one summer, I was answering all the Sub Pop mail and starting to do K [Records].

ART CHANTRY: Calvin Johnson was a huge influence on Bruce. There came a point where Bruce was basically "Calvin Jr." He would even walk like Calvin. If you take enough MDMA, it starts to, like, rot away at your joints — the cartilage in your joints. You start to get this loose-limbed, weird walking way. Both those guys had that walk after a while — you saw them walking down the street, and you couldn't always tell who it was, because they were both shaved-headed.

CHRIS PUGH: The Supreme Cool Beings, Calvin and the Cool Rays — Calvin Johnson had a thing going, Beat Happening came out of that.

CALVIN JOHNSON: Living in Olympia at the time, I had been playing music with people. I felt that I needed to try something a little more straightforward. It was a band with five people — that seemed cumbersome and hard to manage. So I was in this band with my friend — just the two of us. Then [my friend] left town for a while, and I thought, "Maybe I'll add something to it — three people." So we had me, Heather [Lewis], and this woman Laura — that was starting in February of '83. Sometime over the summer Laura moved away, and we just said, "Hey Bret [Lunsford], do you want to be in our band?" By the end of the year, we played our first shows as Beat Happening — December 1983. That's when we recorded our first session with Greg Sage as well.

We played a [house] party in Olympia — we didn't have any equipment. We asked if we could borrow the equipment of the other band, and [they] said, "Yeah, no problem." But then when we got there, the other band said we couldn't. We decided to play anyway, without their equipment — I think Bret found a guitar in the house somewhere, and we just used garbage cans or boxes as drums — and without a PA. I felt with Beat Happening, we would never be relying on equipment or technical issues to be who we are, to perform. That was tested early on, at that party. And we were able to proceed on our own terms — without the performance suffering. It was probably even *better* that we didn't have the expensive drum kit.

KATHLEEN HANNA: The stuff that I was really into was K Records — the Go Team, Beat Happening. They were really influential.

TRACY MARANDER: Everyone in Seattle seemed like, "We're hipper than everyone else." In Olympia, the people at the shows seemed somewhat more friendly; people in the audience seemed more nerdy. Most of the women in Olympia wore skirts — kind of that '50s style, with little bobby socks, skirts, and shirts. Everything was more quirky and laidback.

ALICE WHEELER: The kids from Olympia . . . it was almost a precursor to "the grunge look" — the really long, straggly hair. We all had thrift store clothes. But I think the punks liked to have more vintage stylish clothes, and the headbangers just had flannel shirts and ripped up jeans.

TINUVIEL: I moved to Olympia in '88–'89 — I was in New Mexico before. I was sick of the desert, so I wanted somewhere "watery" [laughs]. The first person I met was Slim Moon, and the next [people were] Kathleen Hanna, Kurt Cobain, Calvin Johnson. Everyone was in at least three bands.

JACK ENDINO: There were two people involved in starting Sub Pop — Jonathan Poneman and Bruce Pavitt. Bruce and I, we never really connected. I've hardly had more than a couple of conversations with Bruce — in twenty years. He's a hard guy to talk to — he's very reserved and private. Whereas Jon Poneman is the opposite — the "public face of Sub Pop," the guy I've always talked to and had a good relationship with. Bruce was "the idea man," and Jon was "the nuts and bolts" — the guy who made the deals happen. They were an interesting couple.

LARRY REID: We were at a house party — the U-Men were playing in this basement of this house near the University District — and Bruce had just moved to Seattle. He walked up to me and said, "The Seattle music scene is going to take over the world" [laughs]. Under those circumstances, to make a preposterous statement like that . . . but he said it with conviction. He

PIC BY KRISHA AUGEROT

The architects of Sub Pop Records, Bruce Pavitt and Jonathan Poneman

wasn't laughing. Damned if he wasn't right — and again, this was 1983. [Pavitt] is a bit of a savant — kind of a genius.

STEVE FISK: No one understands that [Sub Pop] was a cassette magazine first.

KIM THAYIL: Sub Pop was a magazine. As a matter of fact, the volume numeration that you find with [the] magazines continued with the record label — to this day. I think the first four magazines were all paper with different sizes and formats. "Number five" was a cassette magazine where they had a small little pocket magazine insert, along with the cassette. "Number six" was a paper magazine, "seven" was cassette, "eight" was a Xerox copy magazine, "nine" was a cassette, and then "ten" was vinyl — [1986's] *Sub Pop 100* — which had Sonic Youth, Steve Albini, Shonen Knife, Skinny Puppy, and the U-Men.

BRUCE PAVITT: I'd also opened a record store, Bomb Shelter. So I was pretty active at the time.

MARK ARM: I'd known Bruce and Jonathan for a number of years. I was a DJ at KCMU — both Jonathan and Bruce worked there. Jonathan hosted *Audio Oasis*, which only played local artists. He was also very involved as a local promoter, scrounging up new places for bands to play.

JONATHAN PONEMAN: I was at the University of Washington, when I stumbled into KCMU, and discovered it was easier than I had thought to become a DJ. This woman, Rhoda Mueller, owned a tavern, the Fabulous Rainbow — it's now the Rainbow Tavern. [She] called and said, "I have Tuesday nights free in my bar. You're playing all this local music, you guys need money, why don't you turn this into a fund-raising night for KCMU, and you can affiliate it through your radio program?" So through that, I started to see a lot more bands, and gave a number of these bands their first Tavern shows. It coincided with a time where the bands were really starting to gel, and the other thing — when you add alcohol, everything gets a lot crazier. And when you add X, things get crazier still. There was a lot of that going around. I was pretty much just off to the sidelines playing in my band, doing *Audio Oasis*, and putting on some shows. But it became very clear to me — around 1985 — that the music scene in Seattle was going from being a dismal/backwater music scene to something original and inspired.

BRUCE PAVITT: First met Jonathan in '86 — Kim Thayil introduced me.

KIM THAYIL: Both Jonathan and Bruce wanted to put out a Soundgarden record. They had different resources — Jon had the financial resources, Bruce had established a network of magazines and record labels. So he was tied in with any national or international indie music scene. That was an important resource for us. He couldn't afford to make a record at that point in time, and I thought, "Well, both of you guys are interested in making this record, and you guys have two different capacities which could be useful to us. So why don't you work together?"

JONATHAN PONEMAN: I'm not the most gregarious guy in the world — I never really knew [Bruce] on the social basis. But we both had the same idea at the same time, which was these bands are really great, they need to be documented — there needs to be a label to do it. And then Kim said, "Bruce is talking about doing Sub Pop on a more full-time basis." I had interviewed Bruce on *Audio Oasis* at the release of *Sub Pop 100*, and I had put on the *Dry as a Bone* record release party at a club that I had been booking.

Finally, Bruce and I got the idea that we would work together on doing a Soundgarden record, and take it from there. We found as things were coming together for the Soundgarden single and for [1987's] *Screaming Life*, that we enjoyed each other's company, and complemented each other. Bruce said, "I'll take you on as a partner in Sub Pop." So we went into business formally, where we quit our jobs and made this our day job. We moved into our first office in the middle of March 1988, but the lease began on April 1, 1988. We've always seen that as "day one" as Sub Pop.

JACK ENDINO: They borrowed a bunch of money from various gullible people and somehow set the wheels in motion to start an indie label. I was already working in this eight-track studio from the middle of '86, and I had been working with Soundgarden almost from the moment the studio opened its doors. So some of the recordings we had been making anyway, wound up on the first Sub Pop record — Soundgarden's "Nothing to Say"/"Hunted Down." And that became the *Screaming Life* EP, those two songs plus four others. Sub Pop had a strange rationale when they started — "Let's just do EPs at first. They're cheaper to record and you can put a lower list price on them, which means more people will take a chance on buying them." The other side of the equation is you make less money on it [laughs]. So Sub Pop did a lot of seven-inches and EPs in their first few years.

STEVE MANNING: When Sub Pop started, it was in the Terminal Sales Building on First and Virginia. There were lots of rental spaces available at that time in the city.

JEFF GILBERT: Their warehouse was all the way in the basement, so there's constant elevators and stairs. You'd take the elevator, it would stop at the tenth floor, and you'd have to get out and walk up another flight and a half of stairs to get to their offices. They were in "the Greg Brady room" [laughs]. The Sub Pop Singles Club was a brilliant marketing stroke on Sub Pop's behalf. Fucking genius man. Even the metal guys would go out and get the singles, just because they thought it was cool — metal is all about collecting [laughs]. I remember telling some of the metal guys around town, "You should look at what they're doing, co-opt it, and 'metal it up' for your side."

JONATHAN PONEMAN: The Singles Club really was a natural evolution. We were making far more commitments than we could afford. What started happening was there was a handful of record stores that were buying most of our singles. We were trying to open accounts and people would get mad at us, because they would try to buy records from us and we would already sell them out before we even placed an order with some of these accounts. The one way people could ensure that they would get a single and we would have cash flow was to have people pay up front. I don't remember who actually came up with the name "Sub Pop Singles Club" — Bruce came up with original text for the advertisement. I remember after work, we would go to this place, the Virginia

Inn — across the street from our old office. Bruce and I would have a couple of beers and talk about this kind of stuff.

BLAG DAHLIA: Chris Cornell sang like the guy in Zeppelin — so did everybody in Los Angeles. Kurt Cobain frowned a lot, and acted sad like the Replacements, and a lot of the Midwestern Touch and Go bands. All of this stuff is more derivative than it's generally portrayed. Sub Pop essentially completely copied the artwork of Touch and Go, and that "grunge style" started with bands like Butthole Surfers and Scratch Acid. They were good at promoting their scene as something unique. If you look at Sub Pop, what they did with their Singles Club — they signed the one good band in every town. There was no Chicago scene, but you could get one thing out of Urge Overkill. There was no San Francisco scene, but you get one thing out of the Dwarves. L.A. had L7 and Ohio had the Afghan Whigs. Basically, "Grab the one band that's touring and hanging out, and make it into something."

KIM THAYIL: The Green River single with "Ain't Nothing To Do" on it — the Dead Boys' song — came out on green vinyl/green sleeve. Then the Soundgarden "Hunted Down"/"Nothing to Say" single came out on blue vinyl/blue sleeve. To complete the set, you had Blood Circus on red vinyl/red sleeve, and I think it was Swallow with yellow vinyl/yellow sleeve. And Tad did a clear vinyl/clear sleeve thing. The Green River one is part of that set, but the money spent came out of Green River's pocket, so they put it on Tasque Force Records — the Green River killer had yet to be found, so Green River's fan club was called Tasque Force — a French spelling. But the distribution and promotion was pretty much Sub Pop. Then our single came out alongside Green River's *Dry as a Bone* EP — that must have been "eleven." In some cases, they'd stick a copy of the Soundgarden "Hunted Down" single in with [*Dry as a Bone*] — "Here's what we want you to play, and by the way, we got this coming up." That was "twelve A," and "twelve B" was *Screaming Life*. So we were the twelfth Sub Pop magazine [laughs].

MARK IVERSON: It was exciting — I wanted to buy everything they put out. I basically did buy everything they put out for a year or two. I remember the first time I saw the "Loser" T-shirt, and I just thought, "That is the funniest thing I've ever seen in my life — I've got to get that." They did a good job of creating anticipation, desire, and demand.

JEFF GILBERT: The coolest club you could never get into. Those guys were almost too smart for their own good — they ignored all the rules. They would promote the negative stuff, like "Loser." If you were dysfunctional, disaffected, or didn't have a crowd to call your own, that was your crowd.

ART CHANTRY: The thing you've got to remember about Bruce is that guy was stoned all the time. He was one of the earliest guys you ran into who was really into MDMA. His eyes were like fucking sparklers — I swear to God, they had sparks flying out of them. So he was like this marketing genius, but what he was, was like, *stoned.* He kept jumping ship with graphic designers. He was always a sampler — a kid in the candy store constantly. Whoever he was working with, you could talk him into anything. I quickly learned with Bruce is the way you worked with him, is you made it *his* idea. I tried to talk him into not putting the title of the band on the cover, and just have the logo to promote the label, and how important it is to promote the label. And he'd look at me like I was crazy. And then the next time I saw him, I'd say, *"Remember when you had that idea?"* And he'd go, "Yeah, that was good, wasn't it?" And then it would happen. After a while, I could get anything done [laughs].

STEVE MANNING: Over the years, as Sub Pop grew, they expanded to three floors in the building. Probably grew to twenty full-time staff. It had great views, [but] it wasn't very conducive to an office space — it was really hodgepodge. The conference room was huge — it was really unnecessary — and everybody's offices were cramped and closetlike. You'd have to walk through a little maze to get to each desk. Nobody seemed to know what they were doing — shit stacked everywhere. People signed graffiti on the wall, there was garbage sitting around. They were completely learning on the fly — and really struggling to keep the doors open.

BRUCE PAVITT: I have memories of the phone company calling us up and telling us they were going to disconnect our phone line because we couldn't pay our bills.

DANIEL HOUSE: I was driving home, and who do I see at a bus stop — Jonathan Poneman. I pulled over and said, "Hey, let me give you a ride." We got to talking, "Do you know anybody that's looking for work? We need somebody to spearhead our sales efforts and distributions stuff." And I said,

"I do — *me.*" So the following week I started working at Sub Pop — it was Bruce, Jon, and me. Bruce and Jon were probably two of the most disorganized and flakey people I've ever known. Bruce and Jon also have some of the most remarkable luck of anybody I've known. They were terrible about paying bills, hitting deadlines. They were losing things — masters, artwork. I was basically building their direct-to-retail account base, which by the time I left was, like, 400 stores nationwide that we sold direct to, on a COD-only basis. Eventually, I was billing out approximately $30,000 a month. Frankly — not to take too much credit — had it not been for that money made during that time, I'm pretty sure that Sub Pop would not have been able to weather their debts. They would have had to foreclose and declare bankruptcy, because they were hemorrhaging money like crazy.

GRANT ALDEN: Total disorganization. Luck? You make your own luck. Those guys gambled every time — without fear. Every time they had a chance to walk away with an extra $10,000, they blew $20,000 doing something else.

JEFF GILBERT: They owed everybody in town money. Everybody around town ended up working for them, and ended up getting stiffed by them. Their famous saying — "What part of 'We have no money' don't you understand?"

BLAG DAHLIA: I used to describe it as "Starving to death in a really cool suit." It was the kind of place where they would rather give a fat girl from the bar a job and a paycheck than give any money to the bands on the label. That's why no bands stayed for any length of time — but there were always new and tremendously useless Seattle townies working there. Bruce had good taste in music and could grasp an interesting concept. He was just so high and confused that often only the bands Jon liked got any help selling records — because he showed up at the office once in a while and occasionally did something.

JEFF AMENT: It was impossible [to get paid]. When Green River broke up, the hardest thing was we played on Saturday night, drove home all day Sunday, and then I went to work on Monday. And on that Monday morning, Jonathan Poneman came down and said, "We just got a bunch of money — we're going to buy a van, so you guys can tour on this next record." I thought,

"Wow, just when we decided we're not going to do the band anymore, somebody is actually offering to do something for us."

ART CHANTRY: They did everything exactly wrong — it was astonishing how stupid their moves were. I remember [the poet] Jesse Bernstein coming to their office and threatening them. Jesse was a scary dude, because the guy had *been there.* He walked in the office, and wanted his money for that recording they put on [1988's] *Sub Pop 200.* Some people said there was a gun, some people said a knife — probably not, because he didn't do that. He walked into their closet office, grabbed them, took them down to the bank, made them withdraw every penny they had in their account, and give it to him — it was a hundred bucks or some pathetic amount. And that's the only way he got paid. I mean, Girl Trouble immediately pulled their fucking record from Sub Pop — they were the first ones to walk.

GARRETT SHAVLIK: As time progressed, things started getting a little more tight, and Jon and Bruce started getting a rift between them. Jon was "the yes man" and Bruce was "the realist."

CONRAD UNO: Early on, they bought studio time and eventually product from me. Over the course of their first five/six years, they always owed me money — it got to be a slight source of tension. I'm not sure it ever got paid either. Can you speak to Jonathan? I'm sure you have his number . . .

JIM BLANCHARD: They paid me $150 for a piece of artwork. Although I never got my original art back.

SCOTT VANDERPOOL: I remember buying Sub Pop's first stereo system — it was a ghetto blaster they put on my credit card, because I had one. And a hand truck, to move boxes of records around. It would be like, "Jon, Bruce — can we get paid?" "Oh, I'll write you a check — but don't cash it for a week or so." I quit working there, because I thought they were going to fail at any minute.

JONATHAN PONEMAN: We started off the business with about $19,000 — what we were able to accumulate between money that Bruce and I borrowed from people. We spent that money within one month. We were in a situation where we were calling up record stores and trying to say, "Hey, if you buy from us direct, we'll give you a discount, but you need to pay COD." At the time, there wasn't anybody else doing that. The most critical connection [Bruce] was able to establish at the time — the Sonic Youth/Mudhoney single — was something he and Mark orchestrated. And then the Nirvana single, because we knew there would be . . . not a huge amount of fanfare, but a certain amount.

I remember Bruce and I would pray to UPS — *"Oh please!"* Because the checks would come in clumps. There would be days where there would be no checks, and then suddenly, there's $400 worth of checks. We could pay rent and give ourselves a paycheck. That happened for like a year, year and a half. But we were on the ropes, because we were always being ambitious. Two times in particular that I can remember we cleared out our bank accounts to buy vans for our bands. One was the $600 we gave to Mudhoney to buy their first van. We bought this monstrosity — I can't remember if we bought it for the Fluid, or L7 and Cat Butt — but they both ended up using this van, and Sub Pop paid thousands of dollars.

And the third time, we had like $3,000 in the bank, and Tad was about to go out on tour with Primus. This was seen as being a big deal, so they strong-armed us at the time, because this was between when we had regular business affairs and contracts, and the handshake deal. So the implied threat from Tad was, "If you guys don't get us a van, then when we become big pop stars after this Primus tour, we're going to split." Which all seems kind of amusing now. We all lived in a perpetual state of paranoia.

ROD MOODY: Sub Pop began hosting "Sub Pop Sundays" at the Vogue. This series began to solidify the whole scene that they were developing. Everybody knew and supported each other, we all recorded at the same place, with the same engineer, and we all went to and played the same three or four clubs. We all toured in the same "Sub Pop van," the first of which Swallow blew up in Texas. Probably slept with a lot of the same girls too.

KURT BLOCH: I remember one time, seeing [Jonathan] at a show, and he was like, "Hey, I don't have any money, can you buy me a coffee? Come in tomorrow and I'll give you a single that will just blow your mind." Went down there, and it was the "Love Buzz" single.

TRACY MARANDER: I remember when Sub Pop called to tell them that they wanted Nirvana on their label, Kurt was so excited. At the beginning, he thought that they were really cool. He was like, "There's this independent record company, they're from Seattle — they're not from somewhere else." Touch and Go at that time was his favorite label. He sent tapes to them, but they never contacted him back. It was just validating the fact that he was actually starting to get his music somewhere. [Later on,] I think he felt like they were ripping him off, and they were not willing to pay the money that they deserved or other bands deserved. The thing is, at the beginning, they couldn't afford to.

DYLAN CARLSON: All of a sudden, there's starting to be a lot of British journalists at shows. Articles on Seattle in British music papers.

JOHN LEIGHTON BEEZER: The infamous story of Everett True. [True] ends up writing for *NME* — but not their marquee/flagship author. He's, like, a dude that managed to write a few articles for them. So the Sub Pop single comes in, a promo package, and it says, "If you'd like to come out to Seattle and see what is happening here . . ." Everyone's like, "Eh, where's Seattle again?" And he's like, *"I'll go!"* They're like, "Do you realize that there's no budget for a hotel? They're just going to fly you there and you're going to sleep on people's couches." So he comes out, and I think in the movie *Hype*, Bruce Pavitt says, "Everett basically came out and invented the myth."

So what he did is he found kindred souls — drank with all these crazy people and slept on floors. Went back and wrote what turned out to be a cover article in *NME*, that said, "Holy shit, amazing things are happening in Seattle!" And the British public bought it [laughs]. So Mudhoney immediately went to Europe to tour. That was chaotic — it was mayhem and insanity. I wish I could have seen some of that, because that was probably some of the purest, best example of what it was all about.

BRUCE PAVITT: I felt that the British audience was really hungry for music that was decidedly more American, more physical, and more rocking than what was going on in England. The timing was really good.

DANIEL HOUSE: C/Z was a label that was started before Sub Pop started. What really inspired [Bruce Pavitt] — by his own words — to launch the label was the release of the *Deep Six* compilation. Never grew as big as Sub

Pop, but at one point, C/Z did have thirteen people working for it — it was a full label, and definitely "the number two label" in Seattle for many years. Even though I didn't put out the *Deep Six* record personally, it was the record that was the launching point for Soundgarden, the Melvins, Green River. Certainly, there are bands that may have never ever broke, or left a mark, had it not been for C/Z. We had the Gits, 7 Year Bitch. C/Z was around for fifteen to twenty years.

CHRIS HANZSEK: I borrowed and scraped together enough money and gear, and started a studio called Reciprocal Recording — right at the beginning of 1984. And ran the studio for a year. I had my day job, and then I'd work until two in the morning in the studio. Met all kinds of great bands. The idea occurred to me, "There's bands — the city is still forming its identity." I had a partner at the time, my girlfriend, Tina Casale, and we lasted a year in our first studio building, before the old Swedish landlord decided to kick us out at the end of our lease year. Then I had a year off, where I put the studio in my basement, and started C/Z Records. Talking to some of the musicians that I had been working with, the idea sprang up that there should be a compilation record to expose all of the talent in Seattle.

During the making of [*Deep Six*], there was a little bit of friction — the bands took the "democratic thing" really seriously. And Tina started to rub people the wrong way — she was an abrasive person early on. I think I had the ability to be the deal maker, but she had the ability to be the deal buster. She ended up pissing some people off — including me — and then we ended up splitting up in the middle of the record. I lost my day job too, because they went Chapter 11 — I was totally out of money. When the record came out, people were pissed at me, because I wasn't promoting it very much. I think I was branded a guy who talked a lot and didn't put his money where his mouth was. I got out of the record business pretty quick. I did another record with the Melvins, their first [1986's *Six Songs*], and I developed a bit of a distaste for dealing with the distributors and all the high expectations coming from artists. I more or less gave the label away after a year and a half — I gave it to a fellow who promised to be good and run it with all his best interests and my best interests put forward.

DANIEL HOUSE: I went to Chris, who probably still had over half of his thousand record pressing sitting under his bed, and subsequent release, which was the Melvins record. I offered to take the whole thing off of his hands, take over the label, buy his inventory. He was more than happy to say, "Here, fine."

CHRIS HANZSEK: I went back into the studio business after that. For a brief time, I partnered up with Jack Endino — for about a month — when I started the second version of Reciprocal Recording. He decided he wanted to be a producer, and didn't want to have anything to do with paying the bills, buying the equipment, or making any of the business decisions. So he went off on his angle, and I stayed with mine, which was studio owner/manager/chief engineer.

LARRY REID: I think Endino sort of engineered the Seattle sound.

JACK ENDINO: I knew all the bands, and they already knew me, because I was in Skin Yard. I was already "one of the guys." Bands have an instinctive distrust of people in studios — especially if the people in the studios are not musicians themselves. Because there's no qualifications really for being a guy who works in a studio — plenty of idiots can do it. You can go to recording school or you can have a rich dad, who buys you a bunch of equipment, and you open a studio. The most important piece of gear in the studio is the guy running it.

People had heard my four-track recordings, which sounded like albums. All of the stuff I'd done in my basement was circulating around the city because I'd been making demo tapes for people in my basement studio — literally the basement of my house. Malfunkshun could come in, and they knew that I wasn't going to be like, "You're going to have to play with a click track." Nobody was covering this sloppy, noisy rock music that was happening. And nobody had any money. The studio I was working at was one of the cheapest ones — it was just a little eight-track studio. We charged fifteen dollars an hour — that included me.

Mid–Late '80s

CHAPTER 11

"If we can just keep it a secret": Mid–Late '80s

By now, it could no longer be ignored — Seattle was the location of a fast-growing, fertile local music scene. With a straight-ahead/un-glamorous approach, grunge was a much-needed antidote to what was going on with overblown mainstream rock at the time . . . but it would still take a few years for the rest of the world to catch on.

JONATHAN PONEMAN: Seattle was a much smaller city at the time — much more "user friendly." The roads weren't as busy, the neighborhoods weren't as cluttered. Nobody was thinking about houses so much — apartment and house rentals were cheaper.

MARK ARM: All-ages shows were completely shut down in Seattle in '84–'85. So as soon as these musicians became twenty-one, their bands started playing in the bars — mostly for each other.

JERRY CANTRELL: It was a very supportive type thing, without being a real blowing-smoke-up-your-ass/ass-kissing fest. It was a healthy community of pissed off, fucking young guys, and a lot of shit that was weird in the world. Music could become really stagnant, and the last part of what was playing out was already played out.

JONATHAN PONEMAN: To this day I don't really believe that there was ever "a Seattle sound." There were some pivotal events, bands, [and] shows that shaped the listening habits of probably a dozen bands that played together frequently.

ART CHANTRY: What I was going to see back then were those monstrous mid '80s touring punk bands — Sonic Youth, Hüsker Dü, Big Black, Butthole Surfers, Live Skull, Scruffy the Cat, the Replacements, Pussy Galore, Camper Van Beethoven, Tupelo Chain Sex, the Cramps. These are the best fucking bands I've ever seen *in my life.* The Northwest was part of the network, and they all passed through here. There were just some astonishing performances — mind-boggling stuff. If you never had the chance to see Scratch Acid or the Butthole Surfers at their very peak, you don't know what you missed.

JEFF GILBERT: Before the floodgates opened, our bands were starting to get on major tours. There was a very palpable sense of electricity, excitement, and "in the know." Like, "God dang, this is happening right here, right now." It was funny, somebody said, *"If we can just keep it a secret."* Because at any given night, you could go downtown, and see 7 Year Bitch, Tad, Love Battery, Mudhoney. I was blown away by how fun it was. I'm still surprised I'm still standing. My liver — I'm surprised that still works. Because it was not uncommon to go to a club three, four nights a week here during that period. The word would get out, and they wouldn't even have to advertise it — it was all word of mouth. "Hey man, Alice in Chains over at Graceland." "Cool!" Well, you'd walk through a dog-poop-filled alley, and it would connect up with RKCNDY. So in between sets, you would go over to the next club to see what was going on over there. It was like everybody was on their game. The girls were starting to look better, the places started to smell a little better.

KURT BLOCH: Nobody would come to see us. It was like, "OK, great — another show with thirty people." By the end of '87, I think Lulu was out, and we were playing as a three-piece, which could have been good, but ultimately, we were just tanking. Kim was off in another world, and the drummer was off in another world. I kept trying to book shows, and couldn't find people. "Where's Nate? Where's Kim? Can't practice, don't know where they are." So by the end of '88, I was like, "Forget it — there is no Fastbacks." Which is really too bad, because we recorded a song for *Sub Pop 200*, and it was great. We recorded the three-piece with Jack, and everything turned out pretty good, but everybody was off doing other things. The curse of being twenty-seven.

So that fizzled until late '89, and by that time, there's tons of Sub Pop records coming out. I remember running into Jonathan, and he's like, "You guys should do something." We were going to put out our second album, thinking, "This will either get us going again or it will be the end." Around the same time, a label in England put out our first record, and put out a couple of singles. The singles got back to Seattle, and got some plays on underground shows in England. So we scrounged up the three-piece recordings we'd done before the band blew up. I remember being at Sub Pop talking to Jon — he's like, "Can you give me a ride to the U District? I want to take some records to the store." Jon didn't even have a car.

So I gave him a ride, and I was playing the Fastbacks thing. He's like, "Wow, this sounds really great. Are you guys going to be playing again?" I was like, "This label in England put out our record, and they're putting out this one too, and we're thinking of trying to go there to do shows." He's like, "If you guys can get a band together and start playing, I'd love to put out a single." So I call everybody up, and was like, "Let's try to do something." So we had two albums out, which Sub Pop was distributing, and we went in and recorded more stuff, and put out that first Sub Pop double single. They're like, "That's pretty cool — would you want to put out a compilation? Do you want to make a new record?" Sub Pop and that label in England, Subway Records — that's what revitalized the group.

JIM BLANCHARD: After seeing what happened in Minneapolis, you could tell something similar might happen in Seattle — in terms of it blowing up nationwide and getting a big media response.

SCOTT VANDERPOOL: Another band I would list on the "should have made it" thing — Feast. Feast [included] Danny Peters, who later ended up in Mudhoney, on drums. They were one of the first bands to go real slow and heavy. Black Sabbath/Zeppelin, and still kinda punk. That was in the real early days, and they would play the Vogue a lot.

KIM THAYIL: Too bad they never made a record. Sub Pop was getting ready to do a Feast single and EP — all the other bands were really into supporting them. They just fell apart.

TIM HAYES: The Nights and Days were fantastic, and then morphed into the Night Kings after that. Rob Vasquez was the kingpin of those bands, and he had many bands after that, like the Gorls, Ape Lost — the list goes on.

DYLAN CARLSON: Slim [Moon] had this rock band called Lush. Then there was Heliotrope, that was sort of all the Evergreen students' hippie band.

BEN LONDON: Hammerbox were selling out 1,000 seat venues before they'd even put out a major label record, and their record didn't really translate what their live show was. They were a great live band. And Gas Huffer.

MEGAN JASPER: Gas Huffer should have been huge. They had such a huge local following, but they were a band for twenty years. I can't say that they didn't fulfill whatever it was they needed to — they had a great life for themselves as a band.

CHRIS PUGH: Young Pioneers played a lot of shows — we were a drunken college band. We were influenced by a number of the bands going on at the time — the Wipers, Green on Red, REM. One time our guitar player didn't show up for practice — he was three days late or something. I wanted to be a little more serious — that's when I started Swallow. Swallow played quite a bit in that era, opening for other bands. I don't think we ever had quite the draw as some of the other bands — we wrote some good songs. There was a yellow vinyl single, and then a record [1989's *Swallow*] — I think it was one of Sub Pop's first CDs. We were young and [had] certain substance abuse issues — we could have been volatile at times.

ROD MOODY: [Swallow] went on to play shows with Mudhoney, Blood Circus, Soundgarden, Nirvana, Cosmic Psychos, and more. One of these shows, at Capitol Lake in Olympia, featured Nirvana opening, Swallow in the middle slot, and Soundgarden headlining. Something to tell the grandkids about.

JIM TILLMAN: Coffin Break was as hard — if not harder — than Nirvana. Those guys were never home — they'd tour nine months out of the year. But somehow, never got past the C/Z sort of punk rock credibility to break wider.

ROD MOODY: Coffin Break was the hardest working band around. They had a cool mix of metal and sing-songy pop. Cat Butt put on amazing, drink and drug–fueled shows that were always on the verge of going out of control. The tension between bandmates sometimes resulted in onstage flare-ups. Front man David Duet had the grunge rock star bit down pat, and the combination of his gravelly whiskey-soaked vox and Brother James's twisted

PIC BY MIKE LEACH — BESTROCKPHOTOS.COM

L7's Donita Sparks in Melkweg, Amsterdam, 1992

blues guitar rave-ups made them an unstoppable force. That is, until they stopped.

BLAG DAHLIA: I used to stay with the Cat Butt guys a lot. They were always good for some insane fucking dope addict shit. There would always be some weird stripper chicks over there. You'd hear stories. I never actually saw this one, but I remember Dave telling me about a guy that stayed at their place, and got so strung out and crazy that he pretended that a piece of cat shit was dope, tried to melt it down, and shoot it — but they stopped him. Very fucking sick.

DONITA SPARKS: [L7] had already toured the country in '88, but we had never played Seattle. We were fortunate enough to hook up with Cat Butt — we met up with them for some shows in Northern California, and headed up to Seattle. My first impression of the town was flyers everywhere — flyers on every phone pole and street lamp. It just seemed very alive — very youthful. The music community seemed really connected from my eyes. We stayed at [Cat Butt's] house, we danced to the Sonics — literally every night. Danny from Cat Butt booked the bands at Sub Pop — he worked at Sub Pop. I think he was kind of a "tastemaker" over there.

So we stayed over there where he lived, with his bandmates pretty much, in this place called "Blaine House" — which was filthy. The shower stall was covered in mold — you had to stand in the middle of the shower to not touch the mold on the walls. I guess our first time up there we stayed for a few days, and we played a place called the Hollywood Underground. We swapped clothes with Cat Butt — we wore their clothes and they wore our clothes. I think the next time we went up there, the guys at Sub Pop saw us and decided to do a Singles Club with us.

BLAG DAHLIA: [The Dwarves] first went to Seattle in 1989 to play a two-day event that Terminal Booking was putting on. Seattle was a good town for rock 'n' roll because it was basically a white suburb where young drunks could play music in their basements. Most urban environments like New York, L.A., San Francisco were embracing hip-hop — not rock. In the alternative realm, the Dwarves were the only band to wear women's clothing onstage, perform naked, and jump into drum sets — all cheap tricks that were later copied by various Seattle bands who became much more famous than us.

ROD MOODY: Blood Circus, along with Mudhoney, were the epitome of "grunge version 1.0" — bludgeoning sledgehammer riffs combined with deep guttural growls from singer Michael Anderson. Like Swallow and Cat Butt, Blood Circus was a train wreck, and one never knew what to expect at their shows. Sometimes they were phenomenal, other times, too sloppy and drunk to do much more than make din.

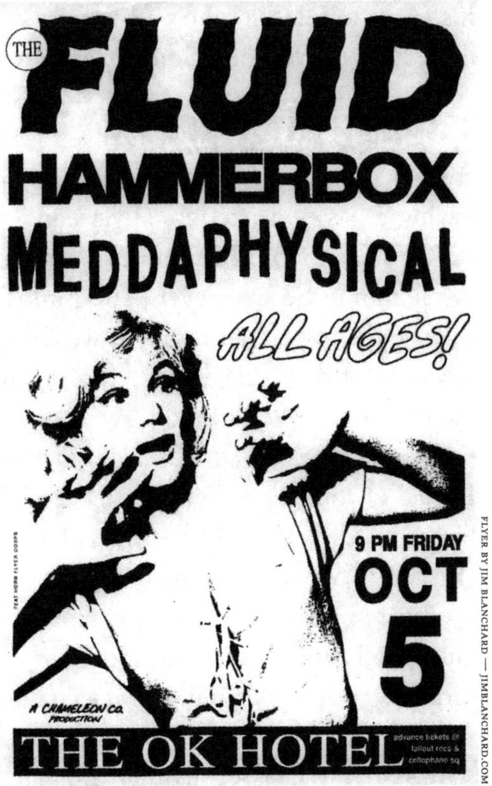

Lookout, the Fluid is coming!

BLAG DAHLIA: We couldn't get over the fact that girls in California were so much better looking than the ones in Seattle — so we didn't like hanging out there very much. Although you could always get good weed up there. We recorded with Jack Endino who thought we were amusing, but rude. He was right. We hung out with Mudhoney, Dickless, Tad. The Supersuckers — or as we referred to them, "Dwarves Jr." — opened many shows for us.

RON HEATHMAN: [The Supersuckers] were under the impression that we were just going to take it over. Because that's what we knew in Tucson — you form a band, you're instantly the best band in Tucson. So we figured that's what's going to happen. Our second show, we played a two-day event at the COCA Art Gallery — Nirvana, Cat Butt, Tad, Mudhoney, Gwar, and the Dwarves. We were just like, "Oh my God, all these bands are amazing!" It was all the little simple things — the beer was stronger, the pot was stronger, there was, like, four or five different clubs that bands played, whereas in Tucson, maybe one would stay open.

ROD MOODY: The Fluid from Denver sounded like no other band on the roster — a killer combo of Stonesy swagger and melodic hooks that stayed imbedded in your head long after they were done playing.

GARRETT SHAVLIK: Denver was very violent — the pit was out of control and people would get hurt. Then you'd come up here and people were having a gas — there was always an after party, and you had a place to stay. Me and Dan from Mudhoney became best of friends — it turned into this lovely family. So whenever [The Fluid] came back up, not only would it help finance the rest of our tour, but we always had a lovely time. So we would take a couple of days off just to hang out with Bruce and Jon. This was like our second home. We did a St. Patrick's Day show at the Backstage, in Ballard. We played with Coffin Break, and there was some dirty acid going around. I usually wouldn't partake in that before I had to play, but my two guitarists, James [Clower] and Ricky [Kulwicki], and sometimes our bass player, Matt [Bischoff], would "drop in." I look at them and they look like children — their eyes were really huge like those crazy paintings — biting their nails. Pavitt, I guess, had given it to them, and Pavitt's tripping his head off. But then all of a sudden, we start playing, and it's just perfect — kids were all over the stage.

GRANT ALDEN: The other thing, it's important to remember that it wasn't just Sub Pop and grunge. At that same time, Sir Mix-A-Lot was happening in the Northwest and nationally. There was a substantial garage rock scene being led by the Mono Men and Estrus Records out of Bellingham. There were the Walkabouts that were huge in Europe, and never made it in the United States. Even if you go back to *Sub Pop 200* — there is a great variety of sound there. There was a substantial pop scene, led by the Posies.

KEN STRINGFELLOW: Jon [Auer] and myself came from Bellingham — we went to school there. I moved to Seattle to go to the University of Washington. We had been friends and played music together all through high school. Then after my first year of college, we reconnected. Found that we were in a similar vein, and our thing was very melodic and "sunny." A naive version of another area of music that was inspiring to us — Squeeze, XTC, and Elvis Costello.

One thing that also brought skepticism to our cause is a band that's really popular in Seattle locally, in some weird, fluky way. Jon had a home recording studio — we made this thing that became [the Posies'] first record.

In our wide-eyed, don't-know-the-rules-enough-to-be-intimidated way, we brought them to local radio stations. There was an AM commercial alternative radio station, KJET. They played Soul Asylum, the Replacements, They Might Be Giants, Suzanne Vega. Local bands they didn't play much. We walked in with this cassette, like, "Hey, do you guys want to play our music on your radio station?" Like total dweebs. "I'll give it a listen."

Normally, "give it a listen" means they'll chuck it in a wastebasket. Four or five days later, I heard our song on the radio. Then an hour later heard it again, and then an hour later heard it again. Not only are they playing it, they're playing it *all the time.* So being that we had found our way into an area where some other local bands had not, I think it was assumed that we were more calculating than we actually were. It took us a while of playing shows where people were like, "They do something really different than what's going on. They're not totally out-of-the-loop musically; they're just on a slightly different trip."

MARK ARM: The "Seattle explosion" was weird — to us we thought it had peaked in '89. It hadn't cracked the mainstream consciousness and there was no reason to think it would. We just figured it was the latest underground hype.

DUFF McKAGAN: That talent was always in Seattle — the industry finally went up and tapped it, that's all. It wasn't like there was some sort of genius stroke that just hit Seattle in '87 with Mother Love Bone, and continued on for the next six, seven years. It was there since I started playing music and seeing bands in '78.

DAVE DEDERER: Who would have ever thought? I flash back to the moment I described of being on the U Dub campus with Stone in '84–'85, and he's talking about his look, and how he's not washing his hair anymore because he wants it to look like Johnny Thunders. Who would ever think five years later that kind of bullshit would actually come true? And it's even more unbelievable that it comes true not just for one person or one band!

ART CHANTRY: Even bands that were really smart got screwed. Not just by Sub Pop — when the majors moved in, the professionals got in there and started screwing *everybody.*

CHAPTER 12

"How do three guys sound like nine?": Nirvana

Unquestionably, one of the most popular and enduring grunge bands of all time is Nirvana. But judging from their early years, there was little evidence that this unlikely group of misfits would eventually completely alter the landscape of rock music.

KEN STRINGFELLOW: The scene in Seattle was staying a bit harder and not melodic. Like, you know how Mark Arm is monochromatic melody-wise? Seattle wasn't bending towards that "pop sensibility" really. Until Nirvana. Nirvana was far more melodic — almost insanely so. Even though they had really noisy stuff too.

LARRY REID: I remember when [Kurt Cobain] was this homeless waif who was tagging along as a roadie for the Melvins. I remember him being at the last Big Black show. He was a really interesting, creative little kid — I was smitten with him from the get-go. He had these tattered bell-bottoms — he didn't look like he'd washed his clothes. I think he literally was a runaway kid. This was like '84. He kept popping up at these things — he kind of stood out. He was always a good-looking kid.

ART CHANTRY: Kurt was one of those guys that always hung out and was always carrying everybody's equipment. He was Buzz's friend.

DALE CROVER: I met Kurt — he used to go to the high school I went to. It was probably a month after I joined [the Melvins]. Buzz was telling me they saw this kid that they knew from Montesano on the bus, started talking to him about music, and invited him to go see Black Flag. I met him down at the smoker's shed at Aberdeen High School. Became friends, and he started hanging out with us. We knew he played guitar, and he even kind of tried out for our band — we were thinking about adding a second guitar player. But in the end, we decided not to, because he didn't have an amp. Didn't really seem reliable [laughs]. But we were still good friends — he'd hang out and we'd jam occasionally.

I'd work on songs with him sometimes. In '85 or '86, for about a week, I wasn't in the Melvins. They were thinking that since I was still in high school, they were going to tour, and I wouldn't be able to get out of school to do it. That was always a problem, because we had gigs, and I'd be missing school the next day because we wouldn't be coming back. They decided that they would try to get another drummer. It didn't work out, but in that brief week that they tried to get another drummer, Cobain and I went to his aunt's house and recorded the Fecal Matter demo [1985's *Illiteracy Will Prevail*]. His aunt had a four-track. I don't think he had an amp then either. I remember him plugging in direct, but I can't remember how the hell I would have heard the guitar. People talk about that demo like it's this unreleased thing that must be amazing. But not really. A crappy four-track demo. We basically had formed a band — I played drums and bass on the demo. We may have even been playing before that, with a friend of ours that lived across the alley from me. He played drums and I played bass.

We were in various different bands with Cobain too, like we had a band called Stiff Woodies. Modeled the name after the Limp Richerds — a great Northwest band that nobody knows about. Sometimes Kurt would play drums, sometimes he'd play guitar. There was a point where Novoselic was the singer, which was great because he's this big seven foot tall dude, with a Jimi Hendrix fringe vest, who'd do big high kicks — who couldn't sing at all [laughs]. Someplace floating around, there's some radio show with us doing a bunch of those songs. We did that demo, and I don't think we played any shows, but that's how he got Krist to play with him — I was back playing with the Melvins. He wanted to put a band together that was more a band, not just a side project. He even tried to put something together with Buzz playing bass, and the old Melvins drummer playing drums. They rehearsed for a while, and it fell through.

DYLAN CARLSON: I met Kurt at a show; it was this side project that Buzz and Dale were doing with him — Brown Cow. It was him doing spoken word stuff, while Buzz played bass and Dale played drums.

CHRIS HANZSEK: [The Melvins'] roadie was Krist Novoselic. I remember thinking that he was a really tall kid, and he wore these size fifteen basketball shoes — he didn't have the laces laced up beyond about the fourth row. So he had eighteen inches of lace hanging out. Kind of goofy looking — fifteen-year-olds never quite look right. I remember ironically thinking, "Oh jeez, this poor kid, he's got to get his act together," because it just seemed incongruous that this band was bringing this guy along. And then they told me he was in a band himself. I remember thinking, "Yeah, OK — *good luck buddy.*"

SLIM MOON: Krist had this crazy VW van, that was decorated like a zebra, and he would always drive the Melvins to shows.

JOHN BIGLEY: Hoquiam — a very depressed area. The fact that they bumped into each other . . . Kurt had that "stuff" in him — they got it together and got it recorded. The whole spectrum, it's almost movie script shit. *But it's not.* They got good fast too. The first few shows, everybody was talking about them. Real sweethearts too. Then, I don't know, they started drinking protein shakes or eating Wheaties or something.

ALICE WHEELER: I saw them at the HUB Ballroom, and there were probably more people with the band than there were in the audience. My friend Tracy was taking pictures — she was dating Kurt.

TRACY MARANDER: I'm not really sure the first time I met him. I remember two times — one time was at a party at the Fifty-Sixth Street House in Tacoma. Jim May, who ran the Community World Theater, him and a few people lived in a house right by there and would always throw parties. They would charge two or three bucks to get in, and have bands playing. [Kurt] was with the Melvins, and I remember talking to him — he had a pet rat on his shoulder. And then the other time, I was in the car with my

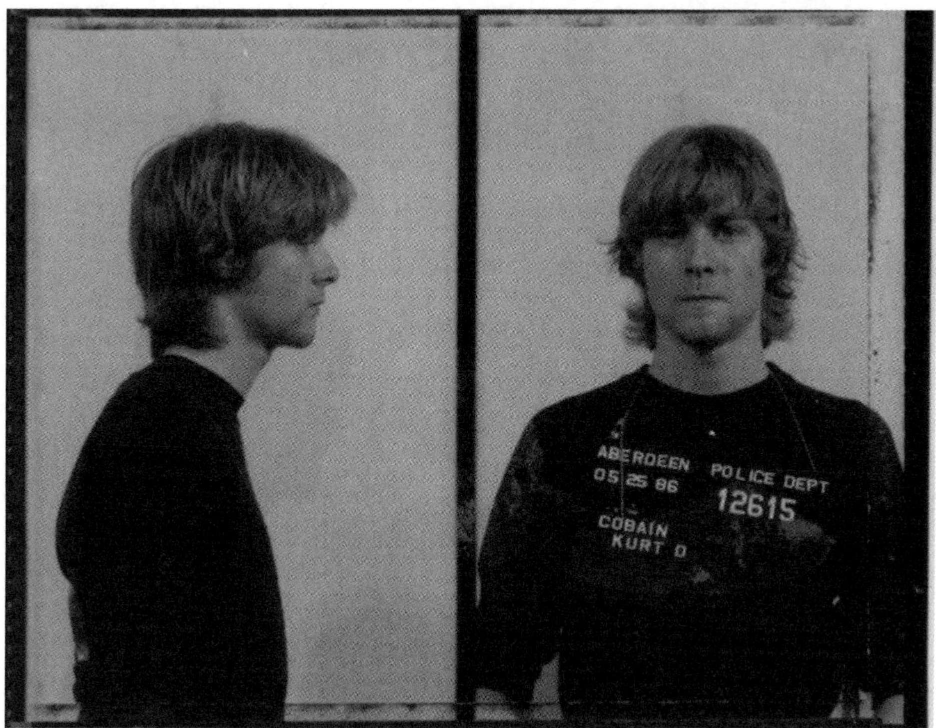

Kurt Cobain after being caught spray painting on a bank wall, and charged with "malicious mischief in the third degree." (Kurt spent eight days in jail.)

boyfriend at the time in the parking lot of Gorilla Gardens. Him and Buzz were talking to us — I remember how blue his eyes were, and he had a nice smile. And was really friendly. He had a long trench coat on, and had kind of short, feathered hair. I was friends with Shelli [Dilley, Krist Novoselic's girlfriend and later wife]; we worked together. I'd go down to Aberdeen to visit, and we'd see Nirvana practice in Kurt's living room. Kurt's voice was a lot different then — more gravelly and deeper. I had a crush on him — I'd go hang out with Krist, Shelli, and him. I would try and hit on him every so often [laughs]. Shelli's like, "He likes you too, but he's kind of shy." Eventually, we hooked up and started dating.

Shelli started working the graveyard shift with me; Krist was doing some painting job during the day. They were trying to find a house in Tacoma or Olympia. During the weekdays, they stayed in our studio apartment. Shelli and I would sleep in there during the day, Krist would be at work, and Kurt would wander around Olympia. Then we'd all have dinner together, and eventually, Krist and Kurt would go to sleep later, while Shelli and I went to work.

Kurt liked to watch TV. We didn't have cable at that time — we only had one channel. He'd play music — sit around and play his guitar — or paint pictures. If we could afford to, we'd go to the art store downtown and get canvases for him. If we couldn't, he would paint on the back of board games. He also did a lot of oil pastels and stuff, where he'd draw cartoons and things.

We drove in their friend Ryan's panel van [to Nirvana's first show, a house party in March 1987] — we all crowded in the back with the equipment. I remember drinking a lot of beer and stealing beer from the fridge. I think a lot of the people at the party really didn't like Nirvana. At one point, Krist was on top of their big, '70s sorta TV, encased in a wood box. Krist was standing on there shirtless. Shelli and I were in front of him, running our hands up and down his chest — just to be goofy, because everyone seemed like they were uptight. We were trying to be as outrageous as we could. Krist was jumping off the TV, and they'd run around the living room, and jump off the coffee table. Everyone's like, "You're going to break stuff!" Eventually, I think they kicked us out. At first, he had a really good time. But later on, he was critical of the mistakes they'd made. I thought that was kind of stupid, because like I said, everyone was drunk, and at some point, they just decided to make it more outrageous — to make an impression — than to play well. [Kurt] liked Aaron Burckhard's drumming. He was a really good drummer, it's just that he had lousy equipment, and instead of buying new equipment, he'd just spend it all on alcohol, drugs, or whatever. He was always flaking out on practices.

JACK ENDINO: An unknown band called me up, and a guy said, "My name is Kurt Cobain, and I'm friends with the Melvins. Dale from the Melvins is helping us out because we don't have a drummer right now. We want to record some songs for an afternoon — we don't have much money." I said, "OK." I figured, "If Dale is playing with you, you must not be bad." They came around noon, and they were out the door by 5:00 or 5:30, with ten songs recorded and mixed. You can call it a demo — some of the results are on the box set [2004's *With the Lights Out*]. Actually shocked at how good they sound.

I think they only played one gig with Dale Crover — that night at the Community World Theater. Literally, they left the studio, drove to Tacoma, and played a show. There's bootlegs of the show, and they played the same songs they recorded with me in the same order [laughs]. Plus a couple more we didn't record because they didn't have money for any more tape. Then Dale moved to San Francisco to be with Buzz who had already moved down there. So Nirvana did another gig or two with this guy, Dave Foster.

MARK ARM: I heard a tape that Jack Endino recorded — I didn't really think much of it at the time. Jack thought it was great, brought it to Sub Pop, and Bruce and Jon thought it was great. I was really into simple, primitive, aggressive, stripped down rock, and that early Nirvana demo somehow sounded too busy to me. The first time I saw them was at the Vogue, and they weren't very good. I mean, *honestly,* they weren't very good — they had a crappy drummer.

SLIM MOON: They seemed to have a different name every time they played — Skid Row, Pen Cap Chew, or Ted Ed Fred. It was clear Kurt was really talented, and Krist was a favorite. They were a great band, but they always had these drummer problems — they'd go through drummers every few months, and then end up back with the drummer that they had fired a while before. It was really a frustrating situation, because they had started out making their original recording and playing a few shows with Dale from the Melvins, which was one of the best drummers in the world — for that kind of music. And then they'd have these really bad drummers, who couldn't really even keep time.

DYLAN CARLSON: You could definitely tell [Cobain] was into Gang of Four at that time — a lot more complex rhythms. A herky-jerky kind of sound.

ALLISON WOLFE: I remember the first night I saw Nirvana play. I believe that was '87. It was also the last night of this club that was about to close down — a student project from Evergreen, GESCCO. There was maybe twenty people, and Nirvana was called Skid Row. I was excited to see Skid Row, because I had a tape — I think they played on the radio and I had taped it. It was great. I remember feeling like something big was happening. Even though no one was there, that band was the perfect blend of '70s punk, but it also had this Zeppelin feel to it. And of course, Kurt Cobain was very cute. From there on, I started seeing Skid Row whenever they played. I remember this one show at Community World. They played a cover of CCR's "Bad Moon Rising" — that was the end of their set, and everybody went crazy and was dancing. A whole bunch of people who I had assumed would have been at the show, showed up — when the show was over. I was like, "Oh my God, you missed [it]!" And they're like, "We went to Seattle to see a concert. This new band from L.A. — *Guns N' Roses.*"

CHAD CHANNING: I remembered seeing their show when they were Bliss. You've got this one guy who's really, really tall, just hammering this bass, and then there's Kurt. He had some kind of . . . it looked like crushed velvet, silk, purple or blue, bell-bottom pants, and I think he was wearing platform shoes. He was a really colorful character up there. He's louder than hell, screaming, and then there's Krist, who's standing the size of the Eiffel Tower on one end. Krist was the talkative one; Kurt seemed on the quiet side, almost timid.

JACK ENDINO: Nirvana the first time I saw them weren't very impressive [laughs]. In fact, in their early shows, they weren't very good because Kurt hadn't really figured out how to sing and play at the same time. In the studio, his voice blew me away. The first few Nirvana shows I saw, they were nobody — which means most of '88 — because the first demo I did for them was in January of '88, and then I was doing the "Love Buzz" single in June or July of '88. And that didn't get released until a couple of months later. So there's the first three-quarters of '88, they're out there playing shows, but there hasn't even been a seven-inch yet. They played a lot of empty rooms.

DAWN ANDERSON: [Jack] ended up passing the tape on to Sub Pop. He doesn't remember this anymore, but I was in the room when Jack was talking to them on the phone, and Jonathan was telling him, "I really loved it — Bruce thought it was a little too arty for him." Jack got pissed off — he said, "He's into mediocrity!" [Laughs.] Then I went to see them, at the Vogue. They weren't as great as I expected them to be, but they were good. After that show, [Kurt] was whining, because he thought he sucked. He was talking about how he was sick and his stomach hurt — he had puked, and all the precursor of things to come. I remember telling his girlfriend, "You need to tell him that he's awesome, because he thinks he sucked." And she sort of rolled her eyes — "Yeah, *that's Kurt.*" I wrote this thing that ended up getting quoted quite a bit, where I said, these aren't my exact words, but "With enough practice, these guys can actually be better than the Melvins." Like saying, "The Beatles may become as good as Badfinger."

CHARLES PETERSON: The first time I saw Nirvana, I thought they sucked. I didn't understand why Jonathan wanted to sign this band. They just seemed like a bunch of mopey shoegazers. The music seemed off, it didn't do it for me. And stupidly, I didn't take any pictures of them that night. I just thought, "This is probably the first and last time I'll ever see or hear from this band."

KIM THAYIL: They had no damn stage presence — at the time. They seemed a little bit nervous. They were opening for us outside in this park in Olympia. We really liked the songs, but Kurt just stood there — his hair was in his face. He didn't move.

TOM PRICE: I remember smoking dope with Kurt at a U-Men show at an art gallery. I remember going to a party at Susie Tenant's house, and all these guys came in. I didn't realize who they were at the time, but it was Kurt and some of those guys. I remembered thinking how funny they looked — they were kind of shorter, stocky — they looked like lumberjacks. It was funny being at a party and there's all these hipster, punk rock freaks, and then here's these guys wearing what would later be "the grunge uniform" — caps, flannel shirts, Parkas. They were all smoking weed.

REGAN HAGAR: The last Malfunkshun show in Olympia, Kurt came up to Kevin to see if he wanted to join Nirvana. Kevin told him, "No," and thought he was just some fan. I'm sure Kevin wishes he would have given it a shot.

MARK ARM: Nirvana didn't start to get good until they got Chad Channing in the band.

CHAD CHANNING: I first met Kurt and Krist at a Malfunkshun show. They were playing the Community World Theater in Tacoma — I'd been friends with Kevin. We actually had been working together for a while as cooks in this seafood restaurant. I went up there, and a friend of mine, Damon, introduced me to Kurt and Krist, because they were looking for a drummer. Before that, I was in this band called Tic Dolly Row, which actually had Ben Shepherd — in fact, that's how Kurt and Krist heard about me. A friend of mine, John Goodmanson, had this radio show at the college station, and Tic

Dolly Row went up there. As I would later learn, Kurt and Krist were listening to that show, and thought, "Wow, that was some pretty cool stuff."

JACK ENDINO: They got Chad in the band, and then came up with the name Nirvana.

TRACY MARANDER: I think [Kurt] liked Chad's drumming quite a bit — although they thought he was a little hippie-ish. Kurt's problem was, if you get a good drummer, they're going to have their own ideas. But then Kurt wanted to be the one to control, tell them how to play the drums.

CHAD CHANNING: The thing that lured me in was how simple the music was, yet with the vocal melodies, was just really cool. He did a really good job of taking something simple and making it sound really, really good.

JEFF GILBERT: They didn't play much around here, but when they did, it was an event. Three guys making a sound that totally belied the band members. I mean, how do three guys sound like nine? It all came from attitude, power, and volume. But it was punk rock — *their* version of punk rock — and you couldn't get more pure than that. And they would go on so stinking late — every freaking time. You'd get burned out waiting. Like, *come on!* The sets wouldn't be that long, because as punk rock songs are — like the Ramones — you can squish twenty-four songs in twenty-four minutes practically. You hit that first note — Kurt would do a power chord, and the drums were starting to smack around a bit, and the bass would rumble for a minute. And then in one second, it would all come together, and just explode. It was like a lightning bolt hit. You saw more feet than hands in the air, because people would go upside down. And you couldn't even see the band — except for Krist — you could never see the drummer, you could see the top of Kurt's head, because the Vogue's stage was maybe just a foot and a half off the floor.

The audience would be pushed right up against the band. Half the time, the band would have to play on the dance floor, just because there's no room. Band and fan became one at those shows. Just horribly loud. The Vogue and the Central are big cement rooms, and the echo . . . you'd have tinnitus for three or four days. I was amazed at how much beer could be drank and spilled simultaneously. The floor when you would walk in — Monty would have the floor perfectly mopped, swept, and before any of the bands came on, nobody was standing out on it. Stick to the perimeters. Once the bands came on, you'd go, "Where were all these people thirty seconds ago?" You didn't think they could fit all in there. Then when you were done, you'd look at the floor . . . the grunge guys wore Doc Martens, the metal guys wore white tennis shoes. Big mistake — they'd be *brown* by the time you got out of there. Again, the stench. *Ugh.*

Those were the days: Nirvana opens for Skin Yard

GARRETT SHAVLIK: Probably one of the worst live acts ever. They were really good people, but they were just terrible. It was a chaotic mess — gear falling apart. Chad had these crazy North drums — they're made out of fiberglass and were usually duct taped together. He had to play hard because Krist and Kurt were so loud, and he's a little fella. All of a sudden, his rack tom would fall off — I'd run up onstage, wrap it up in duct tape, and put it back on. Obviously, they got a lot better. But God, in the beginning, it was horrible.

CHARLES PETERSON: Consequently, the next time I saw them, which was at the University of Washington HUB Ballroom — a big place, probably could hold 1,000-plus people — they were on a bill opening for some local bands. From the very first chord, they got me. There was just something that changed. Kurt was just absolutely an amazing performer. He was doing these fantastic leaps in the air, just all over the place. They were playing that gig with the second guitarist, Jason Everman, who was also totally crazy and out of control. I don't know if that inspired Kurt maybe, but it was like "Wow!" Their songs were much more distinct and worked out. They just blew me away.

BRUCE PAVITT: The amazing thing about Nirvana that a lot of people don't understand — the way they matured and grew in such a short period of time.

ROBERT ROTH: The loudest band I had ever heard. This was at a *rehearsal.* [Cobain] reminded me of a cross between Charles Manson, Jesus Christ, and Johnny Rotten.

LILLY MILIC: For me, they would be really sloppy some nights and difficult to listen to — possibly too drunk to play. And then other nights they would just blow you away — they were amazing. It was just really inconsistent.

MARK PICKEREL: They were playing at this little community center — Hal Holmes Center. At some point during the show, Krist's girlfriend was up in the front, knocking about with a bunch of her friends — they were breaking the "no slam dance" rule. The guy who ran the center, came into the crowd, and he tried to intervene, and get the girls to mellow out. Krist's girlfriend started getting in his face — kind of pushing him. I remember this guy tried to reach to contain her — nothing aggressive — just trying to protect himself from her. When Krist saw this, he threw his bass down, jumps from the stage onto the guy, wrestles him to the ground.

GARRETT SHAVLIK: Krist was crazy, which was awesome. We had a Tad show and Krist showed up. Tacoma had a thugish sort of crowd — leather jacket fuckups with mullets. A brawl started happening around the Tad camp right after they got done playing, and I was breaking down my drums. Krist says, "Hey, do you mind if I borrow that cymbal stand?" And I go, "No, that's cool." He pops down the legs, and starts swinging at this guy. I was like, "OK — *that's another use for a cymbal stand.*"

BEN REW: Novoselic was always a kick in the pants. We all went to this big "love family" party someplace. After we polished off the beer, there was all this boysenberry wine — hippie wine. This shit must have been twenty fucking proof. All of a sudden, Krist is naked, and he's jumping over this bonfire. *And* *he burned his sac!* People had to tackle him and hold him down. But yeah, he roasted the sac-i-moli.

STEVE TURNER: He's a real character — you can get really spacey talking to him.

MARK PICKEREL: I remember [Novoselic] and I wrestling onstage during Tad's performance, when Tad opened for Nirvana at the HUB Ballroom. He used to always arrive everywhere with a big jug of wine — it seemed like there were *a couple* of jugs of wine with him that night. I remember helping him polish off a jug or two. There's a picture on the live Nirvana CD [1996's *From the Muddy Banks of the Wishkah*] of a guy stage diving in mid-air. That picture was actually taken during Tad's set.

CHAD CHANNING: [Kurt and Krist] always had a pretty good relationship. It was like a special little brotherhood sort of thing. Kurt was a quiet character a lot of the times. So if something was bothering him, you'd never know it, and if he talked to anybody about it, it would always be with Krist. Those guys really cared for each other quite a bit.

NILS BERNSTEIN: What struck me is that all the Seattle bands were such "a guy thing." There were a lot of girls that went to shows and liked all the bands, but you wouldn't go over to a girl's house and she was playing Green River. But Nirvana — all the girls liked Nirvana. And that was real evidence to me that they were going to be big.

ART CHANTRY: I worked on Nirvana's very first record — [1989's] *Teriyaki Asthma: Volume One* [the song "Mexican Seafood"]. [Daniel House] had been dumped by Sub Pop, and he wanted to get this band out before Sub Pop, because he recognized their greatness. Kurdt [Vanderhoof] spelled his name old school — K-U-R-D-T. Nobody knew how to spell [Kurt Cobain's] name. When Daniel tried to get a hold of Kurt or anybody, nobody could give him a straight answer. If somebody wouldn't follow through, I would follow through for them. So I sat down and spelled out his name as extremely as I could — like Kurdt Vanderhoof's name. I guess that's where Kurt started misspelling his name.

KURDT VANDERHOOF: I'm the other "Kurdt" from Aberdeen [laughs].

JACK ENDINO: I gave the tape that I made to Sub Pop, and by and large, came the offer for the seven-inch. That's when you had the "Love Buzz" seven-inch.

TRACY MARANDER: I think originally, Krist wanted to do the other song [by Shocking Blue], "Venus," but then Bananarama did it. Kurt liked the Beatles a lot, and '60s music, and Krist was really into '60s bands.

KURT DANIELSON: I'll never forget the day when Jonathan was at the studio, we were doing mixes for [1989's] *God's Balls*, and Jack was there. Jon says, "I got this tape — I want to see what you think of this." He put it in — I had no idea what it was, I never heard it before. And it was the "Love Buzz" single for Sub Pop. Just the eight-track recording, raw, on a DAT tape. I was completely blown away from Krist's bass playing, first of all. And secondly, by the great singing — everything else was just right on. Jon was like, "The band is not sure that it's tight enough."

MARK IVERSON: I was at Fallout Records. I used to go there almost weekly. In fact, that's where I bought "Love Buzz" by Nirvana — just because they were an Olympia band — and I was able to get number twenty out of a thousand. It's in my closet in case I ever need money.

CHAD CHANNING: The first time we toured, *Bleach* hadn't come out yet, we just had the single out — "Love Buzz"/"Big Cheese." That was an interesting tour — it was hit or miss. We could end up playing Tucson for twenty people, and be lucky to come out of there with thirty dollars to get us enough gas to make it to the next town, where maybe the next town would be a different story. There were these people that would come out — "We're on the Sub Pop Singles Club, and we know all about you guys." It's like, *"You do?"*

JACK ENDINO: After the "Love Buzz" seven-inch came out, they started getting a few more people to their shows. Then when we started working on [1989's] *Bleach* — over the holidays of '88. They didn't really start taking off and having a lot of people coming to their shows until after *Bleach* came out, which would have been spring of '89. And Kurt was still trying to figure it out

— he would play guitar and his singing just didn't have the power. Ultimately, I think he concluded that he needed to play simpler songs, so that he could sing better.

CHAD CHANNING: Recording *Bleach* happened fast. We were in there for I think a week. Recording at Reciprocal — a really cool scene. I always remember Jack sitting there and he had a circle of snacks around him — chocolate bars. We did a lot of weird experimenting with snare sounds. We actually took two snare drums, took the bottom head off one of them and the top head off another, combined the two drums together. So there ended up being this gap between the two snares, but I used double-sided screws to link them together. Another thing — "Blew" was a song that initially was played in D. So when we went to record that song, it had turned out that we were already in D, and that everyone tuned down, or at least Krist did, to C — it was even *lower.*

TRACY MARANDER: Kurt chose that shot [for the cover of *Bleach*]. I had the negatives, he decided he liked that one the best. And it was his idea to make it a negative image — he'd seen some picture somewhere of a negative image, and liked the way it looked. I think he liked the way everyone looked like they were rocking out — they weren't just standing around playing. Kurt had wanted me to make sure I got a picture of all four members in the photo for the album — even though Jason hadn't played on the demos. I was secretly thrilled because Kurt was so happy that it was finally out. When he got the first copy, he was clutching it in his hands. Just so happy — couldn't stop smiling.

ART CHANTRY: The *Bleach* cover was one of the last album covers [Lisa Orth] designed for [Sub Pop], because by this point, they owed her thousands of dollars. They were jumping from printer to printer, because nobody would print their stuff — they owed so much money. I think they drove a couple of people out of business — they were awful. But because they were friends, you kept doing stuff for them — for nothing or next to nothing. And Lisa only charged them like $300 — the *Bleach* cover. I remember when she was working on it at *The Rocket* — in the production room — I was standing there talking to Grant Alden, who set the type and edited the magazine. He set type for me on this old computer typesetting device called a Compugraphic, and Lisa came up, and said, "I'm working on this band for Sub Pop. They said they're going to pay me up front this time, but they're not going to. I'm going to do it anyway. They're a band with a terrible name, Nirvana. They're from Aberdeen." It's like, *"Oh Jesus."*

She had this not great photograph — it was another live shot of a band. Another "hair shot," and she didn't know what to do with it. She didn't want to put a lot of effort into it, because she knew she was going to get shafted. So she just put the photograph in, and couldn't crop the photograph, because it was long and skinny, and the record cover was square. She ended up sloping in some type above and below the photo, and reversing the whole thing on the Photostat camera. She went up to Grant, "Can you set the type for me?" "OK, what typeface do you want?" "I don't know, whatever's on the machine." What was on the machine was a typeface called Onyx, which is a bad design that was only available on Compugraphic. He goes, "What's the name of the band again?" "Nirvana." And he goes, bam! "There you go." That's how Nirvana's logo was made. Got paid fifteen bucks [for "designing" the logo]. How many millions of dollars were made on swag? And the joke on the back about the $600 was her joke — she put it on there as kind of a jab at Sub Pop.

Later, they used that "blissed out" happy face image. That particular image was actually the logo for a strip club in downtown Seattle, across the street from the New Art Museum, called the Lusty Lady. They had buttons with that image that they gave out on the street that were really popular. Many of the Seattle rock scene girlfriends made money to support their boyfriends' bands by dancing at the Lusty Lady. It was crucial in the support system of the Seattle grunge scene — as was prostitution. Many early Seattle rock bands were even managed by notorious pimps. One of the dirty little secrets of rock.

JERRY CANTRELL: I think I heard about Nirvana from Chris — Cornell would wear Nirvana T-shirts. The first time I heard *Bleach*, I hated it. I can say the same for a lot of my favorite all-time records. It was like, "This guy fucking sucks. He can't play guitar, blah blah blah." Self-righteous shit, and also having some attitude about your own band. One particular listen at one time, and everything changed — I'm like, "Oh, I get it. *I fucking get it.* These guys are great." But it took a while. I didn't know a whole lot about them. I didn't see a whole lot of their gigs. I remember the guys in the band were really stoked on it — Layne [Staley] and Sean [Kinney] really liked it a lot. I was a little bit hesitant — it took me a couple more "bites" to realize that I loved it [laughs].

KIM THAYIL: When I heard *Bleach*, I thought, "Holy cow, this is one of the coolest local bands I've ever heard." Not just a cool local band, but a cool band from *anywhere*. We did one of our first major van tours — it might have been the SST tour — where we were touring with Sylvia Juncosa. I believe during that tour, the two cassettes that got the most airplay in the van were Nirvana *Bleach* and the first Fugazi EP [1988's *Fugazi*]. Everyone in the band loved *Bleach* — it was just so amazing. The whole thing — the songs, the guitar, the vocals, the bass, the drums.

JON AUER: I must admit the first time I heard "About a Girl" I thought it was "Blood and Roses" by the Smithereens. Of course, as soon as the vocals came in it was a different story.

ART CHANTRY: Everybody loved that record.

TRACY MARANDER: I remember one time going to a show at the Vogue, and it was *so* jam-packed. At that point, realizing how big they'd become. They were too big to be playing small clubs like that anymore.

ALICE WHEELER: Instead of being exclusive, it was an inclusive movement. I think in my mind, that was one of the main differences between say, Soundgarden and Nirvana — was the exclusivity versus the inclusively. The rock star thing versus the everybody's-in-it-together thing.

CHAD CHANNING: When *Bleach* came out and the second tour [began], things were definitely a lot different. It was generally packed houses. We spent a lot of time hanging out with people that would come to the show, and almost always get hooked up with a place to stay. Some of the most fun places to play were in the Midwest. I think it's just because they didn't get a whole lot of bands coming through there — except for really big major acts at whatever coliseum.

One of the bigger memories was when we played in Dallas, and we got caught in that massive rainstorm. It's on the DVD [*With the Lights Out*]. We ended up staying at somebody's house, but it seemed like there were ten or eleven people living at this big house. And then we had that show in San Antonio, where we didn't end up staying at anybody's place. We ended up camping out. When we were out there — some sort of campground — we woke up and heard these ducks that sounded like they were getting ripped apart. Crazy noise, huge splashing in the water. I think Jason was walking down at night with a flashlight, looking around the water, trying to see what the hell is going on. We're like, "God, could that have been alligators?" Hell, it's swampland, I wouldn't put it past it. Kurt or Krist might have decided to sleep inside the van after that.

Milwaukee is where I think some of the footage on that DVD came from. The Pixelvision stuff — the really weird black-and-white, grainy, small screen stuff. That clip is a time when we were driving down the road at night — we put up a blanket to separate the two front seats. Krist was driving, and me and Kurt had the Pixelvisions going. Just started doing random things, and saying random stuff. I think we were drinking Jim Beam — wine and whiskey. [On tour] we listened to a lot of Talulah Gosh, Vaselines, Lead Belly, Shonen Knife. Those guys hadn't been familiar with Shonen Knife until I brought in a tape. In Boston, I'd picked up *The Man Who Sold the World.* I know those guys — Kurt anyway — weren't big David Bowie fans. But I popped it in one time, and Kurt was like, "Wow, this is really cool. This is David Bowie?" I'm pretty sure that's where he got the idea of doing "The Man Who Sold the World." We listened to some Pogues, and people would give us their demos.

STU HALLERMAN: One time I saw them play at Evergreen State College at K Dorm. There was a place called the Pit, which was the bottom of the staircase, kind of a lounge. This little octagonal room. I didn't want to be near the mosh pit, so I went up three or four steps, so I could see a little better. The band gets onstage, they play about three notes, and the entire crowd is pushing on each other so hard that everyone fell over! Just this massive heap of people. I'm like, "Oh man, people are going to get hurt." I reach down and start to pull people up, and there was this human cooperation thing — everyone grabbed the person on their right and leaned up. The entire crowd went from collapsed to up and dancing again — in half a second.

SCOTTY CRANE: It was amazing seeing that any of those bands were playing the Moore [for Lame Fest '89]. Very exciting, but seemed like the apex/pinnacle of any of their careers — like it could not go any higher. And actually, I don't think it was sold out. I remember the crowd was light for Nirvana, pretty packed for Tad, and thinning out during Mudhoney's set. No one knew who Nirvana really were. Chad was at the merch booth — gave me the white vinyl version of the record.

JOE NEWTON: They scared me a little bit [laughs]. I always thought that Kurt was going to hurt himself — and he probably did. The first Sub Pop/Lame Fest thing that they did — I think that was when he was spinning the guitar around his neck, by the guitar strap.

ROBERT ROTH: There's another interesting synchronistic event that always struck me as being eerily symbolic of the coming "new age" — the first tour Nirvana did of Europe with Tad. It included dates in both East and West Germany, if my memory serves me right, and coincided with the fall of the Berlin Wall. Johnny Rotten wanted to "Go over the Berlin Wall." Nirvana went through it, metaphorically speaking.

CRAIG MONTGOMERY: I really got to know them when we went on the European tour. It was then on that Nirvana started viewing me as their sound guy, and really wanting me to be there at their shows. Krist had been to Europe before when he was a kid. Everyone reacted to that pretty differently. The insanity of the crowds was pretty striking. The way that people would react to the music — jumping off the speaker stacks, going into an uncontrollable frenzy.

KURT DANIELSON: We got the opportunity to tour in Europe for the first time, and not only that, but sharing a van and the bill with Nirvana. We got to know them well and become really good friends. We did seven weeks — forty shows in forty-five days, something like that. Your standard hellbent-Kamikaze-hellride-straight-to-hell-in-a-handbasket kind of action. We were young, flexible, and able to bounce back. I wish I would have known then what I know now. What was really great was watching Nirvana play every night. At the time, it felt like prophetic experiences — like watching a tidal wave approach from a great distance. Transcendent — just wonderful.

BEN REW: Chad was über hyperactive. Tad calls me, and he goes, "They stuck me and Chad in the same room. Chad jumped up and down on his bed — *for three hours*. I swear to God, I wanted to kill him!"

TAD DOYLE: I remember [Cobain] struggling with stomach problems all the time. We'd always make jokes, "I'll hold the barf bucket for you, if you hold the barf bucket for me." We actually ended up doing that for each other on many occasions. We'd both laugh our asses off when the other guy was blowing chunks out his nose and mouth. Tears streaming down our face because we were so sick. You get in a van, it's as cold as hell in winter in Europe, every night's a show — it wears you down physically, I don't care how healthy you are. Certainly rock musicians who smoke and drink aren't the healthiest of people. I remember one time we went to get our visa for going into Budapest, Hungary, and we had to get photos taken for that. Kurt and I exchanged photos. I still have that photo, and I don't think anybody else in the world's got it, except for me. That's pretty special.

CHAD CHANNING: I think [Kurt having an onstage breakdown] was in Italy. I guess he was questioning the whole band thing, and everything else. My perspective on it is kind of a lot different, because pretty much after I was born, I've spent most of my time moving. I've moved so many times it's ridiculous, so I'm very accustomed to being on the road. When I'm touring, I'm completely comfortable, and happy when I'm out of my element. I may have been the only one on that entire tour that enjoyed myself all the time. I know it was tough — the other guys would complain being sick of eating bread and bologna spread. There were nine of us in this passenger van, so we were all in pretty close quarters.

When Jason joined the band, the idea that Kurt was thinking was, "I'd like to get somebody in there so I don't have to worry about always trying to keep that rhythm up, or if I mess up there's someone to back me up. So I've got freedom to concentrate on what I'm singing." We had the one tour with him, and to this day, nobody's really sure — except for Jason himself — what went on. Halfway through the tour, when we got to New York, he got really quiet on us. We tried asking him what was up, and never got much response. We had a lot of fun with him until whatever happened changed — then it got kind of weird.

BEN SHEPHERD: I was supposed to play the other guitar [after Jason left] — but I really didn't do anything, except be a friend on tour. I was always like, "You guys should just stay a three-piece." They came home for a little while, then I went on the road with them. Before we left, we rehearsed everything that basically became *Nevermind,* and never played that shit live. They only played *Bleach* back then.

ROBERT ROTH: I almost joined Nirvana — we ended up setting up a session and it went really well. But they stayed a three-piece.

SCOTTY CRANE: I was always really amazed by the sheer gusto they took the stage with, and how much everyone poured into the performance. I was in San Diego, and I crossed down into Tijuana to see Nirvana. This is the end of their West Coast tour — they knew they had no money — and they still destroyed Chad's drum set! It's like the stories of the Who and Pete Townshend having to go steal guitars after shows. Why did they play cheap equipment? Because they couldn't afford it.

DANIEL HOUSE: One of my favorite stories which really reflects both [Sub Pop's] remarkable lack of competence and their amazing luck altogether was when they put out the *Bleach* record. I joke that I sold the first 50,000 copies of that record, because I pushed it to every store in America, and made sure it was being reordered. It was vinyl-only, and they decided, "Well, it's time to put out a cassette." They had earlier done this licensing thing with [Tupelo Records'] Gary Held for a four-song EP that came out of London, *Blew* — two of the songs were on *Bleach*, and two of the songs were non-released tracks. So they literally cut the tracks out of the *Bleach* master, recut them to a new master, and sent that off.

They then decided to put out a cassette, so they sent the masters out for the cassette. We had to approve the master first, before they could start manufacturing. And Jonathan [was] like, *"I'll do it."* And I kept bugging him, "Jonathan, I need approval," because I also took care of all the manufacturing and all the production issues. He kept going, "I'll do it." I'm like, "Jonathan, you're too busy on the phone. I'll do it." He was just too disorganized to focus on it. The deadline came, the deadline went. Two weeks later, we're pushing the whole thing back. "Jonathan, what the fuck? This is ridiculous — we need to get this out, we already have our distributor pissed at us because we're behind deadlines." He goes, "I'll do it tomorrow." So he finally puts the tape in, listens to it, but it's really just playing the background — he's on the phone the entire time. He tells me, "Yeah, it's great. Go for it."

So I think we manufactured 50,000 cassettes, maybe it wasn't that many

— it was a lot though. Two tracks that had been pulled from the *Bleach* master and sent to London for [1989's] *Blew* EP had never been reedited back into the tape. So, we had this *Bleach* master, with two songs missing from the record. The artwork reflected the full track listing — the actual tapes had two songs missing. The entire run got manufactured, all the orders went out, everything got sent out. Probably something crazy like sixty percent of the whole run was ordered straight up. It was probably a month or two later before it even became clear that there was a problem. So we're like, *"Oh shit."* We're getting ready on taking a huge hit on returns of basically the entire amount — which we had to eat, because we approved it. *We didn't get returns.* People actually went out to the store and began buying them up — because it was a mistake and a collector's item! All it did was serve to sell the entire rest of the pressing out in record time.

MARK PICKEREL: I also worked at Sub Pop during those years — I was a salesperson and did junior A&R — from '89 through '91. I was literally on the phone all day, selling hundreds of Nirvana shirts and CDs just in the average sales day. So I was aware of this movement bubbling under, and it was about to turn into something massive.

MEGAN JASPER: Of course, their music was amazing. There'll be no one who can dispute that. But the thing that was so great about them truly — they had a *spirit* that was so unique. The one moment that really sort of captures that for me, it was not even a Nirvana show — it was a Fluid show in Tacoma. There were these huge spools, without cable — they could have been used as a table. Krist and Kurt were at the show, and somehow, Kurt wrapped his body around the inside of the spool, and Krist pushed him. He was rolling across the venue. When he got out, he was super dizzy and clumsy — falling a bit. Then Krist wrapped his six and a half foot body around it, and Kurt was pushing him. They were having the best time in the world.

ALLISON WOLFE: One night I was hanging out, I believe this is the summer of '89. I was at Slim Moon's house, which at the time, there was this duplex house with a basement, and Slim, Dylan, and some other guy lived on the right-hand side, and Kurt Cobain and his girlfriend, Tracy, lived in the basement. I remember I was hanging out and we were playing records. Kurt and Krist came in, and they always made a big entrance when they came

— especially Krist, because he was so tall, loud, and obnoxious back then. They came booming in — like, *"Hey! Hooo!"* I remember all of a sudden the atmosphere changing from mellow and depressing to really fun and energetic. Those guys had a really good feeling about them. Kurt was jumping around off of tables and couches, kind of leapfrogging — pretending to be a frog. They were really sweet and fun.

TRACY MARANDER: Basically, he just fell out of love with me. I think because I didn't play music was a factor in it. I think he wanted to be with somebody he could play music with, and collaborate with. He started dating Tobi Vail before we officially broke up, and I found another place to live. Kurt and I went out for three years. A few months after we broke up, I was angry and didn't want to talk to him at all. It was weird — one day I woke up and I wasn't angry anymore. He came over one time and stayed the night — nothing happened — we just hung out, went to the Java-Jive, and he went back home the next day. Another time, he came over — he was dating this girl Sheryl — my boyfriend and I were watching a movie. It was *Jacob's Ladder* — they ruined the ending for us. He was like, "Is this the movie where blah blah blah?" We're like, "Hey, *thanks*."

CHAPTER 13

"The sloppiness was essential": The Thrown Ups, Mudhoney

After the breakup of Green River, former bandmates Mark Arm and Steve Turner united once more as garage rockers Mudhoney. But just prior to Mudhoney, the pair was part of an improv band called the Thrown Ups, whose unpredictable — and often messy — performances are still legendary according to bewildered and stained bystanders.

SCOTT VANDERPOOL: Before Mudhoney started, the other guys [from Green River] had started Mother Love Bone. But before they were Mother Love Bone, they were going to be called the Lords of the Wasteland. And Mark decided to put together what we'd call "a fuck band," which was just a one-off thing. There was one he called the Wasted Landlords. Because of that, those guys dumped Lords of the Wasteland immediately! There was another fuck band show he did, as "Beergarden."

MARK ARM: After he quit Green River, Steve joined the Thrown Ups with Ed Fotheringham. The Thrown Ups were the brainchild of Leighton Beezer. Leighton decided that he loved to play, but hated to practice. So the Thrown Ups never practiced. In the beginning, the Thrown Ups had a rotating lineup, which centered around Leighton. Ed wasn't the first singer; Steve Mack, who moved to the U.K. and joined That Petrol Emotion, was the first singer.

STEVE MACK: I had to go back to college either the third or the fourth of January, and we had this huge party [on New Year's Eve, 1983]. We decided for some reason that it would be a good idea instead of going to sleep to stay up nonstop until the start of college. We built up this arsenal of as many drugs as we could find, and then decided not only were we going to stay up, but we were going to make music continuously. And who should walk in, but Leighton Beezer — out of his mind on drugs. He joined in, and we kept playing and playing. We actually managed eighty-four hours before I said, "I can't stay up any longer! *I'm dying!*"

JOHN LEIGHTON BEEZER: We finished playing and somebody said, "How did that sound?" And Ed said, "It was the audio equivalent of throwing up."

MARK ARM: Ed became the singer after a couple of basement parties. Leighton grabbed three people and began playing on someone else's gear — just making stuff up. I know that sounds pretty horrible, but with Ed as the front man, it was one of the greatest things ever — a truly great band. I eventually weaseled my way into that band. Their drummer was a better drummer than me, but he didn't really listen to what the other guys played. He would just get bored and randomly change the beat, throwing the rest of the guys off. In a band like this, the drummer's got to keep it together as much as possible. I convinced the rest of the Thrown Ups that I could do that — although I'm a shitty drummer.

Ed would do the goofiest things — he would come up with a different concept for each show. One time, he decided, "I'm going to make 'zit pants.'" He made pants out of garbage bags — they looked like leather pants from a distance. He crafted these little pockets that he filled with shaving cream, and attached to the inside of the pants. He would stab one of these pockets with a pencil, flex his leg, and shaving cream would squirt thirty feet! [Laughs.] One time, we played wearing boxers and giant daisy heads, and we had a couple of friends who had horns so one of them was the sun and one of them was the moon. Just totally retarded stuff, but funny and interesting — at least to us. Apparently, Steve's ball sac hung out of his boxer shorts the whole time. No one knew this except for the poor folks in the front! [Laughs.]

Another time, Ed's concept was, "Let's be beatniks." So we all dressed in black and wore berets. Ed decided he was going to be a beatnik girl, so he

PIC BY MIKE LEACH — BESTROCKPHOTOS.COM

Mudhoney's Mark Arm at the Paradiso in Amsterdam, May 19, 1992

strapped cups to the bottom of his shoes, wore a long straight black wig and a little mini skirt, and most bizarrely, cut a Ping-Pong ball in half, put each half in his cheeks, and sang the whole show like that. Since the Thrown Ups didn't have any songs, we would have to make up a set list for every show. The process for this consisted of getting drunk and brainstorming. The titles that made us laugh the hardest became the songs we would play that night. Ed would make up the words for these songs on the spot. We did another show where Ed's concept was we would be the dirtiest band on earth. We filled up a guitar case with dirt and bark from the median strip in front of the club, smuggled it into the men's bathroom, shook up a bunch of Pepsi, sprayed it all over each other, and then threw the dirt all over ourselves. This of course, completely befouled the bathroom and the stage. The club was none too pleased with us. And I'll tell you what — it was gross! [Laughs.]

LARRY REID: The Thrown Ups were a great opening act, because they would play until they got unplugged, and that was my job [laughs]. They were horrible, but fun.

MARK ARM: I joined [Steve] in the Thrown Ups about six months after he left Green River. When Green River broke up, I immediately called up Steve and asked him if he wanted to start a new band. He'd already been playing with Dan Peters, who, along with Greg Gilmore and Matt Cameron, was one of the three best drummers in town. Steve was really surprised he got Dan to play with him [laughs]. Steve, Dan, and Ed had been dinking around in the fall of '87. Steve wanted to play written songs as opposed to making stuff up. But Ed's heart wasn't really into it — he wanted to do art and be an illustrator. It was very easy for me to worm my way in there [laughs]. With Ed's disinterest, there was this instant band for me to join. When the three of us began practicing in late '87, we didn't have a bass player. We considered asking two people — Jim Tillman and Matt Lukin. Steve and I knew Matt pretty well since the Metropolis. We heard that the Melvins were moving to San Francisco and leaving Matt behind. So we asked Matt first since we knew him better than Jim. He was into it, and the next time he came into Seattle was New Year's Eve. We had our first practice on New Year's Day. So that's when we mark the birth of [Mudhoney] — January 1, 1988.

SUSAN SILVER: I remember it was New Year's Day, and Chris and I were at my apartment by the Pike Place Market. Somebody called to say that Green River was breaking up — it was devastating news. And to learn that Mark was going on to do this other band, Mudhoney.

JERRY CANTRELL: Green River was a band that I really dug a lot, and

Mark continuing on with Mudhoney — a band of great importance to Seattle, and to me.

LIBBY KNUDSON: We were all crazy about Russ Meyer, it was like, "Oh Mudhoney, *ha ha ha.*"

STEVE TURNER: We were definitely way more in sync again with what we wanted to sound like. We were both turned on by a lot of the Australian stuff — feedtime, and the Scientists. If we were going to do a band, I wanted him to play guitar — I didn't want him just jumping all over the stage. Because he was such a terribly cool guitar player — he was an idiot savant on the thing. It came together really easy.

MARK ARM: The very first show Mudhoney played was opening for Das Damen at the Vogue. I remember being super nervous, because I hadn't played guitar in a band for a while. I'm not even sure if I picked up a guitar after I stopped playing in the first few months of Green River. I had gotten this baby blue Hagström II off a friend — Tom Mick [from Feast] — for eighty dollars, because he was in desperate need of some quick money. I felt bad that I was taking advantage of Tom's proclivities, but he was going to sell that guitar for next to nothing to somebody, and it might as well be me. I really liked that guitar because it had a small, thin neck. It was easy for me to play a chord on it. I was partially inspired to use slide by feedtime — "Sweet Young Thing" has a pretty pronounced slide part in it, and the part I play in "Touch Me I'm Sick" is slide too. In the earliest days of Mudhoney, Steve and I would get together in my apartment with our guitars not plugged, just trying to show each other what we have. It sounded way better with a bunch of distortion.

JONATHAN PONEMAN: There was a sloppiness to it, but the charisma was undeniable. The sloppiness was essential, because there was a real chaotic frenzy to what they were doing. The way they were using distortion pedals at the time — it harkened back to Lee Stephens and the Stooges. But there was a sense of humor. It was loose. It was menacing and playful — all at once.

MARK ARM: In the earliest days of Mudhoney — we would play maybe once a month, so there would be all this built-up energy. We would just go ape shit. We would be bouncing off the walls.

STEVE TURNER: They were really just a drunken mess, for the most part. But it was really fun. It was our friends and us basically, so it was very communal. A bunch of happy, sloppy, drunk people rolling around. Once we started touring, it was a little different. We were drunk at least.

MARK ARM: I worked with Bruce Pavitt at Muzak. Jonathan Poneman worked there before I started — a lot of musicians worked there. I played Bruce a tape that we recorded on a boom box at a Mudhoney practice. It was so distorted that you couldn't tell what was going on. He had us go into Reciprocal and record a few songs with Jack Endino, just so he could hear what we were up to. He trusted that the combination of the four of us would be a good one. Our main goal was to put out a single. We figured that we could get either Amphetamine Reptile or Sub Pop to release it. AmRep head Tom Hazelmyer was a Marine stationed on Whidbey Island [and] played bass in the U-Men for a while. AmRep released the Thrown Ups singles and Sub Pop released Green River records. Our first single, "Touch Me I'm Sick" with "Sweet Young Thing Ain't Sweet No More," and the song "Twentyfour," which appeared on [1989's] Amphetamine Reptile seven-inch compilation *Dope Guns N' Fucking in the Streets Volume One*, came from that very first session. It was weird to record a single before we even played our first show. We were super, super lucky.

JONATHAN PONEMAN: Everybody thought "Sweet Young Thing" was *the song* at first. We were told by people who knew better than all of us, "No, no, no — *it's 'Touch Me I'm Sick.'*" It was a double A-side — such a galvanizing single.

NILS BERNSTEIN: One of the few memories I have is of sitting in Danny Blossom's truck with Mark Arm shortly after Green River breaking up. He said, "I'm going to do a band with Steve Turner, and it's going to be the best band Seattle's ever seen." About a year later they made "Touch Me I'm Sick." He was totally right.

BRUCE PAVITT: Mudhoney was the band that I was most excited about. Put out "Touch Me I'm Sick" almost as soon as we started doing the label full-time. But the shows were unbelievable. I don't think any of the records really capture the looseness, vitality, and insanity of those live shows.

STEVE TURNER: The "Touch Me I'm Sick" single I remember having to wait for it forever. It disappeared fast because it was such a small pressing. That was a riff of mine — it was trying to be "garage punk." It was inspired by this guy, Rob Vasquez, who had a band, the Nights and Days, at the time. Just really fast chording, but he never used very much distortion — I just kind of hyper-fuzzed it. In retrospect, it sounds like some Stooges song [laughs]. It was real instant. For me, usually the best guitar things I come up with are really instant — they're not labored.

ART CHANTRY: I can't tell you the impact that single had. I remember the first time I heard it, I was driving down Broadway, and this song came on the radio. I'm going, *"What the fuck is this?!"* It was on KCMU, and I had to pull over to the side of the road and listen — I couldn't drive.

CHARLES PETERSON: They spoke to our basic instincts. Mark sang about dogs and sickness a lot — it rocked, it was funny, it had that insouciance of punk rock, but without the fashion posturing that a lot of it devolved into. And live, Mark was just incredible — contorting and twisting himself. They certainly didn't go as far as Nirvana — destroying instruments or anything — but just as far as Mark being some sort of "punk rock yogi," without knowing it . . . I have pictures of him all sprawled out on the stage. Jumping into the air, jumping into the audience — really going for it.

BRUCE PAVITT: I would say from '88 to '90, they were the driving force in the Seattle scene. I could definitely see Soundgarden's commercial appeal — I thought they might be the most commercially successful. But I thought Mudhoney might be the most significant group.

MARK ARM: Sub Pop had hooked up with this German label, Glitterhouse. Glitterhouse wanted to release a Green River record in Germany, [and] put out a record by the Fluid. The labels just did a swap — "We'll swap you Green River for the Fluid." So Sub Pop put out the Fluid records. There was this thing called Berlin Independence Days, which was a CMJ/South by Southwest sort of thing in Berlin. Sub Pop and Glitterhouse chose us to represent both labels. They couldn't afford to each fly out a band, but they could combine their resources and fly one band out. This was bizarre considering the fact that we hadn't played outside of the Pacific Northwest and had been together for less than a year. We flew out to Berlin with Bruce and Jonathan, and we stayed there for four days — we played one show. We never even tried to adjust to their time — we slept all day and drank all night. We embarked on our first U.S. tour two days after we came home from Berlin. We went to the East Coast and back on our own. Then we hooked up with Sonic Youth in Seattle, and went down the West Coast, and over to Texas with them. With the exception of Lexington, Kentucky, where we got paid fourteen dollars, a six-pack of pop, and two packs of cigarettes, this tour was a million times easier than any of the Green River tours. This tour paid for itself! I quit Muzak to go on this tour, and I didn't have to work another day job for over ten years.

JONATHAN PONEMAN: I remember them playing at Berlin Independence Days — in October of 1988. There are tapes of that show around, but I don't think it caught the overall impact of this runaway rock band. There was the whole "Mudhoney thing" being let loose on unsuspecting Germans. Some people had heard the hype, some people were familiar with Green River, but there was nothing quite like Mudhoney at the time. I remember watching that show, and going, "*This is an event.*" This is the sort of thing as a fan of rock music you hope to experience — at least one show like this. Where you see a bunch of people's lives being changed.

STEVE TURNER: We had already recorded the EP by that point — [1988's] *Superfuzz Bigmuff*. So it was more about waiting for that to come out, and then we were supposed to go on tour once that came out. We went on tour and it *still* wasn't out. It came out while we were on tour.

KIM THAYIL: I liked Mudhoney right off the bat — it was kind of Green River plus more attitude. The music was a little simpler — it left a lot more room for some of that "Mark attitude," and more of the rock power. A little rawer and more spontaneous — especially *Superfuzz Bigmuff*. And live, it was certainly that way — those guys were really animated, jumping all over the place. It had this element of chaos — it was certainly a wild band, and that seemed like what rock 'n' roll was supposed to be.

STEVE MANNING: There was no line between the band and their fans during the show. People were on the stage, they were in the crowd. It was a very interactive experience. One of the photos that's in [1990's] *Superfuzz Bigmuff and Other Early Singles* CD is a picture of me laying on the stage with Steve Turner, sort of spooning, in the midst of the show — and his guitar over the top of both of us. That, to me, is what I remember about those times. I remember a Fluid and Mudhoney show on my birthday — it must have been '89 or '90 — and it had snowed. When snow is here, the city completely shuts down — nobody knows how to deal with it. We walked down to the Vogue to see the show, and I thought there weren't going to be many people there. It ended up being packed. In the midst of Mudhoney, a big snowball fight breaks out in the middle of the club, and snow's flying everywhere. It must be ninety degrees in the club and twenty degrees outside.

RON HEATHMAN: A wall of sound, and this guy that has a voice that comes out of this tiny little body — at that point, the skinniest. The only thing I can compare it to — when the first time someone saw the Stooges. I never got to see the Stooges back then — it was probably the same thing. You walk into a club, in this case, it was a club called the Backstage, we're like, "We're going to see this band Mudhoney. Great, whatever." You go, and all of a sudden this guy gets up there, and this voice comes out — you're like, *"What the hell is going on?!"* Your jaw is on the floor for the whole show. They're like the Muppets [laughs].

MARK IVERSON: Seeing Mark Arm, and I say this facetiously, but his "rock star pose" — knees bent, leaning back, those beads hanging, the striped Bobby Brady T-shirts. And their distortion [pedals] — they were totally on fire. Amazingly energetic. Matt Lukin was always shit-faced and telling jokes — he was the guy who talked a lot between songs — and Mark Arm was totally witty.

KATHY FENNESSY: No offense to Nirvana, but they didn't look in the early days like they were having much fun. Mudhoney did.

MARK PICKEREL: There were two bands that I was jealous of, in terms of their live shows — Nirvana and Mudhoney. Their ability to make crowds go crazy, in four bars of the song, was pretty amazing. To see the crowd go from being anxious but reserved to absolutely ape shit was always so exciting.

JENNIE BODDY: They had a manager who was into the "personality" himself. He would go to the shows wearing Santa costumes — for no reason.

MARK ARM: We made our friend Bob Whittaker our manager. We took him with us on our first tour for entertainment. He couldn't run sound, tune a guitar or anything, but he was pretty good at finding people for us to stay with. He worked on and off at Sub Pop too. He became our tour manager and when we were meeting with the labels we made him our manager. I think it's way more important to have someone who is ethical and understands you be your manager — managers get their percentages from video budgets, and record deals, as well as other stuff, so shyster managers will steer bands towards bigger budget deals so they can line their pockets. We could trust that our friend Bob would never have pulled that shit.

STU HALLERMAN: Sitting in some park in San Francisco, watching Mark Arm carving a table out in this park — "Mudoney was here" — he misspelled the name of his own band! The night before, [Soundgarden and crew] were walking down the street. Everybody was exploring Haight, and we ran into Matt [Lukin] — he was blitzed drunk. He was wearing this long overcoat, and he was like, *"I better tie my shoe."* He bends over, and two bottles fall out of his coat. They were both bar bottles, with the "pourer" on there, that he snagged off a bar when the bartender wasn't looking.

ART CHANTRY: There was one summer of "Mudhoney mania" — it must have been about '89 or so — where Mudhoney was *the band.* When they played in town, there were lines that went around the block. For miles.

JEFF GILBERT: You never knew what was going to happen. They didn't really sing songs, they shouted them. People went to see them to get into the music as much as to "get it out of their systems." Because at a Mudhoney show, there were no rules — *anything goes.* If you could throw it, drink it, eat it, fuck it, stomp on it — it was all fair game. They wouldn't care if you got up onstage and dove into the crowd. Metal guys had been doing that forever. In fact, we used to laugh at the pitiful attempts at the grunge guys to stage dive. It was like, "No, no, no — it's done like this, *you weenies*" [laughs]. Metal taught punk how to play their guitars, and punk taught metal how to say "fuck."

JENNIE BODDY: I was very intimidated by them. Mark just had a glare — like he could see right through you. You just knew if you said something stupid, he would look at you like, "*You asshole.*" But he actually wasn't like that at all. Sub Pop wouldn't have stayed in business whatsoever [without Mudhoney] — they wouldn't have released a Nirvana record, anything. They were always the ones who brought us back into, "Oh, the phones got turned back on." They were our cash cow.

SUSAN SILVER: Really, the credit in a lot of ways deserves to be theirs. They were the world ambassadors that took this noise that was coming out of the Pacific Northwest, and took it to Europe. And suddenly, the world noticed. The noise wasn't being heard outside the Pacific Northwest — until Mudhoney played a show in London.

STU HALLERMAN: One of the best memories was London — Soundgarden was a young band at the time, and Mudhoney was huge in London. They played the School of Oriental Studies — an old-fashioned ballroom kind of place. Soundgarden plays, gets a nice response from the crowd — totally full house. Mudhoney hits the stage, the crowd goes nuts, and the band is having a great night — they're flying all over the place. Jumping and moving around so much that Steve's guitar gets unplugged. And Mark at that point, I don't know if he did a stage dive, but I remember him coming back from the audience up on the stage. They'd only played half a song so far. Kind of crumbles, comes to a stop.

Meanwhile, while Mark went back onstage, a couple of people followed him — crouched by the monitors, which were sitting on these little wobbly tables. I don't know if they played the same song or they're going into the next song. About halfway through it, the guitar becomes unplugged again, the song grinds to a halt, and Mark's out in the crowd with the microphone. He comes back onstage again, and a few more people follow him onstage. By this point, there's like a dozen people onstage. Mark gets on the microphone, and says, "I'd like to personally invite each and every one of the audience members onstage!" About twenty more people climb onstage. They start to play the next song, and as these people are walking up onstage, the monitor tables broke. The monitors are kind of collapsing, and people are pushing on the light poles — so the lighting rig is shaking.

I'm halfway backstage and halfway in the crowd, on the outside of the main PA speakers — just watching all this mayhem. I notice the monitor guy is unplugging everything, putting the cover on the mixing board, and loading everything out. The lighting guy is cranking down his lights, taking them off, and unplugging them. The band's looking over, they stop, and they're like, "What are you doing?" And they're like, "This is crazy, we're getting out of here." At this point, I'm looking at the stairs and the back door, because the crowd is *seething* — they're not going to put up with three halves of a song and call that a show. There was going to be a riot. The way we settled it was the main PA stayed up, the monitors [and] lights packed up and left — they just turned up some houselights, and finished the show with no monitors. A great show — some very memorable moments. One guy climbed on top of the PA stack and did a dive with an SLR big camera — flashed on the way down. To this day, people would like to get a hold of that picture.

MARK ARM: Our first European tour went on for nine weeks, which was an eternity for an unknown band with a dozen songs [laughs].

KURT DANIELSON: Later, at the climax of Tad's first European tour with Nirvana, both bands had the honor of opening for Mudhoney in London at Lame Fest II, a reenactment of the fabled original Lame Fest — held in Seattle about a year before. The lineup was the same both nights — Nirvana opened, Tad held the [middle] slot, and Mudhoney headlined. This gig is hard to beat memory-wise — Tad and Nirvana had been stuck in a van together for seven weeks, doing shows practically every night. It was a transcendent experience to play this show at the end of this seemingly endless and grueling journey, because both bands once again had a chance to open for their Sub Pop brothers. Towards the end of Mudhoney's set, a few of us — along with a member or two from the Cosmic Psychos — ended up rushing the stage. Tad grabbed Dan, and threw him from the drum riser into the seething crowd, and [Cosmic Psychos' drummer] Billy and I tried to nab Lukin, who resisted. We ended up stage diving *en masse.* I can still feel the crush of that crowd slamming me to the beer-soaked concrete floor.

MARK ARM: Word of mouth spread. From then up to about '95, our shows in the U.K. were great.

STEVE TURNER: The first full-length [1989's *Mudhoney*], in retrospect, we didn't spend very much time on it. It just wasn't as good as it should have been.

MARK ARM: There were a couple of songs that ended up on our first album that we'd had since before *Superfuzz*. "You Got It," "By Her Own Hand," and "Dead Love" were among our first songs. It might have been a hurried process — the stuff we were writing was not that different from the stuff for *Superfuzz*.

EMILY RIEMAN: I've known Mark since I was nineteen — I think we met in about '84. When I was in L.A., Mudhoney would tour. It was right around the time [*Mudhoney*] came out. So when they would come down, they would stay at our house. When I was in L.A. I saw Mudhoney was on the cover of *Melody Maker*. I was like, *"What the hell?"* We were really happy for them. Once when Mudhoney was going to play in Hollywood, we called up Jonathan at Sub Pop, and said, "They can stay at our house if they need a place to crash." Jonathan said they wouldn't need to sleep on our floor because this was "the big money tour." They slept on our floor.

MARK ARM: Bruce and Jon decided to put a show on at the Moore Theatre. I thought they were nuts because the Moore holds, like, 1,500 people. The only underground band to play there was the Dead Kennedys — regular underground bands didn't play there, and local bands certainly didn't play there. When Green River opened for the Dead Kennedys at the Moore, I couldn't figure out where all these kids came from. How come they don't go to other punk shows? Black Flag was kind of like that — they'd pull weekend punkers out of the woodworks. [Bruce and Jon] booked the Moore, and we headlined. Nirvana played second, Tad opened — and the place was sold out. Where did all these people come from? This is '89, before things got *really* out of hand. Playing for 200 people just a few months earlier was a huge show. Next thing we know, there are 1,500 kids at a show of all local bands.

CHAPTER 14

"*GET OUT OF THE WAY!*": The Melvins, Screaming Trees, Skin Yard, Tad

The Melvins and the Screaming Trees continued to gain momentum during the mid–late '80s, the Jack Endino–led Skin Yard offered a prog take on grunge, while another promising group, the larger-than-life Tad, also appeared on the scene.

SLIM MOON: The Melvins were *the* band. They were the first band that made any impression on me. It was just sort of widely accepted that they were the great band that we could see. Everybody was like, "The Melvins are going to be huge, the Melvins are geniuses, the Melvins are going to leave their mark on the world — we're lucky to see the Melvins." We would go to every Melvins show. Wherever they were playing, all my friends would pile in a car, go see the Melvins, and get wasted. Sleep in the car, and drive home in the morning. The Melvins was more the story of my teenage years than any other band.

CHRIS HANZSEK: [The Melvins' 1986 debut *Six Songs*] was done initially just to make a seven-inch. It was later on, when Daniel House was running C/Z Records, that he decided to reissue it as a twelve-inch record. And that's when I got called up to edit together some of those missing songs. I really liked that record — that was all recorded live to two-track. That's what 200 bucks would buy me — to get the band into the studio, set up really fast, throw microphones up, and record to tape. Mixing it live, no overdubs. After

I recorded it, I listened to it, and kept hearing some awful sound on the bass. So I had them come back two weeks later and record the whole thing again. Put that record out, and called it quits on being a record label after that.

DALE CROVER: For our first few records, it was "blast through things as fast as you possibly could," because you've only got a limited amount of time. Not like live at all — it definitely took quite a few years to get comfortable with being in a recording studio.

SLIM MOON: [1987's] *Gluey Porch Treatments* came out, and my best friend, Dylan [Carlson], got so depressed. The process that went on in his head is that that record was so good that there was no reason to be in bands, because he could never be as good as them. So he had this crazy freak-out where he destroyed his guitar and amp, and moved back to Seattle.

TINUVIEL: The thing with the Melvins — especially in Olympia — you've got the little Olympia scenester kids, skinny punk boys, Riot Grrrls, and artsy kids. And then you've got all these people crawling out of the woods that you've never seen in Olympia most of the time. They only show up when the Melvins are playing — these huge, scary guys, who are probably the offspring of loggers. It is a little bit intimidating. Every Melvins show has that extreme audience.

XANA LA FUENTE: [Malfunkshun] went to do a show in Tacoma with the Melvins, and there was this cheesy metal band there. We kept telling them, "You guys are way over your amount of people you can have free at the door." Somehow the way it worked at the end, not only were they not making money, but they owed us money for the sound system. I remember grabbing all of the cash and stuffing it down my bra! The Melvins were living in their van at the time — the guys from Malfunkshun said, "Just give it to the Melvins." So I handed the Melvins $500, which in '88 was a lot of money. They were like, "Xana, you saved our lives!"

MARK IVERSON: I thought they were gods, [but] they were assholes to interview. This was on the *Ozma* tour, and I thought *Gluey Porch Treatments* was one of the best albums ever. Dale answered nearly every question with the word "Satan!" so loudly that the meters would peak into the red. Buzz didn't want to give a straight answer, he kind of did, *"Memememememe!"* — baby talk. I was easily intimidated at that young age on the air.

KIM THAYIL: They were working a lot harder than the other bands. They were doing tours before the rest of us had really acclimated to the national punk rock tour network.

JOE KEITHLEY: We played with them down in Atlanta, at this real shit hole place — the Metropolis. There was this burned up building across the street that was occupied by Nazi skinheads, and they had all these slogans spray painted — all this racist crap. Every time you pulled up, you'd go, "Who booked us here again?" We got there around seven in the morning, didn't have any place to crash, so we banged on the door [of the Metropolis]. We thought, "Well, let's sleep on the stage — at least we won't have to sleep on the ground." It turns out the fucking Melvins were sleeping on the stage — they beat us by a couple of hours.

DALE CROVER: We had played as much in Seattle as we could. The band broke up for a short time, and Buzz was moving to San Francisco. He had a girlfriend there that ended up playing in our band for a while, Lori Black, and he was thinking of starting something with her. I'm like, "Do you need a drummer? I'd like to get the hell out of this place." And he's like, "Sure, move down!" It was really hard to get shows, because nobody knew who we were. We didn't move there thinking, "Oh, the music scene is great here!" It was more like, "Let's get out of this piss hole that we live in, and move somewhere nice." Eventually, we built up a pretty good following.

NILS BERNSTEIN: [1991's] *Bullhead* really floored me, it was this already really extreme band going even more extreme, and it was at least ten years ahead of its time. On three occasions I got free beers after Melvins shows 'cause the bartender thought I was Buzz, which I don't see. But I'm still thankful.

DALE CROVER: I don't think it was until *Bullhead* where we were starting to feel comfortable [in the studio], and starting to understand how the whole thing worked.

KATHLEEN HANNA: We went to see Screaming Trees, Dinosaur Jr., and Mudhoney — stuff like that. I was too young though — I had to sneak in. The guy was like, "Tell me the truth — how old are you?" I said, "I'm nineteen." He's like, "OK . . . go in." *I was so psyched.*

MARK PICKEREL: [1985's] *Other Worlds* was born out of Lee's home demos. I was really excited when Lee handed these demo cassettes to all of us. I was amazed to find out he had this talent, and until then, hadn't really shown its face before. Since I had just befriended Steve Fisk, it was only natural that we book some time in this studio, Albright Productions, and record these songs. This was maybe a few months after Lanegan started singing with us, so he was still figuring out his strengths and weaknesses.

I remember that there's this song — I believe "Pictures in My Mind" — he was self-conscious about his voice, so we ended up speeding up the tape, to give his voice a different edge. It's funny considering most people, including myself, think of Mark as being one of the best singers of our generation. The *Other Worlds* EP gained some interest outside of little old Ellensburg. The next thing we knew, *The Rocket* was writing about us, and we were getting added to a few playlists — little college stations. To us, this was absolute validation. *Clairvoyance* was also on Velvetone, which was a label that was really just an extension of the recording studio — Albright Productions. The opening track, "Orange Airplane," was a really great introduction for us nationally. It had the best elements of your paisley underground bands, but it had the intensity and urgency of Hüsker Dü. I wish more of the record had been as strong — we rushed everything.

VAN CONNER: After [1986's *Clairvoyance*] was done, *then* we played a show — because there was no place to play in Ellensburg. Our first-ever show was at a group home for the mentally handicapped in Ellensburg. There was an old video of the Cramps playing at a mental institution [released on DVD in 2004 as *Live at Napa State Mental Hospital*] — and we thought, "Hey, *we* can do that!" We couldn't get a gig at the mental institution, so we went to a group home [laughs]. Played a show there and videotaped. That videotape is somewhere — it's lost. It was totally crazy — people jumping all over the place. Then our next show — our first show at a normal club — was an all-ages show with Beat Happening, I think. I remember going up onstage, and being scared and nervous. I looked over, and Lee was going totally crazy. As soon as he walked onstage, he started doing that "odd behavior" that he always did when we played — jumped all over the stage and rolled around. He'd never done that at practice. I was just standing there like a statue.

CHAD CHANNING: Lanegan — that guy always had long hair! With the punk rock thing evolving into what they coined "grunge," the Screaming Trees were different from all that. Seeing something like that in the mix, it opened things up. Nothing has to be totally hardcore all the time or whatever. Mark's just got that eerie, melancholy type of voice.

TAD DOYLE: Mark — an incredible singer. That voice of his is really low, warm, and full of pain.

TRACY MARANDER: [Lanegan] would usually stand with his eyes closed — reminded me of Jim Morrison.

DAWN ANDERSON: Mark Lanegan was one of the shyest guys I've ever met. When I interviewed them, it was really difficult, because they were afraid to talk to a girl [laughs]. Later on, they loosened up.

HIRO YAMAMOTO: I remember those two big guys — Van and Lee — shaking their hair. Those guys were so big and had so much energy. An awesome band — Lanegan is something else. Pickerel was just a kid — he was, like, a sixteen-year-old back then. A lot of big bodies and hair flying.

MARK PICKEREL: I was in awe of [the Conner brothers' relationship] — it was so much fun. That was the most entertaining aspect of the band — watching those guys try and function together. I think they really loved each other, but they sure didn't like to show it. Like most brothers, they fight and talk a lot of shit, but at the end of the day, they end up eating or watching a movie together. The next morning, it starts all over again [laughs]. I witnessed maybe four or five physical confrontations onstage. It usually was the result of Lee borrowing Van's guitar. Lee would lose his mind at these shows, and start swinging Van's guitar — smashing it about. So Van would throw his bass down, and start punching Lee, and kicking him — and Lee would fall over! The crowd loved it, but it wasn't staged. I don't think Van ever threw a punch at Lee that he didn't mean.

MARK IVERSON: The Screaming Trees at the Central Tavern were always fun. But Mark Lanegan would be a bit . . . he would take his time showing. So the whole band would be onstage, and it's like, "Where's Mark?" One time, it was probably midnight, and all of a sudden, he comes tearing through the crowd. His hair is flying, his flannel is flying, he jumps onstage, and they just launch into their thing. Who knows what he was doing outside.

MARK PICKEREL: Van, Lee, and I came to see Black Flag play — about '84 or '85 — in Seattle. I timidly approached the stage as Greg Ginn was plugging in his amplifier, and tossed him our demo cassette, at his feet. He picked it up, and put it on his amp, and nodded his head in acknowledgement. That, combined with Steve Fisk being friends with this guy named Ray Farrell at SST, who he had also sent some music to, had ultimately led to us getting signed to SST. This is around my senior year in high school, or right after I graduated.

By the time we went on to record [1987's] *Even If and Especially When*, we had a couple of major tours under our belts — a tour with fIREHOSE, and we shared the stage with Sonic Youth, the Meat Puppets, and Dinosaur Jr. In doing that, we gained a lot of confidence, because we went over really well with their audiences. It gave us some confidence to follow our own instincts, and worry a little bit less about what some of the "professional people" were suggesting we do. By the time we recorded *Even If*, even though it was in the same studio, we'd all become more proficient with our instruments, and I had a clearer idea of what to do as a drummer to make the songs more meaningful, and further the best aspects of each song.

I think a lot of people have the misconception that the Screaming Trees were always in turmoil, fighting, unhappy, and miserable. There were days when that was true. However, we laughed together constantly. The self-deprecating humor was always in the house. We were always making jokes at each other's expense. For the most part, we were all there in support of each other, and encouraging to each other. We were all big fans of each other — I loved every individual in the band. So, that was a very prolific period for us — we were recording at least one record a year, sometimes more. Most of that was due to Lee being such a hermit — locking himself in his room and writing a song every day. I would guess he wrote at least three quality songs a week. At least a few really amazing songs a month. I must have another thirty to fifty great, classic Screaming Trees songs on cassette — that Lee recorded at home — that really should have come out. That were as good as anything else available. I regret that we didn't record more records.

VAN CONNER: When we did [1988's] *Invisible Lantern*, we were probably ready to call it quits. We all had crap jobs, and had no future. You weren't making any money in a band like that — we were supporting our "band habit" by having a job. You had to take it really seriously to keep it going, and sacrifice everything. And you had to be willing to drop everything at the spur of the moment — like quit your job. I did quit at one point. I left before [1989's] *Buzz Factory* for a while — about half a year — when I had my first son. I freaked out, I was like, "I can't do music anymore!" Of course, then I realized that life sucked even worse without music, so I started doing it again. At that point, we'd done a bunch of tours — we'd toured Europe and the States.

STU HALLERMAN: [After a Screaming Trees performance] we all went out to eat together, at the Rib Eye, this little greasy spoon place up the hill in Olympia. It's the two Conner brothers, Mark Pickerel, and myself. It's Pickerel and myself on one side, and the Conner brothers on the other. The waitress takes mine and Pickerel's order first, then turns to the two other long-haired, baby-faced guys, and says, "What would you ladies like?"

MARK IVERSON: I saw them at Evergreen State College. They were playing, I think, a gay and lesbian benefit, and there was nobody there. The stage was one foot off the ground, and [Lee] rolled into the crowd while viciously playing his guitar. *He's at my feet.* I remember still feeling that adrenaline the next day.

STEVE FISK: Gary Lee Conner doing lots of high volume air stuff — crazy Pete Townshend moves. Things you wouldn't expect a big guy to do. Somersault stuff — crazy shit. Everything was always too fast and chaotic, and didn't resemble the records remotely. Kind of got out of hand — a scary vibe. Even the pop songs were fast and crazy.

MARK PICKEREL: We had a common objective, and we wanted similar things. Where we differed was in our personality types. I'm a pacifist, I'm passive-aggressive — the type of person that when faced with confrontation, [my] instinct is to turn and walk away, hide, or just not deal with it. In hopes that it will dissolve and disappear. That's the kind of household I was raised in. From what I understand, Lanegan had a troubled childhood. Mark was always reluctant to get into any details, but I seem to remember hearing that one of his parents had a problem with alcohol — this might have contributed to Mark's own early use of drugs and drinking. Mark could put away booze faster than anyone I've ever met. There's worse cases out there, but I get the impression that his childhood was not as rosy as my own. And therefore, Mark's natural instinct is to put up his fists if things aren't going the way he wants. Or if you've done something that doesn't sit well with him, or pisses him off, his natural instinct is "to go to the mats." Mine is to go sit and feel sorry for myself. It's hard for such opposing personality types to exist together — day in, day out.

I felt that Lee was jealous of the attention Mark gained from the Screaming Trees. Lee, knowing he'd written so many of the songs, and that without his songs, the band wouldn't exist, was jealous of the attention Mark was getting from the press, and from the females in the audience. So there was some resentment there, and like I said before, Lee was "socially challenged" back in those years. He really led a sheltered existence, that mostly consisted of being at home all the time, which is also what led to him to write so many great songs. So the Screaming Trees was really his first introduction to a larger social life, that was very active and put us into a lot of different situations. This created a really awkward environment for the band, to see the way Mark might react to something Lee might have said in a certain situation, that might have embarrassed Mark.

Van and Lee were incredibly competitive. It was easy for Van to become frustrated or impatient with Lee, and occasionally, would result in Van punching Lee, or at least getting into a verbally abusive fight with him, if not physically. This is just day in, day out — this started to take its toll on me. I was also seeing a girl at the time — it's funny, she had a very similar personality type to Lanegan's. She was very confrontational, very demanding of me mentally and emotionally — but it was also my first real live-in relationship, that I was also happy about. I discovered myself in a situation where I could really only be emotionally, physically, and mentally available to one person at a time. To try and appeal to Mark's demands and to have to be mentally available to what was going on in the band all the time, and emotionally available — it was hard to do. I was already trying to give so much to someone else, who was at least providing me with some of the other luxuries in life, and some of the other comforts that I wasn't getting from my own band anymore. I really have such great love and respect for everybody in the band, but that's just the reality of the situation — it was tough and dysfunctional. I was probably as much a part of that as anyone else.

KURT DANIELSON: Jack's well known for a producer, but Skin Yard was an extremely important band. As important as Soundgarden or any of those other bands were at that time.

JACK ENDINO: I met Daniel House, who was playing bass in Ten Minute Warning at the time. Ten Minute Warning was falling apart, so he and the drummer, Greg Gilmore, got together and jammed — just the three of us. I had a demo tape of some songs I had recorded in my basement with myself playing all the instruments, and Daniel really liked it. He called and said, "Why don't we start a band?" Greg played with us a couple of times, in January '85 — we had three or four practices with him. Then he decided, "This isn't going where I want to go with my music; I want to do something else." So Daniel said, "There's this other guy I was playing with in a band called Feedback, Matt Cameron." He got Matt to come over, and Matt liked it. The three of us rehearsed for a few months, while we decided, "Let's look for a singer." And around May, we found Ben McMillan — I think we played our first show as Skin Yard in June.

The band as initially conceived was probably a bit too on the progy side. We gave Matt free rein to his Bill Bruford impulses, and I gave free rein to my Robert Fripp impulses, *because we could* [laughs]. There's nothing you can conceive that Matt cannot play the drums to. So that was like a challenge to me — to come up with the weirdest shit I could. So Skin Yard was a really weird, arty band when we started. We were a little out of step with what was going on, but we got noisier and sludgier. And before we knew it, everybody else was doing that too — not because of us — it was just the direction the scene was going. We quickly realized, "It's fun to play all this intricate stuff, but it gets old fast. We should be playing stuff that's more of the body, and not so much of the head." Once we got that out of our systems, we turned into a regular rock band. [Matt Cameron was in the band] about a year and a half, maybe a little less. I think he left the band in spring or summer of '86. We got to open for a lot of interesting people. We played for a lot of empty rooms [laughs].

PIC BY CHARLES PETERSON — CHARLESPETERSON.NET

Photographer Charles Peterson and Tad Doyle

KIM THAYIL: Skin Yard was more into King Crimson and prog. They weren't aware of the SST/Homestead scene — they weren't listening to Sonic Youth, Black Flag, or the Meat Puppets. And Jack Endino knew very little about the punk rock underground — he pretty much learned a lot about that stuff from borrowing my records. I remember loaning a bunch of records to Daniel House — Big Boys, Butthole Surfers, the Minutemen.

SCOTTY CRANE: I remember sneaking into shows at the Comet before I was twenty-one, just to see Jack Endino play and Ben McMillan sing. Those guys were amazing.

NILS BERNSTEIN: In retrospect, there's like five important bands. But at the time, everybody was equally important. We all thought that Tad was going to be the big band. *They had it all.*

GARRETT SHAVLIK: Tad was trying to be so fucking heavy — but with a tongue firmly in cheek. He was so funny onstage, he'd be like, "Alright all you kids, come up and sit on my lap!" And "Come up here and shit on me!" They played super-low and super-tight — drop-D. He's like, "I just want to get that note, where people *shit their pants.*"

BRUCE PAVITT: Amazing presence, brilliant sense of humor, and an incredible musician — he could drum, play guitar. Super heavy — probably had the heaviest out of any of the groups.

JONATHAN PONEMAN: He had a reputation as being a computer geek. He always looked very menacing. I remember him as being an unbelievable drummer.

NILS BERNSTEIN: Tad was the butcher at QFC on Broadway. Once they found a finger in the meat section . . . but I think that was after Tad left.

JIM BLANCHARD: The particular Kinko's I worked at was like "Rock 'n' Roll Kinko's" — Mark Arm worked there for a while, Tad worked there. Tad was the guy that greeted you when you walked in, and took your order — this big, scary looking guy.

TAD DOYLE: Worked at Muzak for a while. And during this time, I was meeting people in the music scene. Being a guy from out of the city, it took a long time to meet people and have them warm up to you. I grew up in a farming area, so I'm really outgoing, and pretty happy-go-lucky. There was this "big city attitude" people were giving us when we moved there. I figured out later that it was just Seattle, and it was dark there all the time. Music was very important to me — I went to see bands on any night of the week, and put together my own band after I was a drummer in H-Hour for a while. I just got tired of being the first guy in/the last guy out with playing drums. It's like being in the Marine Corps — you have all this equipment to mess with. Tad started because I got sick of playing drums.

KURT DANIELSON: About 1980, I was living in a small town in Seattle, about an hour north, and started my first band — playing bass — and eventually moved to Seattle, about '83. The band that I started in the small town still was in existence [Bundle of Hiss]. It was kind of important, but I was also

PIC BY CHAD CHANNING

Prepare to binge: Tad's Kurt Danielson and Steve Wied, plus Kurt Cobain

going to school at the University of Washington, to get my degree in English. There were various different members in the band — I was the constant member. The drummer we had was really great — Dan Peters — who ended up being the drummer for Mudhoney. About '86–'87, that band did a lot of shows with Green River, Soundgarden, Skin Yard. Another band we played with was H-Hour. Tad was something to watch onstage. Amazing drummer — a big physical presence. Came to pass that Bundle of Hiss broke up.

TAD DOYLE: I bought a Fender Jazzmaster, and decided I was going to play guitar. All I did was go to work, come home, and play guitar in my room, on this little Fender Champ — my first amp. I had a drum machine that I'd play with. I decided that I was going to write some songs, and a few months later,

I got my check back from taxes being taken out that year — I spent all the money on recording at Reciprocal with Jack Endino. I recorded the guitars, the drums, vocals, and bass all by myself — three songs. I took it to Muzak — we had this really pimped out, ridiculous stereo that we put together out of parts from different Muzak machinery. We used to crank it up and play all kinds of cool music. I brought it in and played it for people, and they're like, *"Who the hell is this?"* I kept quiet — I was just beaming. I liked it, and they seemed to like it, and Bruce Pavitt came in, and said, "This is awesome. Who is this? Is this the new Butthole Surfers?" And then it was *on*. He says, "I want to put this out," and I said, "Cool, this is always what I wanted to do, and do that only."

JONATHAN PONEMAN: Bruce had heard a demo he had done, which became "Ritual Device" and "Daisy," the first single. He equated it to Killdozer and a little bit of a Foetus vibe. I was surprised how great this single was. I never thought in terms of, "We can't market that." I thought, if anything, Tad was probably going to be the easiest thing to get across — heavy dude/heavy music. *Connect the dots.*

TAD DOYLE: I started writing more songs, and it quickly became evident that it was a lot of work to play alone — I was going to record drum tracks, bass, and guitar, and then play live with a guitar and sing vocals over the recorded material. I decided I needed a band. I got Kurt Danielson, and I knew this drummer from a band called Death and Taxes, Steve Wied, and Kurt knew this guitar player, Gary Thorstensen. We started jamming, writing songs, and it became Tad. Shortly thereafter, we had a single out, and we were offered to open for Pussy Galore.

ART CHANTRY: Tad was this big fat musician — he was *huge*. His big guitars looked like toys on him. Bruce decided he was going to turn this guy into some kind of lumberjack thing, and the fact that he actually made a living as a butcher at one time was all part of the joke. So he was trying to create this persona that was, quite frankly, insulting to Tad. Tad hated that, but figured, "Bruce is my friend, and he's putting my record out — I'll let him do what he wants to do." When he got onstage, here was this huge man, but he seemed weightless. He just floated around, making this huge, heavy music. Everybody thought they were going to be the next big thing.

KURT DANIELSON: Went into the studio almost immediately. Recorded three songs — one of which came out on *Sub Pop 200*. We were also able to go in the studio with Pussy Galore and do a split single. We did "Damaged I" and they did ["Damaged II"] — that was part of the Sub Pop Singles Club. Then we had our first record, *God's Balls*, in '89. We toured the States for that.

TAD DOYLE: The first Tad record we did at Reciprocal, again with Jack. I think there's only one song that wasn't in the same key, and that was something that Gary was worried about — "All these songs are in E, they all sound kinda similar." We had fun doing stuff — we were using saws on metal, and bows on cymbals.

BEN REW: I met Tad at the Vogue. There was a little spot in the back of the Vogue — they didn't say you could smoke weed back there, but everyone smoked weed there. He would always get us pitchers, and I didn't find out until about three years ago that those were all the "run-over-pitchers" — all the beer that ran out of the pitcher when they would pour them. I was like, "Ugh, you nasty bastard!" I saw the guy drink a pint of beer in one gulp — he was my idol immediately. I started hanging out with him, doing road stuff with him. I remember when Tad met his Canadian agent, James McLean, he'd just played a big show in Vancouver. I go, "This is James." James goes, "I'm a huge fan." Tad goes, *"GET OUT OF THE WAY!"* "But I'm a huge fan." *"MOVE!"* He shoves him and just *projectile vomits* into the corner.

CHAPTER 15

"Dark, black, and blue": Soundgarden, Alice in Chains

Soundgarden got the nod as the first grunge band to sign with a major label. At the same time, another band, Alice in Chains, eschewed their early glam rock ways, and quickly followed Soundgarden up the ladder.

NILS BERNSTEIN: I went over to Danny Peters' house. He was like, "Oh, you got to hear this," and put on a test pressing. It sounded just like Bundle of Hiss — one of the bands he was in at the time. It sounded incredible. Listened to it over and over again — both sides. "Oh my God, you guys have outdone yourselves!" And he's like, "Oh, you think this is Bundle of Hiss? No — *this is Soundgarden.*" It was the first Soundgarden single — "Hunted Down" and "Nothing to Say." Blue vinyl. It was one of the best things, if not *the* best thing I'd heard from one of those Seattle bands.

JACK ENDINO: I had a little four-track recording studio in my basement, and Kim used to come over and mess around in the studio. I ended up recording some demos for them — actually took my four-track machine to Chris Cornell's house at one point. By 1986, I wound up working at Reciprocal Recording, and they were about ready to record something. So I wound up doing their first EP and single which became one of the very first records on Sub Pop. I think we started recording some of [*Screaming Life*] in late '86 — kept messing with it into early '87.

MATT CAMERON: We only had three or four days to get the rhythm tracks done — me and Hiro — because we had day jobs. I remember that being a very quick recording session — we recorded everything live, other than the vocals. At the time, we were a pretty ferocious live act — that record really captures our live sound at the time. It's holding up wonderfully. I remember listening back to the mix of "Nothing to Say," and I just couldn't believe that I was playing in a band so good — at such an early stage of development.

KIM THAYIL: "Tears to Forget" was a very popular song — that was the one song on the album that was a regular part of our set. All the other songs we back-burnered, to hear what these new ones sounded like. It was not entirely representative of what we were doing live then. "Entering" was a song we had been playing for a few years — "Entering" and "Tears to Forget" were certainly part of our live thing. And then we'd come up with "Nothing to Say," "Hunted Down," and "Little Joe."

BEN SHEPHERD: *Screaming Life* is still my favorite record of theirs. That's what Soundgarden sounds like to me — dark, black, and blue. Like the overcast days of Seattle.

KIM THAYIL: I think it was — up until Ben joined the band — [the recording] that captured our spirit and sound best. Even though the music is somewhat dark, it seems sunshiny to me.

MATT VAUGHAN: I was crashed out at my friend's house on Capitol Hill, and he was playing *Screaming Life*. I was laying there for thirty minutes thinking for sure this was the greatest Zeppelin bootleg I'd ever heard — I had no idea it was a band from Seattle. Then we all went and saw them — it was frenetic, it was mayhem. They were easily the heaviest band, and came across as pretty serious. It was pummeling.

JEFF GILBERT: Usually, when the Melvins or Soundgarden would play these small clubs, you couldn't do anything. You couldn't jump around. That's why on the *Screaming Life* back picture, you see Chris Cornell on the ground. That's how I saw him mostly at the Vogue. You couldn't really move. Well — *hit the floor then.* I remember thinking, "I can hear him, but I can't see him." And then you'd see Kim, and he'd be looking down for his cue from Chris [laughs].

STEVE FISK: It was Bruce Pavitt's idea [for Fisk to produce Soundgarden's 1988 EP, *Fopp*]. They played in Ellensburg — Faith No More played an under-attended show, and they opened. They closed with "Iron Man," and Faith No More opened with "War Pigs." This is before anybody knew who the fuck they were. Cornell had the best sense of humor — it was really wicked. Kind of vicious but also funny at the same time.

SUSAN SILVER: Soundgarden always has had a sense of humor and a sense of irony that I think was lost on a lot of people.

MATT CAMERON: We were playing in this big empty theater — it was kind of cool to me, but I didn't really understand how we were going to get a record out of it. But lo and behold, we did. That was like a one day session, and Steve did a remix at his studio.

STEVE FISK: At one point, a jackhammer crew went to work on pavement, and we couldn't hear anything in the truck. We got the crew to come back later in the day — they knew Seattle bands were starting to get some attention. So they did it to be cool [laughs].

SUSAN SILVER: Things were moving really fast and furiously for [Sub Pop] *and* for Soundgarden. Jonathan and I had become really good friends. Then when Soundgarden got together with Jon and Bruce and decided to put a record out, the friendship just deepened. There was a really exciting memory — standing on the corner of First and Pine downtown with Jonathan. *Screaming Life* had already come out, *Fopp* was about to come out. The guys — even though lots of major labels had called by that time and we'd gone to L.A. and had meetings — still wanted to be on SST, that was the goal. I remember standing on the corner, with Jonathan saying, "Soundgarden should stay on Sub Pop." They hadn't really formalized their business enough to where they had an office yet or people helping them. I remember looking at Jonathan and saying, "Soundgarden is a juggernaut, and it's taking off. *It's got to go* — I've got to move as fast as I can to keep up with it."

JEFF GILBERT: Certainly, the Melvins had all the elements in place. Soundgarden were the ones that brought it into more of a focus.

JERRY CANTRELL: Soundgarden is like "the granddaddy." There's a lot of other bands, but when I think about Seattle and what was going on, I think it pretty much begins with Soundgarden. Those early EPs, and going to see them, the way that Chris sounded, and the way that the band sounded together was an amazing thing. It was very inspiring.

ROBERT ROTH: The first time I saw them was in '88, and they blew me away. I don't think I heard a major scale that whole night. And at that point as a musician, a lot of the music I liked was based on major scales — a lot of punk rock, a lot of post-punk. This was just really dark, and really different.

BEN SHEPHERD: They were playing a show down in Olympia — one of those daylight shows. Seattle was totally cool back then — the music scene was happening, people were fun, life was cool as fuck, and there they were. Chris was just singing, and Hiro and Kim — that was the *true* Soundgarden.

STU HALLERMAN: Slim Moon was eventually a proprietor of the Kill Rock Stars label, but at first, he was just a guy in a band — and he liked punk rock. This little thing he did every summer — he would hire me and my PA system, get some guys to bring out a flatbed truck, and get three or four punk rock bands to play free — in the park. Slim sponsored it, he also got the Olympia Parks Department and the police department under their DARE unit to cosponsor this thing, and help pay the bills for this free show. He asked me if I knew any bands. I was like, "Well, I know some guys up in Seattle, maybe they can play the show." "Who is it?" "Oh, these guys called Soundgarden." And he got all excited — "*Soundgarden?* You know these guys? What's their phone number?!" It was like, "Come on, it's just these dopes in their basement." I called them up, and since they never played in Olympia, they did agree to play. So two weeks later, we did do the show. The lineup was My Eye, Nirvana, and Soundgarden.

Towards the end of [Soundgarden's] set, I stepped away from the mixing board to hear what's it like for the audience. I happened to find myself between the Park Department guy and the DARE Olympia Police Representative. The police officer is like, "There's no cussing coming offstage; it's really good music!" They were playing "Fopp," their encore. We all wistfully look up at the stage into the sunset there, and Chris is bending over, yelling, "SUCK MY COCK! SUCK MY COCK!" into the microphone. We looked at each and shrugged, like, "Eh — *so much for being nice.*"

After the show, the band pointed out that they were about to hit the road for a West Coast tour and Europe in the spring. They're like, "Hey Stuart, you've got a PA, and you got your old Dodge van. You sounded good tonight — do you want to come on the road with us?" I'm thinking, drag my PA to all these beer-soaked, smoky, nasty punk rock clubs? Sure, I'll go! [Laughs.] Hiro I'd known for almost my whole life by that point, and Kim I'd known for nine years or something. Chris I'd known for about three or four years. I was struck by how much of a kid he was at that point — he had these little rubber birds and GI Joe–ish kind of things that he would fly around the van. He'd be the cassette jockey — playing Aerosmith, Butthole Surfers, and Fugazi. [And] weird mainstream things I'd never think he'd be into.

MARK PICKEREL: I was instrumental in getting Soundgarden signed to SST. They came out and played a show in Ellensburg in about 1987, and the Screaming Trees' soundman, Rob Doak, recorded the show on his soundboard and made me a tape of it. I was so impressed that I sent it to Greg Ginn. A couple of months later, SST signed them.

MATT CAMERON: We were tickled pink, because at that stage, we were being courted by major labels quite extensively. But instead of going down that route right away, we decided that we wanted to do one more record on an independent label. We chose the coolest independent label of the '80s to be on, so we saw that as a real honor. We had a little more money to record with. We went down to record in this kind of homemade studio that was pretty good. It was in Newberg, Oregon. Again, we didn't have a lot of time — I think we had two weeks to do it all. We recorded some up here in Seattle, in an abandoned warehouse; we got a mobile truck. Recorded some drums there, then we finished the rest in Newberg.

JACK ENDINO: There's eight-track demos of most of the stuff on [1988's] *Ultramega OK* that sound better than the record — that sound more like *Screaming Life*. In fact, probably *better* than *Screaming Life*, because we did it much later. A lot more lively.

MARK IVERSON: I thought *Ultramega OK* captured their live sound better than *Screaming Life*. At Fallout Records there was this poster that

PIC BY CHARLES PETERSON — CHARLESPETERSON.NET

Soundgarden caught in Charles Peterson's trademark "flash and drag shutter effect"

had been put up, because the Fluid had been robbed — their van had been broken into and they had lost a lot of equipment. It was a fundraiser put on the next day. We went and saw them at a super-small theater in Seattle, it was used more for plays than for live music. I remember hearing two of my buddies from KCMU who were standing behind me, and one of them said, "This'll be the last time we'll ever see them in a club even close to this size." He was right.

CATHY FAULKNER: Performance-wise what totally stood out was [KISW] did "a rising star show" at the Paramount Theater. Jane's Addiction was headlining — we put Mother Love Bone and Soundgarden in to open. Combine all three of those bands, and there was a magic in that — beyond words. You could cut the energy in the room with a knife.

DUFF McKAGAN: I remember hearing a lot about Soundgarden. They finally came down and played L.A. — I want to say '88. Maybe they played while we were on tour for *Appetite*, but the first time I saw them was at the Scream in downtown L.A. *That* was a rock band. There wasn't many gigs of bands I wanted to go see at that point. '88 was a pretty shitty time for music

— a lot of White Lion, Whitesnake, and Warrant. *It was terrible*. So when I heard Soundgarden was coming down to play, I went, and I was really hoping that it would still be the Soundgarden that I remembered and heard such great things about. And they just fucking blew my mind. For some reason I always look at the drummer — if the drummer is good, the rest will follow. And Matt was just insane; playing all those different meters. And Kim Thayil, wow — what the fuck is that? And Cornell's voice was fucking Robert Plant on acid. They were menacing, beautiful, musical — the whole thing.

HIRO YAMAMOTO: That was exciting — going around the whole country. What an adventure. I remember [being] crammed in the van, getting hotel rooms — someone would always sleep in the van to watch the gear, and it was four or five of us crowded in the room. It was always like, "Man, I need a break from these guys" [laughs]. We went all the way down to Florida, touring the South, and up to New York. The thing with the South I remember is that they weren't as into us — they didn't know as much about us. But the big cities, like New York and Los Angeles, we were pretty well-known. There was the whole Los Angeles/music industry deal, because every time we went towards Los Angeles, the wining and dining started.

JACK ENDINO: Soundgarden may have been the first to actually get the deal. By the time of their second record, they were already talking with A&M. Well before anyone else. Their [third] record came out on SST, and A&M said, "Why do you want to do this?" And they said, "We don't want our career to stop for a year while we're negotiating with you. So we're going to continue and release this other record on an indie label — to have something out." Because most bands would start negotiating with a major label, and it would take six to eight months. Then they would record, and the label would sit on it for three or four months, and then a year goes by. Suddenly, the band lost all its momentum. Soundgarden, very cleverly, said, "We're going to release one more indie record."

KIM THAYIL: We'd do ten-week tours — we'd be gone for two and a half months. I was in Pioneer Square — I went to see some band, I don't know if it was the Melvins. Kurt was there — I think Kurt was by himself and I was by myself. I went over to tell him how much I loved *Bleach*. He was very quiet and subdued. He said, "Thanks — that means a lot coming from you.

Consider yourself our biggest influence." I was like, "Whoa!" We'd always been a "younger band" — we'd always been an "up-and-coming band." Now, we'd made a record on SST and were playing nationally, and to have a guy you consider a peer put out a record that you absolutely love, and to have him say, "You're a big influence," was head-spinning for me at the time. It was one of the many things that gave us a new perspective about ourselves.

SUSAN SILVER: We were in negotiation with A&M. They really wanted to have an album on SST, so that happened.

HIRO YAMAMOTO: Faith No More was one of the big reasons we got signed. Those guys had just gotten signed, and they were really into us. I think they were in their record label's office, saw a demo of ours, and were like, "You should check this out." And then once that started, everybody was interested [laughs].

JOHN LEIGHTON BEEZER: The first time I ever heard the words "bidding war" was with respect to Soundgarden.

SUSAN SILVER: A&M — as its reputation — was a really artist friendly place. People were genuine and cared. There was no bullshit. They had a way of hiring people there that were genuine and music fans — that had a history of doing cool things in the music business. Everybody was really supportive. We met with Geffen several times, and then negotiated with Epic for quite a while — but nobody felt the same as they did about A&M. There were days where we thought Epic would be the way to go — and I probably wouldn't be here today telling you the story if that had been the case, because I'm sure they would have knocked me out for a bigger manager somewhere in the early days. Whereas A&M was really supportive of young bands *and* managers.

MARK ARM: When Soundgarden got signed, there were basically two paths you could go if you were a rock band on a major label. You could take the "metal route," or this "alternative rock route" — defined by the Cure and REM. For some reason, Soundgarden decided to take the metal route. If they'd waited a year or two and Nirvana broke through, they could have taken the third path. They could've stayed true to themselves. Soundgarden recruited their friend Eric Johnson to be their tour manager — Eric's a great guy and he knew where they were coming from. But for some reason, he got canned when they got more pro. By the time they were doing bus tours, they had this big, gross dude with laminates, who had tour-managed Aerosmith. He was the kind of guy who would trade blow jobs for backstage passes. It's like, why would you get rid of your friend Eric, and hire this gross asshole with this old-school-music-biz attitude?

Eric was [later] snapped up by Pearl Jam, and he worked with them for years until that period when they backed off of touring. Last I heard, Eric was Neil Young's personal assistant. It seemed so weird to me that Soundgarden would surround themselves with a crew of rock-pigs, dudes [who] would just as soon go out with Bon Jovi and Poison — and probably even prefer that, because those bands pull hotter chicks. I never understood why Soundgarden let themselves slip into that world. I mean, Kim is nothing like that. The thing is, in the end you make the final decisions for yourself. You don't have to go out on a certain tour because some manager or label flack thinks it'll be good for your career. And you don't have to hire unlikable people just because they have touring experience. There are plenty of good people out there.

MATT CAMERON: [1989's] *Louder Than Love* was produced by Terry Date, and we recorded here in Seattle at London Bridge, which was in Lake Ballinger. It was a good experience, probably our first time in a professional studio — a real big-time studio with a 24-track machine. We didn't want to fuck up — we were well rehearsed. We knew what songs we were going to do. So we treated every recording session as a chance to bust it out quick, and try to get our live sound down as much as possible. I think later on we tried to use the studio more as a composition tool.

TERRY DATE: There's a lot of quirky little memories — convincing Kim to buy a second guitar, which was difficult. Trying to decide if we were going to go with the equipment he was using, or if we were going to buy some new stuff. As far as my production memories, we experimented with layering guitars. I think the band felt like it led to too smooth of a sound. We were also doing that record at a time when Metallica's *. . . And Justice for All* was coming out. So there was a very different sound in "heavy metal." Soundgarden, Metallica, and Mother Love Bone were all being lumped into heavy metal — they're about as different as I can imagine.

HIRO YAMAMOTO: Terry Date could make things . . . things just *shimmered.* It boomed and it shimmered at the same time. I remember being skeptical about Terry, because his big thing was metal bands, and I was always like, "Are we a metal band?"

TERRY DATE: They all got along great. I think the only argument I can remember is when I finally did get Kim to get a new guitar, and somebody picked it up to play it in the morning, after they'd been eating powdered donuts. They got white powder all over the guitar. Kim kinda got pissed off.

ART CHANTRY: They didn't have a name for the record. We were talking about it and joking — I said, "You should really call this record 'Louder Than Shit.'" They go, "That's a great name!" I go, "No . . . call it '*Louder Than Fuck.*'" "Oh, that's great!" And Susan Silver goes, "My band isn't putting out a record with 'Fuck' in the title." That's where *Louder Than Love* came from.

GRANT ALDEN: Susan Silver was the most difficult manager I dealt with and most controlling. She and I banged heads repeatedly with Soundgarden. But I don't mean that negatively — if I were in a band, I would have loved to have her manage them. She was a really competent, aggressive person. And she got what she wanted. The problem she had with me is I'm hardheaded too. I can't remember specific arguments, but they would be about what photograph of her band we were going to use on the cover. And she would want to exert her right to make that choice. She was not the art director of the magazine — it's not her place. Well, we'd bang heads on that — life goes on.

ART CHANTRY: Susan Silver is an est head. That was her powerbase, and she ran that band with an iron fist. She was "the fifth Soundgarden member," and was married to Chris Cornell — who was a doormat, *oh my God.* I remember when I was working on the *Louder Than Love* record cover, Chris wouldn't talk to the band. He talked to Susan, who in turn talked to the band. And when they would talk to Chris, they would talk to him directly, but he wouldn't respond — he'd respond to Susan, and Susan would talk to the band. And that is the way communication worked.

Soundgarden was a monster, and Susan Silver was Dr. Frankenstein. It was another one of those astonishing things to watch. Watching the way these organizations emerge and the dynamics. Like, the dynamics of the Nirvana camp were so "junkie." The mechanics of the different labels, and the way they instinctively began to structure their organizations were always dependent upon the personality foibles. Like any organization. It's like Ken Lay and Enron — their personalities dictate everything down below. And Soundgarden, Nirvana, Alice in Chains, and all these bands, no matter who they were — Mudhoney, the same thing, in a different way.

Watching the structures work, it was like sociology at its finest. Basically, it was "the Susan and Chris dynamic," with these three guys that were sitting around following them, because they had no choice. This is back when Hiro was in the band — I never met Ben Shepherd. There were these three guys that were obviously the band, and then you had "the lead singer syndrome" in the corner. They were stuck. That was the dynamic — resignation. But at least they were getting money. So it was resignation *with cash.*

MATT CAMERON: After *Louder Than Love*, we were going to start promoting our record. Hiro decided he didn't really want to be a part of that machine. He left on good terms.

HIRO YAMAMOTO: I guess the reason why I left was the whole deal about metal — "I don't want to be in a metal band." To me, that's still the most embarrassing thing in my life. We were a hard rock band, but I don't know if we were ever a metal band. We got bigger than I ever imagined we could have — I wasn't really ready for that at the time. That wasn't what I wanted out of music. I guess promotion scared me — advertising and promotion are things to me seem very foreign. Mixing music and the two of them was something that was hard for me to grasp at that point. I was unhappy before we left for Europe. And then halfway through Europe, I was like, "I can't keep doing this." A&M was telling us to tour 350 days a year, and I was like, "I'm not doing this, *you can't make me!*" [Laughs.] I remember being in Italy somewhere — that was pretty much near the end of the tour. That was it. [*Louder Than Love*] had been recorded, it just hadn't been released yet.

KIM THAYIL: It was certainly heartbreaking for us, because he was a founding member, and such a significant creative part of the band — in our sound. What we were about, and the style that all our peers and friends had come to love was founded on certainly a creative interaction between Hiro and I. And definitely the three of us working together — not leaving Matt out of that. With four people in the band, there are six different two-man relationships, there are four different three-man relationships, and there's one four-man relationship. So that's eleven relationships, I guess. Having Hiro leaving the band, you have now changed the nature of seven relationships.

HIRO YAMAMOTO: I keep in contact with Kim every once in a while. I haven't talked to Chris, except for running into him a couple of times since then. I've seen Matt a few times.

JIM TILLMAN: I played with them several times — trying to figure out if it would work. They had a tendency to tune everything down — *way down.* They'd take an E string and tune it down to a C. I promptly blew up Hiro's bass cabinet. So we went bowling instead.

BEN SHEPHERD: They were crunched for time, they had deadlines — they had these make up tours they had to do. Once we got to the rehearsal room, I didn't say anything; I just walked over to the amp, turned it up, and started playing. Then we jammed for three hours, we didn't play any of their songs. They went, "The next time we get together, *we've got to work on the songs.*" And they took Jason [Everman] because he knew the songs. He was more connected and on-beat with it.

MATT CAMERON: [Jason] was the best guy at the time. We had seen him play in Nirvana — thought he had a cool look.

KIM THAYIL: We chose Jason because he knew a number of the songs, so we thought he could learn them really quick. He was a good player and had a good attitude. When Hiro left, it was a big hole in the band. Hiro leaving the band could have broken the band up, and we certainly needed stitches or a Band-Aid. What was unfair to Jason is we were unaware of what we needed, and the demands that we were going to put on him. And he was certainly unaware of it. We didn't realize that we needed some major surgery on the band — to keep the band together. That's a lot to put on one guy. We needed a creative and emotional presence to hold the band together — we didn't realize we needed that.

MARK IVERSON: They're the band I saw grow the most. To be honest, I think Soundgarden and Mudhoney were better than Nirvana live. Mudhoney and Soundgarden were more energetic and charismatic onstage. And Chris Cornell would do his thing — like on the cover of *Louder Than Love*. Seeing them at the Central, then they played the Moore Theatre when they were doing the Voivod tour, then they played the Paramount. At the Paramount, some people were handing out these flyers, and if you're familiar with the poster of *Rattle and Hum* by U2, they doctored the photo so [the spotlight] was shining on Chris Cornell. It implied that they were local — putting together this hand-made flyer. *But they were on A&M Records.*

JACK ENDINO: I was pretty disappointed with everybody's first major label record, to be honest. I don't think *Louder Than Love* is a very good record — it's not produced well, it's not mixed well. The later records blow it away. The problem with all the indie bands — they had come up making records in a week, two weeks. Suddenly, you're presented with two months to make a record. What you wind up doing — if you're not familiar with the process and have never done it before — is basically instead of using the technology, the technology uses you. You wind up making a record with all the rough edges removed. You wind up making everything perfect. That's alright if you're making a Radiohead or Police record, but not if you're trying to make a rock 'n' roll album. So you ended up with *Louder Than Love* — a fairly safe-sounding, not very exciting-sounding record. But they were the first to get "the nod." And then you had Alice in Chains.

JEFF GILBERT: Alice in Chains — who is the evolutionary link between grunge, hard rock, and metal up here — started out as a glam band. And I'm not kidding — *they wanted to be Poison.* In fact, when they finally grew their hair out, quit bathing, and put on flannel shirts and Doc Martens, they took a lot of grief. People used to call them "Kindergarden," because they tried to copy Soundgarden so much. The irony is that Alice in Chains got more airplay than anybody once they got their sound down.

JERRY CANTRELL: It was my dream to be one of the guys that I dug, and to play music for a living. It appealed to me from an early age. I actually started playing guitar fairly late — about seventeen. That was out of I never could afford a guitar — we didn't have a lot of excess cash around. My folks were divorced, and my mother and grandmother raised me. My cousin scored a shitty Mustang copy [and] a Sound Design stereo — an eight-track tape, a turntable on top, with a couple of speakers that had a guitar plug in the back. You could record onto the eight tracks as well, so it was kind of my own little studio. He brought it over, and I convinced him to loan it to me for a weekend — I never gave it back! [Laughs.] There was stuff going on in Tacoma too — some of the Seattle bands would come down and play. I'd seen Layne [Staley]'s band, Alice 'N Chains, at the Tacoma Little Theater.

NANCY LAYNE McCALLUM: I'm a second soprano, so Layne learned harmonies. Our friend had a drum set, and offered to let Layne use it. Layne became a drummer — drums in the living room, in the bedroom, in the garage. He loved it. Then our neighbor sold him a drum set. That was what he played the last couple years of high school. He was in a band with his friend, Tigger Giles. They'd get dressed up in their rocker costumes, and be in somebody's basement or bedroom. He wasn't in choir in school, and our church didn't have a choir. The whole congregation would stand up and sing. Every Sunday and every Wednesday our family attended — so, he heard lots of good, non-professional singing.

I think Layne went to his first concert in high school with his step dad, Jim, who raised him. It might have been Van Halen. One day, his stepbrother, Ken, was at the house and said, "Layne, there are a couple of guys over at Shorewood High School looking for a singer." Layne said, "Well, I'm not a singer," and Ken said, "Why don't you try out anyhow?" I think Layne was out of high school and probably had turned eighteen. So they zipped on over there, and he tried out. When they heard Layne, they said, "You're it, no more auditions," even though they had a long list scheduled. It was a band called Sleze — Johnny Bacolas, James Bergstrom, Nick Pollack, and Ed Semanati were in that group. They practiced at James's house.

YANNI "JOHNNY" BACOLAS: The first song we jammed was "L.O.V.E. Machine" by WASP. Then we did an Armored Saint [song], a Mötley Crüe song, and after doing a few songs together, that was the band. We were just blown away by him — he had "star qualities" even then. He was much more timid — he looked down while he sang. But the grain of his voice was there, the soul was there. From that point, we started playing local gigs around town.

MATT VAUGHAN: I first met Layne when I was in high school. He was hanging out with my sister, who was a year younger than me — I think it was because he knew my folks managed Queensrÿche. I remember him posing in the mirror — we were in our kitchen — and he said, "I'm going to be one of the biggest rock stars in the world."

JERRY CANTRELL: I went to concerts, played with people. I didn't have a car, so I would carry my guitar case and little amp on a bus. I'd get to practices and learn. And then things took a turn for my family. My grandmother and mother both passed away in about six months of each other. At that point, I was on my own — I had no home, no immediate family — except for aunts and uncles. My mother left me a little money from an insurance policy — enough for me to exist on for a while. I bought some gear, put together the Diamond Lie band. We probably were one of or *the* biggest band in Tacoma.

DAWN ANDERSON: Those poodle bands used to play at this steakhouse out in Lynnwood — total white trash — and stand around comparing each other's equipment and haircuts. One of them was Diamond Lie. I always thought they were one of the best of the poodle rock bands — for whatever that's worth.

BEN REW: Jerry is an OK guy . . . he's not really my cup of tea. He's always been into "the strippers and ho's." That's not my fucking biz. Remember those little guys in school that were "the rock guys," that were skinny as fuck but were always trying to bully you around? *That's Jerry.* I was big, but I was always nice, and I could never understand how you would be having a party, and he'd all of a sudden decide he was going to be screaming at somebody twice his size — just because he was in some band. He was the only guy out of the scene that I ever met and remember [at] parties being a jerk.

YANNI "JOHNNY" BACOLAS: One day, myself and a guy named Russ Klatt — he was the singer of a band called Slaughterhouse Five — we were at this party, and we were talking about different concepts for backstage passes. It would say, like, "Sleze: The Welcome to Wonderland Tour." That ended up turning into a discussion — we were talking about changing the band name. And we were saying, "Alice in Wonderland? How about this, how about that? Maybe . . . Alice in Chains? We could put her in bondage stuff!" I liked the ring [of] "Alice in Chains" — I remember I came back to the next band rehearsal and I told the guys. The issue was the reference to bondage, which our parents would not go for. Layne's mom was very hardcore Christian. So we ended up changing it to Alice 'N Chains, which made it more like "Alice *and* Chains."

JEFF GILBERT: They used to be "Alice 'N Chains" — like "Guns N' Roses."

NANCY LAYNE McCALLUM: I had a sense of humor about the name Sleze. But when he came home and said they were changing the name to Alice 'N Chains, *I was not happy*. I said, "Honey, that is female bondage. You don't want to choose a name like that — it's going to push your female audience away. I really feel strongly about this." He was adamant and I was adamant. For the first time in my life, I didn't have much of a conversation with him for about two weeks, because I was concerned, and also offended. How could my child possibly choose a name like "Alice 'N Chains"?

YANNI "JOHNNY" BACOLAS: About 1988, we were jamming in this place called the Music Bank, and Layne — to pay his portion of the room rent — was the guy with the keys. If you were to come knock on his door at three in the morning, he would look through the peephole, walk you in the room, unlock your band room, and you'd get to jam all night long. It was this warehouse in Ballard.

TIM BRANOM: I worked days and Layne would work nights. A bunch of girls would bring you food, and let you go take showers. That's how we survived. And then we made four dollars an hour *credit* at the rehearsal room. The place was huge — I don't know how many rehearsal rooms were in there, maybe a hundred. So at night when we turned off the lights, me and Layne would be sleeping in there. He was on the couch and I was on the floor. If you had to walk all the way to the bathroom — it was gross and dirty — you can't see, it's all pitch black. A couple of times, we were so tired, we'd just pee in this big Slurpee cup. One time, Layne peed in it — I don't know who did it, I was sleeping on the floor in a sleeping bag — it spilled. I was so tired and it was so pitch black, *I just had to lay in the pee.*

JERRY CANTRELL: I had met Nick Pollock, who was the guitar player in Alice 'N Chains at the time — Layne's version of it. He knew what I was going through, and he invited me to come up to Seattle. He took me to a house party — somewhere in West Seattle. I walked in the door, and he introduced me to Layne immediately. We just clicked. He was really cool and he looked great — he was really funny. I think he had his hair flat-ironed, so it was all crimped and teased up. He offered, "Come down and live at the Music Bank with me. Maybe we can get you a gig, running keys." I moved up there the next day. And I have to also say about Layne, the very first time I heard him sing — at the Tacoma Little Theater — it was one of those "lightning bolt moments." I just knew, "I've got to be in a band with this guy."

PIC BY YANNI "JOHNNY" BACOLAS — YANNIBACOLAS.COM

Layne Staley . . . or Vince Neil?

TIM BRANOM: Jerry played with [Gypsy Rose] for a short time — all the music sounded like Dokken. That's kind of what Diamond Lie sounded like — really polished. They always used to talk about Mike Starr because all the women loved him. He wasn't a great bass player, but the women loved him.

JERRY CANTRELL: I was in band with Mike Starr — Gypsy Rose — for a minute. We both got kicked out because we didn't have good gear.

MATT FOX: [Mike Starr] was like "the sergeant guy" in a World War II movie. If you were in the desert, out of weed, out of gas, out of girls — he could find all three. He was a good guy to have around if you were a band living in your band room — he could scrounge up the girls who would buy you pizza. They were total "band bum guys."

PIC BY YANNI "JOHNNY" BACOLAS — YANNIBACOLAS.COM

Layne Staley . . . or Bret Michaels?

JERRY CANTRELL: We ended up at the Music Bank jamming. Our second or third rehearsal, there was some dude running through, looking for bands to open up this show he was throwing at Kane Hall. We had maybe two or three songs. He's like, "Hey man, can you do a forty-minute set?" And we're like, "Uhhh . . . yeah, sure!" That was our first gig. [Layne] was working with his band, which I think was disintegrating at the time, and he was working with another guy in another band. It became apparent that we had similar goals — we really liked each other as people and we all had a lot in common. We were like, "We need to get Layne to get out of these other bands and commit to us."

SEAN KINNEY: I met Layne at a place in Seattle called Alki — the closest we have to a beach. You can't go in the water — it's cold and shitty — but people cruise around in cars. I was down there and I saw Layne hanging out. We got to talking — he had this band going on. "Cool man, I'm a drummer. If you know somebody who's looking for that, give me a call." We exchanged numbers. Probably six months later, Jerry called me out of the blue. He said, "Hey, I got this thing from Layne." So I came down to meet him at the Music Bank. My girlfriend at the time was Mike Starr's sister. He was like, "I want to put a band together — I'm thinking of a bass player, this guy Mike Starr." And I was like, "That's weird — *this is his sister!*" I was sleeping in a car in front of [the Starrs'] house for the last month. So I called him, and he came down that night. We hung out, had some drinks, and started jamming. Kept trying to coax Layne into doing it.

JERRY CANTRELL: We staged fake auditions with some super shitty singers — just to piss him off. One of the guys was a male stripper! [Laughs.]

This redhead dude — we didn't think the guy was talented at all, we were just trying to get [Layne] to make a move, like, "OK, you're not going to jump in? We're going to get somebody else." After the guy left, he was like, "OK, fuck it. I'm *not* going to let you guys get in a band with that dude. I'll quit my shit — I'm jumping in." And from then on, it was any gig we could take. Any VFW hall, we did a lot of gigs at the Kent Skate King — we did some shows there with Mother Love Bone.

BRUCE FAIRWEATHER: When Love Bone was first starting, we played a few shows with them, and they were full-on, bad glam. They were white trash dudes. We were playing somewhere down south in Seattle, a roller skating place. We played, and then afterwards, Layne's up onstage — I think they did "Suffragette City," but a horrible version of it. He's like, "Bruce, Andy, come up here! *Come play with us!*" Andy's just like, *"Jeeez!"* He's hiding behind me — we ran away [laughs].

JERRY CANTRELL: That was kind of the music of the era and the look. I don't know any of my buddies that play in bands today that weren't involved in that — some shape or form. Spandex and the fucking hair — I had all that shit. My whole thing before I even was a good player was just trying to get attention — the more outrageous I could look, and the more people that could call me "fag" as they drove by in their cars.

JEFF GILBERT: These guys would get bigger gigs, because they had an insane female fan base. These guys had women like you can't believe — all over the place. And not just good women, *skanky broads* [laughs]. The dirtiest women you could find. And the guys would go, because the girls were going, and would go, "Hey, that guitar player's pretty freaking good!" Sean Kinney on drums — he's very Bonham-esque live. I mean, he throws his whole upper body weight into it. When he hits a drum, you can feel it in the back of your head. But they were very tongue-in-cheek. I don't think they had any aspirations to be anything but. They'd come out and do this shtick — they'd bring mirrors out and primp. They had this one song, "Queen of the Rodeo," and it made the circuit. The underground trading and grunge guys liked it, because they thought, "Oh, these guys get the joke." They were, in a sense, making fun of themselves.

There was a bidding war for Soundgarden that was just stupid-crazy.

Suddenly, bands started to stop and take a look around to see the changing face of the music scene. Alice in Chains did that almost overnight. It was that quick. That sounds like that was a very patented move on their part, and for a large part I guess it was. But I also think that they had run out of steam on the glam thing, because their buddies, who were all in metal bands, kept giving them shit. "Hey, you guys are better than this — why don't you really play?" Because Jerry, my God, can play *anything.* So I think it was, for them, a natural progression, to just slide right in and bring their hard rock roots. They had no problem saying, "Yeah, we listen to KISS, Aerosmith, and Ted Nugent." They weren't from a punk background at all — they could care less about punk, because punk guys never got any girls. So these guys got the best of all worlds — they got the credibility *and* the chicks [laughs]. All the grunge guys were butt-ass ugly, but Alice in Chains were good-looking guys, scored all the women, and got good street cred. Once they got serious, their whole sound got serious. Their sound got larger. The bass got thicker, because it's that "drop-D tuning thing." [Jerry] brought in his love of Joe Perry and Ted Nugent, and just thickened up that sound. When you put Layne's vocals over top of it — you couldn't miss.

GRANT ALDEN: I thought Alice in Chains were posers. There was an organic scene and sound, which did develop in Seattle. Alice in Chains looked around at what was happening and changed who they were. It was like Soundgarden-lite. They had the same management, they'd clearly been watching Soundgarden a lot, it was the same stage moves. It just wasn't honest.

JERRY CANTRELL: Everybody starts off emulating someone else — that's just the way it is. That's how you learn — you emulate other people. And hopefully at some point, you become yourself. You take the best elements of stuff that turns you on, and you add your own thing to it.

SUSAN SILVER: Ken Deans was managing them with a fellow that was a hairdresser by day, coke dealer by night — who ended up going to jail. Ken asked Kelly [Curtis, Mother Love Bone's manager] and I if we'd like to work with them. I'd been helping them already with various things locally, and loved the tape they'd made. I loved their personalities — they were some of the drop-dead funniest people I'd ever met in my life. Sean Kinney is one of the funniest human beings I challenge *anybody* to meet. They all lived together in Des Moines, Washington. It was a ridiculous scene — totally trashed party house that had a sun bed underneath the coffee table. A couple of grey cats running around. And four funny, crazy guys that survived [by] getting girls to buy them food and other people to buy them drinks. And played this music that was so catchy and so cool. When Ken said he didn't want to do the management, I said, "*Absolutely* — sign me up."

NANCY LAYNE McCALLUM: That kid onstage — I just didn't know him. Layne was a great actor — and I was completely unaware or completely unprepared for any kind of drug involvement. He struggled a bit in high school for a couple of years, but had quit using. Then he was off and running with the band. Other than one of the moms screaming into the phone at me, "You've got to do something!" — I didn't have the faintest idea what she was talking about. I had no idea how to help my son, and I didn't know how severe his use was. I just didn't know how much to be alarmed. Layne was a smart boy with so many wonderful qualities. We came from a family and church that didn't use drugs. There was just no reason in the world to think that this would persist. I wanted to stay calm, to support Layne, and know that he wouldn't go in that direction or be harmed. I thought that the songs he was singing about drug addiction were about people he was observing.

The show I remember the best was when they performed at the Renton Fire Hall. At that point, evidently, they were being scouted. He came up to me, and his eyes were glistening with tears just on the rim. He looked down at me, from his six feet, and said, "Mom, *I'm going to be a star.*" I put my hands up on his shoulders, and I looked him straight in the eye. I wanted him to go for his dream, so I said, "Go for it, honey. Somebody's got to do it." I would have said that to him if he wanted to be a roofer or anything else. It was in his heart. I was so naive. If I had any idea what the entertainment industry is like, and what would happen to him . . . I would have hidden him.

JERRY CANTRELL: We had been living in the Music Bank for a while. I paid for a demo that we did in a tree house on the side of a mountain — that's no joke, we borrowed Coffin Break's van to drive up on top of this mountain in Issaquah, and recorded a demo in a fucking tree house! We killed their van in the process, and lost all our gear halfway down the mountain because the back doors came open. But we recorded the demo. And then we were going to record another demo — for the record companies. And that night, while we're sitting there — we have all our gear ready to go — the Seattle SWAT team comes down and takes over the whole place! It turns out the party scene that was the Music Bank — we'd been living next door to a fucking *forest* of pot. I can't remember how many times we'd been like, "Man, we need some weed," and it's right through the wall.

They seized the whole building — including our gear. We woke up to guns in our face. Of course, they think we're all involved [laughs]. We spent most of the night trying to [convince] the cops into, "Just check our gear. There's no drugs in here — we're going to get *signed,* dude. We've been working for-fucking-ever to get this to happen, and now you guys are going to lock our shit down, the night before we've got to go make a demo."

So while that's going on, we were bored, and Sean and Mike went around to a couple of the local Zippy Marts, and ripped off some beer. We figured all the cops were busy, and we needed something to do in the meantime [laughs]. So they brought it back, and we washed the whole thing down. As the night went on, they realized we were just a bunch of kids — we weren't connected. When we ran out of the beer, we actually talked the officer-in-charge into kicking down twenty or forty bucks for some more beer! [Laughs.] So we sat there and got toasted, and as the night went on, we were the only band they let take gear out of there. We'd spent enough time with these guys — they checked our shit to make sure there was nothing in it. We took it out, and stacked all of our shit in front of the front door. We had to sleep *on* the gear outside, so nobody would steal it. Then in the morning, Ken Deans came in a van to pick us up. We went down, made the demo, and the rest is history.

CHAPTER 16

"He's going to be one of the biggest rock stars in the world — no question": Mother Love Bone and Andy Wood's Death

After the split up of Green River and Malfunkshun, several members of each band united as Mother Love Bone. While the majority of grunge bands were punk-based, the Andy Wood–led Love Bone modeled a sound and look akin to arena rockers, and were poised for success. But shortly before the planned release of their major label full-length debut, *Apple*, tragedy struck.

XANA LA FUENTE: If you saw Mother Love Bone, you were rocking out and laughing your ass off at the same time.

REGAN HAGAR: Stone and Jeff were determined businessmen — they were going to make it. Those guys were buckling down, practicing, making connections, and planning tours on their own. So those guys, mixed with Andy's charisma and stage presence, it was like a match that sparked and took off.

GRANT ALDEN: Love Bone wanted to be rock stars. Nobody else in that scene wanted to be a rock star — they wanted to make music.

JEFF AMENT: [Playing with Andy Wood] was mostly Stone's idea. I had known Andy pretty well — I had seen him around a bunch. I knew he partied pretty hard, and at that point, I was still pretty straight edge. I saw Andy and Stone play a show at Tug's — this gay bar about two blocks down from the Vogue. I thought they were frickin' amazing — total T. Rex. They had a

PIC BY KAREN MASON-BLAIR — KARENMASONBLAIR.COM

Mother Love Bone (L-R: Stone Gossard, Greg Gilmore, Andy Wood, Bruce Fairweather, Jeff Ament)

drum machine, Stone was playing his acoustic through the PA — it had this kind of distorted sound. And Andy was just being Andy — he was doing his whole campy T. Rex/Freddie Mercury thing. At that point, it made total sense. We played a couple of shows with Regan — Regan and I had a little bit of a falling out, and Stone ran into Greg Gilmore, who was in Ten Minute Warning. We thought Greg was the best musician in the whole scene. The fact that he wanted to play with us — he was by far the best musician in the band, so it raised the stakes a little bit.

BRUCE FAIRWEATHER: Green River was starting to get pretty popular, so [Mother Love Bone] started out with pretty big crowds.

JEFF AMENT: It was *so* different. Mark had such a heavy, cynical thing going on, and Andy's thing was pure comedy. It probably took me like ten shows to make a transition, because before that, both bands I'd been in were kind of like gangs, and we were kinda all the same. I'd never been around anybody like Andy.

DUFF McKAGAN: With Mother Love Bone, it was like, "OK, Andy's not playing bass — he's just singing. Well, that's *perfect.*"

CHRIS PUGH: Compared to Malfunkshun, they had real songs. They were a good band — once again, they were barking up the classic rock tree in a way.

JEFF AMENT: Playing four-quarter notes over and over started to get old — we were starting to develop "groove." We were aspiring to mutate beyond just the hardcore/super up-tempo thing.

KIM THAYIL: I liked every damn person in Mother Love Bone — I've always felt uncomfortable about the union. I don't know what it is. I think because I really liked Green River, and I was a *huge* fan of Malfunkshun. It eventually led to the demise of Malfunkshun, and that's kind of how I saw Love Bone. I saw Love Bone as trying too hard. And one of my best friends on the planet played in Love Bone — Bruce Fairweather. We would always give each other's band shit. I *liked* Love Bone — I liked the songs, I loved hearing Andy's voice. I wanted to see them do well — but then at the same time, I didn't like seeing the ultimate demise of Malfunkshun, or the disintegration of Green River. [Andy's] stage presence with Malfunkshun seemed like a good dose of parody and homage. It was campy, witty. With Love Bone, the parody seemed to be missing. It seemed more serious, more professional — which would make record companies and management happy. It just didn't seem right — it always seemed awkward. It seemed like it was forced — like they were *trying.*

CHARLES PETERSON: Boy, *not my cup of tea.* We did a photo shoot at my place, and Stone had brought a tape of Guns N' Roses. He was like, "Check this shit out!" I was just like, "This is just fucking garbage. I mean, *'Sweet Child O' Mine'?* Give me a break!" At the time, I was listening to Public Enemy and Mudhoney. There was always this sort of rivalry — the scene broke down into two camps. There was the Mudhoney/Nirvana/Tad camp, and then on the other hand, there was the Mother Love Bone/Pearl Jam/Alice in Chains [camp] — a little more MOR/hard rock.

STEVE MANNING: Much more reminiscent of what was going on in L.A. at the time. The music was new, but they still seemed like they were some crossover to both sides.

JEFF GILBERT: Still a little on the glammy side, because of Andrew. He didn't care about grunge — even though they were lumped into that, they weren't really. He was a very soulful singer, very melodic. Probably one of the more melodic bands, outside of Alice in Chains, of that era. Andy wanted to be a rock star — he didn't care how, he was just going to do it. Truly, nobody would have been able to touch him, in terms of being "the charismatic front man" he was back then. The potential he had was just sick. To see it in person would be to understand it better. You stood there, and you're going, "Oh, he's going to be one of the biggest rock stars in the world — no question." The band wasn't really even that good per se — they were all just like everybody else, trying to make some noise. Not him. He had his sights set on big, big things. No matter what stage they were on, it would be like the biggest gig they ever had. I remember Ann Wilson from Heart came to see them. He had a glass of beer — and I can even tell you what beer it was, it was Schmidt Animal beer. Because at the Central, they sold one dollar sixteen-ounce cans — "a pound of beer for a buck." He was dancing around, grabbed the beer, sees Ann, and gets that weird look — very mischievous. He threw his beer at her — just *drenched* her. She looked really stunned. He looked over, smiled, and winked. And right there, you knew they were going to be best friends. She "got it" — instantly. It was one of the coolest rock moments I had ever seen down there.

BRUCE FAIRWEATHER: The first show we played was at the OK Hotel. I remember a girl being high on ecstasy, knocking my amp offstage, going, *"Where's Stoney? Where's Stoney?"* I think we bummed out a lot of people — it was totally different than Green River. We ended up getting a new following.

DAWN ANDERSON: I was thinking, "These guys are going to lose a lot of fans, and they're going to get a lot of new ones. They're going to probably be a lot bigger than Malfunkshun ever was."

STU HALLERMAN: I met Andrew through Chris years before. And I'd see him up at Susan's office, just being this little smiley, helper, gnome guy. KISW used to do these rising star concert series shows, and one of those was Mother Love Bone, Soundgarden, and Jane's Addiction. The band's jamming, the singer is not onstage yet, and all of a sudden, here comes this guy with a cape and a mic stand with no base. He leaps up on the guitar cabinets and yells, *"HELLO SEATTLE!"* Like he's some star from out of town. People either scowled or cracked up.

PIC BY LIBBY KNUDSON

Andrew Wood: January 6, 1966 – March 19, 1990

LILLY MILIC: Everybody I knew wouldn't go to a Mother Love Bone show — that was a completely different scene. That was the big hair and hairspray. You couldn't go into the bathrooms because there was so much hair-spray everywhere.

JEFF AMENT: Any contacts I made on the Green River trips, I sent tapes to, and said, "Can you help get us a show during these two weeks?" We were starting to line up shows, and Dayle Gloria, the woman who booked [Green River] at the Scream with Jane's Addiction, was friends with Anna Statman. Anna called me back — she was working at Slash. Right in the middle of all that, she quit her job at Slash, and started working at Geffen. She called and said, "We want to sign you to a demo deal" — they give you a couple of grand to record a few songs. Kind of a test run. We did that — it was just *on*. People started calling me at work. Within a month, there were seven or eight labels that were trying to get up to Seattle to see us play or take us out to dinner. I think it's what Andy termed "the Seattle Dinner Tour."

JOHN LEIGHTON BEEZER: At the time, it blew my mind — I think it was Polydor [that] gave them a quarter of a million dollars to record a record. Only later did I think, "It's going to take them a year, they're going to spend it all on recording, and how much do five guys make a year?" So great — they got ten dollar an hour jobs [laughs].

XANA LA FUENTE: I did Andrew's wardrobe — I literally made every stitch of clothing he wore. Or I'd find stuff and sew stuff on it, or paint stuff on jeans. I made lots of hats and jackets that were worn by other bands — whether it's Chris [Cornell] or the chicks from Heart.

KEN STRINGFELLOW: I took some of his shtick at face value. So I was like, "What the fuck? This guy is stupid [laughs]. *Just shut up.*" But now I've come to appreciate it a lot more. I did have a "watershed," when they played at the Vogue. They were definitely past the point of needing to play there, and man, the show was totally amazing. I was like, "*Oh* . . . OK. This band's great *and* he's funny." I got close enough to realize what his shtick was consisting of — it was with a wink.

NILS BERNSTEIN: Sub Pop flew J Mascis to town, which resulted in the "The Wagon" single, and all he wanted to see was Mother Love Bone. Which technically, would have been uncool at the time — except we *all* wanted to go too.

BRUCE FAIRWEATHER: We were playing in Montreal I think, and [Andy] had a wireless microphone. He went running into the crowd, and was singing and dancing around. He came running back to the stage, whispering in everyone's ear, *"Ian Astbury's here!"* He was totally excited — he almost wet his pants. Afterwards, we got to meet him, and every time Ian Astbury was looking away, he'd start dancing around.

SCOTTY CRANE: I remember [Andy] calling up Slam. He used to call him Chadwick — he was literally at every single show. That guy put up posters for every single band in Seattle — he would plaster all of Seattle. Part of the deal was ten bucks and a guest pass. In the early days, he would jump off the PAs and monitors. I remember a show at the Gorilla Gardens — it was either during the Accüsed or Malfunkshun — Chad jumped off the monitors, everybody moved, and [he] landed on his head! If you listen to Mother Love Bone bootlegs, you can hear Andy call out "Chadwick" at almost every show. But if you watch [the movie] *Singles*, at the very beginning — you see Chad putting up flyers around town. That's how much of a staple he was, that they had to include him in that.

JONATHAN EVISON: Slam Hate — now known as Chad — who I've long considered something of a mascot for the Seattle scene, used to have this big butch girlfriend named Wendy. On the back of Slam's leather coat, in the handwriting of a dyslexic eight-year-old, said, "Slam + Wendy = Sex." I always thought that was eloquent. It's still my favorite math equation.

DUFF McKAGAN: Greg Gilmore I'd played with before. I was pretty good buddies with [Andy]. They'd gotten a record deal just after we got our record deal. For me, it was only a matter of time before people on a national level started realizing Seattle talent. Mother Love Bone was great — they made a great record.

JEFF AMENT: It took *so fucking long*. We never dealt with a major label at that point, and Michael Goldstone, who we signed with at PolyGram, was probably the most thorough and partly neurotic of all the people we could have signed with. That's one of the reasons why we signed with him — we could tell that he really cared about what we were doing. He was so meticulous about every little aspect that it just took us forever. We recorded with a bunch of different people. We put out an EP [1989's *Shine*] that we recorded with Mark Dearnley, who was an engineer with AC/DC — which seemed like a great idea at the time. And then we recorded a couple of songs with this guy Davitt Sigerson, who was a really super-bizarre choice — he did David & David, and the Bangles. We went through that whole process, and we were like, "We want to record with somebody that we know." That's when we started talking to Terry Date.

TERRY DATE: We recorded the basic band tracks [for 1990's *Apple*] down in Sausalito, at the Plant. We were down there for the big earthquake in '89. Bruce Fairweather and I were doing guitars when it happened, or we were actually taking a break — we were in the lounge. Running out into the parking lot when that thing happened, and seeing Carlos [Santana] and some of his people out there, with a cooler.

That was a lot of fun working on that record. We all lived in the same condo — we shared a couple of condos. Andy was a blast — he almost burned the studio down once. He always leaves candles burning on his keyboard. He came in to check the vocal parts, he was sitting next to me, and all of a sudden, he jumps up, and runs out of the studio. I look out there and there's four-foot flames on the carpet below his keyboard — the candle had fallen off.

JEFF AMENT: We went to Sausalito for, like, three months — recording at a studio that was a thousand bucks a day. In retrospect, it wasn't the right way to make a record. What we should have done is practiced more and actually gotten to the point where we could have played the songs better, and then cut the record more live.

TERRY DATE: Andy was like your little brother . . . or big brother. He was like a brother that you couldn't quite get to know. He was the nicest guy I'd ever been around, but also the hardest to get close to. He was always open to trying things. We were doing the middle break [of "Holy Roller"] that he always ad-libbed live. It's very difficult to do that in a studio, obviously. So I suggested that he take a huge poster board, and just randomly write as many words on there as he could, then when he went to do the part, just open his eyes and whatever word he saw, he'd ad-lib off of that. That's what we ended up doing.

SHAWN SMITH: There was a point where my two favorite acts in the world were Prince and Mother Love Bone. Both did something to me that few other acts had done — gave me chills. "Stardog Champion," there's a breakdown right before the big outro, and it just felt like electricity came down. It was a show at the Central, I think. The other moment was at a sound check, at that same venue — "Gentle Groove." It was the first time I heard the band play it. That was just a huge leap in understanding what's possible.

PETE DROGE: They had the cool, slinky, guitar interweaving thing down really well. I wasn't so used to, at that point, hearing friends' records that sounded like real records.

KEVIN WOOD: I knew that he always wanted to have "the Andy Wood Band." He felt guilty and sad about breaking up Malfunkshun, but he was excited about the possibility of making some money playing rock 'n' roll. In retrospect, I can't see how that band could have been the vehicle for his ultimate success, because it was so . . . I don't know, *cliché-ish.* The only way that he would be artistically happy was if he were calling the shots as far as the compositions — like he did in Malfunkshun. I think Malfunkshun would have been the better vehicle for his talents. He did get the nod to do [a solo album]. I was working with him on some of that material — we were doing preproduction at his apartment. He wanted me to be the guitar player on his solo thing, which was pretty goddamn cool, after all was said and done. I felt like, "The guy's got a heart after all." I mean, I knew he always had a heart — it broke his heart to break up Malfunkshun. He was going to redeem himself.

SCOTTY CRANE: I don't think Mother Love Bone was "it." Stoney was working on [Andy's solo songs] too. I have recordings — it was really rough four-track demos. I don't think that was the solo album that would have made him famous. Really where you can hear a hint of what was to come is on "Crown of Thorns," "Man of Golden Words," or "Chloe Dancer" — the ballads. I think Andy had had his time with his obvious influences with KISS, but ultimately, it was his Elton John that was going to come out. And that's what he was going to be — a ballad singer/songwriter. He didn't have the voice Elton John does, but it was getting better and better all the time. He did possess the charm to do it.

JEFF AMENT: We were getting ready to put the record out, and talking about touring — we were so anxious to get out and play. We were tired of being in Seattle, and tired of getting ready to do it. We just wanted to get out and do it. And then Andy died.

KEVIN WOOD: He was a hundred days out of rehab. I had a premonition that he relapsed — I had been off alcohol for probably two years at that time, and I was tuned into that way of thinking. I called him on it and he denied it. Then the day after that, my dad called me from Harbor View, saying that he had overdosed and was in the hospital. It's still hard to believe it actually happened — it's one of the most horrible things I've ever had to deal with. You just never get over that kind of thing.

XANA LA FUENTE: I just came home. The band was supposed to tell me if there was anything fishy going on. He had called Kelly [Curtis], and said he wasn't going to be able to make it to practice, and that Xana was going to think he did drugs. He said, "Did you?" [Andy] said, "No," and he said, "You have nothing to worry about." That would have been the time to call me, but they didn't. I was at a meeting at work, and I couldn't answer my phone. I don't know if he tried to call. I took a couple of friends from work home, and that took about a half an hour out of my time. That always bothered me, because the nurses at the hospital kept saying, "If you had been there just *ten minutes sooner*." Because he wasn't dead, or blue, or anything — he was just asleep — unconscious. They pronounced him dead — they told me to go to Harbor View. And then he was alive again — in a coma for three days. Then they said his brain had swelled too much. It was weird, because another guy came in, in worse condition than him. His brain was swelled too, and he lived.

JEFF AMENT: That night, Kelly Curtis, Greg, and I were talking to a guy that was going to be our tour manager. That was about as big of a punch in the gut as you could possibly have at that point. Andy was doing so good — he was working out every day, going to meetings, seemed really stoked to live out his rock dreams . . . *fuck.*

STU HALLERMAN: Just prior to [Soundgarden's] show, the crew was in the bus and the band was not. We got a phone call from Xana to our tour manager. I'm not sure how we got this message from her, but she said she had gotten back from the hospital. Our tour manager said, "Don't tell the band, we'll tell them after the show, I don't want to ruin this last show." So we held our tongues, did this last show [with Voivod and Faith No More at New York's L'Amour]. We had a lot of fun onstage — in the back of our minds, knowing that we had to tell Chris that our friend was gone. So that was pretty bad. Susan Silver was there that night, which was good, because Chris was very attached to Andrew.

SUSAN SILVER: We were in this crappy apartment-hotel place that we stayed at, because it was eighty bucks a night and had a kitchen. A bunch of people lived in it — you always smelled liver cooking and heard people practicing instruments. It was by the Beacon Theater. I got a call, and it was Kelly, and he said that Andy was in a coma, and they weren't sure if he was going to make it. We were all in a daze. It was scary — everybody was in shock. I remember after sound check, sitting at this table and there was a TV playing — waiting for the doors to open. It was during that period that Sinead O'Connor had done "Nothing Compares 2 U." For some reason it seems like that was playing over and over — that stark video with her face taking up the whole screen.

REGAN HAGAR: A lot people overdosed that particular weekend — there was bad heroin in Seattle at that time. So I think it was a huge mistake. I think he had been clean for a number of days. He was with this guy from Bainbridge, who had the drugs, and had given them to him. I think he just didn't say no. I remember being really frustrated at the hospital. He did not die immediately. They ended up saying he had an aneurysm — the aneurysm was apparently moved forward by the drugs. It was kind of hard to figure out what the hospital was saying. But he was on a life-support system for a couple of days.

I remember going to the hospital and getting really angry, because there was "a scene" there. People that to me were his new friends, because he was successful — which bothered me. I had no right to be bothered by that — that's fine, everybody has the right to be there that cared about him. But I was being selfish at the time. I remember going into the room, and his hair was all fucked-up — just really messy. I remember being in there with my now-wife, venting to her, and she had a brush. We tried to clean him up a little bit, because he looked really bad. In a way, I wish I had not seen him in there — he looked all pale, sick, and bloated. It's a terrible memory for me.

SUSAN SILVER: We came back the next day, dropped our bags at home, and went right to the hospital. All the band was around, and his girlfriend. They told us when we got there that they were going to take him off life-support. His family was there — his parents, his brothers, and his little two-year-old nephew. I remember holding his hand, giving him a kiss on the forehead, and saying that he was an angel. None of us will ever meet another human being that looks more like an angel — a cherub. Gorgeous, cherub, porcelain skinned face, with long blond hair. A really surreal moment. I said, *"Goodbye angel,"* stepped outside the curtain, and they turned off the machines.

JERRY CANTRELL: When Andy died, that was a serious reality check. We all had our fun, but it was pretty young and innocent at that time. It was a real slap in the face. I didn't even realize he was struggling as much as he had.

SUSAN SILVER: Somewhere in the days ensuing, there was a memorial service at the Paramount Theater, which we thought was a fitting place for such a theatrical guy. One friend put together an amazing video tribute. It was the beginning of a lot of "rites of passage" that we've all been through since then. *So many more.* More than most communities could ever endure.

REGAN HAGAR: Then there was a memorial service that further fueled my fire — there were these people talking all this smack about him onstage. I got up, went to the mic, and started venting. Me and another friend couldn't take the guy who was hired to deliver some service, or something — I don't know what the hell he was doing. But he obviously didn't know Andy, and was talking a bunch of shit. Talking about Andy being a junkie, and that really made me mad. Because I knew lots of junkies. There were junkies in the scene, but he *wasn't* one of them. It seemed so derogatory. So I went up to defend Andy at his own memorial service, and say some good words about him. Even his father referred to Andy as a junkie at the service, which bums me out. Maybe he was. That's a term that . . . I just can't accept that.

SCOTTY CRANE: I remember Andy's memorial at the Paramount, everybody was being really serious. And of course it was — Andy had just died. But I remember Chad [aka Slam] holding up the Mother Love Bone EP *Shine* and a lighter, at one point during this service. And yelling something — I don't know what — like, "Andy, we miss you!" Someone told him to sit down. And I got pissed. I was like, *"He's the only guy here who even gets it."* Andy would have wanted him on the podium talking about Andy instead of what really happened. Because that was the spirit of Andy. Fuck yeah — hold up a lighter and an album of his. Do you know how much Andy would have loved to see that?

SHAWN SMITH: I'll never feel a death like I felt that one I don't think, personally.

XANA LA FUENTE: He told me when I met him that he'd been in rehab. But I really didn't understand addiction at that time — I was really naive about it. Whenever he would use, he would tell me. It wasn't like the typical junkie boyfriend that was, "Do you want to try some?" He never, ever used with me. The one time I was like, "Screw it — bring some over here, I want to see what it's like," he was almost going to, and then he didn't. He would tell me every time he did it — it's not like he was strung out and I just put up with it. I had an idea he was doing it, and then he would say, "I used again last night." I would freak out, and then he would start crying. He must have had some idea that he was going to die, because he would start crying — literally, *every single time.* It was really weird — I've seen a lot of junkies since then, and I've never seen someone use, run and tell their girlfriend, and then cry. Usually when you use, you're like, "I'm not going to do it again," or you try to keep it hidden, because you get busted, and then you still lie about it. I really believe that he had a sense that something was going to happen to him.

JERRY CANTRELL: Jesus, what a terrible thing to happen — especially losing Andy, and then the ones that remain. All your dreams and everything in one mix — friend, buddy, partner, band member — down the tubes from top to bottom.

KURT DANIELSON: One of the saddest stories, because it's one of the shortest.

KIM WARNICK: He was just such a sweet guy. It's a shame when anybody dies, but God, that guy — if anybody wanted the whole rock 'n' roll fantasy thing, he wanted it as much as anybody I've ever known. His whole wall in his bedroom was a collage of Paul Stanley and KISS.

DUFF McKAGAN: He was really on his way to becoming a superstar. Nobody will ever know. But I would have had money on it — those guys would have been huge.

SHAWN SMITH: Andy had that spark, y'know? That "David Lee Roth thing."

TERRY DATE: He was one of the great losses. That's one of the ones that just hurts really bad for me — still to this day — and I didn't even know him as well as the other guys did. I just saw a little sliver of his life. But that was a personality that was really, really sad to see go.

JACK ENDINO: He was such a ray of sunshine — a supremely talented and very funny person. I called him "the Heavy Metal Standup Comic of Seattle." He was like a standup comedian onstage between the songs — he would say stuff that was so off-the-wall that you would just crack up. Even offstage he was funny.

XANA LA FUENTE: I was twenty-one when he died. Those guys never remember how young I was. I thought he was extremely talented — I loved his music right away. I've only met one or two people since then that I can sit down and say I love their music immediately. My uncles were all musicians in New Mexico, but they were rockabilly musicians. This was totally different — dreamy Zeppelin-type stuff. And he was hilarious. He was so fun to live with — a total comedian.

JEFF AMENT: We lost our friend in a horrible way, and the two years working to get to that point was gone. I really miss him.

REGAN HAGAR: Incredible loss — I don't think in my lifetime I'll have a best friend of the caliber that Andy was. I think you have best friends when you're kids. When you become an adult, you have relationships with people, but you can never have the chance to have that intimacy with someone again. I could be completely wrong — life is always changing — but Andy was a guy that he and I could hug each other in a loving way, and I didn't know any other guys like that. There was no weirdness there. We knew who we were, we knew that we loved each other, and that we were very close. I think that's a rarity that you find between heterosexual men. We were very close. I think of him still.

SCOTTY CRANE: For years it felt like I would see him in Seattle, out of the corner of my eye. I'd turn, think I'd see him, and it wouldn't be him. It felt like the Seattle music scene died when Andy died. It just got ugly after that — it got to be about money and fame.

1990–1991

CHAPTER 17

"OK, this thing is going to happen": 1990–1991

Due to the breakthrough success of several bands 1991 was the year that "grunge" became a household word. But as scene goers recount, the prior year was just as important to its growth.

PETE DROGE: I remember the first *Rolling Stone* feature about "the Seattle Sound." It was like a one page thing, and I think the big picture was of the Posies. At the time, a lot of people were banking on that band to break big. I can't remember who the inset little pictures were, but I want to say Alice in Chains and Love Bone. That was one of the first things where you go, "Wow, *Rolling Stone.* This isn't some fanzine in the U.K."

BEN SHEPHERD: I always saw it as *all* of America. When I went on that tour with Nirvana [as a roadie], you could see everybody was "on music" at that point. Music was suddenly alive again and doing something. Sometimes it's film and writing that does that culturally. That time, it was music.

GRANT ALDEN: I remember going to CMJ in New York — I have distinct memories of Screaming Trees following Galaxie 500 at CBGB's, and they absolutely *destroyed* the band. The same year, I saw Soundgarden at the student union building at NYU. They had a really low ceiling over the stage, and Cornell got in a trance — he took the mic stand and tore up the ceiling a little bit. People from campus freaked out, and there were cops ready to arrest. Susan said, "Look, *it's just sheet rock*, we can get it fixed. We'll pay the bill. Life goes on, don't freak out about it."

The day after CMJ ended, Mudhoney played a show at a converted church — they opened for Gwar on Halloween. There were all these kids there who weren't there for CMJ, weren't from the Northwest — just *screaming* along with the songs. I came back from that trip, and I was like, "OK, this thing is going to happen. These acts are compelling outside of their own market. They're really good — when I forget they're from my hometown." That meant [*The Rocket*] covered local music — virtually to the exclusion of everything else — to the best of our ability.

JIM BLANCHARD: I remember going to the first Lollapalooza — I had no clue that this "alternative nation" had been building up. There were all these people with crazy hair and tattoos — young people — and it blew my mind. I'd been into this music for so long, and now, everybody's into it — everybody knows about it.

JONATHAN PONEMAN: Bruce and I kind of made fun of the whole idea. There were a couple of instances — we did a "grunge fashion show," like, nine months before I wrote an article in earnest for *Vogue* magazine about grunge fashion. We were always sending stuff up like, "Once we're rich and we've retired, and we've got our Gulf Streams and swimming pools . . . " All this seemed ridiculous. But on a certain level, *it happened.*

ART CHANTRY: I'm still trying to figure out a lot of the interactions and players, and how they crossed paths and created new things. It was [like] the narrow point in an hourglass — Seattle for a brief period was that narrow point. Everybody passed through here, and bumped into everyone else. Very few cities get to experience that. San Francisco obviously had it in the late '60s, Swinging London was like that, New York being such a powerful and big city has it happening on a constant basis. Fucking Seattle? Why did it happen here?

COLLEEN COMBS: Not only was there a huge scene change, but Microsoft got huge, and then Amazon came in. That changed the skyline — it changed the way the city was. When I first moved to Seattle, you could call a bar and page someone. You could write a check for your bar tab. I mean, Los Angeles is such "I want that, I want it yesterday, and of course I can pay for it." You try to get something done in Seattle with that attitude, and you'll be *blocked.* The scene was the same way. Seattle also had this scene where people in the audience would talk to the band, and the bands would talk back to them. Where in L.A., people are trying so hard to be professional; you didn't really get that sort of thing.

BRAD SINSEL: I think a pivotal thing that happened is Seattle stopped taking its cue from outward. We stopped drawing on other people's ideas for a moment, but we also created a hell in the process. It was a great revolution, but in the end, what did we do? Kim [Thayil] — who's a really nice guy — but in his arrogance of being early in the game of success, said to the world, "We put the final nail in the coffin of butt rock." And my thought was, "*How dare you.* You borrowed heavily vocally from Dio, and musically from early Sabbath." As you follow their stuff further down the road, it's like, "OK, now it's starting to sound like Foreigner — what happened to all this musical revolution?"

When "the great revolution" occurred, I was signed to Columbia at the time under War Babies — that was the last deal I did before I left the business. I remember the A&R guy, Nick Turzo — who was Alice's A&R guy — had set up a radio thing in Seattle, where we were going to go out with the Columbia or Sony radio guy. He said, "Warrant is in town. I know we're doing dinner — would you mind them coming?" I went, "Sure, why not." We go to Benihana's, and the guys from Warrant show up — their hair is big. "How's it going?" "Oh, great!" I start pouring a little sake, and all of a sudden, "Y'know . . . *things aren't so great.*" The guy fucking fell apart on me!

JEFF GILBERT: You know what else really connected the dots between the metal crowd and the grunge crowd? Kirk Hammett from Metallica. Huge Nirvana and Melvins fan. Would talk about them in the Metallica fan club newsletters — collected everything Sub Pop put out. He might as well have just opened the floodgates — the metal guys go, "Well, if Kirk Hammett likes it, of course we do." Kirk was a great sales tool for Sub Pop, without even knowing it. Huge Mudhoney fan. In fact, when Metallica played at the Key Arena here in town, they had that "Snake Pit," where you could go in and be onstage with Metallica. Kirk got all the guys from Mudhoney and Nirvana in there. Kirk would keep coming over, and handing beers down to Matt Lukin. Matt would start slugging them, and Kirk yelled over, "Share it!"

DYLAN CARLSON: All of this weird focus on Seattle. Suddenly, there was press, and people moving to Seattle to start bands. People that you knew were gone more and more, because they were on tour. MTV showed up at all different shows with cameras. Even [Earth] got interviewed by Tabitha Soren.

LIBBY KNUDSON: [MTV] interviewed Mark and Steve, and I think Mark is like, "Isn't grunge the stuff in your kitchen sink?"

MEGAN JASPER: "Grunge" became a normal word, which grossed everybody out.

ART CHANTRY: I hate that word — that's a marketing term, not a descriptive.

JACK ENDINO: "Grunge" is just another term for a certain kind of classic hard rock. I don't really see a discontinuity; I see a continuation of styles that began in the '70s, continuing as a thread really, that was interrupted by new wave in the early '80s. But to younger people who didn't live through the '70s, they would see this thing happening in the late '80s and early '90s, and think, "This is a whole new phase of rock 'n' roll, we'll call it something new ... *we'll call it 'grunge.'*" And it really wasn't. It was a resurgence of classic rock — with classic rock song structures, chord sequences, melodies. All the ingredients

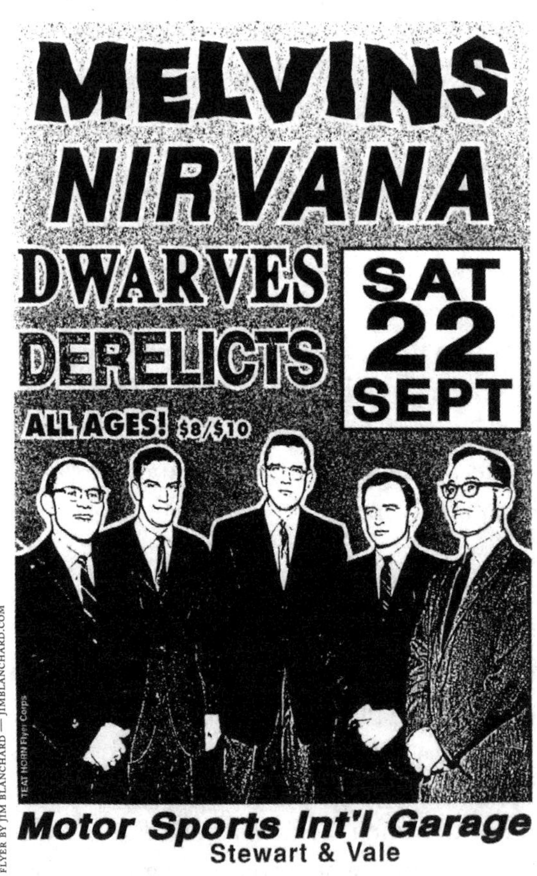

FLYER BY JIM BLANCHARD — JIMBLANCHARD.COM

Middle-aged/bespeckled businessmen really dug the Melvins and Nirvana

of classic '70s rock, with maybe a little bit of '80s punk rock attitude thrown into the recipe. Nobody dressed funny, and nobody had funny haircuts . . . nobody had *any* haircuts [laughs].

But I feel a little strange about the "grunge" thing, because nobody's quite sure who was the first person in Seattle to be using the term. I've discovered belatedly, years later, there's some circumstantial evidence that it might have been me. I've also seen evidence that it may have been some other people. Lester Bangs used the term as early as 1972. I could show you an article he wrote about the Groundhogs in 1972 where he used the term grunge. And the Groundhogs fucking sounded like Mudhoney — just by coincidence. I don't know where it came from, I just think it was a term — my mom would use it to describe the stuff in the drain in the kitchen. What's that stuff in your bellybutton, y'know? It was not an unknown word, it's not like someone made up the word, it was just a descriptive word for something really dirty and nasty. "Get the grunge out of that pan, scrub the grunge out of the bathtub." You think of the first couple of Stooges records in a lot of ways as being proto-grunge.

LIBBY KNUDSON: To this day, I still go, "*Huh*? Those stinky boys . . . what?" I don't know if I'm the only person — I still shake my head in shock. Who would have thought?

EMILY RIEMAN: I moved back in '91, and it actually really sucked. I came home, didn't even recognize the skyline, traffic had doubled — I think the whole Microsoft thing was happening. Everybody was moving here for all kinds of reasons. I had this notion that I would go back and hang out with my old friends. It just wasn't like that anymore. You couldn't even get on the guest list. You couldn't even get a fucking ticket to a Mudhoney show, unless you were "in the know" or brownnosing somebody.

I've got this distinct memory — my roommate when I lived in Seattle was Jim Tillman, and he was in Love Battery. Love Battery was playing at the Off Ramp. He said, "I'll put you on the guest list." I go down to the show, and he forgot to put me on the list. And it was totally no big deal, it slipped his mind. I still thought, "Maybe if I stick my head in, I can see somebody I know who can go find Jim for me, and get me in." But it was crazy — this show turned out to be sold out. I remember old friends of mine walking past me, and they wouldn't even give me the fucking time of day. They were just whipping past me, because it was so important to get in that show, be VIP, be who's who, and where it's at. I was just *appalled.* I remember that night going, "GET ME OUT OF SEATTLE AGAIN! I HATE IT HERE!"

DAVID MEINERT: Around '91, police started using [the Teen Dance Ordinance] on rock shows. As the Seattle rock scene blew up, I think it made the powers that be in the city scared, and they wanted to shut it down. So they used the Teen Dance Ordinance, saying, "When kids are moshing, they're dancing — this law applies to them." I worked at the Odd Fellows Hall, and Mudhoney was playing a show. The police surrounded the building with riot gear, came in, and said we had to shut down because kids were dancing. We're like, "*It's a Mudhoney show* — they're not really dancing." They're like, "It looks like dancing to me." And that was at the height of moshing. They really started to go after all-ages clubs at that point — rock clubs and punk shows. That turned into a big battle that we eventually won . . . but not until 2001.

ED FOTHERINGHAM: People were taking the piss out of everybody. There's that story of the *New York Times* writing a fluff piece about "grungy Seattle." They wanted a youth lexicon, and they called up [Megan Jasper] at Sub Pop — she was the receptionist at the time. She spun this bullshit, and it got published! And this is the most venerable paper in the world. That was a victory for Seattle.

MEGAN JASPER: I remember thinking it was a joke that someone was playing on me. Because it's too dumb of a question, for someone to say, "Share the grunge lexicon." Dude, *come on.* When I realized it was a real phone call from a real reporter, I figured I should have fun with it, and make a joke about it. I tried to give more and more whacky grunge synonyms, thinking that the reporter would go, "Oh, come on!" But that never happened. Then I thought, "That story will just end internally at the *New York Times*, because someone's going to read that, and say, 'This is retarded.'" All I could hear was the sound of the keyboard — the reporter was so busy accurately trying to get the information. I'm sure he's a smart enough guy, but his brain was turned off. He just became part of the telephone wire — my words went directly into the keyboard, and it skipped his brain.

ART CHANTRY: We clipped that thing off the front page of the *New York Times*. Daniel House at C/Z put it on T-shirts, and people were wearing them around town. It was really hilarious. But the more and more outsiders came here to partake of the explosion, after a while, *those words became real.* You'd walk down the street, and people were actually using those slang terms. And then years later, *Harsh Realm* becomes a TV show, for Christ's sake! Then you begin to realize the power of what happened. Here's this scene that didn't exist, that was created as a hype. It was a fraud — it didn't exist. And then, it became real. And then out of it, it became a vehicle for enormous talent that had been pent up in this crappy little part of the world forever. It got a venue. These talents that had been living like rats up here in the Northwest for decades all of a sudden had a place to show their stuff. And *blam* — it's like they had the chops to back up the bullshit. It's one of those incredible moments.

JERRY CANTRELL: To see what it turned into — it was incredible. Turned the world on its ear — *the fucking planet*, dude. That's heavy [laughs]. Not me, not us, *all of us* — we all did it together, without doing it together. We were just doing our own thing. That's the beauty of it. It wasn't some planned thing — it just happened. And it happened because the shit was good.

CHAPTER 18

"If you can sell 40,000, they'll let you make another one": Pearl Jam, Temple of the Dog

Still reeling from the death of Andy Wood, ex–Love Bone bandmates Stone Gossard and Jeff Ament decided to continue to work together. On the recommendation of a mutual friend, singer Eddie Vedder was welcomed aboard — resulting in the formation of Pearl Jam. At the same time, a one-off tribute album was put together for Wood — Temple of the Dog.

JEFF AMENT: Not long after Andy died, Susan [Silver] and Kelly [Curtis] shared offices, and she mentioned that Chris [Cornell] had recorded a couple of songs that pertained to Andy, and wanted us to hear them. I hooked up with Chris, and he gave me a tape — I was blown away. I thought initially that he could just release them like that and they would have been great. The demos of "Reach Down" and "Say Hello 2 Heaven" are really not that much different than what ended up on the record [1991's *Temple of the Dog*]. Chris had all these songs together, and there were a couple that Stone had — we knocked them out in five or six days. We were down and out, and those guys picked us up for a minute, and helped us out. It was pure music, it wasn't anything else.

Right around that time, I ran into Mike McCready. He said he'd been playing with Stone, and I needed to come over and check out what they were working on. As soon as I started playing with Stone and Mike, it seemed like that was more what I wanted to do. At every party I went to, Mike was playing guitar in the corner of the room — I just remember him *shredding*.

I've never been across the room from somebody that could play blues and Hendrix that well. He and Tim DiJulio also helped keep me alive by flowing me leftover pizza at Piecora's, which was right across the street from my apartment.

Things happened pretty quickly after that with Stone. I think we practiced together a few times, he and I hung out, had dinner — talked about what we wanted to do. Because the end of Mother Love Bone wasn't that creative — it was super passive-aggressive. I remember saying, "I want to be able to throw out ideas and not get laughed at. We should be able to play whatever we want." That was probably the main thing we took into Pearl Jam — we wanted to be a really good, diverse band. We wanted to be able to play a country song, a hardcore song, or a groovy, mid-tempo rock song.

REGAN HAGAR: I remember feeling like, "Alright, Stone and Jeff, *I know you can do this.*" They were "the Paul and Gene" of Seattle — very matter-of-fact.

JERRY CANTRELL: I always liked Jeff a lot — he was a real business-oriented guy. A serious individual. Really into the graphic art part of the band, as well as the musical direction.

KRISHA AUGEROT: Stone is one of my best friends — one of the funniest guys I know, in a different way. He's not self-conscious — he's very open and smart. He's your classic smart, funny guy, who isn't your typical rock star in any way. He remained himself through his entire career. Stayed true to himself — he has all the same friends.

JEFF AMENT: Stone and I were in Los Angeles, promoting the Mother Love Bone record — which was a horrible, arduous task. I don't think it was something that either one of us wanted to do, but we felt that we wanted Andy's legacy to be heard. Somehow through [Michael Beinhorn], we got in contact with Jack Irons — who we loved as a drummer. We heard that he had quit the Red Hot Chili Peppers. Got his number, and ended up meeting him down there. Gave him a tape, and didn't hear from him for three months.

One of us finally called [and asked] if he was interested, and he said, "Nah — I have this other band, Eleven. I've known these guys all my life and I've got to do this." I remember one of the last things I said to him was, "If you know another drummer that plays like you — or if you know a singer — that's where we're at right now." Within a month or so, Jack called back and said, "I've become friends with this kid from San Diego. He's got a lot of energy, and I think he'd be perfect for what you guys are doing." So we got his address, sent him a tape, and within four or five days, I got the tape back with "Once," "Alive," and "Footsteps."

EDDIE VEDDER: I got this tape through Jack Irons, who I had become friends with while he was playing drums with Joe Strummer, on [the] *Earthquake Weather* tour. I started hanging out with Jack, and we went on this camping trip with a bunch of guys through Yosemite — Flea; John; Dix Denny; Nicky Beat, who played in the Germs; Dick Rude, who just made a documentary about Joe Strummer [2006's *Let's Rock Again!*] and was in a band called Two Free Stooges; Cliff Martinez, who was one of the Peppers' drummers. This really cool gathering of the underground Los Angeles scene. This twelve-day trip — or maybe it was six days and twelve guys, I can't remember. Just hiking and backpacking out into no man's land. One of the greatest trips *ever.*

When I got to Jack's house in L.A., he gave [the tape] to me — I played it on the way home to San Diego. Then I'm sure I went right to work. I was a glorified security guard/gas station attendant doing midnight shifts. I had been doing midnight shifts for quite a while — maybe five or six years. I'd also work three shifts at this club called the Bacchanal. I had the music in my head. I went out for a bit of a surf in the morning, and then wrote the songs in this shack that I had a four-track sitting in. I sent the tape off that day — my version of three songs. Two days later, I saw a little article in *Rolling Stone*, that had a picture. I think it was Bruce, Stone, and Jeff. It was the first time I could put a face to it.

JEFF AMENT: It was so much more intense than anything we'd ever done. I remember when he came to Seattle, the thing he told me before he left was, "When I get there, I want to go straight to the rehearsal studio and play. I don't want to hang out and chit-chat."

EDDIE VEDDER: I had no business making any demands — but I felt it was a gentle one.

JEFF AMENT: That's all we did for about a week — we'd take a break once or twice a day and go eat, and the rest of the time we're in the Potatohead basement, working on songs. On the sixth day, we went in and recorded the ideas we had. We played them all at the Off Ramp on the seventh day, and then he went back to San Diego. We were buzzing — I remember not being sure of what had just happened. During that whole process, we wiggled our way out of the PolyGram deal that Stone and I were still signed to. We knew it was good the first day that we played. It felt like the kind of band that I would want to see. And I knew Ed was the type of guy who would have my back if I was getting my ass kicked . . . I don't know if I had felt that way in other bands — i.e., the Detroit Samhain show.

EDDIE VEDDER: I took a week off work and did that. I was excited, because it was a kind of music that I hadn't really heard before. I could hear things in it. When the vocal got on there with some of the songs, it felt like something different. I was thinking, "We'll play a song — one of the ones they've heard, or one of the ones I've just written," because I'd written three more before I got up there. And . . . they were more concerned with the drummer! [Laughs.] This guy Dave Krusen. They'd talk to Dave for ten minutes, or try maybe a half hour to figure out a part or a bridge. I'd say, "What about my bit there?" "Oh that's great, that's fine — let's do it again." I was looking for some reinforcement one way or another, so I could work on it. By the end of six days, we had probably ten songs — maybe eleven.

JEFF AMENT: There was never any doubt in my mind that he was the singer for us. He was *so* into it — so dedicated and uninhibited when we were playing. The first time you play with people, it usually takes three or four times until it feels right. With him, it all locked right away.

SUSAN SILVER: Kelly and I were in New York. We were waiting for some Alice meeting, and he played me this cassette. This guy, Eddie, had put some melody and lyrics to this song — it was "Alive" — and I go, "Oh my God, *it's amazing.*"

KRISHA AUGEROT: Kelly's relationship is really tight with the band. Kelly is not your classic businessman/manager. He's very personable, it's a very democratic situation — they all decide what's going to go on. He's more like a representative of the band — like a sixth member. Pearl Jam is really his number one priority, and always will be. He's not looking to become a corporation, where he's managing all these acts and making millions. He's just devoted to Pearl Jam.

I remember when Eddie first came to Seattle. The first time I met him, was at a party down in the Pike Place Market — I don't remember whose house it was at. He stood out a little bit, because his whole style was different. He had a long, grown out Mohawk thing, that hadn't been cut in three years or something [laughs]. It wasn't a mullet, it was a Mohawk. I guess it was [a] really early "grunge look" — tie-dyed big pants and a hat. He was really sweet — very personable.

Eddie likes to be one-on-one with somebody. If he meets you at a party, he would take you to a corner, or sit down somewhere and have an intimate conversation with you. People were drawn to him for that, because he would really focus on you and have this talk. He was back and forth during that time, then he moved up here, and he was staying in their practice space — below an art gallery on First Avenue. Living there — perfectly content. He was nice, friendly — also very funny.

SUSAN SILVER: They were getting to know Eddie, so they brought him in to the studio, and he sang on "Hunger Strike."

EDDIE VEDDER: It was during that same week that I was up there. Day four maybe, or day five, they did a Temple rehearsal after our afternoon rehearsal. I got to watch these songs, and watch how Chris was working, and watch Matt play drums. It got to "Hunger Strike" — I was sitting in the corner, putting duct tape on a little African drum. About two-thirds of the way through, he was having to cut off the one line, and start the other. I'm not now, and certainly wasn't then, self-assured or cocky, but I could hear what he was trying to do, so I walked up to the mic — which I'm really surprised I did — and sang that other part, "Going hungry, going hungry." The next time I was up, he asked if I'd record it — so it was just me and Chris in the same studio that we made [1991's] *Ten* record. I really like hearing that song. I feel like I could be real proud of it — because one, I didn't write it, and two, it was such a nice way to be ushered onto vinyl for the first time. I'm indebted to Chris time eternal for being invited onto that track.

MATT CAMERON: A&M really liked [*Temple of the Dog*] and put it out there — so it was once again, organically produced.

SUSAN SILVER: They went in the studio, and eleven days later, came out with that *entire album*. It was just an unbelievable, cathartic experience. An amazing record — a big, powerful record.

XANA LA FUENTE: Chris gave me pretty much the first copy of it. I loved it — I still love it. I'm just not happy about the fact that they made money off of it — I think they could have asked Kevin and Brian to be on it. I know they have some hard feelings about that.

KEVIN WOOD: Me and Brian were bummed that we didn't get asked to play on it. I never really listened to it until I had to go to Italy last year, and they asked me to learn some of the songs. Otherwise, it struck too close to home for me to go out and buy it, or even listen to it. You pick yourself up, you go on, and then somebody says, "I wrote a song about your brother, and it's really sad." "OK, well, don't play it, buddy, *I don't want to hear it*." Chris and all those guys who played on it are awesome musicians and did a wonderful job.

GRANT ALDEN: I was in L.A. on the A&M lot, which were the Chaplin Studios. I was picking up an advance of the *Temple of the Dog* record, and Rick Gershon, Soundgarden's publicist, had this promo photo. He said, "Grant — who the hell is this Eddie Vedder guy, *and why is he in my picture?*"

EDDIE VEDDER: The end of the week I was there, I think day six, we played a show. And day seven we recorded the ten songs that we had — maybe it was twelve. Then I went back, and it seemed like all a blur, but I had this tape — which was not just the instrumental tape now. It had the whole deal going on. So we played a show on day six, and that was at the Off Ramp. That was in late October — I'm guessing.

JIM BLANCHARD: I saw the Mookie Blaylock show, before they were Pearl Jam, at the Off Ramp and hated it. They're great musicians, super-professional, talented, charismatic. You can tell they're on their way to becoming superstars, but don't ask me to like it. It's the vibe they were mining — it brought back memories of all those awful '80s heavy metal bands that we sought out to destroy. It had a little bit more passion going, but it wasn't that different.

STU HALLERMAN: I remember leaving that show, and for months afterwards I would tell people, "I have a favorite new unknown band in Seattle, these guys Mookie Blaylock" [Pearl Jam's original name].

EDDIE VEDDER: The first show was interesting because we opened for I don't know who — we snuck on this bill. During sound check — of which we were the last band to sound check, since we were the first one on — I had my eyes closed. We had only one song to play before they opened doors. I kept my eyes closed and sang the song — I don't know if it was "Release" or "Even Flow." The club's empty, I sing the song, I open my eyes right at the last bit of music is playing, and the club's half full. They had opened doors. It's kind of an interesting analogy of just what it was being ushered into Seattle, and the kind of interest Stone and Jeff already had in their group, and me getting to share in that. After years of playing to ten or fifteen people that you had to coax and call to get to show up, it was interesting to start a song with your eyes closed, wake up, and there was a crowd. It wasn't lost on me — having a crowd was a new experience [laughs].

After the show, I was getting some positive reinforcement from a few folks that I knew were part of the family and scene. Cornell coming up to me, and he just happened to be standing under a black light. He was talking to me, and his eyes and his teeth were glowing — *he absolutely looked like Satan.* He was saying he thought it was great, and was happy for Jeff and Stone. Andy was a friend of his and this felt like a good thing. To hear it from Chris, especially from his connection with Andy . . . but to hear it from *Satan* at the same time, it left a really strong impression.

SUSAN SILVER: [Alice in Chains] filmed the show [at the Moore Theatre in December 1990], and that was the show that this new band opened for them. Everyone was still reeling from Andy's death — it had been nine months, but it was such a shock. They hadn't really played out yet. The band came on, and Chris carried Eddie onto the stage — he was on his shoulders or something. It was another one of those super powerful moments, where it was a big healing for everybody. He came out as this guy who had all the credibility in the world — in terms of people in Seattle — and Malfunkshun and Mother

Love Bone were loved bands. Andy was such an endearing personality. It's a hard thing to do — to show up after people die. And Chris bringing Eddie out, and pointing at him, as much to say, "*This is your guy now.*"

JIM SORENSON: [Eddie] was nowhere near as over-the-top as Andy had been. He was much more intense.

REGAN HAGAR: Andy was a coliseum-big-arena-rock-guy, Mark Arm was an Iggy Pop–small-club-guy. Vedder came in, and it was like, "Wow, they got another 'Iggy guy.'" Because he was flailing around, breaking shit, climbing on stuff — it's exciting when you're in a little place and somebody's going ape shit. So I enjoyed the energy Pearl Jam created since day one. There wasn't a build there — they put him in place, came out with a show that was on fire right away.

SCOTTY CRANE: When I did see those early Pearl Jam shows, I was blown away by Eddie Vedder. I was blown away by his stage presence. Eddie was *a wild animal* onstage — insane. He was fearless. It was like, "He's going to die!" The way he was jumping off huge things and throwing himself into the audience like a madman.

GRANT ALDEN: The next time I saw Eddie, he was at RKCNDY scaring the hell out of Epic executives, because he'd gone hand-over-hand up into the lighting rig, two stories up, with nothing but concrete underneath him. I remember seeing that show and thinking, "Boy, these are nice guys . . . it's too late, they're never going to happen." *Wrong again.*

JEFF AMENT: [Alice in Chains] were kind enough — they took us down the West Coast. We probably played about ten shows opening for them. That was huge at that point.

RIKI RACHTMAN: Alice in Chains played the Cathouse [and] brought Pearl Jam. They're like, "Can we let our friends open up? They're from Seattle too." Eddie Vedder was all over the place. I think he hit the microphones hanging from the ceiling — he might have broken some of those. He was climbing all over.

KIM THAYIL: There were a lot of strong hooks. When I first heard Pearl Jam, I saw them live. As much as I loved Andy and his stage presence, Eddie's voice and some of the melodies he was singing actually sent shivers up my spine. That's not an experience that I would have with any degree of regularity. It was his voice and the way he presented it. I thought, "There's something there too."

JEFF GILBERT: There wasn't anything loose or jammy about them. The songs had real solid structure. Very meticulously arranged. Choruses even [laughs]. These were actual songs you could hear on the radio.

ART CHANTRY: Pearl Jam was never considered really "a Seattle band" — they were "an industry product band." Nobody really respected Pearl Jam as a band. They liked the individuals and they were all their friends, but they were never really respected. Whereas Mudhoney was the real thing — they were like *fucking Iggy Pop* — beating their heads and doing all these crazy things. Really making an impact.

CHRIS PUGH: With Pearl Jam, pretty good songs — for me, it's mostly about Ed's singing. It's not that the rest of them aren't good players and songwriters, but his voice really carries that band. It's such a distinctive sound to it — passionate, provocative. And their live shows were really good too. They're rock stars, and they were from the get-go. It's not like they developed into them, they just had a lot of those necessary elements.

STEVE TURNER: I remember thinking it was a lot better than Mother Love Bone. I was excited to see them doing stuff.

EDDIE VEDDER: At this point, I'm done working at the gas station, I'm living in Seattle, and I think we're getting 700 bucks a month. I'm not really paying rent because I'm living in the basement of the little art gallery/artist space we were renting for practice. And every couple of days I'd go shower at Kelly Curtis's house, or sleep in his basement. I didn't have a lot of money saved, but I remember getting a certain amount of money for giving Matt Dillon guitar lessons [for the movie *Singles*]. So I did that, and they gave me a nice check — at least 500 bucks. And then I got another call, and they said, "We need you to come down right now — there's 500 bucks in it for you." So

I ran downtown, and they took Polaroids of my head — kind of mug shots, from the back as well — then they cut a big chunk of my hair out. I think I might have gotten 1,000 bucks for that. Then they made a wig for Matt Dillon. I think I also bought a twelve-string Rickenbacker, because a couple of the other guys were getting some guitars and amps for recording, and what did I need, a mic? It was on sale for 600 bucks. I thought that that was going to be what I got from making the record. The guitar that *Ten* got me. We had no idea it was going to be anything different.

JEFF AMENT: After the process we went through with Mother Love Bone, I didn't want to do that ever again. We decided we were going to spend a lot less money making *Ten* — we probably spent about half as much money as we did the Mother Love Bone record. We rehearsed really hard and recorded at a local studio [London Bridge] with Rick Parashar. Part of the compromise with Michael Goldstone at [Epic] was he wanted somebody to professionally mix it — we probably spent as much time in London, England, with Tim Palmer mixing, as we did making the record.

EDDIE VEDDER: If I remember right, our drummer at the time, Dave Krusen, I think [when] we recorded some of the songs, like "Even Flow," his wife or girlfriend was having a baby. We played the song, like, 120 times, because of the tempo. All I remember was singing it, thinking each take was going to be the one that ended up on the record. Trying to really sing it with everything I had. And not realizing that I would do the vocals *later*. I remember losing my [voice] a lot in the early days, because I was going for it at all times — thinking, "This could be the take."

JONATHAN PLUM: I did hear that Eddie was living on the couch [of the recording studio] for a while, when they were making the record.

CATHY FAULKNER: They were recording *Ten* — one of our former disc jockeys was down there when they were mixing, and I went to give him a ride home. Got to listen to some initial tracks. The first time I heard them and really thought, *"Oh my God,"* was in the studio. Instantly, I knew they were the real deal. They were raw, passionate, and there was a certain reckless abandon that Eddie had onstage that I hadn't seen a lead singer have in years. It was not only refreshing — it was infectious.

PIC BY MIKE LEACH — BESTROCKPHOTOS.COM

Pearl Jam's Jeff Ament and Eddie Vedder in Melkweg, Amsterdam, February 12, 1992

EDDIE VEDDER: Our record is getting mixed, and now it's getting ready to be put out. It was like, "What's the goal here?" There was the magic number of 40,000 — for some reason I remember that. "If you can sell 40,000, they'll let you make another one." I don't know if that was true or not — that was what we were being told. Then we made our "Alive" video and did a couple of things. It seemed like we were getting opportunities. You could start to feel the pot simmering.

CATHY FAULKNER: When they recorded the "Alive" video at RKCNDY, it was 120 degrees inside, but there wasn't a person you could talk into going outside and getting fresh air. They didn't want to turn it into "a Hollywood video shoot," so they just played it twice — at the beginning of the set and at the end. Whatever they got, they got.

EDDIE VEDDER: I think with the advent of MTV and us putting stage diving in "Alive," [it] was regretful, because then it was like training videos for how to jump in the crowd — like that was the mode of expression. It wasn't the same version that was happening at early Social D or X shows. It got to be a distorted MTV version, and now it was like every frat boy buying a pair of spikes from the corner novelty shop, putting spikes on their big white gym shoes, and doing it. And guys that were way too big to have any business landing on people. It got out of control real quick.

SEAN KINNEY: It was really amazing to hear that record before it came out. Just knowing it's going to be huge.

PETE DROGE: We did a show with them at the Off Ramp — it was after their album was out, or right before it was going to come out. They did an unannounced show, and they were fucking *so loud.* At that point, they'd been playing bigger places, and they were really firing on all cylinders. I remember having the impression, "These guys are *loaded for bear.*" Not only from the band really playing well together, but all the buzz and energy surrounding their ascent — success-wise and on an international scale. There was so much anticipation and titillation around that. I remember sitting there and watching them from the side of the stage — really super powerful. They sounded like a great rock band.

KRISHA AUGEROT: Dave Krusen was out early — he was out before they even went on tour. Matt Chamberlain played for a while — he came from the *Saturday Night Live* band. He was a little more like, "I need to be taken care of." It was more of a side project for him — even though they really liked him a lot and he was a great drummer. So they started auditioning drummers, and I could *not believe* when they hired Dave Abbruzzese. It didn't make any sense at all. I remember seeing him in the lobby of our office, and walking back to my house, going, "*Who is that dude?*" He was wearing a matching running suit and really long hair. He's a rocker from Texas. I'm like, "Is he that good? Because he doesn't fit in the band."

KIM THAYIL: The record came out — it was great to hear a lot of the songs, because there were so many great hooks that Stone came up with. And of course, "Jeremy," which was Jeff's riff. Initially when I heard the record, it didn't seem to have the immediacy of their performance live. They remixed a lot of the singles, and it had a better sound. If you listen to the radio or MTV mixes of those songs, they seem to be a lot better sounding than the record. *Ten* benefited ultimately from good singles mixes.

DUFF McKAGAN: That record was killer. It was more in line with what I was into — anything that wasn't fucking Whitesnake or White Lion.

CHARLES PETERSON: At the time, I really did not like the first Pearl Jam record, which is funny, because a couple of years back, I started listening to it again, and I was like, "Some of this stuff is pretty good." Part of it is your mindset at that age, being oversaturated with stuff — I always was more into being on the cutting edge of things. That said, back in those days, the few times I did see Pearl Jam play, I was totally blown away. It's that when I was home, I didn't reach for "Jeremy" to put on the turntable. *Superfuzz Bigmuff* spoke to me more than *Ten*.

ROBERT ROTH: I don't want to sound snobby, but I *was* a snob at the time, so why not — it wasn't punk rock, it wasn't underground, it wasn't rebellious to me. I saw it as being very mainstream. Now had I been living in the Midwest and was bored with everything on MTV, and didn't realize there was all this other cool stuff going on, maybe I would have been charged by it too. I mean, they imported their singer from San Diego, they had auditions. It just seemed like a weird kind of way to go about it. It wasn't quite the organic, "from the streets" thing that the other bands were.

EDDIE VEDDER: We had two options that were being looked into. One was a European tour with the Cult, or this tour [in] support of the latest Chili Peppers record [1991's *Blood Sugar Sex Magik*], and do the States with them and the Smashing Pumpkins. We were lucky, because the Peppers allowed us that option, and we were able to go on tour with them, instead of the Cult. And the one thing at the time too — I didn't know if I would ever get to see Europe. So it wasn't as much the Cult, it was, "Am I passing up my only chance to go to Europe in my life?" But if it wasn't for that Chili Peppers tour . . . that really helped us reach a crowd.

MARK ARM: We met with an A&R guy who said, "This Nirvana record is doing well now, but the one that's *really* going to blow up is the Pearl Jam record." We thought he was nuts because we'd heard the record once, and nothing jumped out to us the way that "Smells Like Teen Spirit" or "In Bloom" did. Lo and behold, he was right.

EDDIE VEDDER: A lot of what Seattle was — "Don't try." That's what's on Bukowski's gravestone, "Don't try." So, the first time I didn't try, everything just opened right up and said, *"Come on in."*

CHAPTER 19

"A 'testosterone period'": Alice in Chains, Soundgarden

The first grunge album to hit big was Alice in Chains' debut, *Facelift*, while Soundgarden broke through with their second major label album, *Badmotorfinger*. But each band reacted differently to its initial success.

DAVE DEDERER: [Alice in Chains] was the best of all those bands. *Just the songs.* They had the most distinctive sound — in terms of taking it in a new direction. Jerry and Layne's harmonies. Jerry's probably the best guitarist from that whole era by miles.

KRISHA AUGEROT: Jerry is super loyal — very talented musician. He was responsible for ninety percent of those songs. I remember him playing me eight-track versions of all the songs on [1990's] *Facelift*. They were exactly the same — it wasn't like they went in the studio and rewrote anything. It was those really catchy riffs — really impressive. With Layne singing, it was just an amazing band.

SUSAN SILVER: They'd lived a pretty crazy rock 'n' roll life, so they were ready to buckle down and start working hard. The only one that was difficult to manage was the original bass player — he had that notion that if you sign a major record deal, you can go and spend a lot of money. The rest of the guys were really great about being money conscious and realizing that the money you get is *your* money, and the way you spend it is going to be how much you have at the end. Dave Jerden produced that record — he was no help in terms of having them be money conscious. He would say, "Just go to the music store and *get it.* Tell them to put it on your bill." We had a few rounds. They made it in L.A.

YANNI "JOHNNY" BACOLAS: With regard to their success, I think that [Layne] was happy. He was similar to me — he wanted to make Mom proud, and show everyone what he's accomplished. "Look at me, I'm not a bum." Because he had lived in cars for a long time — doing odd jobs before they got signed — and I think he got a lot of judgment from his parents. Then all of a sudden, he gets a deal with Columbia Records. He had a different vibe about him.

SEAN KINNEY: I played [Alice's debut, *Facelift*] with a broken hand — I broke my hand right before. I almost didn't play on the record — they started rehearsing with the drummer from Mother Love Bone, Greg Gilmore. I was sitting there playing with one hand, guiding him through it. Dave Jerden came in and they started to try to do it. He was like, "Screw it — pull the plug. This is not going to be the same." Luckily, we took a tiny bit of time off. I had that cast on for a while, and was like, "I can't miss this." I cut my cast off in the studio and kept a bucket of ice by the drum set. Kept my hand iced down and played with a broken hand. I tried not to do that again — your first big break, and you fuck it up.

NANCY LAYNE McCALLUM: Layne called me one day after he'd given me *Facelift* and said, "So, what do you think about the tape?" And I said, "I think there's a sleeper on that album" — a song that was going to creep up on people. "It's called 'Man in the Box.'" And he said, "Mom, *I wrote that song.*" I said, "Layne, it's so beautiful." But I didn't know *he* was the man in the box. I'm sure he just kept wanting me to get it.

KRISHA AUGEROT: Alice in Chains — I hung out with that scene in particular one summer. I don't remember exactly what year it was, but I was dating Jerry off and on, and hanging out with Demri [Layne Staley's girlfriend]. We'd all go to the beach every day during that summer at Magnuson Park, hang out, then have a barbeque at a friend's house. It was this constant party for the summer. It was a very free, loving time. I remember when they got

PIC BY KAREN MASON-BLAIR — KARENMASONBLAIR.COM

Alice in Chains (L-R: Mike Starr, Layne Staley, Jerry Cantrell, Sean Kinney)

their first tour bus. Alice in Chains played a show [at the Vogue]. Waiting outside when they got done was this big tour bus that had a Corvette or some cheesy thing airbrushed on the side. It was probably one of the cheapest buses they could get, because it was so dated. But they were so psyched — everyone got on the bus. They were ready to take off and be rock stars.

JERRY CANTRELL: We were a great live band. We had a lot of energy — Layne was an amazing front man. Me, Mike, and Sean were like Tasmanian devils — headbanging, spinning all over the fucking place. Out of all the bands, I always admired our ability to not only play the stuff well, but to bring *a show* — and to get that energy to translate on a stage. At the same time, we had a "fuck it" attitude. If we got a gig that nobody else would take — like, Soundgarden's not going to go open for Poison in the Seattle Center Arena. But we would. We'll go play with *anybody* — that was our vibe. I don't care what style of music it is — we've got a gig to play in front of people, we're there. We opened up for Helix, Poison, Warrant — stuff that was on its way out, and also something that we had grown past.

MIKE INEZ: The first time I saw Alice in Chains, they were opening up in an empty Long Beach Arena — it was one of those KNAC radio shows with a hundred bands. I happened to be walking through the arena, looked up, and saw Alice in Chains. I was like, "This band is *amazing*." I couldn't take my eyes off of Layne — he was such a compelling front man.

JERRY CANTRELL: Again, starting out with a real lame tour for us — opening up for Extreme for thirty days. *Jesus Christ.* A couple of the guys were cool, but there were others that had egos. At the end of that thirty days, we had enough. We had been playing to empty rooms too — they didn't have their "More Than Words" hit yet. We'd gotten attitude about what we could do, what we couldn't do on their stage. I remember there was no drinking or smoking onstage, because the singer did his set barefoot. So we drank, spilled shit all over the place, smoked. We were like, "What are you going to do, kick us off the tour? It's the last gig!" And Mike Starr would get a case of the nerves and puke. I think he had some beers in him, so he turned around and puked all over the drum set. That was our last gig with Extreme, and we went to Iggy Pop — so that was a nice step up.

GRANT ALDEN: We never did a big Alice in Chains story when I was at *The Rocket*, because I hated them. I did my very best to squelch their career. We can all see what a good job I did.

JERRY CANTRELL: I think the first gold record out of Seattle was *Facelift*.

CATHY FAULKNER: A lot of people nationally at radio stations were freaking out — not only by the band's name, but thinking that they were too hard. I would get calls from people in New York going, "Aren't you scared to play 'Man in the Box'?" It's like, "What is there to be scared of? It's fine!" That was my first memory of the band — other people initially at radio stations were scared to play it.

SUSAN SILVER: They'd gotten up to the level where they could play the Moore Theatre — which is 1,500. Alice played, and it was amazing. And it got filmed. Donny Ienner had the idea to bundle it for 40,000 copies with this concert video on VHS with *Facelift*, and that coincided with "Man in the Box" taking off at radio. A million records later, they were on the map.

JERRY CANTRELL: "Man in the Box" hit, and everything changed. When that song hit, we sold half a million records. I think we toured for eight fucking months, and sold 40,000 records. Then that song hit, and *boom*, there it went. As far as "Man in the Box" goes, I've had conversations with the record company about this, and everybody conveniently forgets the fact that nobody really liked that song [laughs]. They thought it was too slow and dirgey. There was some discussion about it maybe not being on the record, and we're like, "Fuck that — that song is killer."

SEAN KINNEY: I thought it would have been "Sea of Sorrow" more. I mean, there were other songs, like "Sunshine," that I thought would have been a bigger radio type of tune. That one just latched on for some reason. Somebody paid somebody somewhere! Isn't that how it works? Somebody pays somebody a shitload of money to play it all the time [laughs].

JERRY CANTRELL: "Man in the Box" hit in the middle of the Clash of the Titans tour — you talk about a tough fucking tour, opening up for Slayer, Megadeth, and Anthrax. They had a revolving headlining set, but still, Slayer's fans would out-chant any of the other fans in the arena. "*Slayer, Slayer, Slayer!*" I remember playing Red Rocks, and the place is built "up" — you could hit the stage with pretty much anything you throw from a certain distance. That was one of those landmark moments for the band. *We got fucking massacred, dude.* They started throwing stuff from the moment we came onstage. It was un-fucking-believable. We were playing just looking up — watching shit come down, trying to avoid it, without running off the stage. After a while of getting pelted with all this shit — I don't know how someone did this, but they snuck a gallon jug of some liquid, and they hocked this thing. It came down and crashed on Sean's set.

Layne got fucking pissed. He started grabbing shit and throwing it back at the audience. He jumped the barricades, and started spitting back — throwing shit and flipping people off, just like they had been doing to us. So we all did the same thing — we all followed Layne's lead. We got right in their face, started kicking the shit they were throwing at us right back in their faces. And we finished our set. We're like, "Fuck, man, we better get out of here — we're going to get killed." After that show, there were a bunch of Slayer fans out by the bus. We're like, "Oh shit, here we go." We walk up to the bus — they were blocking us from getting to the bus — and they're like, "You guys are alright. You guys didn't puss out."

EDDIE VEDDER: It was interesting to watch a band change the mood of people, 'cause we were doing our first little tour with them. Not really any backdrops or whatever — they were small places — but just with songs being able to change a mood, some of the darker stuff. Layne, you'd see him with sunglasses, you didn't really know what his eyes were doing — he wore sunglasses the whole tour, including playing and at night. If you were to take him from his lyrics, you thought, "Well, I certainly don't want to bother him with small talk." And it seemed hard to get to know him, but all you had to do was say two words. He's really gentle, incredibly warm, and childlike — in the best of ways. That seems so different than how you'd anticipate him being, or how you expected him to be from the songs.

NANCY LAYNE McCALLUM: Alice in Chains opened for almost all of Layne's heroes. I remember he told me one of the guys had admired Eddie Van Halen's cowboy boots, and Eddie then bought them a pair. Sometimes Layne would name somebody he was opening for, and other than maybe having heard the name, I wouldn't have the faintest idea who they were. Sorry to tell you, Iggy! [Laughs.] I had a job to do. I had a family I was raising. We have great humor in our family, but I was serious about doing a good job of raising my children. If it's bad pride, than I apologize, but I'm very prideful about raising your own children — I really believe in it. So, that was Layne's world. And yes, he ran names by me, and I was thrilled for him, because he was thrilled. It was extremely difficult to communicate with the band, because they weren't available . . . no e-mail, no cell phones. They were in different time zones, they were in different countries, they were busy because they were at a photo shoot, an interview, on a plane, touring, and traveling.

JERRY CANTRELL: I remember going to New York City — I went with Layne. I think coincidentally, it's the week I started smoking [laughs]. Our album was on the cover of *Billboard Magazine*. I think we were there to do a press thing. Me and Layne picked up a couple of homeless guys that were hanging by our hotel. We got into a conversation with these guys, and we figured, "Fuck, we're doing good," so we invited the guys up to our suite. We had a kick-ass room, so we ordered all this room service and booze, and hung out with these two homeless dudes all night — and gave them train fare to get back to where they were going in the morning.

MATT FOX: When *Singles* was being shot in town, I was an extra. Alice did their thing at Pier 48, which is down on the waterfront, just south of the ferry terminal — big old pier. They did a shoot for the song "Would?" It looked like RKCNDY kind of. We all had fake beer — for atmosphere — and of course, some of us had brought in *other things*. It was a little party, and we got to see them lip-sync to "Would?" about twenty times. They had everybody show up at a parking lot at Seattle Center, and then they bussed everybody over there — to keep the mystery and keep it from being swamped with people.

VAN CONNER: Talk about debauchery — they made the rest of us look like Catholic schoolgirls! They were out of control, in a fun way too. But it served to their demise as a band, eventually.

YANNI "JOHNNY" BACOLAS: [Layne] told me that he started his "abuse" [during] the Van Halen tour. That's when he was introduced to heroin. I asked him, "How did this happen?" His exact words were, "Johnny, when [I] took that first hit, for the first time in my life, I got on my knees, and I thanked God for feeling good." From there, it just didn't stop.

MARK IVERSON: I saw [Nirvana] with Jason Everman, and then saw Soundgarden with Jason Everman. Then of course he left, and has to be the unluckiest man in show business.

MATT CAMERON: [Jason Everman] recorded one single with us. I guess it just didn't work out musically.

KIM THAYIL: He certainly could do the musical thing, but it wasn't keeping the band together. We were at a point where Chris and I realized, "I don't think we're going to be able to be on the road all the time." We really weren't identifying or behaving as a band. We had our moments where everything was great. But we weren't like four fingers curled up into one fist. We realized we had to make a decision. Chris's suggestion was Ben. He'd been thinking of Ben's ability and personality, and thought that could be the thing that gets us back to where we were — personally and creatively.

MATT CAMERON: We had actually auditioned him once, when we were auditioning bass players, and picked Jason. So after Jason didn't work out, we all figured, "*We chose the wrong guy!* Let's see if Ben is still interested." Luckily, he was.

KIM THAYIL: It certainly gave a creative and emotional punch. It was the spark we needed — we felt like a team, like brothers.

TRACY MARANDER: [Kurt Cobain] loved Soundgarden. At one point, when they were looking for another [bassist] — I think it's maybe when Ben Shepherd joined the band — he actually thought about quitting Nirvana. He wanted to try out for them, because he liked them that much.

TERRY DATE: Different dynamic — they were just two totally different personalities. Ben carries a lot of fire, whereas Hiro was more cerebral. It didn't change the band musically that much, other than Ben would bring in his own songs — a new style of songs. Ben had a different writing style than Hiro. It seemed like a really nice injection of a different song style than what they had. The band had done four records to that point, I think it was nice to have some fresh ideas come in.

BEN SHEPHERD: We rehearsed for a couple of weeks, then we went straight to touring in Europe. The first place I played was Copenhagen, at the Roskilde Festival. We did this three week tour, then we came home [and] had another tour all ready to go. It was like jumping right into the fire — it was awesome. So fucking fun. [A show at the New York's Beacon Theater with Danzig] was one of the best times we ever played "Beyond the Wheel." I met the guys from Queensrÿche and flipped them shit after. "Whoa, I've never seen anybody play bass like that before!" I was like, "Well, you've never seen us then. *Why are you talking to me?*" Then I went and hid in this room in the dark and smoked cigarettes.

KEN STRINGFELLOW: We opened for Soundgarden in Bumbershoot. Locally, they were really big. But nationally, still kind of "a club band" — but getting there. Typically, the headlining act of the festival would play the Coliseum, and Soundgarden was a headliner — but by accident. The Psychedelic Furs couldn't make it. They put Soundgarden in there — they really took a big risk on them. Y'know, 15,000 people — that's quite a stretch for Soundgarden at the time. But they really lived up to it — they did a great job. Spinal Tap had played Bumbershoot some years previously, and left their biggest prop there. Soundgarden hoisted this big horned skull with glowing eyes over their stage.

DAVID MEINERT: It seemed to be the show that tipped them over the top. It was the point where I knew there was something much bigger starting to happen, than just some great local rock bands.

SUSAN SILVER: It was more of a "testosterone period," somehow. Things were rolling so fast by that point.

MATT CAMERON: We rehearsed our asses off. We did a lot of [1991's *Badmotorfinger*] at our friend's studio, Avast! Our old soundman, Stuart Hallerman, let us hole up in his new studio for what seemed like months — at least three or four months — rehearsing these songs, working on music. So by the time we got down to Sausalito, California, we recorded at this place called Studio D — that was suggested to us by Faith No More. We used Terry Date again. We never really went into the city — we were very workmanlike. I think we recorded the bass and drums down there for two weeks, then we came up to Seattle again, and overdubbed the guitars and vocals at Bear Creek Studios in Woodinville, Washington. They had a really cool Jack Russell Terrier there. The sessions were pretty quick and efficient.

TERRY DATE: It was spring or summer — we were playing some game with a Frisbee. It wasn't normal Frisbee; it was some sort of full contact Frisbee. Two guys would get on either end of the field, someone would throw the Frisbee up in the air, and the other guy would throw the Nerf football at the guy trying to catch the Frisbee. I think you had to catch them both, or if you dropped them both — there were points involved. I have video of it. I remember Eddie Vedder came up, with the first test mixes of the first Pearl Jam record — being pretty concerned if it was any good or not.

MATT CAMERON: [*Badmotorfinger*] was a lot darker sounding. We got a heavier guitar sound, and we used Ron St. Germain to mix it. He did a lot of records we liked — *I Against I* by the Bad Brains. So he mixed the drums dry, and the bass is really loud — it was a cool sound. It's certainly different than *Louder Than Love*.

TERRY DATE: They felt *Louder Than Love* was a little too smooth — they wanted more of an edge. At the time, most of the stuff I was doing and what they were doing wasn't getting a whole lot of radio play. Nobody took it very seriously. Which gave us a lot of freedom to do whatever we wanted to do. I had no expectations — I knew it was a good record.

KIM THAYIL: We kind of knew prior to the album's release that ["Outshined"] was going to be slated as a single. I actually thought they'd work more on "Somewhere" or "Mind Riot." I don't know how big it was as a single — I wasn't a big radio listener or MTV watcher. I didn't get cable TV until '94 or '95. So when I saw our videos, it was on tour in a hotel.

SUSAN SILVER: That was the symbol of things changing in the industry, and the dedication of A&M to really help break Soundgarden. ["Outshined"] at a label with less support — maybe it wouldn't have gotten the sort of radio play, because the promotion staff wouldn't have been so focused on it, or the relationship with MTV wouldn't have been into play on that track. Amazing song and all the right circumstances surrounding it to have it promoted properly.

MATT CAMERON: We did a fucking eight-month Guns N' Roses tour around the States. Then we were in Europe with them for a while. Then we toured with Skid Row — we were in "the metal trenches" at that point, just fully paying our dues. We were like *the* opening act for '91–'92.

SUSAN SILVER: [The Guns N' Roses tour] was a call I got, that I was so excited to tell them about. I had a bunch of T-shirt designs in a box that I needed to show them. So I went to this studio that they were at — Avast! — doing some B-sides. I get there and I can barely contain myself. "Guys, guess what? You got offered the Guns N' Roses tour today!" *Dead silence*. Finally, Kim pipes in. "What's in the box?"

SCOTTY CRANE: Axl Rose name-dropped Chris Cornell in *Rolling Stone* as "a great singer to look out for . . . from some band in Seattle called Soundgarden." I'm paraphrasing, but that was the gist.

COLLEEN COMBS: I really loved a lot of the music that was coming out of Seattle, and every once in a while, Axl would ask me to pick up new music for him — when I was working for him. So I gave him all the Soundgarden stuff, and also Nirvana. Did anyone ever tell you the story of him crowd surfing at

PIC BY MIKE LEACH — BESTROCKPHOTOS.COM

Soundgarden's Kim Thayil, Chris Cornell, and Matt Cameron at Tivoli in Utrecht, Netherlands, March 21, 1992

a Soundgarden show? It was like a Concrete Convention gig in Los Angeles. I was at that show — I missed him crowd surfing — but I experienced some of the fallout the next day, because he lost his wallet [laughs]. I don't know why, but Axl's a little bit older than me, and he always seemed like an adult to me. When I heard that he was crowd surfing, it seemed to me that he was too old to do it. In my mind, Seattle was, like, everybody was so much younger — which isn't true — but by this time, it seemed like Axl was a rock star and established. He was supposed to go over there with Aerosmith and the Rolling Stones, and he shouldn't be part of anything to do with Seattle.

SUSAN SILVER: Once they got on the tour, they were treated so well — the Guns N' Roses crew was incredible, and everyone was really accommodating. The hospitality was just great. It didn't take long before the Guns N' Roses crew dubbed them "Frowngarden" [laughs].

BEN SHEPHERD: We had a blast, man. Because the whole crew of theirs and their whole band are really fucking nice. Me, I'm like a punk rocker fuckup, and I'm all cantankerous — my nickname was "Manimal" back then. We weren't rock stars; we're not like that. Totally like the kids you'd think we'd be. And I'm all grumpy — "Goddamn it, these guys are nice, I can't even hate 'em! I hate their music, but they're nice." Same thing with Skid Row — fucking hated their music, they knew it, but they're all so cool. Pissed me off, now I don't even have a reason to be pissed off. What the hell is this? My life is going to shit and it's beautiful at the same time! I didn't have a home life anymore — that's what happens when you tour all the time. But you've got to go for it when you have a chance.

KIM THAYIL: When we toured with Guns N' Roses, we alienated some of our Sub Pop/punk rock/indie fans. They thought, "Soundgarden was on the fence — kind of punk rock, kind of metal. But now they're touring with Guns N' Roses, they fall into that side of the fence." It's like, "No, *we didn't.*" At that time, who were we supposed to tour with? When we signed up to tour with Guns N' Roses, Nirvana wasn't bigger than us yet. Who was there in that genre for us to tour with, that we could open up for, and play cities that we couldn't command ourselves? A lot of the cities we hit with Guns N' Roses and Skid Row were places that we probably couldn't have gotten gigs ourselves. We weren't big enough to get a gig in Omaha. We could play a small club perhaps, but promoters wouldn't have taken a chance with us, necessarily. It was an opportunity for us to play in front of a larger audience. Those tours were certainly a lot of fun. I think in retrospect, everyone understands it now. But back then, some people thought it was weird that we were taking that tour.

BEN SHEPHERD: That whole year of *Badmotorfinger* seemed like "*Whooom!* Where did it go?" It was like stepping into a fucking dragster and going for it.

CHAPTER 20

"You guys will be bigger than Hüsker Dü": Nirvana and *Nevermind*

It took one specific album to open the grunge floodgates, and Nirvana's classic *Nevermind* was it. By the end of 1991, Nirvana was one of the biggest rock bands on the planet, with unexpected superstardom bestowed upon them.

CHAD CHANNING: Half the songs that came out on [1991's] *Nevermind* were songs we recorded with Butch Vig, that was to be the next album for Sub Pop. But we didn't know at the time — at least *I* didn't know — that Sub Pop was talking to Geffen. A deal was made that this wouldn't be quite a Sub Pop release, and Geffen would take over and put out the album. They ended up doing that — but rerecorded the album.

CRAIG MONTGOMERY: Them firing Chad was way before *Nevermind* came out — before they [re-]recorded it. I was disappointed, because we liked Chad. They liked Chad personally, but there were times — like in the earlier tours — where you could see Kurt frustrated with Chad if he would drop a beat. Chad would be the first one to tell you that he wasn't the most solid drummer in the world.

SCOTTY CRANE: My memory of Chad and Nirvana was that he didn't think they were really going to do anything. In all honesty, a lot of people felt that way. They were amazing to see live, but I don't think even Sub Pop at first thought they were going to be anything. Cool songs, great performance — that was about it.

CHAD CHANNING: Everybody's heard things like, "He left" or "He was fired" — it was actually a combination of both. I was hoping to get the opportunity to chip in with some songwriting. After *Bleach*, Kurt talked about it — he wouldn't mind having some help [with] writing. And of course being a songwriter, I was like, "I'm all for that." But over time I realized that wasn't going to happen. What slowly happened was I just started losing my inspiration to play — it shows. Ultimately, I didn't give them much choice but to kick me out of the band.

DALE CROVER: I played some shows with those guys when they were getting attention. We opened for Sonic Youth on a West Coast tour. They were talking about having me play on the record, but then they decided they were getting Danny from Mudhoney.

NILS BERNSTEIN: There was that period where Dan Peters was in Nirvana, and I thought they were amazing with him. He's such an interesting, distinctive drummer. That was a really exciting period — right between *Bleach* and *Nevermind.*

KURT DANIELSON: We were demoing songs with Jack. During our lunch break, Nirvana came in — Krist, Kurt, and Dan — and recorded "Sliver." That's a little known fact — all the amps and drums are Tad equipment. We were only too happy to let them use the gear, because Krist brought a big spleef and we smoked it. They did that in three or four hours — diligent and workmanlike, no bullshit in the studio. They were just like everybody else — even humbler. I think Kurt was the humblest person I ever met — at the same time, a complex person.

JON AUER: The first song that really did it for me was "Sliver," probably because it reminded me of the Replacements — one of my all-time faves. Only amped-up with a serious metal edge, which, having metal roots myself, really drove it home.

ALICE WHEELER: The show that really changed everything was the Motor Sports Garage — all of a sudden, there was a ton of people, and you had to have a backstage pass. I didn't have a photo pass, but I brought my camera. Dylan came up to me during the Dwarves, and said, "Here's my pass, Kurt wants you to come backstage." I went, and Kurt said, "Save some film for the end, *I'm going to have a surprise.*" It turned out he was smashing his guitar. He used a different guitar to smash, not the good one [laughs].

BLAG DAHLIA: We played at the Motor Sports Hall. Nirvana was the big buzz band — I liked their singles and thought they were the only catchy songwriters in a sea of sad and tedious bands from Seattle. We got added to the bill at the last minute because we were on Sub Pop, and because Cobain and Novoselic were fans of our bass player, Saltpeter — the only guy in our band who could really play well. Their friends at the show were mostly dirt-head-beer-gut-heavy-metal-type guys, from their dreary suburb of Aberdeen — the kind that they would later claim to be much more sensitive than.

We never used to ask what we were getting paid, but it turned out to be $100. We really needed some money for gas so we asked Novoselic if they could give us money. He got really nervous and fidgety, but he finally said he'd give us $100 if we promised not to ask the Melvins for money. We said sure . . . and then went and asked the Melvins for money. We had played a few shows with them and got along fine [and] had more shows with them that month, so we figured they would be understanding. We were wrong. I didn't realize that everyone up there needed money for dope at that point. Near the end of the show, Saltpeter got hit with a beer bottle, and it knocked him to the floor. Vadge threw his sticks down and jumped randomly into the crowd. I took Saltpeter to the emergency room and got him stitched up. Because we had to leave the show, we never got paid anything . . . but I'm sure a check will show up any day now.

CRAIG MONTGOMERY: We saw Dave Grohl playing at this show in San Francisco, with his band, Scream. Kurt said, "Wow, I wish we could get a drummer like that." And then later, word got out that [Scream] had broken up. So they got a hold of him, and the rest is history. I wasn't there for their rehearsals [and] Dave living with Kurt. But when they first came out to do shows, it was a breath of fresh air. He was really solid — he hit solidly and he could sing — he fit in really well.

JENNIE BODDY: I remember the Nirvana shows where Dave Grohl was drumming for the first time, at the Off Ramp. Two a.m. was the cutoff time. They played and played, and they used to have a thing called "Hash After the Bash," where there were really terrible scrambled eggs — greasy food. So they closed the place down for a minute, let everyone back in, and they played for another two hours.

STEVE MANNING: They kicked everybody out, because of the liquor license. They cleared the club of all the alcohol supposedly, and then came back in to continue playing. Krist came up and said, "OK, there's no alcohol, who's got weed? No, *I'm serious* — I need to smoke some weed if we're going to keep playing." So I got up onstage and broke out my proto-pipe — all brass and on the side is a little holder for your weed.

JEFF AMENT: I remember we came back home and I saw them at the Off Ramp. It was a *totally* different band. To this day, I think Dave Grohl was at least as much of a reason why they were great as Kurt was. Kurt was a poet and had an incredible knack for writing a melody, but Dave gave them all the power. He gave the songs a ship to sail on.

STEVE MANNING: Even now — and it seems crazy — Dave Grohl seems like "the new guy" in the band.

STU HALLERMAN: Five bands played upstairs in a cafeteria-ish room [at Evergreen State College], the fourth floor of the library. It was Nirvana, Bikini Kill, and other bands. There's this one guy who kept looking at me — a little guy with white face makeup, really messy mascara and lipstick, and torn flannel shirt. I don't know what was on this guy's mind, so I avoided him. A couple of hours go by, all these bands play, and it's Nirvana's turn. They get up, and who was that "guy"? Kurt!

TINUVIEL: One show that really sticks out is when they played at Evergreen — it was right as we started the Iran–Iraq War. They were opposed to the war — they put black charcoal or makeup on their face, looking ghoulish. In terms of the audience, the general atmosphere was we were all frightened, and wondering what we were doing bombing the Middle East. I really appreciated that they would bring that into what could otherwise have been just another stupid rock show.

SUSAN SILVER: Before Nirvana signed, they had come down to my office. Krist was always the spokesperson, and was asking about labels and lawyers. They really wanted to meet Peter Paterno. I said, "I'm going to L.A. tomorrow. If you guys get a ticket and meet me down there, I'd be happy to introduce you to people." They whispered and conferred with each other, and said, "OK. We'll drive — we'll meet you there tomorrow." Krist and Kurt got in their van and off they went. Twenty-four hours later, met me at A&M. Unfortunately, it didn't work with Peter's schedule — he had an emergency and had to go out of town. So I introduced them to Alan Mintz, who became their lawyer.

JONATHAN PONEMAN: When we did our deal with Geffen and the band — to be bought out of the contract — what was important to us was when people buy the records, it would help the band to have the Sub Pop logo on a certain level, because the band wouldn't be considered a sellout. These sorts of things mattered, or so we thought. But what was really going [on] — we were interested in getting the Sub Pop logo out to as many people as we could. That was just part of the settlement and agreement — for two records, which ended up being *Nevermind* and *In Utero,* that were supposed to be the second two records in the Sub Pop contract — we could get logo identification. You see that logo on other records — *Incesticide* has it because there are Sub Pop masters on that record. People thought that we released or co-released the record, but we had nothing to do with it. We just had a logo stamped on there.

SLIM MOON: In Olympia, there was a feeling against major labels. And Kurt was conflicted. As soon as he signed, he really started downplaying that and not talking about it much. It became sort of taboo to talk about.

SUSIE TENNANT: The first time I met them, I think they had just signed to Geffen — they hadn't even started recording [*Nevermind*]. We hung out when they came to Seattle — hit it off immediately. From that point on, whenever they would come to Seattle, they would stay at my house and hang out. Dave was happy-go-lucky, really fun to hang out with, Krist the same, and Kurt was Kurt — he was great. A lot of times, they'd be here for a couple of days. [Kurt's] girlfriend and Krist's girlfriend would stay — we'd pull out the futon and everyone would crash.

ROBIN TAYLOR: Krist Novoselic called me a couple of days before they were going down to L.A. to record *Nevermind*, and asked if I would book a show [at the OK Hotel] the next day. I was like, "Dude, give me a break — I want to promote, I want to get it on KCMU." There was a line around the block at a quarter after three to see the show.

EDDIE VEDDER: They played these shows at the OK Hotel, which is right down the street from that basement I was sleeping in, and somehow [managed] getting into the first one of those. Which I think was the first night they played "Teen Spirit."

SUSIE TENNANT: The place just exploded. Across the street in a warehouse, they were filming the music scene from *Singles*. I remember trying to get some of the radio people in town — "You've got to go see this band, they're really great!" "No, we're going to go see Soundgarden."

STU HALLERMAN: Midway through the set, Kurt gets up to the mic — "We're going to play a song we never played live before, but we recorded it for our upcoming record. The name of the song is 'Smells Like Teen Spirit.'" The audience cracks up, because it was kind of a funny name. They play the song, and everybody's blown away. The quiet/loud stuff — they just nailed it. You see a punk rock band play, they say the names of their songs, but the next day, do you remember any of it? In this case, *yes* — the funny title and the glory of that song were unforgettable.

STEVE MACK: When Nirvana played the Reading Festival that first year, it was on a Friday at two or three in the afternoon — they were, like, ninth on the bill. But after that, everyone was walking around going, "The festival's over. We just saw the best [band] — nothing's going to top that." That was one of those rare times in your life when you see a band, and go, "I guarantee they are going to be the biggest thing next year."

CRAIG MONTGOMERY: It was a very steady progression. You would hear them working on ideas at sound checks. You could see him moving away from the really heavy, noisy stuff, towards more pop melodies. I mean, on the first European tour, we spent just as much time listening to ABBA as to any kind of noisy punk rock or heavy metal. Kurt definitely had an appreciation

PIC BY MIKE LEACH — BESTROCKPHOTOS.COM

Nirvana's Kurt Cobain, at the Paradiso in Amsterdam, November 25, 1991

for pop song craft. The first time they played me their rough demo of "Teen Spirit," my first thought I said to Kurt was, "Wow, *Pixies!*" And he said, "Yeah, I know. Do you think it's too obvious?"

EDDIE VEDDER: Nirvana's record — people were passing around advance copies of that. Like it was a keychain — *everyone* had one. Everyone's office, you'd just hear it playing. Really exciting. But that was based just on music — everyone was excited about the songs. That was months before it came out.

ART CHANTRY: I was working at *The Rocket*, and a guy brought in a cassette tape. These two records by Nirvana and Soundgarden were being released — we had this 90-minute cassette in the production room, it was *Badmotorfinger* and *Nevermind* on the other side. So we started playing it — "Hey this is a great record!" Flipped it over. "Hey, *this* is a great record!" We flip it over. "Hey, this is a *REALLY* great record!" After a while, we quit flipping it and just played *Nevermind* over and over.

VAN CONNER: Krist came over to Dan Peters' house — we were having a party. Dan, him, and I listened to *Nevermind* right after it got done. We were like, "Wow, this is really good man. You guys are going to sell . . . 100,000 records [laughs]. You guys will be bigger than Hüsker Dü."

SLIM MOON: What I remember more was not the general impression of "This is a great record," it was, "OK, this is the new Nirvana record — *let's parse it.*" Like, "Smells Like Teen Spirit," the original first feeling was,

"Wow, he's using 'the Mudhoney rhythm,'" because there is a Mudhoney rhythm that all the early Mudhoney songs had. I remember picking it apart, like what's going on in Kurt's head — what his influences were, why he wrote this record. We were trying to figure out which people we knew that the songs might be about. I don't really remember [thinking], "Wow, this is going to change the world."

KIM THAYIL: I already loved *Bleach*. Many of those songs are my favorite songs ever — of *any* rock band. I was really looking forward to hearing *Nevermind* with great anticipation. "Smells Like Teen Spirit" stuck out immediately. I remember they sent us a demo, and Ben really liked it — he started laughing, pointed at the boom box, and said, "That's their fucking hit!" It sounded pretty produced — it was definitely a very "wet" record. A lot of reverbs and delays — whereas *Bleach* seemed punchy and dry. I know people like to think of *Nevermind* as being all punk rock and raw. Anyone who doubts that should put their headphones on and listen to it — it's a very wet, slick, polished record.

STEVE TURNER: I thought that they had overproduced it. I heard the demos they'd done with Chad on drums — some of the same songs, and I thought it was great. I was a bit disappointed with the sound of *Nevermind.* It sounds like a really big, almost '80s hard rock record, the sheen that's on it.

CHAD CHANNING: Overall, all the parts were the same. In fact, when I heard that, I was like, "*Wow.*" I was flattered that they kept my stuff, the things that I had done. Kind of the greatest compliment I'd ever received. For instance, "In Bloom" — I had the single kick drum thing going on for the main verses, and then Dave added an extra one. But the majority of that stuff is all pretty much the same.

JERRY CANTRELL: I thought it was amazing. It was a serious step up from the record before. It was like *three or four* steps up.

CHRIS PUGH: My girlfriend at the time gave me a cassette of it that she'd got from Kurt. I remember thinking to myself, "These guys are going to be bigger than Guns N' Roses."

DUFF McKAGAN: *Nevermind* was kick-ass. I had one cassette copy of it before it came out, and my girlfriend and I kept stealing it out of each other's car — we wore it out. It was a really loud, well-produced, punk rock record. With something extra — a great drummer. Nirvana was straight up, they had three-minute rock songs that were perfect.

CURT KIRKWOOD: *Nevermind* was like Aerosmith or something. I thought it was still hard rock — not realizing that there was another group of disgruntled teens coming out. I kind of started seeing that scene like that too — playing to the disenfranchised youth again. That's alright — they can cloud it with their Mardi Gras beads and stuff. I was pretty cynical about it.

NILS BERNSTEIN: Personally I didn't think they were markedly better than any number of other bands, until *Nevermind.* Not that *Bleach* wasn't fantastic, but so was *8-Way Santa.*

EDDIE VEDDER: There was something about those songs — not only was there an immediate connection, but you didn't get sick of them. It was an incredible bit of playing, songwriting, and focus of energy — having it seem natural. And where they were coming from, and what he wanted to say — even though you didn't [know] what he was saying.

We drove out to the Mojave Desert to see Fugazi — free show in the middle of the desert. You get there and there's a van, two work lights set up, they're playing in the sand amongst these dunes. It was quite a drive out there, and I think we listened to [*Nevermind*] all the way there and back. All that was on our minds was Fugazi, but then we would listen to this music. It was like getting doused and lighting yourself on fire — in some kind of celebration.

KIM WARNICK: Probably one of the funniest [memories] was going to their record release party for *Nevermind.* They got kicked out of their own record release party for starting a food fight and throwing a cake around.

VAN CONNER: Those guys would get *so blasted.* I remember dancing with Novoselic that night — he had a pitcher of beer and he started going in circles. Dumping it over the whole bar. Right after that, they got thrown out.

ROBERT ROTH: We were hanging out with Kurt early on — we were smoking cigarettes. The party was pretty fun — I remember "On a Plain" came on, and those guys started throwing food. A mini-food fight broke out, which fit perfectly with the song. We all went to, I think, Jeff Ross's place downtown — a bunch of people drinking and hanging out. Probably twenty-five to thirty people in this warehouse. Another interesting thing I observed about Kurt was certain selflessness. After we all got kicked out of the Re-bar and went up to Jeff's, Kurt spent part of the evening consoling a friend out in the stairwell who was having girl trouble. A very mature gesture, especially just following being evicted from your own record release party. And then somebody let off this fire extinguisher, so we had to leave *that* place. We went up to Susie Tennant's, and everybody got really wasted — at one point, there were, like, twenty drunk people rolling around the floor. A few of us stayed the night there — Susie, Kurt, me, a few other friends.

SUSIE TENNANT: We made a cool, super-long maze [of CDs] — like a domino maze — because I had this huge apartment. We'd stack them up really high and start running from one end . . . [makes crashing noise]. I had some gold records — we had fun defacing the ones that we thought were silly. Goofy stuff — what happens if we put CDs in the oven? A lot of times, everyone would end up going into my closet and trying on all the different clothes.

ROBERT ROTH: I remember that morning [after], hanging out and trying to turn Kurt onto the Soft Boys' *Underwater Moonlight*, which he'd never heard. Dylan was coming to pick him up. They were going to go out someplace in the woods with guns, and shoot the hell out of this pot roast [laughs]. I don't think he lived anywhere — I think he was living out of his car. He'd just edited the "Smells Like Teen Spirit" video, which he played for us that morning. He seemed really focused and really together — which is funny, because then when the Courtney stuff started happening, things seemed like they went in a different direction. He seemed ready to take on the world at that point.

STEVE MANNING: Nobody had the insight that it was going to do what it did — change everybody's lives here.

BRAD SINSEL: There is the theory that rock every few years just implodes. It's had enough, it blows it back down to three chords and simplicity

— minimalist approaches. But once artists have some success with three chords, they start finding all these toys. They start layering tracks, you get money around it, and a producer saying, "Oh, we can do *this.*" It slicks up. Somebody comes around with three chords, it sounds like "Louie Louie," and it wins. The one thing that always brings super-polished stuff down is "Louie Louie" — *which was Nirvana's tune.* Everything in between is people trying to get back to the three chords.

ROBIN TAYLOR: When I heard the END play ["Teen Spirit"], I just felt a chill up and down my spine — you'd never heard it on regular radio and it sounded so spectacular.

TRACY MARANDER: All of a sudden, you heard it every forty-five minutes.

SEAN KINNEY: I remember being in Europe. After shows, promoters would bring you to "the rock club" in Glasgow, Scotland, or something. The kids stand around — drinking beers and smoking spleefs. When a song comes on that they like, like zombies, they'll get on the floor and start headbanging — like it's a concert. The next song will come on, and if they don't like it, they'll creep back to the wall. When "Smells Like Teen Spirit" came on . . . you knew it was going to take off.

ROBERT ROTH: I remember when they finished *Nevermind,* being pretty sure that album was going to wipe out the Sunset Strip. I don't know if I have a slight bit of clairvoyant in me or what, but I just knew that nothing was going to be the same after that.

SUSIE TENNANT: This is the era of hair bands — there is no way that MTV is going to play this video. The bands that my friends and I liked weren't popular — they were popular in the underground, but they weren't on the radio, and they weren't on MTV.

MARK ARM: I remember starting a tour just as *Nevermind* was about to come out. It seemed like every club was playing "Smells Like Teen Spirit" as we loaded our gear in. We played the last two shows of that tour with Nirvana in Portland and Seattle. The idea was one band would headline Seattle, and the other would headline Portland. Once *Nevermind* got released, it was clear that we wouldn't headline either show [laughs].

MARK IVERSON: Every week, it was like, "Can you believe it's up to this . . . up to this . . . up to this?"

SCOTT VANDERPOOL: I went to Hawaii. I was in this bar, with some classic rock cover band, and there's a bunch of drunken frat boys yelling, "Play fucking Nirvana!" I had to ask them where they were from. They were from Chicago. I'm like, "Holy shit — this stuff is starting to take off."

NILS BERNSTEIN: I used to get their mail. They were getting a couple letters a month, so you handwrite back and send stickers. Then it got a little more — started typing out people's labels, Xeroxing letters and responses. I had to go to Kinko's and copy a hundred letters just to respond. At the mail place, there were these old ladies that worked there, and they thought it was *my* band. It's like watching Nirvana's success through the eyes of old ladies at the mail stop. Kept moving them into bigger mailboxes, until they ended up with this row of the biggest mailboxes. They said people used to come by there because it had a street address, so people thought it was a member of Nirvana's home. People would take pictures of the mail location.

KEN STRINGFELLOW: It's just one of those things — right place at the right time. They connected with one of those "cosmic shifts," as that generation became adults. Nirvana was their representative in a way.

RIKI RACHTMAN: I was so excited to meet Kurt Cobain [on MTV's *Headbanger's Ball*], and it was such a disappointment. He was smashed out of his ass — high on dope. I didn't even get the whole "ball gown thing." "I'll wear a ball gown to the ball." OK, that was really funny, Kurt. It wasn't uncomfortable, like, "Oh, how do I react?" It was more like, "What a fucking idiot." I *loved* Nirvana — I still love Nirvana. I walk into my dressing room, and he's there — laying facedown on the floor. That's something that sucks about meeting people you really want to meet, and then they're just such a letdown. It bums you out.

RON HEATHMAN: I was with Dylan and Kurt on October 30 in Vancouver — they played the Commodore Ballroom with Mudhoney. Soundscan had just started, and the manager had come back and said the record went gold. I remember everyone sitting around, shrugging their shoulders, like, "What does that mean?"

KEN STRINGFELLOW: Nirvana didn't really "get marketed," to be honest — I know from people working there that their marketing budgets were pretty modest. Their sales projection for *Nevermind* was like 250,000. They thought they had another Pixies on their hands. They made the video — which was probably the biggest commercial concession they made. Then the record sold itself.

CRAIG MONTGOMERY: When *Nevermind* came out, obviously the band was proud of it and it was a great album, but nobody knew what it was going to do. The first tour that was booked was not in big clubs — it was just another run through the same punk rock clubs that they'd played before. It was a pretty stressful scene sometimes — obviously, the Dallas show [when Kurt and a bouncer got into an onstage altercation, as seen on 1994's *Live! Tonight! Sold Out!!*]. That was the epitome of that tour — out-of-control, crappy sound systems. It's stressful when the band sees people outside who can't get in because it's already sold out. You feel like you're kind of wasting your time. Pretty soon after that, we went to Europe, where the venues were bigger. And by this time, MTV is all over it, and it's getting bigger in the States. So when things really took off and Nirvana became a household word — we were in Europe.

ROBERT ROTH: Then, things became mega huge. The few times I'd run into [Kurt] at shows, he'd be wearing a disguise or some crazy hat that covered half his face.

SUSIE TENNANT: After a while, Dave and Krist would do all the talking, because [Kurt] just wasn't into it. That happened pretty quickly.

STEVE MANNING: I remember an Urge Overkill show — Kurt Cobain was there. As everybody was leaving, I was walking with him and chatting, and this group of hardcore punk rock skate kids screamed at him, "You killed punk rock!" And just watching his shoulders dip, get quiet, and leave.

ALICE WHEELER: The atmosphere was completely different from when Nirvana first started. Kurt seemed like he was under a lot of pressure — kind of stressed out.

TRACY MARANDER: I remember Alice telling me she went backstage at a Nirvana show, and only got to talk to [Kurt] for a couple of minutes. His handlers were like, "He's got to go do this and this." She felt like people were keeping his real friends away, and keeping the hangers-on — the people that wanted money or [were] giving him drugs — around.

CRAIG MONTGOMERY: It was about this time that he met Courtney [Love]. And also the group on tour gets bigger — we have more crew, we're in bigger venues. I'm not spending as much time with the band anymore, so I don't really have a feel for how he feels about things. I mean, it was still fun . . . *I think.*

SLIM MOON: And then Kurt got this girlfriend who publicly slandered my best friends and my town every time she got a chance, and wrote a song about how my town sucks. That was a point when people in Olympia started to willfully not pay attention to Seattle. We started to highlight, "Well, that's not us. That's a different scene."

TRACY MARANDER: Whenever [Courtney] saw me, she was always really nice. I remember [at] the Crocodile Café show, she was there, and her and I were sitting at the counter talking. It was really funny — people kept walking by looking at us, like they're waiting [for us] to start fighting at any minute. We were just yakking away. Every few months he and Courtney would call me really early in the morning, like two or six. He would talk to me for a while, and then Courtney, for whatever reason.

SCOTT VANDERPOOL: I was at the Vogue, and Kurt and Courtney showed up in this big white Lincoln Town Car. Courtney was dancing on the hood of the thing, I was leaving, and Kurt came over, and said, "Hey man, I just want to say thanks for playing us on the radio."

BEN REW: I met Courtney when she was a stripper in Portland, and we didn't mesh, shall we say. She was really loud — like, "I'M PUNK ROCK!" And I was like, "Oh my God, *you're a dude with a dress.*"

ART CHANTRY: I met Courtney Love once — she's like Godzilla with a skirt. One of the most fearsome creatures. She was with Jonathan Poneman, and Jonathan was terrified of her — you should have seen his expression. Nobody would deal with her when she walked into *The Rocket*, nobody knew who the fuck she was — this was before she was huge. She was really scary — she's a big woman, and she had all kinds of junkie zits on her face. Her hair was greasy and dirty, and she was wearing man's clothes — lumberjack clothes. She just looked terrible. Trying to buy an ad — she was looking for a new bassist for her band, Hole. We had this woman working at the front desk, Anna Woolverton — her nickname was Viva. And Viva was a real piece of work — she knew how to handle anything that walked in that door. So here was this interesting chance meeting between Courtney Love and Viva — I stood in my doorway and watched. She's digging through her goddamned purse looking for money — she didn't want to pay for it because she's "Courtney Love" and it was one of those moments where she was literally emptying out the contents of her purse on the countertop. And the things that came out of that purse, *man* [laughs].

She ended up signing over a check that was one of Kurt's, so it was an awkward thing — they didn't know whether to take it or not. Jonathan basically said, "I'll cover for it no matter what happens" — he was terrified to even talk. Now, Charlie Cross — the owner of *The Rocket* — *hates* cigarette smoke. He's one of those guys that is just paranoid about cigarette smoke — cigarette smoke gets anywhere near him, he will grab the cigarette out of somebody's mouth. That was a totally nonsmoking office — heavily enforced. So [Courtney] was smoking a cigarette ten feet inside the front door. Viva looks up at Courtney, and says, "This is a nonsmoking office." Courtney was taken by surprise. "What?!" "This is a nonsmoking office — you're going to have to put out your cigarette." She goes, "No!" There's this stare-off — it was one of those moments where Jonathan even took a few steps back. But Courtney backed off, and walked to the front door. About eight inches inside our front door, on the rug, she dropped her cigarette and ground it out in our carpet. And that cigarette butt stayed there for like a week — nobody would pick it up! Finally, I made a little sign that said, "Courtney Love's cigarette butt," with an arrow. I taped it next to the butt, and everybody loved that. Eventually, Charlie came in, got pissed, and tore it off the floor.

SUSAN SILVER: Courtney started taking shots at different musicians in the vicinity. It wasn't cool — suddenly, there was tension between people. You don't get far in business or in life by talking out of turn. I was really surprised when I got a phone call from Danny Goldberg, saying, "They just really want you to stop talking about them." It was like, "*What the fuck?* What are you talking about? Talking about *them?* Who would I be talking to them about?" Shortly after that, a woman came from England doing a book on Nirvana. Courtney left a super abusive voicemail on my answering machine — a tape that I still have to this day — just reading me the riot act. It was pathetic more than anything, but it was really clear in that — because she named all the women that Kurt had ever been friends with, and that she had systematically removed from his life — she was really threatened by him having any female friendships. This woman [who was writing the book] came — she was quite disarming and quite lovely — and at that point, *I was pissed.* Like, "Wait a minute, they're talking shit about me to other people? She's leaving me abusive phone messages. She's having Danny Goldberg calling to basically give me a gag order." I don't get angry very well, and haven't many times in my life, but I had said basically what I said to you, to this woman. And at that point, she put it in some book I think. It's nothing I wouldn't say now — Courtney left an abusive phone message and was acting extremely irrational at this concert in Spain. And it was really sad, because she was somewhat instrumental in the undoing of our sense of community here.

BLAG DAHLIA: I'm always fascinated by that phenomenon of people who are talented and good, but get vaulted to these heights that don't seem to be in line with reality. I mean, *I like Nirvana* — I'm a fan. The same way I like Green Day, the same way I like the Beatles. I just don't really see them as so radically [different]. If you compare what Guns N' Roses is to what Nirvana is, you find essentially they're the same thing — cute guys, Geffen Records, heroin, fucked strippers, into 1970s Aerosmith rock. Everything is largely exactly the same, and yet at the time, they were marketed as a different thing. It was time for a different marketing idea.

DUFF McKAGAN: There was a lot of heroin around at that time. So both bands had a lot of success, there was a lot of drugs and alcohol infiltrated into both bands. Both had huge followings that weren't going to die anytime soon. Guns N' Roses had nothing in common with most of the bands of our time. And I think probably the same is true with Nirvana. Even with bands from Seattle — like Pearl Jam and Soundgarden. They were alienated in drugs and über success. Guns was a band that did shit on their own terms, and so did Nirvana. There was probably an awful lot more in common than *dis*-in-common. I never saw it as any different . . . the press certainly made a lot out of it then — and still does.

EDDIE VEDDER: You'd see bands, after the show you'd see somebody smoking and drinking. You'd say, "That drum bit in that song, that's insane" — just kind of picking out parts of the show that are fairly obvious and makes for meaningless conversation. But you couldn't really do that [with Nirvana], it was like, *a Nirvana show.* It's weird, at the time, it wasn't about any kind of extreme musicianship on anybody's part — it was truly this three-piston/three-cylinder combination of everything happening at once. Including the crowd and the power of the songs. It was a real communal experience.

I got a hold of this show at a place called Trees, which I think we played a week later or something. It was this tiny place — posts in the middle of the crowd — it was in Texas. It was booked three months before the records [were released], so by the time we got there, the venues were packed. They're playing on a stage about the size of like a modern day drum riser. The amount of people landing onstage — there's really a grey line between who's in the band and who's in the audience. It's really like the tide keeps going in and out — like a wave going in and out. Just watch the patience — Kurt was so fucking patient with people stepping on his pedals, smacking the mic into his face. And they're not missing a beat. It was part of that energy, which was like a modified and modernized version of Black Flag and Minor Threat. I almost remember those shows as not being exciting, but when I watch them now, it was exciting *on a hundred levels.* I was still thinking you needed a guitar solo or a Pete Townshend jump to be exciting.

SLIM MOON: Nirvana went on tour to support *Nevermind* — those were our friends, people I'd known for five years. When I lived in Seattle, they would always crash at our house. When I lived in Olympia, I lived next door to Kurt. He would come over and borrow my four-track so he could demo songs. Then they went on tour to support *Nevermind,* and never came back, y'know?

The Blackouts at Baby-O's, 1983 [pic by Mike Leach — bestrockphotos.com]

The U-Men at the Golden Crown, 1983 [pic by Mike Leach — bestrockphotos.com]

The March of Crimes at the Metropolis, early '80s [pic by Damon Romero]

Malfunkshun's Andy Wood (with nifty homemade T-shirt) in early '80s [pic by Blaine Cook]

Spluii Numa plays, Mark Arm goes upside down at the Metropolis, early '80s [pic by Mike Leach — bestrockphotos.com]

Green River dig KCMU
(L-R: Jeff Ament, Mark Arm, Bruce Fairweather) [pic by Libby Knudson]

The Melvins rock! (L-R: Buzz Osborne, Matt Lukin, Dale Crover) [pic by Libby Knudson]

Early Nirvana, at the Capitol Lake Park, August 20, 1988
(L-R: Kurt Cobain, Krist Novoselic, Chad Channing) [pic by Rod Moody]

Soundgarden at the Aragon Ballroom in Chicago, November 10, 1996
(L-R: Chris Cornell, Ben Shepherd, Kim Thayil) [pics by Seth Perlman]

This living room will never be the same:
Tad live in Europe, 1989 [pic by Chad Channing]

Matt Lukin and Krist Novoselic in Europe, 1989 [pic by Chad Channing]

Truly underrated, Truly (L-R: Hiro Yamamoto, Robert Roth, Mark Pickerel) [pic by David Hawkes]

Eddie Vedder and a field, 1992 [pic by Krisha Augerot]

Mad Season's Layne Staley and Mike McCready perform (in Eddie Vedder's house!) as part of Pearl Jam's *Self Pollution Radio* broadcast, January 8, 1995 [pic by Yanni "Johnny" Bacolas — yannibacolas.com]

Ladies and gentlemen . . . Bratmobile [pic by John Perry]

Mudhoney outside KEXP, March 2006 (L-R: Dan Peters, Steve Turner, Guy Maddison, Mark Arm) [pic by Bootsy Holler — bootsyholler.com]

Pearl Jam at Easy Street Records, April 2005 (L-R: Mike McCready, Jeff Ament, Eddie Vedder, Stone Gossard) [pic by Bootsy Holler — bootsyholler.com]

CHAPTER 21

"That they didn't reach a broader audience baffles me": Mudhoney, Tad, Screaming Trees, Truly, Melvins, Jesse Bernstein

With the grunge movement in full swing, Mudhoney and Tad each issued classics for Sub Pop, *Every Good Boy Deserves Fudge* and *8-Way Santa*, while the Screaming Trees made the jump to a major label with *Uncle Anesthesia*, and the Melvins continued to rock the underground. Also on the scene was a promising new band comprised of ex–Screaming Trees and Soundgarden members, Truly, while Seattle's local poet, Jesse Bernstein, left an impression on the scene.

STEVE TURNER: We took a six-month break — I was going to sign up for a couple of quarters of classes. It snowballed that we were breaking up, even though we never said that — we kept saying, "No we're not." Looking back at the year that we were supposedly "on break," we did [1991's] *Every Good Boy Deserves Fudge*, me and Mark did the Monkeywrench record [1992's *Clean as a Broke Dick Dog*], I joined the Fallouts, and I did the Sad and Lonely(s) record [1992's *The Sad and Lonely(s)*]. I only made it through one quarter of college.

TAD DOYLE: Mudhoney never failed to stir up the audience and get them excited. There'd be a lot of stage diving — all kinds of shenanigans and craziness. They'd do all these crazy, "skinny guy antics," like bending completely over backwards and touching their head on the floor — still holding their guitar and playing. Athletic stuff that a big guy like me can only wonder about.

BLAG DAHLIA: Mudhoney came down, and we had a party at my place in San Francisco. I told everybody, "We've got to be cool, my landlord lives upstairs — everybody be quiet." And Lukin did something like fucking set off an air horn.

GRANT ALDEN: They were the band I have seen play live the most out of any band, ever. They were capable of being the best band you ever saw, or the worst. But they were — for forty-five minutes — *phenomenal.* That they didn't reach a broader audience baffles me. Although, one of the things that happens in music is what works on a small stage doesn't work on a big stage. I'm not sure what they did was ever going to work in an arena.

MARK ARM: After we recorded [*Mudhoney*], Steve was like, "Dude, no more songs about sickness or dogs!" [laughs] *Every Good Boy Deserves Fudge* was largely saved by Steve. At this point, I was getting heavier and heavier into heroin.

STEVE TURNER: Anyone with a drug problem is going to be kind of out of it, secretive, and weird. I always maintained the position that if someone wants to do drugs, they have every right to do it. It's not like we were pressuring him to stop, really. On tour, he was fine, it was just the first few days would be a disaster, because he'd be sick. It was when we were home that it was a problem — he would disappear. We made him go into rehab once, because we had a tour booked. We were like, "Either you go into rehab or we're not doing the tour." I think you have to solve those problems on your own, in a certain way. He solved his problems on his own, and then it got a lot better [laughs].

MARK ARM: Steve kept the band rolling for *Every Good Boy*. He grabbed the helm and steered the *SS Mudhoney* in a new direction — in [a] more stripped down and, for lack of a better term, "garage rock" approach. Steve was really into Billy Childish — he had been for a long time. Most of the songs on *Every Good Boy* have more of a '60s punk feel. The song "Who You Driving Now?" was originally written for an Estrus comp — Estrus is a garage label. Our aim was to try to write a fake Sonics song. Then we decided it was too good to put on a comp, and that we had to put it on our next record [laughs]. We decided that our first single had the best sound of anything that we had recorded, and since that single was our only record done on an eight-track, we should find another eight-track. Steve called Conrad Uno at Egg Studio — which is in the basement of Conrad's house — to tell him that we'd like to record at Egg. Conrad burst out laughing and asked, "Why?!" Of course, we went to Egg.

STEVE TURNER: That record, I think we were on top of our game. That's still one of my favorite ones of ours. We were trying to do different things — we brought in this Farfisa keyboard. It was more stripped down, and less of "the big grunge sound." Whatever it was, I wanted to get away from it.

SCOTTY CRANE: Mudhoney's set [opening for Nirvana at the Paramount on Halloween 1991] was amazing — they kept making jokes about how poor they were compared to Nirvana. Mid-song, someone in the audience threw coins at Mark's head, and the band kept playing — as Mark scampered around to collect the change. This became the big joke — soon, the band was being pelted with change, while Mark and Matt picked it up.

STEVE TURNER: [The release of *Every Good Boy*] was delayed again, and [Sub Pop was] always struggling financially. It was getting argumentative, and we didn't want it to go totally sour. So we decided we had to move elsewhere.

NILS BERNSTEIN: In Tad, they brought in some more overt '70s metal sounds.

KURT DANIELSON: We hooked up with Steve Albini in Chicago. Recorded [1990's] *Salt Lick*, which was done very quickly and raw-ly. The songs weren't really done — we had the opportunity, Steve had the time, Sub Pop had everything set up. We just jumped at it, and let the chips fall where they may. It ended up being a live record in the studio.

TAD DOYLE: I think we spent two or three days on it. I remember Steve telling me not to sing because I can't, and don't even try. I remember saying, "Fuck you, I'm going to" — I wound up doing it anyway. But [Albini] brought a lot of energy out of us — he got us fired up. He was not of the mind of experimentation in the studio as much as Jack Endino on the first record. So after *Salt Lick*, we just toured — it seemed like we toured nine months out of the year.

BEN REW: I've toured probably one-tenth or one-twentieth of my life. Tad always had really good shows — people used to adore him. The one thing about that guy — out of everyone in this scene, he is the only person that would talk to every single person after a show that wanted stuff signed and wanted to talk. You'd be screaming at him out the door, "Dude, we've got to leave!" He would always stand in the front row of the openers. No other band — Seattle or anywhere else — did I ever see the main dude of the band standing front row to watch his opening act. He was so grateful to other bands. He'd have these parties at his house that were just frickin' hilarious. It would be his birthday — all of a sudden, he would walk out of his bedroom with huge oversized diapers and a Mickey Mouse hat on. Tad was a force to be reckoned with.

You had all these other guys that are really good-looking and really skinny, and Tad was just pure talent. He would get up there and rock harder — he would jump around more than skinny guys. And his between-song-banter was hilarious. That was one thing he really prided himself on — he actually did give you a show. I think he fell into . . . you had all these really good-looking bands that sounded like crap. L.A., the record industry was still in control of what was getting out to people — they still wanted people to buy records on looks and style. Tad was just a guy from Boise, Idaho, that would rock your skull into the ground.

NILS BERNSTEIN: *8-Way Santa* is a great melodic rock record, and was definitely the record to beat in 1991 . . . until that *other one* came out in the fall.

KURT DANIELSON: We drove to Madison, Wisconsin, and recorded *8-Way Santa* at Smart Studios with Butch [Vig]. We'd always wanted to work with Butch — Butch's work with Killdozer was really important to us. One thing that Butch was great at was working with singers, and he had a really great pop sensibility — as you can tell by his work in Garbage. But nobody knew that then — it was just a lucky coincidence. And Butch was like a child in the studio — I'd never seen anybody with so much childlike energy. Loved gadgets and working. We toured for that record, but first, our drummer quit;

it took us like a year to find a replacement. In the meantime, the record comes out, and we get sued.

ART CHANTRY: The band were putting out *8-Way Santa.* It was the best thing they ever did — their breakthrough record. Everybody expected them to be at the top of the charts — the next Soundgarden, the next Mudhoney. I got this call from Kurt Danielson, and said, "We're working on this record cover. We want to use this photo that we found at a garage sale. It was in a photo album that we bought, so that means it's ours and we have the right to use it, right?" And I went, "No, don't do it. Don't fucking use it. If you use it, alter it so dramatically that nobody can be recognized. My advice is don't do it." So, they went ahead and used the photograph anyway — of this guy with sort of a Fu Manchu '70s greaseball haircut, and this petite little woman, with his hand on her breast. Somebody at a record store recognized the dude in the photo and said, "Hey Fred" — or whatever his name was — "Look, you're on a record cover!" That was his wedding photo from back in the '70s. So he showed it to his ex-wife, who had become a Christian singer, and the shit hit the fan. They had to pull the record off the shelves and change the cover.

In the meantime, Bruce decided that he was going to promote the "Jack Pepsi" single — a song about driving drunk in a monster truck, having a wreck, and killing people, or something like that. [Bruce] thought it would be hilarious to do a CD single and use the Pepsi-Cola logo and put the word "Tad" on it — take out the word Pepsi, and put in the word Tad. And [someone] sent several copies to Pepsi Corporate Headquarters. They listened to the single, looked at their logo. They went nova and sued the shit out of the label. Bruce had no money, so his response was to bend over and say, "Do you want it like this, or do you want it like that?" So the record got pulled from the shelves and had to be reissued. Any kind of promotional value was ruined, and any kind of incentive or push the record had, had been dragged out over several months. Pulling it off the shelves and reissuing it killed its momentum.

ANONYMOUS: As part of the settlement, Tad agreed to change the title of "Jack Pepsi" to "Jack" on all subsequent releases. Pepsi did not like their product being associated with drunk driving, natch. Secondly, they also demanded that Tad not talk about the suit or the contents thereof to the press or anyone else — in other words, they slapped a gag order on Tad. There was no financial settlement; these two things constitute the main terms of the lawsuit.

As for the cover art, yes, they demanded that be changed also — that is, the cover art for the single that features the Tad/Pepsi logo. A disgruntled former Sub Pop employee — who had been fired — leaked the whole story to Pepsi's legal division, thereby notifying them of the existence of this so-called copyright infringement, something they never would have known about otherwise, because it would have normally gone below their radar. It took a fink/traitorous bastard to bring it to their attention. Makes for a pretty good story — and a helluva lot of trouble for Tad and Sub Pop.

ART CHANTRY: By this point, Bruce was afraid of this record, the band was pissed off because they were touring a product they couldn't support. Also by this time, Bruce started having bands sign contracts. Because he had already lost Nirvana and Soundgarden, Tad was one of the first bands he had a big release clause in the contract. If the band wanted to sign with another label, the label had to pay Sub Pop something like $60,000. So Tad was stuck — they couldn't jump labels, because no other label out there that would pick them up could afford to pay Sub Pop the release price. The result was Tad was pissed at Sub Pop and Bruce — they would not release any more material on the label. They couldn't release [it] on anybody else's label either. Because of the release clause, they lost all their momentum and lost lots of money.

KURT DANIELSON: We finally went out on the road again, still playing the *8-Way Santa* songs, but with Rey Washam on drums, with Primus. A great drummer — one of my favorite bands, Scratch Acid, Rey played drums for. It was fun — we toured for more than a year in the States, in Europe also. And then things fell apart with Rey — we never recorded with Rey, although we wrote songs that were never recorded with him. That's one of my great regrets.

VAN CONNER: [The Screaming Trees] did *Buzz Factory*, and then after that we did an EP for Sub Pop.

MARK PICKEREL: I'm proud of [*Buzz Factory*], but even more proud of the release we did right after it, which unfortunately is not a full-length. It was a co-production — Steve Fisk producing two or three songs, and Jack Endino producing two or three songs — that would eventually come out as a double single on Sub Pop [1990's *Change Has Come*]. I think that is our best-recorded moment — that period. We must have been fresh off a lot of touring — probably had just come back from Europe. Our confidence in ourselves was at an all time high — we really felt like we were fulfilling our vision. We were being courted by Epic Records. So that, in combination with all the other great things that already existed about the band — Lee's songwriting, and Mark had developed his talents into something that was truly unique — that was the magical moment for us. That was when everything fell into place for us musically.

STEVE MANNING: One of my favorite bands of all time. One really memorable show . . . I was naive at the time, and didn't realize that people were using. I knew heroin was a big deal, but wasn't cognizant enough to know that it was actually happening. I would be hesitant to say that I knew when anybody was using, but I remember a Screaming Trees show where I was sitting on one of the speakers on the stage, and nobody could find Mark Lanegan. They looked and looked, and finally [found him], I think he was sleeping behind a couch upstairs, where the bands hang out. So the band had begun playing without him, and finally, somebody found him, and brought him to the stage. Jim Morrison came to mind, because during the song, he could not have been more *on*, and have that amazing voice. The band was all over the stage, you've got these near-300-pound dudes playing guitar on both sides of him, and then him — this really thin guy, just really interactive and into it. But between songs, he would sink down, behind the speaker I was sitting on, and again, I wouldn't want to say that he was nodding, but seemed to lose consciousness. As soon as the next song would start, he would step out from behind, and be completely going full bore again.

MARK PICKEREL: Mark Lanegan's first solo record was one of the best experiences of my career — [1990's] *The Winding Sheet*. I really hoped that would develop into a Nick Cave and the Bad Seeds kind of environment. I didn't want to abandon the Screaming Trees, because I thought that the Screaming Trees had a lot to offer and were very exciting. But I did picture Mark's record and talents evolving into something that would have been more of a working band/working environment — rehearsals, tours. But that was not meant to be. Now, it has developed into something — it's more palpable than it was at the time.

Screaming Trees (L-R: Van Conner, Gary Lee Conner, Mark Lanegan, Barrett Martin)

ROBIN TAYLOR: I don't think [the Screaming Trees] were overlooked, but were one of the best bands that aren't rich.

MARK PICKEREL: Lanegan and I had become big fans of Lead Belly. And several other blues artists — Lightnin' Hopkins, Robert Johnson. I know that Kurt was a big fan of Lanegan's — they traded a lot of tapes and had conversations about different artists they liked. Apparently, I don't know if Mark turned Kurt on to Lead Belly, or if Kurt was already a fan, but at some point, Mark approached me about playing drums for a project that he and Kurt wanted to start, which would really focus on blues — particularly Lead Belly's catalog. I believe we were also talking about playing songs by all the great bluesmen. I got really excited about it, and was envisioning this super group that was bound for success — sort of be the modern day, Northwest version of Cream. It was funny, because having been in a band with Mark for so long, his personality in the Screaming Trees was he couldn't help but really be the bandleader. He just is a natural leader, is very outspoken, and can be very aggressive. The couple of rehearsals we had, I saw a different side of Mark — one that was much quieter. He seemed to have a great deal of respect for Kurt and Krist. At the same time, Kurt seemed intimidated by Lanegan's talents and vision.

I remember it was my own cassette of "Where Did You Sleep Last Night?" that we used for the example for that particular song. It was really exciting, because I felt like it was a collaborative effort. Funny that it should be easy for me to voice so many opinions to Mark and Kurt simultaneously. I guess because I saw this moment of vulnerability on Lanegan's part, it was a great opportunity for me to finally get excited about all these different ideas. Unfortunately, this was right around the Screaming Trees being courted by Epic, and Nirvana was getting ready to leave for a big tour. We just didn't have the time to make this thing evolve into something bigger, or into more recordings. I think we went into the studio with six ideas, and recorded maybe four or five of them. At the time, there wasn't really a name for the band. Kurt wanted to call it Lithium, and I wanted to call it the Jury. I don't think we ever really arrived at a name, and eventually, the project got shelved, and Lanegan asked Kurt and Krist how they'd feel about using "Where Did You Sleep Last Night?" for Mark's solo record.

VAN CONNER: We all wanted to quit, because we thought we'd done everything we could musically together. And we were all starting to do music with other people — I had that solo album, [1990's] *Solomon Grundy*, Lanegan did his solo record, Lee did his solo record [1990's *Mystery Lane*, credited to Purple Outside]. I think we were sick of each other. When we got together, the stuff was sounding kind of same-y.

MARK PICKEREL: [The Screaming Trees] did the record on Epic [1991's *Uncle Anesthesia*], that Terry Date and Chris Cornell co-produced. There was sort of a self-imposed pressure to produce a record that was exciting, but also radio friendly. We had already seen Chris Cornell and Soundgarden achieve this, so we knew that having him there would benefit us. The problem was I don't think Terry Date had really experienced what made the Screaming Trees so great outside of that experience — nor had he followed us as a fan. I felt like he viewed us as "a project." I think *I* even viewed ourselves at the time like that. Like, "OK, here's our chance to impress the parents." That doesn't help the creative process, when you don't believe enough in yourself to do what's instinctive. And you're not really feeling that you're getting the encouragement to be yourself from the control room. There's some great songs on it, but it just feels a little awkward. It doesn't breathe the way *Change Has Come* breathed, or even the SST stuff.

VAN CONNER: Pickerel wanted to stay at home. We thought we'd try this major label thing, because we got an offer. So we did that and recorded the record. Then Mark decided again that he didn't want to tour anymore. We all wanted to quit at that point — but he was the only one brave enough to do it.

MARK PICKEREL: The demands from the band when they signed to Sony increased. Now not only did we have to make sure that everyone in the band was getting paid and a manager — now it was [also] a booking agent, and making sure the record label's expectations were being met. And their expectations of us were not in line with our own career vision. I wasn't ready to do the amount of touring that they wanted at that time. I met this guy, Robert Roth, through a friend, who had some original songs that he asked me if I'd be willing to develop with him to record. I heard the songs, and thought they were great. They had a lot of the same classic qualities as the Screaming Trees.

ROBERT ROTH: The Storybook Krooks was my first and only band before Truly. And there was that brief time when I tried out for Nirvana. A month after I found out I wasn't going to be in Nirvana, I found Mark. At that point, I was just going to go in and record a solo record, and Mark ended up quitting the Screaming Trees that week. The guy who was playing bass at the time, Chris Quinn, quit his band that day. So once we got to the studio, we realized, "Oh, *we're a band.*" I already had a song called "Truly." Chris said, "How about calling the band Truly?" Mark was at work, and Jonathan Poneman said, "Why don't you call your band Truly?" Two different people came up with the same name — I figured that was fate. Chris and I didn't really get along that well — I'm more of an intuitive type, he's more a studied type. I wanted to be a "Northwest Television" — two guitars doing innovative, cool stuff. So we stayed a three-piece. I left out the part where Chris insisted on switching to guitar, which meant we needed a bass player — Mark calling Hiro.

HIRO YAMAMOTO: I was out of music for a while — I just didn't want to play. I was pretty tired of it. Mark called me, and said, "I'm playing with this guy, and we're looking for a bass player." I was like, "OK, I'll give it a shot." I hadn't played for a couple of years. I listened to their stuff, and was like, "This is kinda cool." I always liked Mark's drumming — it seemed like the right thing to do.

ROBERT ROTH: It evolved into something very effortless — there was not a lot of discussion when Truly was making records or songs. The first EP [1991's *Heart and Lungs*] was made before we were officially on Sub Pop — most of it. That was recorded in the summer of '90. When Jonathan heard the works in progress, he decided to sign us and put the thing out. I think that we were the first Sub Pop band up until that point to do a twenty-four-track recording in a real studio. We broke away from the mold of Jack Endino and eight-track — and we had a full color sleeve. The idea of Truly was to be "post-grunge," even though a lot of the world hadn't found out about grunge yet. That was our intention from day one — to take things elsewhere.

One of the songs [was planned for] the *Singles* soundtrack, although it wound up getting booted from the album a week before it got sent off to press. That was depressing. That's how Mark Arm bought his house, was from that movie [laughs]. The next thing was start recording an album, and we had some budgetary problems with Sub Pop. They were going to give us a huge amount of money to make our record — for their standards — and allow us to do it without signing on for any more records. In other words, they were going to do a one-off, and then let us be free agents. They dumped "Heart and Lungs" off of the *Singles* album — they added another Alice in Chains song, a Paul Westerberg song, and a Heart song. Then Sub Pop reneged. They were like, "You're not getting anywhere near this amount of money, or you're giving us several records." At that point, I was negotiating on the behalf of two guys that didn't want to sign a several record deal with them. So essentially, Sub Pop pulled the plug on the album, but put out the EP. I felt confident enough about the EP that we could get picked up on another label. And we did — we got signed to Capitol.

STEVE MANNING: I saw the Melvins a lot. I think my favorite and most memorable experience with the Melvins was seeing them play at the International Underground Pop Convention in Olympia. All these bands came from all over the world for this four-day conference. They played in the afternoon in the park. All of their family had come out for it — two of their grandmas were there, and had "Grandmas for Melvins" shirts on!

MEGAN JASPER: The best Melvins moment in the world for me was a show they did in Olympia in summer of '91 [at the International Pop Underground Convention]. I wanted to just get away from so many bodies at that time — I walked up around the Capitol building, and there was a wedding set up. They were about to get married outdoors, it was a beautiful day, and they had to postpone the wedding, because all you could hear was the Melvins. Their music was hovering over this wedding — it was fucking great! As sad as it may have been for the people in the wedding party — they were setting up speakers to play easy listening — there was no kibosh that would be put on the Melvins. *They totally took over.* It seemed like one of those moments where even though it was fucking up a few people's lives, everything was right in the world.

STU HALLERMAN: Jesse Bernstein stood out. When *Sub Pop 200* came out, there was a record release party that I think went on for three days — they had each of the bands that were on the vinyl discs. It was at this place called the Underground in the University District. And the emcee I think for all three nights was Jesse Bernstein. I went to a couple of these shows, and he'd read poetry, mock the crowd, and they would mock him back.

NILS BERNSTEIN: My dad was friends with Jesse Bernstein — but no relation. Jesse worked at the Different Drummer bookstore on Broadway, which was one of those SF-style freak-haven bookstores with homeless guys thumbing through couples-massage books. People hated it when Jesse started emceeing or performing at shows, but I liked it 'cause it was familiar — like a thread from the mid-'70s freaks that hung out at my dad's theater, to the mid-'80s freaks at punk rock shows. There's a line in one of his poems — "I am with Jackie O., we are eating oranges from the president" — that still goes through my mind about once a week.

ALICE WHEELER: Jesse was a really interesting guy. He seemed a lot older than he actually was. He was ten or fifteen years older than I was, and he was a real "street guy." He used to tell stories about shooting smack back in the day, he told me he used to be a porn star — all kinds of things. I was never sure how much of it was true and how much of it was made up for the benefit of a young girl [laughs]. What was interesting about him was he knew so many different people from different backgrounds. Even if I wouldn't run into him for six months, he'd sit down and have a great story to tell. He used to talk about how back in the day, he would drink too much, shoot his gun, and drive his car. He said he realized he wasn't going to live long if he kept doing that, so he was on the wagon when I met him. He was really encouraging to me about my photography. One of those first photos I did, he was goofing around — he said, "I'm on medication now, so I drool," and drooled for the picture. A couple of years later, when I gave him the photo, he wanted to give it to his new wife for their wedding present, so she would know what she was getting into [laughs]. With that wife, he lived on a houseboat on Lake Union. It wasn't a real houseboat — it was a barge with a little tiny room on top. Over the years, he lived in a bunch of different hotel rooms.

SLIM MOON: I think he must have been on "crazy money" or something, because it seemed he had a fixed income that was very small. He lived in this tiny flophouse — one room, with a bathroom down the hall, all his neighbors being winos. It was like he was ensconced there. You've got this little room with shelves all the way to the ceiling, a million books, and your manual typewriter. This was like the epitome of "the bohemian lifestyle." He was named the Poet Emeritus of Seattle, and was always reading somewhere — whether it was the Seattle Opera House and a thousand people seeing him, or an open mic with nobody seeing him but the other poets reading that night. Always doing something. His goal was to write a novel that you could print in any order and read in any order — it was irrelevant what sequence you read the pages. He was working on that right up to his death.

He was also a folk musician with sort of a bluesy influence, but he left that behind when he got heavy into the poetry thing. He was just an interesting guy. A cynical person could say he was a Burroughs wannabe, and it certainly was a big influence for him, but he was very much his own guy. He relapsed, and the last year of his life was really like a miserable disaster. The suicide part came as a surprise, but when somebody is as bad off as he was, they either end up in rehab or they end up dead — you don't really go on that way for very long.

STEVE FISK: It's really sad — we only got a song and a half finished before he died [for a Sub Pop/Bernstein album]. He also went into a very bad time in his life when I was working with him — his last big decline. He was just *on* all the time — telling me about himself and all this shit. Nice guy — real generous, real enthusiastic. I don't think I knew him — this period wasn't the best time to know him. There were other times when he

PIC BY BOOTSY HOLLER — BOOTSYHOLLER.COM

Producer Steve Fisk

was a little more focused, and wasn't quite so tortured. Because of the record and everything, people think I'm his buddy or something like that. He'd been having good times and bad times for years. He was somebody that frankly, I was afraid of — because of shit he pulled on friends of mine. He'd done some crazy stuff — bomb threats and pulling out knives [laughs]. Things I don't need in my life. But the work was good, and he's a very talented person. He didn't have to work hard to make interesting things. He more or less told me to finish [1992's posthumously released *Prison*] — I think he knew what was coming up.

ALICE WHEELER: After he passed away [in October 1991], a friend of mine, Jim Jones, and I put out a book of his work [1996's *I Am Secretly an Important Man*]. I have a lot of really nice photographs of him. In fact, some of the first photographs I took were of Jesse.

STU HALLERMAN: I brought *Sub Pop 200* on the road with me, and played highlights of that as [Soundgarden's] warm-up music. At some towns, when [*Sub Pop 200*] got to the Jesse Bernstein stuff, people would be throwing their drinks. "TURN THAT SHIT OFF!" I remember the Whiskey A-Go-Go — [Soundgarden] were filming the *Louder Than Live* video. That was the period I was playing that *Sub Pop 200* CD every night, and the Bernstein piece would always get played — "Come out tonight . . . a picture shaped like my ass." Maybe twenty seconds before it was going to start, I turned to some guy — "The next piece is spoken word, is the crowd going to hate it?" And he's like, "Oh no, people like spoken word here in L.A." By the time we had gone through this much of a conversation, the next piece was starting, and a hush came over the place. They listened to the whole thing, snickered, and laughed at the appropriate moments. And then, they let out this *huge applause* at the end.

CHAPTER 22

"Rebelling against the predominant macho grunge scene at the time": Riot Grrrl

Although mostly male-dominated, the grunge era also included several all-female/feminist bands — including Bikini Kill and Bratmobile — who called their style "Riot Grrrl," and sought to break down barriers and stereotypes.

ALLISON WOLFE: I was born in Memphis, Tennessee — I'm an identical twin. When I was about three or four, my parents moved from Tennessee to Washington State, Mount Vernon. And then my parents had a divorce — my dad moved back to Tennessee. With my mom there was this huge transformation — she came out as a lesbian, and went totally hippie and vegetarian. Playing acoustic guitar and going camping. She got custody of me and my twin sister — I have a younger sister too. All of a sudden we were in this completely different environment. My mom was a nurse, and she went back to school to become a nurse practitioner — a hired nurse — and then we moved to Olympia in 1981. My mom was a huge influence on me. My mom was a feminist, a lesbian/gay rights activist, and also, she started the first women's health clinic, that was for, by, and about women, in Thurston County. She was providing abortions, and also back then, would do rape exams — it was before hospitals did them routinely. She received death threats and people would come and harass us at our house, and harass the clinic all the time. We grew up surrounded by this controversy, feminism, and activism. She used to drive us to "No Nukes" rallies. Also, my mom was pretty broke. So we had to fend for ourselves a lot of the time.

KATHLEEN HANNA: I moved around a lot as a kid. I came to Olympia via Portland — I went to high school in Portland, and then I went to college at Evergreen State College in Olympia. I got into music in high school. Hardcore shows, speed metal was really big then, reggae shows at the Pine Street Theater.

ALLISON WOLFE: In high school, I had this incident. My freshman year, I was sort of preppie — mainstream. I was going out with this guy who was a real jock — had a letterman jacket and all that. He was two years older than me and really traditional/old-fashioned. When I went to his house, it was right out of *Leave it to Beaver*. Creepy. He was really controlling of me — I didn't realize it at first, because I hadn't really had boyfriends. It got to be more and more that he didn't want me to go out with my sister and my friends on weekend nights when he couldn't go, or if he wasn't taking me on a specific date.

So he came over one weekend and I broke up with him. My sister and some of my friends were upstairs, hanging out. He got physical with me — he held me up by my collar against the wall and was yelling at me. He freaked out, took a pan off the stove when he was leaving, and threw it across the room — made a big hole in the wall. It was just crazy and freaked me out. It was also hard for me, because I grew up in a somewhat violent household when I was little — my parents would fight a lot. Something just clicked in me that day, where I was like, "*That's it.* Something's got to change — I've got to wake up." The next Monday, I went to school, and I called up one of my friends that was alternative/new wave — she had been inviting me to hang out at dance clubs. I was like, "Alright, we're hanging out." I chopped off one side of my hair, and started wearing crosses, eyeliner, thrift store clothes. It was an instant transformation, and hung out with alternative people. I already was listening to Duran Duran, but I got really more into music. I'd go dancing at new wave dance clubs every weekend. And then I had this punk friend, who was inviting me to punk shows and parties.

LARRY REID: There would be readings by William Burroughs — these workshops by literary/performance artists. In fact, I remember Kathleen Hanna's first live performance. Kathy Acker, a literary artist who's very influential, did a workshop and a reading — a residence at COCA [Center on Contemporary Art]. We didn't have anybody to open, and I said, "Just pick somebody out of the workshop." Kathleen Hanna was the person she picked. And Kathleen Hanna was *better* than Kathy Acker [laughs].

KATHLEEN HANNA: I remember seeing [Tobi Vail] around, and thinking she was really cool, and wanting to meet her. We met at a Fugazi show when I was in Seattle — I had just done a workshop with Kathy Acker at COCA. So I had to stay in town for a night to open for her on a Saturday, and I think the show was on a Friday. I had never seen Fugazi before. My friend Mikey [Dees], who was in Fitz of Depression, was going to the show, so I was going to try and meet up with him.

I got there and I couldn't find him, and Tobi saw me. I didn't have tickets and it was sold out — I was so stupid. Tobi was already inside — she grabbed my arm and pulled me in. And then kinda disappeared. I watched Fugazi, and it was the most amazing thing I'd ever seen in my life. They played "Suggestion," and I was just like, "Oh my God — boys talking about sexism. This is amazing!"

That weekend, Kathy Acker told me if I *really* wanted people to hear what I had to say, I should stop doing spoken word and poetry, and start a band. So I went home and started Viva Knievel. While we were on tour, I wrote Tobi a letter about her fanzine [*Jigsaw*], and I was like, "Can I write something for your fanzine?" And she said, "Yeah." So I started interviewing all the women I met on tour — asking them what it was like being on tour and what was it like being a woman in a band. I would send the interviews to her, and she wrote me a letter, saying "Let's start a band when you get home."

TINUVIEL: I met Kathleen within a month of being in Olympia — at a party. She had just gotten back from a tour with Viva Knievel. I saw her as a very animated and activated girl, who seemed to really have an idea of what she wanted to do.

KATHLEEN HANNA: There was a place called North Shore Surf Club that later became Thekla. And before that there was a place that Donna Dresch ran, GESCCO. But a lot of things in Olympia happened at parties — at houses. You'd go see Some Velvet Sidewalk play at some party, Unwound — those kind of bands.

ALICE WHEELER: The idea behind GESCCO was it was a project for school — there were about fourteen of us on the committee that ran it. The people that were primarily involved in it were Beat Happening and a bunch of other people from Olympia. At that moment, there weren't a lot of clubs in Olympia, and I think that's why we wanted to start the club and have a place for music. We had art shows there. At that point, the kids from the college were more separated from the community — part of GESCCO's mission was to bridge that gap.

GESCCO went out of business, and then there was another collective gallery run by people from Evergreen State College — Reko Muse. The Reko Muse meetings encouraged free ideas and creativity. A lot of the members went on to be in the original Riot Grrrl bands. I lived in Seattle at that point, so I only went to visit a few times. Kathleen Hanna was really into writing. She wrote a *Riot Grrrl Manifesto*, which was basically we can be in the bands, we can have our own voice, we're tired of not seeing our voice reflected. There was a bunch of bands originally — I saw them play mostly in the backstage area of the Capitol Theater, and they would play in Seattle every so often. I envisioned it to be like being at the 100 Club in 1977 London.

KATHLEEN HANNA: It was a really exciting time in Olympia, because a lot of us were young and idealistic. We were sharing books and records — turning each other on to music. Tobi had the best record collection, and was making everyone mix tapes. We were really excited to be a feminist band. A big part of our mission was to go out and inspire other girls to play music, because selfishly, we wanted a scene. One of the things grunge did for us was it showed us that there could be this strong music scene in the place where we lived.

But we weren't really a part of it — it was mostly guys. There was definitely a lot of sexism. Besides Kim from the Fastbacks, it was pretty few and far between. We just really wanted our own scene. I think that was a really big impetus of why we tried to get more women to come to shows — trying to get women to talk about sexism, to start bands. It was really a selfish intention. We wanted to have a music scene that we could relate to — the same way that Nirvana functioned within the music scene. But it was kind of scattered — Babes in Toyland, Scrawl, Calamity Jane.

ALLISON WOLFE: After high school, I was an exchange student for a year in Thailand. I came back in time for the summer of 1989. I sort of felt separated from my friends — it was like I started over again. I started hanging out a lot more at punk rock shows. And that was the summer I got into Beat Happening and all these K Records tapes. I got really interested in the idea of people making music in their own apartment for themselves and their friends.

Also, Reko Muse was having shows, so I was going to a lot of shows there. I would see Kathleen Hanna on the bus a lot, and at different parties and shows — I was really intrigued by her. She looked like Tank Girl — her hair was all shaved, but she had long bangs. She looked really tough and cool. One time I went by Reko Muse, and she was onstage playing — in Viva Knievel. They were kind of rock, but she was singing and was so powerful — she seemed so crazy onstage. I was really impressed by that. And also, that same summer, I went to see Calamity Jane. That really made a big impression on me. Those were maybe the first girl bands I'd ever seen.

I went off to school in the fall, to the University of Oregon. And Molly [Neuman] was my neighbor in the dorms. She really stood out to me, because she was always loud, bratty, and yelling at people — she seemed really tough. We started doing everything together — I turned her on to all these K tapes. And she got me interested in bands like Public Enemy. She was very politicized for that time, about racism and things like that. We really influenced each other. And this combination of politics mixed with do-it-yourself music got us excited about the Olympia music scene, and the idea of doing our own thing.

We'd go visit Olympia a lot, because my mom and family still lived there. We'd go hang out at all the cool shows. Hang out with Calvin [Johnson], and we got to know Tobi and Kathleen. They were big influences on us too. We started getting more into the idea of, "Maybe we can do this." Molly had started taking guitar lessons, I was writing poetry, and we started telling people we were in a band. It was more like we would hang out on the weekend and make stuff up. It was around the time of the *Batman* movie, with Prince and the "Batdance." We thought, we're brats and we want to be mobile, so we called it Bratmobile.

KATHLEEN HANNA: We were really obsessed with this band, Nation of Ulysses. We went on tour with them and they lived in D.C., so we ended up staying in D.C. for a couple of years. While we were there, in between tours I got bored, and me and my friend Allison and Sharon Cheslow were talking

PIC BY JOHN PERRY

Bratmobile's Allison Wolfe

about feminism a lot. We decided to have a meeting. Molly and Allison were from Bratmobile, and they had a fanzine called *Riot Grrrl.* The meeting started, and it wasn't called anything, it was just like a feminist consciousness meeting — in the punk scene. Somehow, even though we weren't in New York or Los Angeles, we got a ton of press. And then other girls started having meetings. Somehow, the way the press called grunge "grunge," the press called Riot Grrrl "Riot Grrrl."

ALLISON WOLFE: Tobi Vail had coined the term "Angry Grrrl." So she would talk about Angry Grrrl zines. And then this girl Jen Smith, who was from D.C., would talk to her about a lot of ideas, and she told us about this riot that had happened in the neighborhood where all the punk rockers lived — Mount Pleasant, in Washington, D.C. It also had a high Salvadorian population there, and this population was being really oppressed by police, anti-immigrant laws, and treatment.

On Cinco de Mayo that year, which I believe was 1991, there was a shooting — a cop shot a Salvadorian man on the main street corner. People freaked out, and burned down the Church's Fried Chicken. I think it really made a big impression on a lot of people that lived here, and the punk rockers in the neighborhood too. She was talking a lot about the riots and the upheaval in the neighborhood and the city, and she was like, "I think we also need *a girl riot.*" Somehow, between Jen Smith and Tobi, we made this word, Riot Grrrl. We jumped on that, and started having fanzines and meetings in D.C that summer.

TINUVIEL: I was in Olympia then. I remember Kathleen, Tobi, and Allison returning with this wealth of information, like, "This is what we were doing on our summer vacation" [laughs]. And it just *exploded.*

KATHLEEN HANNA: I lived in a house with Calamity Jane, and they were always practicing — they were living in Portland for the summer too. And Kathi [Wilcox's] boyfriend was always at the house. So Kathi started hanging out at the house. Tobi knew who Kathi was, and said, "We have to get that girl to join our band" [laughs]. And she didn't want to — she was like, "I don't want to be in a band, I don't know how to play anything." I just slowly worked on her, and her and Tobi became friends. Finally, she joined [on bass]. We went through a bunch of different guitar players. We really wanted to be an all-girl band, and Tobi used to be in a band with Billy [Karren] — Go Team. He one day showed up, and he was in the band [soon called Bikini Kill].

ALLISON WOLFE: I think Kathleen Hanna and Bikini Kill was the main impetus. Those girls would hang around and talk about feminism and politics a lot. And then the more we would go to Olympia and hang out, we'd all get together and talk. We'd talk about sexual abuse, and not necessarily regarding ourselves — but the problem of it among girls we knew. And also domestic violence — I know Kathleen was volunteering at a domestic violence shelter in Olympia, and I later volunteered there.

STEVE MANNING: It seemed very different than what was going on in Seattle at the time. For a lot of people, [Bratmobile] are considered that first Riot Grrrl band. Bikini Kill came after them — I don't know if there's any contention between the two about who was doing it first.

ALLISON WOLFE: At some point, Calvin Johnson heard about this, because we were probably bragging to him that we had a band, even though we didn't really. And he said, "Why don't you come play this show?" on Valentine's Day 1991. And it was just a month before. He was saying, "This new band, Bikini Kill, is playing, and Some Velvet Sidewalk — why don't you open?" And we're like, "What? We can't — we're not a band!" And he says, "You always *say* you're a band." We're like, "Oh . . . OK." We get off the phone and we're like, "Shit — what the fuck are going to do? We've got to write some songs, play instruments or something!" Also we were influenced to start a band because we were rebelling against the predominant macho grunge scene at the time that was so big in the Northwest. Even though we loved a lot of those bands, there was really a girl element lacking. It was so macho and, "Yeah, I fucked that girl, blah!" It seemed like putting a new face on sexism — but it was still guys stomping on girls, and being gross. We felt like, "Hey, we've got something to say."

And lyrics are so stupid in most of these bands, I'm sure we can do something that's at least more interesting — with a feminine or feminist touch. I already had some stuff written in notebooks, so we put tunes to them, and Molly would go back and forth between drums and guitar, because she learned a little bit of guitar and wanted to play drums. She bought a car used for $400, and we drove up to the first show. It was really scary — we had never been onstage before, and we really had no idea how people could take it. So we were paralyzed onstage, but we played, and it was cool. Bikini Kill was up front, cheering us on. Then Bikini Kill played — that was really great.

I know that Corin Tucker from Sleater-Kinney [was there]. By then, she [had] moved to Olympia, was attending Evergreen, and was a film student. She had asked all of us if she could film that show for her school project. Slim Moon came up to us before we left the show, and asked if he could have one of the songs for a compilation he was going to put out. And this was before [Moon's label] Kill Rock Stars existed — he just had this idea that he wanted to put out a compilation record of local bands. He had asked for "Girl Germs," that we had played that night, we were like, "OK, fine." We were flattered. Kurt Cobain came [to Bratmobile's first show], but showed up right after we finished playing. I gave him our first fanzine, *Girl Germs*.

KATHLEEN HANNA: Speaking of Kurt, he was super-supportive of feminism — he was reading all these feminist books.

TINUVIEL: He loved Bikini Kill. That show at the OK Hotel — when he debuted "Smells Like Teen Spirit" — he had them open. He was very faithful to the people who were his friends and neighbors. Would do his best not to let these people down. Olympia is a small town — you stick by each other as much as you can.

TRACY MARANDER: I remember Kurt kind of making fun of them at the beginning — the Riot Grrrl movement — so I thought it was funny that later he embraced the feminism of it. It wasn't that he felt like feminism wasn't valid, he felt like they took themselves too seriously. He thought they had a very good point about how there weren't enough girls up front being able to be in the pit, because it would be too much of a macho thing. Some shows were so full of testosterone that you couldn't get any girls in the front of the stage. And he thought that was a valid point, and he didn't think there were enough female photographers taking pictures at shows either. But he just thought that they took themselves too seriously.

ALLISON WOLFE: I think one of the main goals of Riot Grrrl was to make punk rock more feminine, but simultaneously, make feminism more punk rock. We were also at the same time taking women's studies courses in college. While we were totally into progressive politics, sometimes the academic nature of those classes didn't necessarily speak to us either. If we would speak in class, everyone was correcting you — "It's not *girl*, it's *woman*." We're like, "Yeah, but don't you value girls too? Are you saying only women have rights and should speak up?" It's like, we're young, we're still teenagers — we just feel like girls, and we want to use our own terminology. I felt like there were ways in which academic feminism was not speaking to common people at times. I think that was trying to find that intersection between punk rock and feminism, or alternative culture and feminism.

DONITA SPARKS: We were not a Riot Grrrl band. I remember once seeing one of those bands passing out flyers, but not passing out any of the flyers to the men in the room. Other than that, I don't really know completely what their agenda was. It was never really my bag.

MEGAN JASPER: The thing that drove me crazy about it — being a woman — was that I hate thinking like that. It's just fucking bogus to constantly think about your sex, what it means, overanalyze, and think of the things that aren't right in society because you have boobs. It kind of grossed me out on that level. I loved that it was happening — I just didn't want to deal with reading another person saying, "What's it like being a woman in the music industry?"

KATHLEEN HANNA: We didn't want to feel like weird outsiders, like the only feminist band on the planet. We didn't, because we were around bands like L7 and 7 Year Bitch — we didn't know the Gits so much, but we knew they existed.

DANIEL HOUSE: The Gits were signed after 7 Year Bitch. A bunch of the folks in the Gits — and some of the seeds of other bands — moved out to Seattle together. The Gits had been a band back in Ohio. A bunch of Antioch students moved to Seattle together as a collective — it was the Gits, and it was Valerie [Agnew], the drummer from 7 Year Bitch, and Ben London, who was in Alcohol Funnycar. When Valerie moved out here, she basically started a band with a bunch of women whose primary influence was the Gits. 7 Year Bitch practiced in their basement. We're talking about a bunch of young women who really didn't play, and this was their first real band. They were barely able to master their instruments and write these songs — sort of "the naive little sisters of the Gits." But whereas the Gits did build a pretty substantial following — they were a great band — 7 Year Bitch hit the scene due to a number of different circumstances.

One — the fact they were all women. Two — they were writing about things that were truly incendiary and very topical. Things like "Dead Men Don't Rape" really hit quick with a lot of people — people stopped, stood up, and paid attention. And they kind of eclipsed the Gits in a large degree in terms of popularity fairly quickly. So we signed them early on. I was really good friends with Stefanie Sargent, their guitar player, before she was even in the band. I saw them and it wasn't necessarily because I thought they were

PIC BY DAVID HAWKES

The Gits (Mia Zapata second from left)

great musicians or had great songs — but they definitely had an energy and a force. It was very clear what it was that people loved about them.

Their big break was getting the opportunity to open for the Red Hot Chili Peppers. Pearl Jam was on the bill to open for the Chilis — they had to cancel two or three Northwest dates, and offered it to 7 Year Bitch. That became the real springboard for everything that followed after that. After that, their first record [1992's *Sick 'Em*] came out on C/Z — it was just explosive. It was amazing how much attention the band was getting, how much more honed their live show was becoming, and how much more confident they were becoming as a band.

BEN LONDON: We were constantly playing together — 7 Year Bitch, the Gits, and Alcohol Funnycar. In a span of about six months, all signed to C/Z Records.

DANIEL HOUSE: The Gits were still playing, still popular, but did not have the same weight that 7 Year Bitch had. 7 Year Bitch, I think a lot of them felt guilty about that. And the Gits felt very angry about that — it wasn't fair. Very few people would disagree that the Gits were a better band. They wrote better songs. And in terms of being able to play their instruments — they were more adept. But 7 Year Bitch, for different reasons, they were the ones that graced the cover of *The Rocket*, and the Gits got angry at me, because we didn't get the Gits on the cover. But it's not that we didn't try. The Gits, I had to spend a lot more time being convinced to sign them. I saw them a bunch of times before finally saying, "Yeah." I totally understood that they were a better band, but I also understood that it wasn't going to be as easy to sell them as a band. 7 Year Bitch was a no-brainer — from a marketing perspective, it was so much simpler. But the Gits's music was undeniable and powerful.

Mia [Zapata] in particular — she was ultimately the reason why I signed them, because she was so much the personality and charm. She really did have a great set of pipes, and she could live in that blues and punk world simultaneously. But they were also a very difficult bunch — one of the most paranoid bands I've ever dealt with. Very mistrustful. So much so, that while we were trying to negotiate a contract, I said, "If you're this mistrustful of me as a label, maybe we shouldn't do this, because there has to be trust. Otherwise, there's no point." They finally signed, but they never did become very trusting. They wanted to approve and control every little thing — no matter how small. The sad part is they were ultimately their worst enemy in terms of their career. They were very tied into who was doing what, and if there was some kind of exploitation going on — what the politics of this other band that they might be playing with would be, and the fairness of the situation. Which in the music business, doesn't exist.

1992–1993

CHAPTER 23

"Be careful what you wish for, you might get it": 1992–1993

This two-year period was grunge's most successful, as Nirvana, Pearl Jam, Soundgarden, and Alice in Chains sold millions of albums, played sold-out shows, appeared on the covers of magazines, and were all over MTV. But success came with a heavy price for most grunge bands and the region that spawned them.

JACK ENDINO: '92 was the year Nirvana knocked Michael Jackson off the charts. Pearl Jam started selling a million records, Soundgarden was doing better and better. The shows were selling out, you had Lollapalooza. The whole thing intensified — went up to another level. It wasn't just the British press talking about it anymore, it wasn't just college radio anymore, it wasn't the indie scenes talking about Seattle. It was suddenly the cover of fucking *Time* magazine. At that point, it was like, "Oh my God, what have we done?" [laughs] Be careful what you wish for, you might get it.

KIM THAYIL: We all went platinum. We were the last ones — we eventually crept up to platinum. We were the horse to bet on for a few years before that. Then all of a sudden, there was a whole bunch of us. We hadn't even gone gold yet, and Nirvana was going multi-platinum. We went gold around the same time as Pearl Jam, and then they just skyrocketed. Alice in Chains . . . there was so much going on. With those four bands, with Sub Pop's growing success, I was expecting the Screaming Trees and Mudhoney to follow suit.

That sense of pride in community and regional identity — and happy for the success of our peers.

EDDIE VEDDER: I was a little freaked out about being, like, "the guy on the side of the bus." All of a sudden, they had billboards with Chicago radio or something, and your face on it — *giant*. This happened fairly quick. It's like, "Do they need our permission for that?" And then they say, "Well . . . *no*." And then you think, "Well, that's strange — I thought people needed permission for stuff like that if they're going to use your image to sell something." And they're doing "All Pearl Jam" or "All grunge" issues of a magazine. "Do they need our permission for that?" "No, they don't." And you're thinking, "We *should* have some control over that stuff — I don't think that's a high quality product right there. Who are these people? And they're associated with porn magazines?" I felt like getting spun around in a washing machine.

JEFF GILBERT: Once the media co-opted the word "grunge," it all went down the shit hole. Horrible. It wrecked everything.

STEVE MANNING: I can remember distinctly being at a show at the Crocodile, looking around, and going, "Wow, I don't know anybody here." Mark and I talk about this a lot — noting the change. All of a sudden, it wasn't our same core of people — it was people from the suburbs.

BEN REW: The pits started to get really violent here. The pits used to be really fun — you could jump in, there would be 150, 200 people, and you would know most of the people.

NILS BERNSTEIN: Everything started to break right when I started at Sub Pop. As media outlets were covering Nirvana and Pearl Jam, they wanted to get Sub Pop's take on it — or access our bands, or get a statement from us. It was this long period where, especially as publicist, every day would be the BBC and *60 Minutes* calling.

One time, a Make A Wish Foundation type of thing called, and they had a kid who was dying of leukemia. He was a big grunge fan, and his wish was to meet Pearl Jam or something — to come to Seattle. Our receptionist, Debby, took it upon herself to make it happen, and ended up scheduling this thing on the roof of Sub Pop, and got people from Pearl Jam, Nirvana,

A meeting of the minds: Pearl Jam and Soundgarden, Lollapalooza '92

Mudhoney, and other bands. People gave signed guitars. And the kid and his friend came — he was just like a high school grunge kid — really cool. Came and had a day of hanging out with all the Seattle rock star people. It was pretty amazing, seeing the kind of impact our bands were having, and also that it was still tight, and egoless enough that Debby could line it up with some phone calls. Ron Reagan Jr. coming to be the correspondent for a *60 Minutes* type show on a piece on the Seattle music scene. So we had to facilitate Ron Reagan Jr.'s trip to Seattle. And going to shows and literally, there being ten people in suits.

JONATHAN PONEMAN: There were some things that were exciting, but it was numbing. The sheer intensity of all these things that were happening — after a while, it was kind of like, "Oh, there's a movie being filmed about the Seattle scene that is going to star Matt Dillon and Kyra Sedgwick? It's going to be loosely based on the lives of people our age living in Seattle at this time? Sure, why not! Chris Cornell and the Pearl Jam guys are going to star in it? Sure, why not! Nirvana's gone to number one? Sure, why not!" Everything was so bizarre that the bizarre became commonplace. Yet life went on. And that's the lesson — no matter what is happening in showbiz at any point in time, you still go home, listen to your music, make dinner, and hang out with your family. Life just goes on . . .

JEFF GILBERT: It's almost like a cruel joke — *Seattle wasn't supposed to be successful.* We were really just supposed to have this cool regionalized music scene, and that was it. That was all anybody wanted to do — the guys in those bands figured they'd do it for a few years, and then go get a job hanging sheet rock, or being an art director somewhere. But it changed a lot of people. People that you would hang out with before, and talk and drink beer with, now were too good to talk to you.

I counted how many people I knew personally [that not only] became millionaires, but *multimillionaires* during that time frame. I counted fifty-three people. You know, Chris Cornell showing up with Susan at a Metal Church gig out in the suburb of Seattle, wearing a burlap sack thing that looked like a shirt, hitting me up for beer money. That's the Chris I know and miss, but after everybody got rich, [it's] like, "Wow, you guys sure changed." Kim stayed the same — he doesn't really care about money. You used to be able to talk to Jonathan and Bruce at Sub Pop — now you had to make an appointment. Wait a second, what the fuck is this? Alice in Chains, I mean, it was all laid out for them. They were touring constantly, their records were selling, they were all over the place — money rolling in. Well, anything you did before, now you did ten times that amount. That could be drugs, alcohol, or your indiscretions of the opposite sex.

DAVID MEINERT: Major labels were looking for similar bands, so there ended up being all these bands that were mimicking. You ended up having Candlebox and this really horrible second, third generation of soundalike bands trying to get record deals and be huge. That was a dark force on the Seattle music scene.

PETER BAGGE: In light of my low opinion of the whole Seattle "grunge" dress code, I was flabbergasted when fashion magazines began marketing it as a specific look that they would deliberately want to copy. It was the height of irony — this antifashion statement become the exact opposite. I still can't fathom who the driving force was behind all this nonsense either, though the Sub Pop guys seemed to be both laughing at it *and* vigorously fueling it at the same time.

DAVID MEINERT: It seemed dumb when there were runway shows of "grunge wear." I would buy $.99 seven-layer burritos and thrift store clothes — not for a style thing, *but because I had no money.*

MIKE INEZ: The cool thing about Seattle bands — they were playing these shit clubs and garages for years before they got signed. Which is completely different than the L.A. vibe back then. People would play two or three gigs, and a record company would give them a bunch of money that they would waste in the studio making a shit record. [Seattle bands] really deserved everything that came their way. They were bands scratching and struggling to make it — it was so cool to hear these masterpiece records come out of those guys.

KIM THAYIL: I think there are obvious repercussions that are pretty well-known. I think Pearl Jam handled it . . . they had their situations as well — they lost and gained band members. We thought we were handling it pretty well. And then of course, after a few years, it does catch up with you — the pressure got to be a bit much. But we thought we were handling it much better than the other bands. We thought the reason why we were handling it better was because everything happened *so suddenly* for Nirvana and Pearl Jam. But Pearl Jam — Jeff and Stone knew what to expect from their experiences from Love Bone. They were working in that direction. It might have hit quickly for Eddie and the others.

EDDIE VEDDER: It's a shame, because I never really remember going, "Wow, this is really great. This is everything you've ever worked for, this is like a dream come true."'Cause in a way, it was. But the whole thing felt like a big wave. The best waves are the fastest, the most memorable. If you can negotiate a big wave — ten foot or bigger — it's something you'll never forget. If that big wave lands on you, it's also something that you'll never forget. I felt like we were riding a big wave, but the analogy works because I kind of knew that it'll break on you. It'll hold you down and some people don't come up. It really felt like you were negotiating this big wave, and you didn't want to take your eyes off it, relax, pop champagne, and celebrate. I guaranteed that never happened [laughs]. It probably kept us from getting swallowed up. I wasn't even drinking at that point — not really at all. It took me a while for my throat to get used to singing five nights a week, so I wasn't smoking. I was kind of a prick about not wanting to be around smoke and blah blah blah. I remember having my wits about me, and living through the experience soberly. And it *was* a sobering experience. I just felt like we're going to lose some loved ones . . . *something*. You're not going to get all this stuff and not have something be taken away — friendships, relationships, whatever it is. In the end, we were absolutely right to be terrified of it all.

BEN LONDON: Any time you'd go into a town, there'd be big letters on the flyer, "FROM SEATTLE." I remember once, we were playing Emo's in Austin, Texas. We're getting ready, and some guy comes up and says, "Are you guys from Seattle? *Fucking play some Chains* — I'll come up and sing with you!" He just assumed that we all knew each other's songs. There was a club in Iowa called Hairy Mary, and literally, the entire inside of the club was covered with flyers from Seattle. Literally, somebody must have been from Seattle and sent them flyers. There were tons of Alcohol Funnycar, the Gits, and 7 Year Bitch — flyers that *I made* were on the wall of this place!

EDDIE VEDDER: In Germany, they put stickers on the *Ten* record that we still laugh about. Big stickers that said, *"The Seattle sound"* [laughs]. You tried to keep your finger on as much stuff as that as you could.

TOM NIEMEYER: The place was getting gross, in a sleazy, "biz" way. Any innocence and sincerity the music community had was flushed by '92. So was that term "community" — there was no turning back now. Hold on to those memories, loyal *Rocket* readers, 'cause that's all you got.

ED FOTHERINGHAM: I made a choice at about '94, when OK Cola came out and all that, and it was obvious this thing was going to become an MTV sort of monstrosity. I went for the mainstream, as fast as I could. I started working for Neiman Marcus for God's sake, which was like the most punk thing I could do — to me.

ART CHANTRY: In the end, as soon as money entered the picture, everybody grabbed their handful and split — and left everybody else with their thumbs up their ass, wondering what hit them. Here they were supporting this community and doing everything to help the community. And it turned out there was no community. There were just a handful of people that were sucking up the money.

Now, to be honest, there were a few people who got rich that were really good about it — Bruce Pavitt was a fine example. He came back and still firmly believed in community. He took his nut, and actually helped a lot of the people from the scene that were struggling to get their foot up and start businesses. He'd finance them, and bankroll them privately and quietly. He helped a lot of people from the brink of disaster. So I really have to take my hat off to that guy, because he really did believe in community. You can't say that for most of the people in Seattle. Community was like something they could buy and sell.

BRUCE PAVITT: I was really impressed that the scene was able to sustain itself for as long as it did.

BLAG DAHLIA: Most of the stories about the Dwarves — they all end up saying it was me. So if someone fucked some ugly girl or shot up somewhere, they say that it was me. I think it's funny — *but not always accurate.* When we were in Europe with the Supersuckers and [Reverend] Horton Heat [in 1993], Jon and Bruce came out to a show in Spain, remarking how lucky we were to have all fifteen of us crammed onto a bus. It was a lot like those drawings of slave ships from the sixteenth century where everyone is piled on top of each other.

We said we had a funny idea, about putting out the story that He Who [Cannot Be Named — the Dwarves' masked/oft-naked guitarist] had been killed in a bar fight. They loved it and thought it was funny — many periodicals reported the story. Once it began to get questioned, their publicist, Nils, quickly cracked. He was afraid that the magazines wouldn't like him anymore, and the label was afraid it might hurt people's feelings. So they issued a press release saying that we had hoodwinked them and that they were dropping us. At the same time, they were parting ways with Caroline distribution and moving to Warner, so our record, [1993's] *Sugarfix*, was effectively unavailable and unpromoted.

Sub Pop has since gone on to claim that it was a trick they pulled on us, but that was a bit of revisionist history to make themselves seem cutting edge and clever. In reality, they were just frightened and panicked. Why would a label screw themselves out of record sales intentionally? For the record, we only had a one record deal at that point — we were not dropped. And despite their attempts to follow up on the success of Nirvana, Bruce and Jon became bitter enemies, fired most of the chubbies, and didn't score another hit until the Postal Service some ten years later.

MEGAN JASPER: I remember feeling like something needed to give. It needed to fizzle out — it was sort of like an old dog that needed to be brought into the backyard and shot [laughs].

CHAPTER 24

"It was on the radio, people were talking about them, people had shirts on and their posters up": Pearl Jam

Nearly a year after its release, *Ten* became one of the top selling albums worldwide, and like Nirvana, Pearl Jam was one of the biggest bands on the planet. The group returned to the studio to record a followup, *Vs.* — which was nearly as big a hit as its predecessor — but the band also had to deal with a supposed "Nirvana versus Pearl Jam feud" in the press.

SCOTTY CRANE: My memory of Pearl Jam was what a slow boiler they were at first. That album basically took a year to take off, whereas [*Nevermind*] was a hit before it was released. And they came out about the same time.

JIM SORENSON: It must have been the beginning of 1992, when the "Alive" video [hit] — my friend Kevin was out doing their merchandise. We'd been selling a couple dozen shirts a night — they were opening for the Chili Peppers. So Kevin calls me one day and says, "We're out of shirts." It turns out the "Alive" video had come out [shortly] before. All of a sudden, *they were big*. It ended up being the rest of the tour was like that. I was working twenty hours a day, seven days a week. My best friends were the Delta Air Freight guys. Everybody that worked for me hated Pearl Jam — "We have to do these things *again*?"

EDDIE VEDDER: We went to Europe, came back, and things had quickly changed. Everyone had heard and seen the song. People were buying the record.

JEFF AMENT: We did our own tour in the States, and we'd gone from playing 200-seaters to 600-, 1,000-seaters. I think the second or third show was in Columbus or Cincinnati. We played a club that was like 1,000 or 1,200 capacity, and it was *packed* — sold out. I went to walk out the back of the club to get in our bus, and the parking lot was full of people. It took me an hour to get to the bus because I was signing autographs — I'd never done anything like that before in my life.

JONATHAN PLUM: About six months after *Ten* came out, they came back — they redid "Even Flow." I think we did a couple of songs then — we mixed and worked on some stuff for the *Singles* soundtrack. I would connect with the mellow guys, like Mike McCready. Hanging out with Eddie Vedder was just impossible for me — he couldn't have a normal conversation with me. He was so caught up in what was happening, and the type of person he wanted to be and project. I think that Stone and Jeff were in control of how the band was being marketed, and they were serious about being big. I think Eddie was really wanting to be more nose-to-the-ground punk. He was worried about people thinking that they were selling out — so that seemed like a constant debate in the band. Just having a conversation with him — he was thinking twice about everything he was saying. I remember sitting down at the table, going, "How's it going?" And he'd give me this big long story about politics or something. It's like, "Man, *I just was saying hi!*" It felt like everything coming out of his mouth was for an interview. And it was just annoying — it was really tiring for me. I just wanted to relax, and I felt really uptight around him. But it was the opposite with Mike McCready — he was a mellow dude, he'd come in, talking about real stuff. He'd be a real person. In a way, I felt bad for Eddie, because I understood what was happening. It must have been complicated.

REGAN HAGAR: I respect Pearl Jam, and love Stone as a dear friend, but they're just not for me. I also don't buy into the Eddie Vedder thing — "Woe is me." I mean, come on — didn't you grow up wanting to be a rock star? *Embrace it.*

COLLEEN COMBS: At the time it blew up, it was done on the road, and me in a little office by myself — being unfamiliar with Seattle, not having any friends, not having very much fun, not being very settled. And Pearl Jam *was* *everywhere* — it was on the radio, people were talking about them, people had shirts on and their posters up. I always felt like I just wanted to get away from it. It was like my whole life alone in an office, and I couldn't listen to the radio. I wanted to listen to just *speed metal* — I was tired of it.

SCOTT VANDERPOOL: I remember being at that show at the Moore Theatre when they filmed that video where Eddie Vedder was climbing all around ["Even Flow"]. He was a mountain climber — he used to hang out with Chris Cornell a lot. I remember him asking me not to talk about that on the radio — "Don't say that I'm hanging out with Chris Cornell, I don't want people to think that we're poser rock stars." You don't get the sense on that video how dangerous that was — climbing in the Moore Theatre. I thought he was risking his life.

KRISHA AUGEROT: I remember everyone constantly panicking about Eddie's antics onstage. The show at the Moore was one of the times where it was like, "Oh my God, *what is he going to do?* Is he going to hurt himself or someone else?"

MATT VAUGHAN: Still to this day, it's maybe one of the best shows I've ever seen. *They were ready.* I recall Eddie coming into our dressing room — we didn't know him — and hands Gruntruck a couple of cases of beer from Pearl Jam's dressing room. Introduced himself — real mild-mannered and quiet. I think he was even thanking everybody in the room for allowing him to be in Seattle and that whole thing. Real modest and nice. He turned away, and we all thought he was going to get eaten alive.

JONATHAN PLUM: Kurt Cobain was saying, "Pearl Jam wasn't legit" and "All the kids beware, they're just another corporate whatever." I remember Jeff Ament got on the mic, and said something like, "Look, just for the record, we love Nirvana. If it wasn't for Green River to make that money to pay for the Nirvana record, Nirvana wouldn't have existed."

JEFF AMENT: The guy that did that interview [the April 1992 *Rolling Stone* Nirvana cover story], Michael Azerrad, called and buttered me up, and then got me to say some things. I'm sure he turned that back around and said something to Kurt. Michael is who I think about every time we play "Blood."

Fucker. If I would have seen him on the street at any point over that next ten years, I would have kicked his ass. At that point, every interview that we did over the course of that year, we got asked at least one Nirvana question. So I'm sure on their end, they were getting asked a Pearl Jam question. After ten or twenty questions about a band that really, neither one of us knew much about . . . I mean, I know I'd seen them play a handful of times, but I doubt those guys have ever seen us play. I'm sure they felt like they were protecting some part of their scene, but I felt totally justified in whatever we were doing, because I was making punk rock music when Kurt was still going to Sammy Hagar shows. It bummed me out, because I knew Krist at that point, and I felt like there was some sort of connection. But after all that went down, there was a real separation at that point. They were still part of that split when Green River broke up — there was two camps, and those guys were part of the Sub Pop scene, and were good friends of Mark's. I'm sure there was still some bitterness left from that whole deal. We'll never know.

EDDIE VEDDER: If Kurt or Nirvana were like . . . *I* didn't want to be out there that much myself. I don't know how [people] were saying we're jumping on a bandwagon when I don't want to be on it, y'know? I mean that was honestly the way I felt. And I felt like, how can I apologize for something that we're not doing? I didn't ask for that. And yet, I might have bought an "All Nirvana" issue, *because I liked the band.* I thought it seemed cool for them to be doing that — it didn't feel right for me or us. And apparently, it didn't feel right for Kurt. But I didn't know. There were people around at that time that were probably making more of a career for themselves off of Nirvana than we ever were. By planting the idea that we were into someone's head, and someone that might have been vulnerable at the time, or justifiably paranoid — which I feel like I was, and Kurt was justified being too — I think they could plant ideas that we were careerists, or we were trying to be opportunistic with their success, to cover up their own agendas. I think that might very well have happened.

CATHY FAULKNER: Soundgarden and Pearl Jam were part of Lollapalooza — saw them both locally and in Irvine, California. It was nice to see how established they were, and how many of the fans were coming to see them — you feel that hometown pride.

EDDIE VEDDER: We played second on the bill for Lollapalooza. They wanted to put us later because the record was doing well, and we just wanted to stay right where we were.

KRISHA AUGEROT: At [Lollapalooza], the general public was just getting to see them. Every show it seemed got more and more crowd response. It just became a bigger deal to see Pearl Jam. Everyone was figuring out that this was "the show." This was the band to see.

COLLEEN COMBS: When the ball was rolling and [Kelly Curtis] could do stuff, his first thing wasn't to buy a fancy car and move his office to Los Angeles. That was one of the things that I really respected and liked about him — they stayed where they came from. And the Pearl Jam guys, I always looked at it like after the heavy metal '80s of Los Angeles, the Seattle scene was such a healthy, great place. I mean, Pearl Jam *did not* have strippers backstage — they had a special road case that had toys in it for the kids. And we had headphones so the kids' ears wouldn't get affected by the sound levels. That for me was a huge change.

CATHY FAULKNER: They did a free show at Magnuson Park, which is a big city park in Seattle. It was on their own dime, in coordination with the city, and it was a "thank you" to the fans. Through three radio stations in town, they distributed free tickets. It was absolute mayhem. They had this kind of canopy over the stage. [Eddie] was climbing up the side, and then [moved] hand-over-hand across the front bar. We all realized that the canopy wasn't fixed to the stage — the rock climber that Eddie was, he was able to do fine. It was pretty amazing. He had thrown the microphone cord over the top bar of the canopy, and had to go up there to retrieve it, because it got stuck — he ended up finishing "Porch" while dangling from the canopy. He hung like a monkey — his head was right above the microphone, so he just sang.

BLAG DAHLIA: I heard Pearl Jam play, and I knew they were really terrible. And yet, when ten million people decided they were good, what are you going to say?

PIC BY KRISHA AUGEROT

Eddie Vedder hangs ten on a muddy wave, Lollapalooza '92

PIC BY KRISHA AUGEROT

Edward E. Neuman

ART CHANTRY: I remember the day when we were told at *The Rocket* that Pearl Jam finally paid off the Mother Love Bone debt. *Ten* had already been at the top of the charts for maybe months.

JIM SORENSON: We all lost the business — the big merchandisers came in with giant advances. I got a call from Kelly Curtis, and he says, "Nice Man offered us a million dollars for the rights for the merchandise." And I go, "You haven't signed yet?" "Nah, we're going to do it, but we're going to wait until the end of this tour." I grossed over $250,000 that year — '92. For a little operation out of the back of a tattoo shop. I mean, my whole place was like 750 square feet — no windows, no ventilation. It would be 102 degrees at two in the morning. There was no name [for the company] — we were "the shirt guy in back of the tattoo shop." I skated around because I didn't have a business license. I used the tattoo shop's resale number for buying stuff — I didn't have to pay sales tax, the tattoo shop owner and I split the money. It went under my name — that's what all the invoices said.

KRISHA AUGEROT: They were worried about being so huge. They were not prepared for that kind of success — especially Eddie. I remember the label wanting to release "Black" as the next single — the fourth or fifth single — and the band wouldn't let them. It would just be an over-the-top crossover song — it was too much. So they made a choice not to do that — and that was a big deal with the label. Obviously, they want them to be a super group, and they were like, "If we could shut down becoming a super group at this point, we would. We want to maintain some reality here." That was the end of that record.

JEFF AMENT: I remember coming back to my apartment by the Seattle Center — my little neighborhood had a coffee shop and a grocery store. All of a sudden, it was totally different. I hadn't been home for a few months, and I remember going to the coffee shop, sitting down and reading the paper, and thinking, "Why is everybody staring at me? What's going on?" Suddenly, this little neighborhood that I lived in for five or six years was different. As it intensified, I just bailed on it. That's when I started going back to Montana, and reconnected with friends there. From that point on, when we had time off, I either went back to Montana, or if we were going to Europe, I would go early to Greece or Paris. I bailed on Seattle for pretty much that whole time

— I spent very little time there for those two or three years. It felt like you were on tour still, even though you were home. It felt like you were under a microscope wherever you went.

We'd all heard about "sophomore slump." We were feeling that, and a combination of all that stuff — it was a pressure cooker. Making [1993's *Vs.*] really wasn't that much fun, even though we were in an amazing spot — north of San Francisco, in the best studio we'd ever been in. There was a swimming pool in the back, and it was in the mountains. It was kind of [like] where I grew up, so I was super-comfortable with the location. And we were recording with Brendan O'Brien — it was the first time we'd ever been in the studio with a real producer who knew his shit. If you told him, "I want the bass tone to be like Motörhead," or "I want the bass tone to be like Funkadelic," he knew how to dial it in. There were all these amazing things happening, but I don't think anybody was really having much fun.

EDDIE VEDDER: It was somebody's brilliant idea to not record in Seattle, and to [record] in a place in Northern California that had rooms, was out in the mountains, had a view. We had been on tour for like two years straight, and it was just the wrong thing to do. I think I was the only guy in a lengthy and serious relationship — probably the most important thing in my life — even though the pressure was making the music have to be the most important part of my life. And that was wrong. It shouldn't have been, but it was. There were times there was pressure, and at other times, it was like, "Look, this many people like the first one, if it goes to *half,* we're still going to be fine."

I had a hard time. I hadn't finished all the lyrics by any means, and I remember thinking being in some kind of idyllic place was exactly not where I wanted . . . I wasn't going to be getting inspiration from the trees. I had this Toyota truck, and had a shell in the back, so I had a sleeping bag. Just going to the park up the street in San Francisco, in skid row, and trying to get inspiration from the conversations of crack addicts walking by or something. I remember it being really difficult — it felt like we were still on tour, and now we're making decisions which to me were more important than "Where's the next show going to be?" It was, "Do we cut out the bridge or lengthen the chorus?" The first record we made not thinking anybody was going to hear it. Now, it's a little different — "Millions of people heard that last thing. I wish we would have changed it then and I'm not going to let that happen again."

And everyone's probably feeling that way on different things. We weren't allowing ourselves space.

You have a successful record, and then they want more. They say, "We're going to do this New Year's Eve show, but then we've got to go in the studio, so you'll have four days to write" [laughs]. I mean, some bands can do it — Robert Pollard is always writing, he never stops. Now, we'll say, "I'm going to take that month, and I'm going to take a month with my family if we can afford to." It's just so different. At the time, we could have afforded to take some time too, but we weren't really advised that way. Maybe people were right, but when I think back now, of them telling us, "You'll be back on Monday, and you don't have to leave until Friday — you'll have four days to write the record." Just stupid — not a good way to not have it be traumatic.

JEFF AMENT: I don't know, because he didn't really talk to any of us about it. It was a combination between, "Hey, are you doing alright?" trying to talk, and not wanting to upset the apple cart. It was a hard time. It was a time where we were all still learning how to communicate with one another. It took a couple of more records before we figured that out.

MARK ARM: Before we toured with either band, we figured Pearl Jam was most likely to play ball with the industry, and Nirvana hung onto its underground roots. I'd known Jeff since he was a hardcore kid with a fanzine, and he had done more in the hardcore underground than anyone in Nirvana. But after Green River broke up, he and Stone had no problem saying, "We want to make it in the music biz. We want to play music for the rest of our lives. *We're going to make it.*" That was such a ridiculous notion to me. You might as well go around talking about how you're going to win the lottery. We were slated to go on tour with Pearl Jam, but after our experience on that Nirvana tour, we almost pulled out, thinking "If Nirvana is this bad, imagine what the Pearl Jam operation is like?"

We went on tour with them anyway because it was just a couple of dates. Our minds were blown. Everyone — from the techs to the band to their management — was super cool. They've got Eric Johnson — who's a great guy — tour managing them. Their manager, Kelly Curtis, used to work with Heart, and I assumed that since he comes from a non-punk old-school rock background, he'd be difficult at best. But he was great to us. You hear nightmare stories of opening bands getting fucked over on arena tours — not getting to use the full PA. Pearl Jam's sound and monitor people worked with us and totally helped us out. Everyone got along. The band had circled its wagons and was dealing with all of that crazy hype on their own terms. It was such a fuckin' dramatic shift from what we'd witnessed a few weeks before with Nirvana.

JEFF AMENT: We learned to do what we did together — Steve, Mark, I, and Stone. The reason that we played together in Green River was because we had similar ideals, and we were all really coming from that "do-it-yourself" mentality. Really being involved with every aspect of the art. When we were in Green River, we played with a ton of bands — I remember playing with Black Flag, and Henry Rollins having his own dressing room. And I remember playing with Public Image, and those guys having a $200 bottle of Bordeaux and La-Z-Boy chairs — we saw their rider. We all knew at that time — we're never going to do that. We're never going to treat bands like shit, the way that those bands treated us like shit. We took that stuff to heart. On the surface, people might have thought we were some careerist rock band put together, but it really wasn't that at all. It was all about playing music and being creative, and pushing ourselves to be better at what we did. We took it very seriously. And probably *so* seriously at some points that it didn't work out with Mark and Steve. I didn't want to work in a fucking restaurant for the rest of my life. I didn't want to be forty years old and dragging my bitter self around to the bars, talking *"Back in the day."* I wanted to be an artist — whether it was in a band, or working for an ad agency.

CHAPTER 25

"Things change, and things change quickly": Soundgarden, Alice in Chains

Both Soundgarden and Alice in Chains continued to build on their success, as Soundgarden appeared on some of rock's biggest tours, and also penned their breakthrough album, *Superunknown*. Alice in Chains' success grew even larger with their second full-length, *Dirt*. But behind the scenes, friction set in for both bands, which ultimately resulted in their undoing.

WHITING TENNIS: I was in New York when [Soundgarden] were huge. They sold out Roseland in New York City — it was such a trip, to see them go from the Central. It would have been a different perspective to see them from Seattle, but seeing it from New York — New York embraced that. They loved it. During that show — this is the split between "the Mudhoney thing" and "the Chris Cornell thing" — Chris stage dived, "swam" all the way to the sound guy, and all the way back. And then Kim Thayil was doing this guitar solo and doing these slides. He would run across the stage and slide on his knees — he was trying to get across that he was making fun of the whole thing. I think a lot of the kids that were at that show *didn't* get it. He was doing a Spinal Tap thing, and they were looking at it going, "Cool . . . rock!"

ROSS HALFIN: I was one of the photographers shooting all the rock stuff in the '90s. So they came in — it was during *Badmotorfinger*. I did a session with them at Epsom Downs — there's a big racetrack. They came and were bored with everything. I got to know them from there, and I shot them quite a lot

— they were very laid back actually. They were very nice, but were one of those bands that as soon as they started drinking . . . when people drink, everybody becomes a wanker. Phil Collen from Def Leppard put it like, "What level of a wanker you are." And they would be a *ten plus* when they started drinking. Matt Cameron, I never saw him like that. Kim Thayil would always get very morose and wanting to be your best friend — crying and stuff. Chris would be alright to a point, and then he'd start doing things like kicking doors or tables. And Ben Shepherd would just go crazy. It would be like, "Fuck you, and fuck you, and fuck you!" to whoever he could. It got to a point where they ended up getting security in England. Ben was walking across Camden Town, there was a bunch of English guys outside a pub, and he's like, *"Fuck you, assholes."* And they came over and whacked him. You never really went out [with Soundgarden]. If Chris was with Susan Silver, you never saw him. But if he was on his own — it was mainly a drinking thing with them. It was not a drug thing, ever. Once you knew them, they were very accessible. They were fairly ordinary, really.

RON HEATHMAN: I saw them on Lollapalooza in '92, and they were great — the transformation was pretty amazing.

MATT CAMERON: That was our payback for opening for all these weird heavy metal bands that we had nothing in common with. Once we got to the Lollapalooza tour, we were back with our friends.

BEN SHEPHERD: That first [Lollapalooza tour] that we did, it was a really bizarre time of life for me. You could see the Pearl Jam thing happening — that Beatles-type phenomenon. It started on that tour — seeing the crowds and the gates, and everyone running in like motherfuckers. I would hang out with Jesus and Mary Chain — I was the only guy that would talk to them. They knew I was all dark cloud and scowling — just storm in the room, share my whiskey with them, or whatever. See — that's the problem. I started drinking too much on that first Guns N' Roses tour. I would get really depressed, and that was the only way out — or so it seemed. A lot of touring is "hurry up and wait." You get there and then you wait. You'd see guys that had been out for a couple of years in a row — you hit this wall where it's like, "Why go home? There is no home, there's nothing! Let's just keep going, we'll play another show!"

Chris Cornell gets down 'n' dirty, Lollapalooza '92

ROSS HALFIN: Pearl Jam, with all their anti-everything, still very much liked the trappings of being rock stars. The bodyguards, the this, the that. Whereas Soundgarden were very accessible, Pearl Jam was "Keep everyone away." In a sense, Nirvana was accessible. Soundgarden always had women around them, which is probably because of Susan Silver working for them. And the women would always wipe their asses — they were always pampered. Everyone around them was fussing and panicking — when you actually got them, they were totally fine.

BEN SHEPHERD: [1993] was a really good year. I tried to make a home life. My life was so fun, because we did the Hater record [Ben's side-band with Matt Cameron, which issued 1993's *Hater*], did *Superunknown*. We were all really connected.

MATT CAMERON: *Badmotorfinger* had gone gold by the time we started [1994's] *Superunknown*, so there was a little more anticipation from the record company to try and up the ante. Creatively, we were peaking. All pistons were firing — we were writing really cool music, and we were playing really good together. We wanted to be prepared, and rehearsed a lot. The label suggested that Michael Beinhorn produce it. We'd never used anyone but Terry or Jack — we were always very guarded and protective with our group. We felt we knew what was best for our music, so anyone who came outside of our group and told us, "Why don't you try this or that," we were like, "No way! What do you know?" So I think Beinhorn was the first guy to make suggestions to us. That helped a little bit, but ultimately, it was our call.

SUSAN SILVER: All the managers that I've ever spoken to who have worked with [Michael Beinhorn] loved working with him. As did I. He was just great to deal with in terms of the business end of things. And every musician who ever worked with him, didn't like the experience at all . . . and came through it usually with the best records of their careers. The process was not particularly enjoyable for those guys, *but goddamn,* they made a good record! [Laughs.]

ADAM KASPER: It was almost six months of recording. My role was an assistant engineer, but it ended up morphing into engineering a lot of it — there was bad friction between the engineer and the producer. There was friction everywhere — but sometimes that creates great art. The engineer tried to mix a song, I think Beinhorn may have tried to mix one, and it was just sounding terrible.

MATT CAMERON: There was a lot of wheel spinning going on — we would spend three days on a guitar part. It got silly. We knew we had a good record in there, but I think we were all just sick of it — we didn't care anymore. And then lo and behold, Brendan O'Brien came in and mixed it — he did it in like a week and a half or two weeks. He worked the complete opposite of the way we were working — just knocked it out. When I took the mixes home and listened to it, I realized we had a really good record.

SUSAN SILVER: When Cameron Crowe was making *Singles*, Jeff Ament worked on the set on the art direction. The set that he created as Cliff Poncier's apartment had stacks of cassettes lying all over — one was Cliff's demos. Jeff went so far as to put song titles on the cassette — something no one looking at a movie would ever see. Chris was visiting the set, saw that, took those song titles, and wrote those songs as a gift for Cameron. The A&R guy at A&M, as a gift, pressed them into CDs. Put the cover artwork that Jeff had put on Poncier's demo, pressed up a thousand, and gave them to us. They got around. "Fluttergirl," "Spoonman," "No One But You," "Missing," and I think there's one more.

ADAM KASPER: A lot of the songs — "Black Hole Sun" — the demos were just amazing. The final product didn't change a whole lot from the demos the band had made on their own.

EDDIE VEDDER: They'd just finished *Superunknown,* and Chris had given me a copy. We went up for a hike up into the Olympic Peninsula — this eight-hour walkabout thing. And I got to talk to him about it *the whole trip* [laughs]. I felt like an apprentice — he was so kind and giving with talking about whatever that process was. "I don't use a lot of background vocals — you use a lot of background vocals, and a lot of effects." He started laughing, like, "I don't know, I don't really think so." And I'd ask him about publishing — all this shit — the poor guy just wanted to take a hike and get away from this stuff! And here we are — looking at the dirt, trudging along these switchbacks going vertically, listening to this shit from me.

Then I remember being on the side of some cliff. We had climbed up real easy, and then on the way back down, we got stuck on the middle of this cliff. He was above me and I was below. I was like, "*I don't see a way out of this*" — we just sat there thinking about it for like five minutes. And then we both started laughing — it was just such a bizarre situation. Both our records were done, and we just started laughing like, "Well, I guess the records are going to sell pretty well!" Kind of like the mystery of whatever had happened. Two nights later they played this club, I think it was RKCNDY, they were playing the *Superunknown* record. I remember that being beyond the beyond — all cylinders were firing.

SUSAN SILVER: The sense of pressure was never there, because the thing about Soundgarden and Alice — they had really clear musical direction within the group. What an outside producer or A&R person had to say about the music was irrelevant — it really just bounced off. In that sense, there wasn't pressure from the outside. Internally, everybody had a pretty strong agreement as to what music they liked. They were making some amazing music. Of course, by that time, a big part of [Alice in Chains'] focus and struggle was drug addiction.

JERRY CANTRELL: We had a meeting one day at the office. Sean came down — he's all animated. He's like, "I had a dream. We put this record out — it's an acoustic EP called *Sap*. People loved it. It was great, I could see the whole thing." [1992's] *Sap*, I think, was off the demo tapes that we did for *Singles*. Cameron wanted a song, so we got him to pay for us to record *ten songs* [laughs]. We gave him an inflated budget. We came up with "Would?" for the movie, and we demoed a bunch of shit. We had all this acoustic stuff, and we're thinking, "What the fuck can we do with this? We're a hard rock/metal band." We figured people might not dig it, also [laughs]. We put out an EP — put it in the stores without any advertising at all. That record, until the movie *Clerks* came out, only a real select, handful of people knew that record even existed — until "Got Me Wrong" got released as a single again years later.

MARK ARM: I was friendly with Alice in Chains, but I didn't know them well. I knew Layne a little bit. I didn't meet those guys until after they had already put out [*Facelift*]. My girlfriend was sort of hanging around Layne's girlfriend. So I hung out with those guys for a while, because we had the same "hobby" [laughs]. But it was Jerry Cantrell who called and asked me to sing on *Sap* [on the song "Right Turn"]. I was surprised, like, "Why would you want me to sing?" I could understand why they'd want Chris Cornell to sing [laughs].

SUSAN SILVER: [1992's] *Dirt* record — the making of the record — started to be compromised. It took longer periods of time to get things done. It started to be undeniable. After Andy died, there's this denial factor. And I was already deep in a struggle with my own brother, who was also a heroin addict. For me, this couldn't happen to someone else who hasn't gone down that road already — because *they'll see* this is where it leads. So I had a certain amount of denial that it was a problem with Layne in the beginning. And then it just became my life as the *Dirt* cycle unfolded. I've spent more hours in every single day focused on and dealing with heroin addiction than I did managing my client's career. It became a behemoth. I lost my brother to the battle, so it was all-consuming. It was a horror show so much of the time — which ultimately led to nothing except pure trauma on my part, to see my own husband go down that road so many years later. *It was shocking.*

By the beginning of the tour cycle with *Dirt*, it was something that I was dealing with every day. And through that cycle, there were many cancellations and incidences. But Layne never gave up hope. He was not a sneaky drug addict — he was open about his struggle. He tried *so hard* on numerous occasions to get clean — through rehabs, and was willing to talk to people about it. He was willing to talk to the press about it. He was really honest about it — often apologetic about it. It kept taking him down.

JERRY CANTRELL: *Dirt* was a heavy record. We came down to L.A., and things had gotten darker around the band. As they will — if you're fucking around with the wrong shit. And we were. We rented a ranch house out in Malibu, and we rehearsed in it. We were coming up with all this stuff that was just *agro*. Super powerful, very heavy lyrical content. It was a serious step up from *Facelift* — I equate it, as far as artistically, [to] what I was saying about Nirvana from [*Bleach*] to *Nevermind.* To many people, it's a record unto itself. I don't think there's a record like that. *Dirt*, from top to bottom, is just an *assault*, man. It's beautiful, it's moody, and it's no-fucking-holds-barred — no punches pulled at all. Beautiful, dark, and ugly at the same time. We came down to L.A., started tracking the record, and that Rodney King verdict came down. *The fucking town went up in flames*. We were staying at the Oakwoods in Venice — so we had to come from Studio City to Venice while the whole city's in a riot. We called up Tom Araya from Slayer, and we went out to the desert and hung out there for a while, 'til the shit cooled down. We had to postpone until the riots fucking chilled out. That's a moment I'll never forget — tied to that record.

JONATHAN PLUM: It was amazing being in the studio with Layne — he was an explosive singer. This is true with all those bands — earlier on they weren't as good in the studio, and later, after they did touring, they'd be remarkably better. In the early days, Layne wasn't super-proficient at singing in the studio. But later on, everything was one take. The latter stuff probably was when he was deep into the drug thing. It was weird — I didn't know what he was doing, or what he wasn't doing. He seemed like a quirky artist at that point. He was temperamental. He'd come into the studio, and be really friendly and funny — and present. And then when he would do his tracks, he got really focused and edgy. When things wouldn't go right, he'd get pretty pissed off. The producer on their later stuff was Toby Wright, and I remember both of us sweating — trying to keep things rolling smoothly, because he would start yelling. Then he'd come back in the control room, listen, and just go back to his happy/normal self. He seemed like he was in a zone — I don't know if that has to do with drugs or not.

SEAN KINNEY: [Drugs] were taking over. We were doing whatever we could get our hands on — and as much. It definitely started working against us. That record, people could probably identify with it — it's all right there. It's laid out — explained exactly what we were doing, what we were going through. It sounds [like] what was echoing in our heads at that time. From then on, some of us continued further down in that direction, and some of us didn't. That's a tough album for me. People are like, "That's your greatest record." It's bittersweet.

JERRY CANTRELL: We *all* partied man, so to point the finger at [Layne] — might as well point the finger at all of us. Unfortunately, he's the lead singer, and the lyrical content of what he was writing — he was putting it out there. I always thought that was very brave of him, and I always stood behind that. It's the type of thing that we always supported ourselves in — going *all the way* with it, whether it was good or bad. I mean about expressing it artistically. We dicked around — I don't think none of us can say we didn't try it, in one form or another. I was first introduced to it in Europe on one of our first tours. There was, like, two days missing that I don't remember very clearly — except all of us being very ill and on a bus. I guess it's something that spoke to Layne, but his experience wasn't anything different than ours. We all had our little vices. If you fuck around with that long enough, it's going to turn on you.

NANCY LAYNE McCALLUM: I didn't relate to it at all. I didn't know any of the code words for the drugs or the lifestyle. It was foreign territory.

MATT VAUGHAN: [Gruntruck] did a couple of tours with them. For Gruntruck, it was double-edged. They went from being beer-drinking best friends to doing it "the Alice in Chains way" — which is a little nastier, and it got ugly in the end. Susan Silver had a bodyguard for Layne. I remember asking her, "Why do you have a bodyguard for him? They don't seem *that* popular yet." And she said, "It's not for the band, it's to make sure fans and dealers aren't getting to Layne." I think the bodyguard slept in the same room, or outside Layne's room. At the same time, Alice in Chains had a lot of young girls that were always hanging on them — as do most bands — but they didn't just walk away, let's say. There was some Mötley Crüe–styled behavior going on with Alice. Guys like me, Gruntruck, and most guys from Seattle, that was *not* our style — to be messing with fourteen-year-olds, and stuff like that. That was more the L.A./Coconut Teaszer/Sunset Strip scene. It was different — at times funny, but after a while, not funny at all. A lot of drugs. It was more of an L.A. trip than a Seattle-style trip.

KURT DANIELSON: Tad did a tour opening for them — right before *Inhaler* came out. Layne was going through one of his periodic attempts to kick his dope addiction. Layne's lyrics remain as naked testimonials of what it is to try to live through being a heroin addict — a story that is difficult to tell, not least because it is almost impossible to survive.

TAD DOYLE: [Layne] was pretty mellow outside of the rock thing. Of course, Kurt Danielson and I did most of the talking when we were hanging out with him. He'd just sit and laugh, make comments every now and then. They're all really funny guys — they had futures in being comedians if the rock thing didn't turn out too well. We were in a van, and they were on a touring bus. They always had us riding with them — playing video games and listening to music.

MARK ARM: I knew Layne a little bit. I remember one time I went to one of their shows at the Coliseum. Layne was trying to stay clean — so was I. He was staying at a hotel, because he didn't want to go back to his apartment where his girlfriend was — he was trying to remove himself from the people who were still doing drugs. So we went back to his hotel, and watched *The Player* [laughs].

MATT VAUGHAN: Silver and Curtis worked together with Alice in Chains the first year or two, and eventually, Susan ended up managing them herself.

SUSAN SILVER: [Pearl Jam's] stuff was taking off so big — [Kelly Curtis] just really wanted to focus . . . it was hard, because drugs were becoming a real issue, and he managed Mother Love Bone when Andy died. It was too painful.

SEAN KINNEY: Everybody was there [two festivals in Brazil, during January 1993] — L7, Chili Peppers. It was a big gig down there. That was another bittersweet moment, because our bass player was leaving — that was the last show we did with him. It was one of the biggest shows we played — probably 100,000 people. You're just looking down the whole time, bummed out, because the bass player [Mike Starr] is leaving. And I'd known the guy since . . . me and him were in garage bands when we were, like, *nine*. It was a sad moment, but hanging out was cool. The parties were always going on. At that time, there's partying where it's fun, and then it takes over. It's not a party, it's your fucking lifestyle. It's a huge dependency, and you're sick if you're not having your whatever it is you're having. It's "the trick" — it's not anything that's glamorous, cool, or fun.

And it's weird down there — Beatlemania kind of shit. That opened my eyes — I don't ever want to be this huge, Beatley kind of band, where you can't go anywhere, with people chasing you and jumping on your car. When you're a kid, you're like, "*That's so cool!*" It's terrifying — "I think these people will kill me if they get a hold of me." There were a lot of eye-opening things there, but it seemed to me it was really a closure of one of us leaving, and the drugs spinning out of control.

BEN REW: The band wanted to fire him when they first got signed, but the label told them to keep him, because he was so good-looking. Poor Mike — it would probably would have done a lot better for his health in the future if they would have fired him.

SUSAN SILVER: His focus became more "lifestyle" than the music.

JERRY CANTRELL: I think we toured with Ozzy for half a year. It was a real family-type thing. Hanging out with Zakk [Wylde], Randy [Castillo], Mike [Inez], and Ozzy was great. So when we decided to make that decision, we made one phone call — we called Mike. If we're going to get another bass player, we're going to have to at least get another guy with the same name, smokes the same cigarettes, plays the same bass, looks the same! [Laughs.]

MIKE INEZ: I had just finished a twelve-month tour with Ozzy, supporting the *No More Tears* record. One of the last bands to open up for us was Alice in Chains. We were in Nevada mixing *Live and Loud* with Ozzy. Sean called me from Brazil, and said, "What are you doing?" They were going to make a move on their bass player. Went up to Ozzy and said, "Is it cool? I hate to leave you in the lurch." It's as clear as day — he says, "If you don't go, we'll have to go to the hospital. It's going to take me about a week to get my foot out of your ass!"

I ended up not going to Brazil. I was going to hop on a plane, and jam with the guys without practice or anything. Then Sean and Jerry called and said, "We'll meet you in London, and we'll do two or three days rehearsal." So I flew to London, and we did, I think, twenty-one shows in sixteen or eighteen countries. It was an amazing schedule, right off the bat. These guys were so burnt from the time travel — going down to Brazil and then to London. We spent the first day just smoking this killer hash [laughs]. We got two rehearsals in — I think it was us and Screaming Trees. We just tore up Europe — it was a trial by fire for me. Looking back, I don't know if I would have jumped in without thinking about it more [laughs]. I mean, I wouldn't take it back for the world, but it was such a crazy thing — to just hop on a plane, and now I'm in Alice in Chains. We put *a lot* of road miles in. I think at the height, there was one year we did 350,000 road miles — and that's not even including the tour bus. That's ten, eleven times around the earth in the air in one year.

STU HALLERMAN: I did some demos for them, and hosted them [at Avast! Studios] for some rehearsals. [1993's] *The Last Action Hero Soundtrack,* they wrote songs for that — Mike Inez was in the band at that point. Layne was having "arm problems" then. He would show up at the studio promptly, but then lock himself in the bathroom almost all day. He would come out, and sing a verse and a chorus, [and say] "Alright, you got the idea?" Then disappear back in the bathroom.

JERRY CANTRELL: Things change, and things change quickly. All of a sudden, we're able to buy houses — we've been living on people's couches for years. Even when we weren't touring, because we were working so hard, what's the point of buying a fucking house? We're never home. So by the time we got home after *Dirt* — this is like *two years*, making that record and touring. We were *done* by the end of that. It puts a wear on you, and you develop a few bad habits here and there that are not conducive to stopping. It's not like, "Oh, you become a drug addict." It's something that develops over time. And it's also indicative to the gig — because *you're* the party in town every night. We had a lot of fun doing it for a lot of years. And then we, all of a sudden, had a lot of time off and a shitload of money.

CHAPTER 26

"We might as well start talking to majors": Mudhoney, Tad, Skin Yard, Screaming Trees, Melvins, Brad

In 1992–1993 Mudhoney and Tad issued their major label debuts, *Piece of Cake* and *Inhaler*. While Skin Yard broke up, the Screaming Trees scored a breakthrough hit with the song "Nearly Lost You," and the Melvins entered the studio with Kurt Cobain as producer for their major label debut, *Houdini*. And at the height of Pearl Jam's popularity, guitarist Stone Gossard launched a side band, Brad.

JOHN LEIGHTON BEEZER: Mudhoney gets a lot of respect, for saying, "Whatever we were doing with Sub Pop, we were doing it right. Why on earth would we want to change?" Well, *several million dollars,* maybe? [Laughs.] They stayed with Sub Pop during that feeding frenzy. I think Nirvana ended up being "the Mudhoney that wasn't Mudhoney." You can't take anything away from Nirvana, but at the time, they were like "the little brother band." When I first saw [Nirvana] on MTV, I thought, "Oh my God, that's Mark Arm playing Steve Turner's guitar!" Steve had that trademark baby blue Fender Jaguar, and that was Mark's hair. It wasn't a coincidence — he really looked up to Mudhoney, and wanted to be Mudhoney. When Mudhoney wouldn't sign with a major, the majors went around saying, "What's the next best Mudhoney?" It was Nirvana.

MARK ARM: We didn't leave Sub Pop because Nirvana got huge. We left before Nirvana exploded. If we knew that would happen, we could've stayed at Sub Pop. We left because Sub Pop was so overextended financially that we thought it would collapse. We decided that we had to get out of there before our friendships were strained over some stupid little thing like money. It was tough for us to leave, but we felt like it was something that we had to do. I know it was tough on Bruce and Jon too — Nirvana had just left. Now Mudhoney, Tad, and the Fluid were leaving.

The first label we met with was Caroline Records. They distributed Sub Pop at the time, and we thought we could cut out the middleman, and deal directly with Caroline. So the president of the company, Keith Wood, came out from New York and took us to lunch. They were having success with the first Smashing Pumpkins album [1991's *Gish*]. He told us that if we wanted to be on Caroline, we would have to do a couple of things. First, we would have to concentrate on Mudhoney, and we couldn't have any side projects. Steve and I had just done the Monkeywrench record. We were just like, "*Huh?* We should be free to do whatever we want to, when we want to!" Then he said we had to sweeten our guitar sound [laughs]. We're like, "If we sweeten our guitar sound, what have we got?" Finally, he said we'd have to tour nine months out of the year, because that's what the Smashing Pumpkins did. That would raise our profile and make shit happen for us. We were looking at each other in disbelief. We could do whatever the hell we wanted at Sub Pop — this sounded insane. We figured if this kind of insane shit is coming from a guy from a minor independent label, we might as well start talking to majors. What have we got to lose?

So we talked to a couple of labels — we whittled it down to Epic and Reprise. The A&R rep at Epic was this guy who wore cowboy boots and a black fringe leather jacket. He was a nice enough guy, but he had this dude-in-the-record-industry vibe. When we did the rounds at the Reprise offices, we met Bill Bentley, a publicist who'd been there forever, and probably still is. He was the first person we met who didn't cover his walls with posters from the label. He's a music fan, a human — not just a shill promoting whatever "hot new release" the label is currently pushing. There were more people like that at Reprise than any of the other labels we went to. It seemed more real to us. Also, Warner Bros./Reprise had this long history of being "the artist friendly major label."

Another weird thing was Sonic Youth, who were on DGC — a Geffen subsidiary — had been authorized to act as A&R reps for that label. So they were trying to get us to sign to DGC through them. We met with their manager, John Silva, who was also Nirvana's manager. The guy always gave us really weird vibes — he seemed a little slimy. We had a lunch meeting with him right when "Teen Spirit" starting getting airplay on MTV. He's facing a TV, we've got our backs to it. He's talking *at* us, not *to* us, staring at the TV. And then the Nirvana clip came on — he starts laughing. He's trying to tell us what he could do for us. "Sonic Youth — in name — will be your A&R guy. But basically, your A&R guy is going to be *me*" [laughs]. He's totally transfixed by the fact that Nirvana is taking off. I swear you could see dollar signs in his eyeballs. It was just the fucking grossest, most transparently icky encounter we had in our label search [laughs]. Of all the A&R people we met, David Katznelson — who wooed us on behalf of Reprise — was the most down-to-earth. At the time, Reprise seemed like it was as cool as a major label could get. We didn't realize that that was only going to last a couple more years.

ART CHANTRY: Mudhoney everyone thought was smart, because they were one of the last ones to sign with a major. They signed for an incredibly low advance in exchange for ultimate creative control. No other band did that — they all took big advances. Advances are loans — they have to be paid back to royalties. So what happens is the bands become indentured servants — they owe money and they work until they pay off the debt. Time and time again, you saw bands from Seattle — hungry for the limelight after years of toiling for nothing — getting this huge carrot on the end of this real long stick. They'd try to resist, but just couldn't restrain themselves. The moment they grabbed for that carrot, man, *they were toast.* And Mudhoney didn't do that. And even then, they ended up getting screwed [laughs].

COLLEEN COMBS: I looked at Mudhoney as being middle class. They didn't become millionaires, but they really could make a living off what they did. Which is what a lot of musicians always said they wanted. And in Seattle, you *could* buy a house and live a decent life at that level.

MARK ARM: The *Singles* soundtrack was another one of those weird things — they offered us $20,000 to come up with a song for the soundtrack. Twenty thousand for one song? That's insane! I'm sure they thought that we would go into a huge studio. Most of the other bands were used to working with major label budgets. They're probably used to spending $200,000 or more on a record, so I guess $20,000 is one-tenth of a ten-song album. We went back to Conrad's, recorded "Overblown" for $164, and kept the rest [laughs]. We recorded and mixed it in one afternoon. I was incredibly stupid with money then — I was blowing it on heroin. Money would come in and flow out like water going over a waterfall. The one good thing about having all this money — I never got to the point where I was stealing from friends or family. God, the stories you hear about junkies who'll do anything to stay high. Luckily, I was in a comfortable enough place. I also supported my girlfriend's habit, and I was fairly generous with other friends [laughs].

We recorded [1992's] *Piece of Cake* in the same studio we used for *Every Good Boy Deserves Fudge* — Conrad Uno's basement. When underground bands from the '80s, like Hüsker Dü and the Replacements signed to Warner Bros., their records got slicker. The main reason we worked with Conrad on *Piece of Cake* — besides the fact that we liked working with him — was that it would prove a point. Prove to ourselves, and to the people who would pick up the next record who had been fans of ours, that we weren't going to radically change our sound. The bonus was that we recorded *Piece of Cake* for $20,000 and got to keep the rest of the money [laughs]. I'm not even sure I was aware that was how our contract was set up until the check came. That was probably one of the smartest things we ever did, because it allowed all of us to put down payments on houses.

STEVE TURNER: We didn't think it was that great of a record after a few years. There was some filler on that record.

ED FOTHERINGHAM: When they signed to Warner Bros. and were putting out a record with them, [they] wanted Art Chantry to design it, and me to illustrate it. So I made money that I didn't think was possible before — I quit my day job and became an illustrator, and stopped painting. Then I went to New York — I'd been doing these record covers, so I had printed work. I went into the *New Yorker*, and had a job in two days. I can't tell you how great it was to be from Seattle in 1992. It opened doors like it was fucking crazy. It was hilarious — a joke. What's wrong with you people? *You suckers.* It was sucker-time.

EDDIE VEDDER: You know who's a big part of Seattle music for me? The obvious answer is Mudhoney — but also Bob Whittaker, who is like the fifth member of Mudhoney. He was the manager, but if you were to make a Richard Lester film about Mudhoney, the other star of the band is Bob. And I think it was becoming friendly with them that really felt like a big part of being accepted. The acquaintances of that facet of Seattle — that was the real deal, as far as from Nils Bernstein to Per Bernstein, to Bob, Charlie from the U-Men, John Bigley, to the Fastbacks and Kurt. Because I definitely did feel like an outsider, and was really malleable as far as, "How do you do this stuff?" I think I knew how to work on music and all that, but I didn't know how much fun you were allowed to have [laughs].

I remember going over to Novoselic's house, and he had two pinball machines in the basement. And I thought, "Well . . . you're allowed to do that?" Like that's not seen as decadent and "Liberace," but cool — having a jukebox. Whether it was or not, they made it that way. It was a blast. So I was highly impressionable and fortunate to be around to not make all my mistakes on my own. And at the same time, not take yourself *so fucking seriously.* You do things, and in the back of your head you could just hear Danny Peters and Matt Lukin laughing at you [laughs]. As they watch some MTV Awards, or whatever the fuck it is. Or seeing them in a pool hall, and them going, "Dude, what was *that* about?" Thinking you did something intense and cool, and they're like, "Yeah — *whatever, guy.*" I owe them a lot.

LILLY MILIC: They played with Sonic Youth at Red Rocks. I remember being backstage with them, and some girls showed up — groupies. I remember all of us looking at them, and they're standing looking at us. Mudhoney, this is not typical rock, in terms of their attitude — rock star–ish or anything. Matt Lukin looked at them and said, "Do you have a beer?" They had nothing to say, they just stood there uncomfortable, and walked away.

VAN CONNER: The Mudhoney guys — similar to the Nirvana guys, in the "taking it to the nth level." I remember after the Reading Festival, all three bands running around and raising total hell. I fell off the stage and screwed up my foot really bad. I remember waking up in the middle of the night in Dan Peters' bed, with their tour manager on top of me in a dress, trying to kiss me — with my foot throbbing in massive pain! Peters had to take me to the hospital. I'm lying there in pain, and Peters stole a whole bunch of latex gloves.

DONITA SPARKS: I think we played the Endfest with them, at the Vogue. I was a little nervous because I could see Mark Arm — he was on the side of the stage. We were doing a cover of Agent Orange's "Bloodstains" — I busted into the lead, and I totally played it in the wrong key. And he put his arms in the air, like it was the greatest thing!

RON HEATHMAN: I don't think a better front guy can be found than Mark Arm. He's everything. Their shows were mind-blowing. And then getting to know them, they never took themselves seriously — at all. I still appreciate that.

EDDIE VEDDER: I probably tried to get the courage to say hello to Mark that first time that we played. There's a healthy sense of intimidation about him [laughs]. We were going to Europe for the first time — I got the courage to ask Mark, "Any advice?" I could see [he was like], "OK, I'll go along with it." He goes, "Yeah, *don't smuggle.*"

I was shooting a lot of Super 8 back in those days — and I have incredible footage of Mudhoney. There's no sound, it's silent. I'd watch this footage, and at one point, they're playing, all synchronized — Matt's head bobbing with Danny's drums — and it's a shot from the side, you can see everybody. All of a sudden, they take their hands off the guitars, they all turn around — as if this is Russian synchronized swimming or something — pick up a beer, take a sip, lean their heads back, put the beer down, back to the song. All four of them — unbeknownst to them that they're doing this. Just magic.

If you go back and listen to tapes of Matt Lukin at the end of shows, he'd walk off, and just as he was stepping to the middle of the stage, he'd see Mark's mic, and look at it as if it was an old friend that he bumped into on the street. He'd just have to say something. The most bizarre, non sequitur . . . y'know, "How about them Cowboys?" I don't even know what that means. Always a real experience — something just perfectly random.

STEVE TURNER: We were doing really well on the college circuit, but we never thought we would be the next "explosion." We knew our place immediately — "OK, *footnote!*" [Laughs.]

TAD DOYLE: We got signed initially to RCA/BMG for about five minutes. They gave us this huge advance. Then they decided they wanted to sell the contract, so we moved to Giant/Warner. Little did I know how good we had it with Sub Pop. I don't regret doing anything I did, but I do regret how it turned out a lot of times. It seems like we could have gotten a little more action out of these labels. They throw 5,000 releases out per year, and the one that sticks to the wall is the one they focus on. We didn't change what we were doing — we kept on doing what we loved. Never once did we let go of our integrity to do something different and out of our comfort zone.

KURT DANIELSON: We found another drummer — Josh Sinder — he used to play drums for the Accüsed. He went into the studio with us to do [1993's] *Inhaler*. I felt now and then that this record was as important as *8-Way Santa*, in terms of the music itself. It was a completely different kind of production — much rawer than *8-Way Santa*. Ironically, it cost a lot more money. But we had a lot of fun making it — it was fun working with J Mascis as a producer. After *Inhaler*, Gary left the band. Gary — from the very beginning — was an integral part, just as Steve was. I can't say what happened with Gary, although I feel personally that I made a mistake, and I wish that we would have continued working with Gary. When he was gone, I realized how important he was.

JACK ENDINO: The final thing [Skin Yard] did as a band was tour Europe in October–November [1991]. We toured the U.S. and then we went to Europe immediately — five weeks here and then five weeks there. Our fourth record came out around the same time, [1991's] *1,000 Smiling Knuckles*, and was our biggest record — it did about 14,000 copies — which is very good for an indie record. At least in those days. We went to Europe, and at the end of our tour, all our equipment got stolen — that took the wind out of our sails. We finished the tour on borrowed equipment. Literally, on the flight home, the band called it quits. We were all tired at that point; my producing career was starting to take off. All these people really wanted to give me money and confine me to the studio for long periods. Our singer Ben was starting Gruntruck — he was getting antsy to get that going.

No more than two weeks after we got home, in January of 1992, I got a phone call from Van Conner of the Screaming Trees. He said, "We heard you guys are breaking up. I didn't want to ask this without checking with you first — but we need a drummer." [Laughs.] He was interested in Barrett, who was the drummer for the last two years of our existence. And I just got this look

PIC BY KAREN MASON-BLAIR — KARENMASONBLAIR.COM

Skin Yard (Jack Endino second from right)

on my face — "Oh my God, Barrett Martin in the Screaming Trees? What an amazing idea! *Yes, take him!*" So Barrett joined the Screaming Trees, Ben started Gruntruck, Daniel had become a father shortly before and had already left the band a few months before that — he was running C/Z Records full-time. And I became a record producer full-time. The funny thing was a few months later, we called each other up and said, "You know all those songs we wrote last year? We really should make a fifth album." So we decided to make one more record — for posterity. We made [1993's *Inside the Eye*], even though we didn't play any more shows. I'm satisfied with what we did — five albums that are dramatically different from each other.

VAN CONNER: When we got [Barrett], we decided, "Let's make a different kind of record." He was a different drummer then we had before — more Bonham-y. We came up with things [on 1992's *Sweet Oblivion*] like "Shadow of the Season," where it was more of a groove, heavier sound than we had before.

MATT VAUGHAN: The Screaming Trees were also on the tour [with Alice in Chains and Gruntruck]. This was the same tour that Mark Lanegan supposedly "went to the hospital." I remember seeing an MTV news report that Lanegan had to go to the hospital and was off the tour for a week. When, in actuality, that's not what happened at all — he was just missing for a while. I think management had to spin the story a bit. I remember him getting in a fight with Mark Naficy — the sound guy for all three bands. They got in a fistfight, but that isn't anything that hadn't happened before — Lanegan was known to throw his fists around. He threw me his coat and was beating up on Naficy. At first it was funny, but then got out of control. I remember Lanegan walking away and he just kept walking — I think we were in the South somewhere. He ended up hooking up with a girl, hung out with her for a week, and was later found in another part of the country. He may have had a stint in the hospital in his stupor or love hangover. Screaming Trees were off the bill for a week or two. Two years later, I get a tap on my shoulder at a Nick Cave show — as I'm wearing Mark's coat — and Lanegan says, *"I want my coat now."*

TOM NIEMEYER: Screaming Trees were amazing, and got a small break for a minute. Image was too important to "the music machine," so they got ignored.

DALE CROVER: We were sitting in a restaurant, and Cobain goes, "Would you guys ever consider being on a major label?" We're like, *"Sure."* We got hooked up with these lawyers from Berkeley, who had done a deal for Mudhoney and Warner Bros. And because of Nirvana and the whole Seattle thing, our name always came up — those guys drummed up some business for us. We talked to a few labels. We went into Atlantic Records — the *Lysol* record was about to come out. We sat in a meeting with the people from Atlantic, Danny Goldberg, and played them this record. Said, "Check out our new record — what do you think? Still want to sign us *now?*" And they said, "We know what your band's like. We know you've been working like this for a long time. We don't expect you guys are going to be some huge band. We like your band, and we'll put your records out. We'll give you this much money, and let you do what you want to do." Sounds good — why not? If this doesn't work out, we could always go back and be on an independent label. We knew we were out of place. It was this opportunity we had to try.

[1993's *Houdini*] was done in so many pieces. We didn't have any new songs when we signed. So we'd write a few songs, record, mix them, write a few more songs. And then we had to depend on other people's schedules. Cobain was getting busy with Nirvana again — he ended up not finishing his producing duties with us. I was against having him do it at first. It was Danny Goldberg's suggestion — "Why don't you get him to produce? Definitely it's good for some records sales." And I was like, "That seems cheesy, like, this guy is famous now, so we're going to have him produce our record." Buzz is like, "Well, we've done how many records now — five or six — and we've never done something like that. We've never had a producer — that might be cool." And they offered to give us more money to do it.

It worked out pretty good — Kurt did some good things. But mostly, he didn't want to do much to change what we were doing. And we were looking for something a little bit more. But y'know, he'd never produced a record before, so it's understandable. He tried to do some things with the drums — they had just worked with Albini, he tried to steal some tricks from him. One thing that stands out about him producing is him nodding out on the couch while playing guitar, and waking up again with his hand playing. Unfortunately, *we didn't get that on tape.*

REGAN HAGAR: I had befriended Shawn Smith from working at Tower Records. Shawn had played me a tape — he was fresh up here from Bakersfield, California. This tape was him and a four-track — drum machines and cheap synthesizers. I was really into Prince, and he was really into Prince. It sounded funky, and I said, "Man, you've got a great voice — we should make a funk band." We tried for months, and we played with a lot of different people in town.

SHAWN SMITH: Me, Stoney, and Regan jammed one day. Regan and I had already started this band Satchel. We came up with the basis for a song — Stoney said, "Let me book a couple of weeks at a studio, and when I'm done with Lollapalooza, let's make a record."

REGAN HAGAR: Pearl Jam had just taken off. I think [Stone] may have gotten his first check. So he's having this success, and he's like, "Do you guys want to go to the studio? I've got some money — I'll pay for it." He flipped the bill for seven days at Avast! We didn't want to use Cory Kane, Satchel's bass player, because then that would basically be Satchel with Stone. So [Stone's]

PIC BY BOOTSY HOLLER — BOOTSYHOLLER.COM

Brad (L-R: Stone Gossard, Regan Hagar, Shawn Smith)

then-roommate — he was from L.A. — said, "My old roommate from L.A. in college was an excellent bass player, Jeremy Toback." The first time we're meeting him really is in the studio. He was an excellent bass player — a true musician. So we do seven days and create everything in the studio as we're there. Stone really likes it when we're finished, and plays it for Sony, who want to put it out. We get flown to New York, we have meetings with Sony, they put us in nice hotels. It's everything you've ever dreamt as a kid. Then they find out Shawn and I are in Satchel. Boom — Satchel gets signed. It's like a dream come true. Sony puts it out [1993's *Shame* after the band is named Brad] and it's a big thrill. By the time Brad's record is officially on the shelf, Satchel is already signed, and now we're plotting our record [1994's *EDC*]. There was some serious tension with Pearl Jam and Brad initially, because some members of [Pearl Jam] were like, "You guys are coattail riding." Which made Shawn and I furious. First of all, I'd been in Seattle trying to make it happen longer than anybody.

SHAWN SMITH: There was some resistance about the record coming out — because it was right at the same time they were doing *Vs.* — in terms of how it got promoted. Which I remember being thankful for. I started to panic, because they were so huge at the time. I thought, "Oh crap, *I'm fucked.* I'm going to be 'the guy in the band with the guy from Pearl Jam.'" Sony held back on the promotion, which I am glad happened.

REGAN HAGAR: We just spent whatever tens of thousands of dollars making videos — why are we not putting them out? I just got the runaround. Then Satchel started being managed by Tony Dimitriades. He happened to be in a room in a Sony office, where this stuff was being discussed. He unraveled a lot of information for me. I guess there was an internal memo at Sony saying, "Don't promote Brad." They put the kibosh on it officially. We talked to Stone about it. Stone was embarrassed I think — asked us not to relay this information in interviews. "Please don't lash back at Pearl Jam — times have changed, we all grow and learn." That's easy to say when you're on top, but I think we basically never tell this story. That's just a little bit of it. Now enough time has passed — I think it's fine to say the reason Brad never did anything was because Pearl Jam didn't want Stone to do it. Now they feel differently. But now, *it's kind of too late.*

CHAPTER 27

"If you were there, you were part of it": Riot Grrrl

The Riot Grrrl movement suffered two severe blows, as 7 Year Bitch and the Gits experienced tragic deaths of a member of each band. Bikini Kill and Bratmobile soldiered on, before eventually breaking up, marking the end of the Riot Grrrl movement.

KATHLEEN HANNA: [7 Year Bitch] were "Seattle," so I knew them from when they would play the North Shore Surf Club, and when we would see them in Seattle. I think we played with them a couple of times. They were super hard partiers, well read, articulate women — kind of amazing. I remember really respecting them, and when [Stefanie Sargent] died, being really confused about why that happened.

DANIEL HOUSE: One thing that is not accurate — I remember *Spin* reported, and I was really pissed off about it — they said that she OD'd on heroin. Which is not the case. It was drug-related, but it was actually asphyxiation on her vomit. She had issues on and off with heroin — she was also a pretty heavy drinker. She had been off dope for quite a while, and one night she was drinking a lot — mostly beer.

She was in West Seattle at this friend's house — somebody pulled out heroin. She talked them into a little taste — not by any means enough to OD, but certainly enough to get high, especially when you haven't been doing it for months. She drove from West Seattle all the way back to her apartment

PIC BY DAVID HAWKES

7 Year Bitch (Stefanie Sargent second from right)

on Capitol Hill. If it had been an OD, she would have OD'd by now. She got out of the car, let herself into her apartment, and lay down on her bed — on her back.

She passed out more from the alcohol, on her back. I think the heroin was enough of a sedative to keep her from waking up, but it also was what caused her to throw up the contents of her stomach, and she choked on that. Terribly awful and sad for a lot of people — she was beloved. 7 Year Bitch was essentially in the studio at that time — had just about finished their record and suddenly, their guitar player is dead. So [*Sick 'Em*] ended up having to be postponed — finally got released in October of '92, when they found their new guitarist, Roisin Dunne. Then they went on and great things happened. By the time the second record [1994's *¡Viva Zapata!*] came out, they were pretty much touring as a headline act.

BEN LONDON: Slowly, the Gits took off first — anybody who saw them was converted into a fan. They got asked early on to open a show for Nirvana and Tad at the HUB Ballroom. That was probably one of their first big shows out of town. Mia was a cook at the Frontier Room — a bar/restaurant. At that point, you couldn't get hard alcohol in clubs, so people would go down there to get shots when they were at the Vogue — she met a lot of people from the scene that way.

STEVE FISK: [Mia] was a really amazing talent — really delivered in the studio. I'd put her in the top five people I've worked with. They were punk rockers, and that's what they were about. In some ways, we had more records in our collection in common then maybe I had with Soundgarden, Screaming Trees, or Nirvana. They weren't pretending to be influenced by Ted Nugent.

SCOTTY CRANE: [Mia] didn't really talk — she was quiet and reclusive. What I remember of Mia — sitting on the stoop [of Soundhouse Recording Studio], trying to write lyrics. Like two days before she was murdered.

DANIEL HOUSE: The night Mia was killed — it was almost a year to the day from when Stefanie died. Actually, Mia and a bunch of girlfriends got together that night specifically in memory of Stefanie. What happened to her that night was so awful and horrible, there's just such an irony about it.

ALLISON WOLFE: It was really devastating and scary. There's so few women in music — especially strong, awesome women doing cool things. I mean, every person is valuable, but I just felt like, we can't afford to lose *anyone.* She meant so much to so many people, and to punk rock music and Seattle. It's so scary to think ultimately, all of us girls could just get raped, killed, and end up in a gutter, which is what we see on the TV all the time. It seems to be accepted that that is what is going to happen to women — no one talks about it as an epidemic. This rarely happens to men. Why does this always happen to women? It was just really horrible.

KATHLEEN HANNA: I was really scared during that time, because I always got a lot of hate mail — but I had gotten some really specifically awful hate mail around that time. And nobody knew if she had been killed because she was in a band — if she had been targeted, or if it had been random. It turns out that it was random. But at the time, both of my parents separately heard about her death and called me, and said, *"Get out of town."* Because they were worried that somebody was targeting . . . she was an outspoken woman in a band, and I was an outspoken woman in a band. I remember a lot of fear around that time in general — it felt like a really scary, violent time. Our shows had gotten really violent. We were getting so much press, and we didn't have any protection or anything — we still lived in group houses. We never locked the door. That happening was really a wake up call, like, "Oh, *we're not immortal.*"

BEN LONDON: They thought it was somebody that she knew — when they were trying to solve the murder case. It was such amazing vindication when they found that guy in Florida and convicted him [in 2004]. In some ways, it was ground zero for some of the political awareness and the grassroots organizing that has happened here and continued to go on. So if you have to say that something positive came out of something like that, I'd say that was the case.

DANIEL HOUSE: She was really sweet, really funny. She was probably the most trusting of them, but still somewhat mistrustful. But once she did, she was warm, genuine, and open. Also very forthright and straight up. She was definitely one of these people that I would refer to as a "no bullshit" kind of person. She'd say what was on her mind — what she thought, what she believed.

SLIM MOON: Bikini Kill did this interview with *Option*, and they hated the way *Option* misrepresented and quoted them. So they burned a copy of *Option* magazine onstage, and swore off doing interviews. Never did interviews again for the next five years as a band. In a way, the more those bands said, "No, we won't do interviews," it made them get more attention.

KATHLEEN HANNA: I was working a full-time job in addition to doing Bikini Kill and activism — I was super-exhausted, and didn't have the time to deal with the onslaught of press. A lot of groups declared "media blackouts." We'd seen what happened to Nirvana — they had gotten really huge, and it was alienating. We didn't want that to happen, either to Riot Grrrls as a group, or Bikini Kill as a band. They wanted to turn it into this weird, sexy thing. Like, "All these young girls wearing short schoolgirl skirts — plaid skirts. We're all strippers who had sexual abuse histories, and that's why we hated men so much."

It was really not complicated or interesting, and a lot of us were very young. We might have sucked sometimes [live], but we were never boring. People were coming up to us every night, saying, "You changed my life — you made me want to start a band," or "You made me get into feminism." We weren't making much money, and we didn't have a tour bus, manager, publicist, or any of that. We did everything ourselves, and we felt really successful. We didn't really want to grow as a band and be on a major label — we didn't want to get bigger and people to recognize us on the street. We felt like we were doing this activist thing, and that's what was important.

ALICE WHEELER: Olympia was an underground parallel scene to what was happening in Seattle. So, I could go see a giant arena concert of Nirvana, but I could still go see Bikini Kill with fifty people backstage at the Capitol Theater. In Olympia, I could stand two feet in front in the band and shoot photos. If you were there, you were part of it — as opposed to what was happening in Seattle, with the "You're the fans, we're the stars" distinction.

KATHLEEN HANNA: People were really freaked out by us. People either really liked us, or really hated us. Our shows were confrontational — I didn't see them that way, because I was the person doing it [laughs]. We were into engaging the audience, and that was disturbing to people. We played at the Paramount, which was our biggest show to date, opening for Nirvana. They didn't even turn the lights on for us — we played in the dark. I don't even know if we had monitors. The people who worked there wouldn't talk to us, wouldn't help us. A really awful experience.

TINUVIEL: [Bikini Kill was] a really great live band. I was always taken off guard by what a negative reaction they would solicit from guys in the audience. It just reinforced how important they were as a band — to speak out for women's rights. I was at a show in Boston, and just as the show was starting, this guy punched out their roadie, who was a girl. Knocked her down right in front of me. I was like, "Why is it that strong, vocal women are still soliciting this response from guys?" *This is the '90s.*

ALLISON WOLFE: We played our second show with the Melvins — the same place that we played our first show, the North Shore Surf Club in Olympia. Calvin again had set up that show and asked us to open for the Melvins. I remember the day of that show — there was all this excitement because the Melvins were legendary in Olympia. So there we were, hanging around Olympia with Kathleen and all them. There were metalheads *everywhere* — so much testosterone on the streets. I swear, it felt scary. There were guys everywhere leering, being gross, scary, and harassing us. We went in to play the show, we played, we did fine, and afterwards, Kathleen came up to us, and was like, "Are you guys alright?" Apparently, people were yelling death threats at us the whole time. Luckily, I'm hard of hearing, so I didn't hear any of it, but she said that she kept hearing guys say they wanted to kill us [laughs].

The funny thing is that after we played, Buzz from the Melvins came up to me. He had this really soft, sweet voice, and he was like, "Thank you so much for playing with us, that was so great! I just love having a band like you open for us. Every time we play shows, they try to put us with these really macho metal or punk boy bands. They don't understand — we don't like that kind of music. I mean look at me, *I like the Cure!*"

KATHLEEN HANNA: The most memorable [Bikini Kill release] was the one we did with Joan Jett and Kenny Laguna [the 1993 single, "New Radio"/"Rebel Girl"]. We borrowed some band's drums — Soundgarden or one of those bands. We did it in Seattle — we did almost all our records in Seattle — with Stuart Hallerman and John Goodmanson. I think we did it in one or two days — probably one day. For us, that was a total luxury. Because usually, we would do all the vocals for the whole album in one day — so there would only be three songs in a day. [It] was really exciting for us — we felt like we were huge rock stars, lounging around the studio. I remember smoking pot near the end of it and goofing around with Joan. And Kenny comes from the Brill Building era of songwriting and recording, so he's used to doing things really professional — but really fast. He made me work on every single vocal line. Being in a punk band, nobody had ever spent that time with me, or given me that attention.

ALLISON WOLFE: Our first album, [1993's] *Pottymouth*, we recorded in Washington, D.C. We recorded with Tim Green from Nation of Ulysses — he had this four-track in his basement — in one or two days. It cost us forty dollars for the tapes, pizza, and a box of hair dye — that's all Tim asked for [laughs]. After that, maybe a year later, we recorded [1994's] *Real Janelle*, an EP. We had just finished touring for a week in California, and I at that time didn't really do vocal warm-ups, so my voice was shot. I sounded like a big smoker — hacking my way through those songs.

KATHLEEN HANNA: For me, it was just time to do something different. It got to be a burden. On any band, there's a lot of expectations. But if you're *a feminist activist band*, you're set up for failure. 'Cause half of the people say,

"You're man haters," and the other people say, "You're not political enough." You're not left enough, not feminist enough, not militant enough. It just always felt like we could never do anything right. Also, I needed to get out of Olympia because heroin was taking over, and I couldn't watch anybody else die. It felt like all areas were pointing towards leaving and starting over for me.

ALLISON WOLFE: It was in 1994 — I think right before Mother's Day. We had had a lot of infighting — there was a lot of strain and tension in the band. A lot of it was a result of pressure — all this media pressure that was coming in from the outside on Riot Grrrls and the Northwest music scene. None of us had a clue how to handle it or how to deal with it. Everybody had a different idea of, "Should you talk to the press, should you not, what can you say, what can't you say?" Everybody was turning against each other and fighting about all these issues. And we had never actually all lived in the same city — we were starting to pull apart. We hadn't performed, or been together, in six months. *Sassy* magazine, I believe, had wanted us to play a showcase for them in New York City, at the Thread Waxing Space. They had agreed to fly us out.

Kim Gordon was there, Thurston Moore, Jon Spencer, and Joan Jett. But we were having serious problems, and I was going through some nervous breakdown at the time, because Riot Grrrl was just eating itself. There were these girls that had been stalking me, who were trying to tear me apart and break me down — try to say that, "We're more radical than you," and "You suck." I was kind of buying it and feeling bad about myself. Some of those girls had followed me up to New York, came to the show, and were causing problems. Kept jumping up on the stage and trying to stop us in the middle of the set, saying, "Some guy punched me — *what are you going to do about it?*" It's true — there was almost no security there, it was way over capacity. But at the same time, I don't see how we should have to be responsible for every aspect of the show — we're just trying to play.

We ended up falling apart onstage. It ended up being this huge circus onstage — girls jumping onstage, screaming into the mic, the manager coming on and yelling. Joan Jett was onstage the whole time yelling at the girls. At one point, Molly and Erin threw their instruments down and were like, "That's it!" Molly left the building, I started crying, and it was totally packed. Someone told me Thurston Moore said that that was the greatest performance he'd ever seen [laughs]. It was more like performance art — we had this really public breakup onstage.

ALICE WHEELER: In the Northwest, even though we're very left wing out here, women have always been sort of second-class. I don't know if that's because it's like the wild, wild West — nature versus humanity, or whatever. It's always been that as a woman, you make a little bit less money — still, that's true. In the rock scene, that's definitely true. I think it gave women a voice. All the bands that counted in my mind were friends with the girls that were doing Riot Grrrl, and were supportive of that. Some of the boy rock star bands probably ignored the whole thing and were too busy on tour — or just wanted their girlfriends to be models and keep their mouths shut.

I think the whole idea about Riot Grrrl is that you could have your own opinion and you could make your own art. And it was equally as valid as anything else — I think that has been proven to be true in history. Part of what happened with Riot Grrrl is that they got a lot of press really early on, and it freaked them out. So then they did a press blackout, and I don't think that helped their position in history any. But I think that people now are wanting to explore what happened with that. Since the '60s, I think it's been the main swing of contemporary feminism — the main underground swing of feminism.

ALLISON WOLFE: I do think that it's important that there were all these girls that were politicized, making a mark in music. And I think we *did* transform somewhat the punk rock scene, and maybe the Northwest music scene and DIY music scene. I think that even if it was through the convoluted sense of *Seventeen* magazine reporting on Riot Grrrl, maybe some girls who live in remote places that might not have a scene to hang out in, could read about Riot Grrrl and feel influenced by that. And to feel like maybe it would give them the strength to tell their boyfriend to fuck off if he was fucking [with] them, or to tell their teacher at school who is being horrible to leave them alone. Or to start their own band, their own zine, or anything productive. I am proud of that.

KATHLEEN HANNA: Everything is "Grrrl this" and "Grrrl that." It seemed convenient, and it was really catchy. We were just like, "*Whatever.*" It's a little weird to still have the "Grrrl" thing follow me around when I'm thirty-seven. I think of myself as a *woman* now [laughs].

CHAPTER 28

"Everything is not OK anymore": Nirvana

With Nirvana still riding high on the vast commercial success of *Nevermind*, the group experienced inner turmoil due to the drug addiction of Kurt Cobain. But the group continued, with an outtakes compilation, *Incesticide*, and the highly anticipated follow-up to *Nevermind — In Utero*.

TRACY MARANDER: Within, like, two years, we broke up, [Kurt] got his own place, became a rock star, developed a heroin addiction, got married, and had a kid. That's a lot of stress in a couple of years.

STEVE MANNING: When Nirvana was on *Saturday Night Live*, I thought it was the coolest fucking thing I'd ever seen — I was so happy for them. And a little sad, because you knew that your little private thing was over. All of a sudden *your parents* knew who Nirvana were. The whole time before that, it was exactly what your parents didn't want you involved in.

CRAIG MONTGOMERY: The Chili Peppers thing was just a four or five day trip. But that's where we were when the album went number one. That was really surreal, like, "What? Nirvana's album is number one?!" We went to Australia — really big, great shows. The shows were pretty consistent. Sometimes [Kurt] might have a shitty attitude about the show, but generally, the show was good and the crowd was happy. Hours of tension, punctuated by moments of brilliance and fun. There was Kurt and Courtney, and the

Hole's Courtney Love in Melkweg, Amsterdam, December 8, 1991

people in charge of getting them everywhere — and then everybody else. There was really a dichotomy. Their drug problems were pretty bad, and they were worried about how they were going to get drugs. They're pretty much sick because they can't get their drugs. And then you go to Japan where it's even harder — he was just *a shell* in Japan. At the end of that tour is where we stopped in Hawaii, and those guys got married.

As much as I could, I tried to insulate myself from all their little dramas. It could be a downer being around them — being around all the tension at times. It wasn't just the drug problem — they were starting to have issues within the band about how they were going to divide royalties. By now, they're talking about real money. So there was tension about that. The impression that I had was that Courtney was in his ear, saying, "You should be more than an equal third of this band, because you're doing all the writing and the singing." The impression I got was he started trying to change the deal.

Then there were the European festivals in the summer. You got the feeling that Nirvana was the center of the universe. They were headlining these huge festivals, and they were the band that everyone was there to see. Nirvana were allowed to dictate the lineup at some of these festivals too — it was a very heady time. They weren't having as much fun, Courtney was having health problems, Kurt was having health and drug problems. I wasn't directly privy to it — I tried to keep my head down and do sound, and hopefully not have anybody get pissed at me. It would be stressful, because there were times that we didn't know if we were going to make the show or not. Kurt's in the hotel room throwing up, or he's worried about his voice — his voice was always a problem. He was not a healthy guy. Every show we got through was a relief.

SUSAN SILVER: [Kurt and Courtney] were incredibly paranoid. She was extremely threatened by any woman in Kurt's life — that was really clear. There were a couple of incidences where I happened to be in the room with a bunch of other people, but I was the only woman, so she took aim at me — unrightfully and unnecessarily. There was a weird incident, where Soundgarden was touring in Europe with Guns N' Roses, and they played Spain. Nirvana was playing the next night, so we all went — it was so fucking exciting to be there with this band that we all loved for several years. And now they're the biggest band on the planet. It was like going and seeing people you think are your really good friends, you see the show, it's amazing, we go backstage, and all of a sudden, it's not amazing anymore.

Krist and Dave were really uncomfortable. Courtney was very pregnant, and was on the couch with Kurt. There were probably fifteen of us or more in this room talking to each other. But there was this real air of discomfort. All of a sudden, she stood up and starts screaming, "Yeah, we shoot dope! We shoot dope every day! Fuck yeah!" It's the elephant in the middle of the room you try not to talk about. It was the moment where I realized, *everything is not* OK *anymore*. Andy died, and that really wasn't OK, but we all pulled through it, and things started to really take off for Seattle — everybody was still in each other's corner. They stormed out of the room. Kurt had an interview going on in the other room, which I found out because I tried to say goodbye to him, and I could see that he wasn't really comfortable with it. He didn't look particularly well, but he'd had a lot of health problems — I wasn't thinking, "Oh, he's high." I just thought he looked sick.

CRAIG MONTGOMERY: [The Reading Festival] was fun. There were a lot of rumors in the British press about Kurt's health and "Courtney this and that." I think it was Everett True — they had him wear a doctor's smock and wheel Kurt out onto the stage in a wheelchair, just to make fun of that.

The band always had a great sense of humor. Nirvana was never about angst, grunge, and being unhappy. A Nirvana show was always the most hilarious thing you ever saw — people forget that. Their main motivation was, "What can we do that would be funny?" At these festivals, they would play, and if some "serious band" had to come on after them, they would just look silly. Because here's Nirvana that's completely taking the piss out of rock 'n' roll, and rocking harder than anybody else.

DUFF McKAGAN: I was never really friendly with them at the time. I think we tried to get them to open on one of those tours during the *Illusion* time, and they didn't want to. And then some bad blood started between . . . well, *Axl* had some bad blood. I think Axl might have taken it personally, and might have said something in the press — although he was a Nirvana fan. And Kurt was a pretty cynical, funny guy. The *punk rock* humor in Seattle — if you didn't get it, you might be offended. I think Kurt said something [at the 1992 MTV Video Music Awards] — they had their girl, and wanting Axl to be the godfather of the child. And Axl got huffy about it, because he thought Kurt was trying to take the piss out of him. It was no big fucking deal. If it was two mid-level bands and that happened, nobody would have heard of it. But because the media eye was so tuned in to both bands, it got blown out of proportion. And then, you can't downplay it. Then it was, "It's a war between the two bands." It's like, "*Oh fucking brother.*"

JACK ENDINO: I was not in touch with the band much during the period when [1992's] *Incesticide* came about. I recall hearing that the record company wanted some product out there quickly to capitalize on the success of *Nevermind,* but the band was not ready to make their next album. So someone must have thought of this other thing. Makes perfect sense really, since the band did have quite a lot of miscellaneous recordings. I did hear about it in time to remind them that I had the master tape for "Big Long Now," a *Bleach* outtake that was sitting on my shelf. They had completely forgotten it. I knew there was an abundance of unreleased tracks because I had recorded an album's worth of them myself! Some others are on the box set [2004's *With the Lights Out*].

CHAD CHANNING: I was actually never contacted by Krist or Kurt during that time — just by [Nirvana's lawyer]. I had heard I was gonna have three tracks on the album — "Dive," "Stain," and "Big Long Now." A lot of that stuff I had heard before, 'cause it was from the demo they had made with Dale — the demo they gave to me just before I joined up. I'd never heard the cover tunes before, so that was pretty cool. I was surprised to see "Big Long Now" in the list — that was a song I thought might never get released. That was a song I actually named — like "About a Girl." And "Stain" was taken from the recordings at Soundhouse with Steve Fisk. There were a number of cool songs from that session which ended up on the *Lights Out* stuff, like "Token Eastern Song."

JERRY CANTRELL: Out of all of the bands, I probably had the least amount of contact with the guys in Nirvana. I think I only met Kurt twice — once in South America, and once in Seattle, when they were doing some MTV show. The first time, we had a great time hanging for a couple of hours in a hotel — partying and talking about music. Kind of digging on each other, like, "Fuck, man, I love what you do" and "Man, I fucking dig your shit too." A cool hang — *in South America*, for God sakes! It took us to go to South America for me to actually meet him.

DONITA SPARKS: The [São Paulo] show was the worst set I had ever seen Nirvana do. They were trading off instruments and doing a lot of covers. I was thinking, "God, *what are they doing?*" I think they knew it when they got offstage. Krist still feels shamed about that show — it seems like whenever it comes up, he hangs his head in shame [laughs]. But then [several nights later in Rio de Janeiro] they were *on fire.* I was almost glad that I got to see them play a shitty show, because I was like, "They're not completely invincible." It was breaking my heart, but it made them seem a little more human.

SLIM MOON: It seemed like they had to promote *Nevermind* for two years or something. Then [Kurt and Courtney] finally bought their mansion in Seattle, and they were home some — they started trying to have a life. Courtney started contacting me, saying, "Kurt's friends are a negative influence." Once she came on the scene, she spent all this time dissing me and my friends in the press — sending me faxes, crank calling me in the middle of the night, all this shit. But then suddenly, she was like, "Oh, Slim — you're OK. You're misguided, and you've been suckered by your evil friends . . . but I like you. You should come hang out with Kurt, because his friends are a bad influence." But I never got any invites from Kurt, so I didn't really take that seriously, and I never took her up on that. I didn't want to be the guy who kisses up to "the rock star."

ROD MOODY: I remained a huge fan up until [1993's] *In Utero,* which was a huge disappointment.

ADAM KASPER: [Nirvana] weren't sure if they wanted Andy Wallace to mix the record again — they were on the fence. I was the engineer who spent a couple of days listening with them. They weren't sure the tapes were recorded very well — the Albini stuff. There were some big questions about it — particularly from the label. So we went in and spent a couple of days EQ'ing, listening to all the tracks, and seeing what could be done with it. It was probably eighty-five, ninety percent finished, but the label had a big issue with it at the time. Nirvana won out in the end, but they had to remix a few things.

MARK PICKEREL: One time, Kurt, Krist, and I ended up sitting on a flight together to Los Angeles — they were flying down to have meetings and to rehearse for the *In Utero* tour, I'm pretty sure. I hadn't seen Kurt or Krist for maybe two years. The strange thing that I attributed to fate — my plane ticket for some reason was separate from Hiro and Robert's. I ended up sitting in the very last row of the airplane — I could see Krist was occupying probably seat D. I was seat E, and sat next to him. The plane was almost done loading, when I heard what sounded like someone with Tourette's, barking out bizarre comments — really incohesive statements, filled with vulgarities. As the voice got closer, I looked up to see that it was Kurt approaching this last row. The only seat available left on the plane was the one next to me. It was strange, because I'd just bought the issue of *Details* with Nirvana on the cover. I was going to read the interview on the way to L.A. [Kurt said] "I haven't had a chance to read it yet. It's really strange that I ran into you, because I was just listening to Mark Lanegan's *The Winding Sheet*, and I love your drumming on it."

So he asked if he could read my issue of *Details*. While he was reading this interview, he started making comments how disgusted he was — or how frustrated he was — with some of the comments Dave made in the interview. He was frustrated with Dave becoming more comfortable with being a spokesperson within the band, or being a voice in the band. I think for some reason that was something Kurt didn't really appreciate, or didn't want to see happening. He and Krist went back and forth — Krist must have become the person in the band who was the peacekeeper. While he might have echoed some of Kurt's concerns, he, I think, wanted to see the band continue to move forward, get along, and learn how to live and work together professionally. This whole *Details* column [and] Kurt being reminded of *The Winding Sheet* sessions prompted this conversation about having me [and] Dale Crover play on the next record. He wanted the drumming responsibilities to be split between Dave Grohl, myself, and Dale. He wanted to hear the band's sound expand, and because of my playing on the Jury sessions and Mark Lanegan's solo record, for some of the songs that required maybe a lighter touch, he wanted to bring me in. It seemed that Krist was a little more reluctant to pursue that. I think he saw it as something that would cause a lot of tension within the band, considering that they were already starting to crack up. But [Kurt] definitely was excited about it.

DALE CROVER: I talked to Kurt about writing some songs together — between *Nevermind* and *In Utero.* He was living in Los Angeles. We had talked on the phone — he was trying to get me to come down to L.A. Maybe rehearsing and possibly songwriting. We both liked playing with each other. Thought that eventually we probably would be able to play together again — or something at some point.

MARK PICKEREL: Of course, I was really excited about it — he gave me his home phone number and address. I remember talking about our different favorite records. I was asking him if he ever spent time listening to the Gun Club's *Fire of Love*, which was a favorite of mine. He hadn't, as well as a few other favorites of mine. Since I owned a record shop, I sent him a package of *Fire of Love*, as well as I think the Gun Club's *Mother Juno,* and — of all records — the most current Talk Talk records at the time. Because he was talking about wanting to do quieter music, and Talk Talk had just released a couple of bizarre, quiet, depressing records — *The Laughing Stock* and *Spirit of Eden.* We talked on the telephone a couple of times after.

KURT DANIELSON: There was a lot of interesting talk — Kurt had a lot of ideas and plans. I'd heard at one point that Kurt was interested in working with Michael Stipe. I had conversations with Kurt myself, where we'd talk about this and that. It would be fun to do more a Butthole Surfers–type thing, with more electronics involved — not a front man — more of an electronic band, with a lot of noise, but also real songs and pop songs. A combination of things.

CRAIG MONTGOMERY: We were getting ready to go out on the U.S. *In Utero* tour. I had chosen the sound system they were going to take on the tour, a bunch of us on the crew were at the sound company preparing the gear and the band's equipment. That was when I found out that they wanted to use somebody else on tour. It was a shock at the time, because I took my job seriously and took pride in it. We always got compliments about the way Nirvana sounded. We had a reputation as a band that had good sound. Things worked out really well — based on my reputation from Nirvana, I was able to get work right way. I think in retrospect, that wasn't a bad tour to have missed.

DERRICK BOSTROM: A friend moved up to Seattle, and he knew those guys. He started calling Curt [Kirkwood], and saying, "These guys are into you, you should reach out to them." The next thing I heard, there was an article in *Spin*, in which [Kurt] was talking about playing *Meat Puppets II* for Courtney, and she wasn't into it, until he explained it to her or sang the songs to her. He was having bands opening for him, giving bands a week at a time. It was for about five shows. We started somewhere in the Midwest. We played with them on Halloween — Cobain dressed up as Barney. I can't remember if this is true or if this is what somebody told me — somebody hit Kurt on the head with a shoe, and he had taken a leak into it and thrown it back into the audience.

CURT KIRKWOOD: He was into the albums — he saw a Black Flag/Meat Puppets show in Seattle early on. It was a formative show for him, in terms of punk rock. It was probably around the time [*Meat Puppets II* was out], maybe even a little before.

DERRICK BOSTROM: We just happened to be the band that was touring with them when they were doing *MTV Unplugged*. They were like, "Teach us 'Lake of Fire.'" They took a couple of stabs at it, and we're like, "Maybe we should just be on *Unplugged* with you." And they went along with it! Mercifully, I didn't have to go — the other guys went.

CURT KIRKWOOD: It was pretty easy to do. We rehearsed for about a week over at a rehearsal studio. It was kinda surreal, having all these out of control idiots in charge of this really big deal. We were the special guest — a "surprise special guest" — and Nirvana hadn't told anybody until we got there. Literally, the night we were there, [MTV] was thinking it was going to be Eddie Vedder or somebody. [Kurt] was amusing to hang around with. He didn't say very much. He seemed pretty overwrought by the whole affair, even though he was doing really good shows and was really good on the *Unplugged* thing.

ALLISON WOLFE: I have a twin sister — she went to see a show of theirs. I remember her calling me and telling me how horrible the experience was. It was like, "I was really looking forward to it, and I was being squished and pummeled the whole time by sweaty, shirtless, long-haired guys." It felt like another excuse for guys to have their male bonding — be sexist and gross. She said that the worst part came when Nirvana was starting the song "Rape Me." She was like, "Can you imagine what it feels like? To already feel completely threatened in this macho environment, and then, all these disgusting guys are screaming 'rape me!' at the top of their lungs. As a woman in a crowd, it was horrifying." Somehow, she cruised backstage afterwards, and told Kurt Cobain exactly what she thought. "Do you know what it feels like being a girl in your audience with all these disgusting guys screaming 'rape me' all around you?" She said he was very disgruntled and defensive, and that he was saying, "God, I'm sorry, it's not my fault. That song is supposed to be an *anti*-rape song." She told me that he felt really frustrated by his audience, and that this audience was out of his control. Also, because she's my twin, she was like, "I'm pretty sure he thought I was you" [laughs].

MARK ARM: Nirvana surrounded themselves with really gross people, like John Silva. He had managed Red Kross, Sonic Youth, and the Beastie Boys, but was still *such a weasel*. My guess is that Nirvana went to John Silva because he managed Sonic Youth, and they suggested him. We did a two-week tour with Nirvana in '93. The Nirvana tour was just *awful*. Everybody was stepping on eggshells trying not to disturb Kurt. Courtney wasn't on that tour. They tried to make it "a dry tour" as some sort of example to Kurt. Kurt's interest had very little to do with alcohol so it was a stupid exercise. They had no booze backstage, but we had beer on our rider. So every night, Krist, Dave, and whoever wanted a beer would come to our little room and take our beer [laughs]. It was ridiculous, why didn't they just get enough beer for everybody who wanted it? Why this pretense that it's a dry tour, when it's not really? Kurt was taking massive amounts of pills. He was totally stoned anyway. The whole idea that this dry tour was helping Kurt in any way was just absurd. Why didn't they take his fuckin' pills?

Communication within the band and the people around them was pretty much nonexistent. On the way to Chicago, someone realized that Nirvana's hotel was far out of town, and the band wanted to stay in town, closer to the venue. They cancelled their rooms, ate the cost, and booked another hotel. So, they paid for two hotel rooms per person on that night, right? Our beer ran out during the Chicago show, so a friend of ours grabs a case of beer from catering, and brings it to our room. Next thing you know, *a federal case* is made out of twenty-four beers! All these guys in their crew are running around with walkie-talkies, like the *Mona Lisa* was snatched. Their tour manager, Alex McLeod, is flipping out over the fact that we stole a case of beer and they're going to have to pay for it. He's calling John Silva back in L.A. — calls are going back and forth, how are they going deal with this situation? They just fuckin' spent how much money on two hotel rooms per person, but they're flipping out over a case of beer that they have to buy from catering? It was the most absurd, insane thing. It was indicative of how that whole group of people were running themselves.

They weren't looking at the big picture at all. They weren't looking at, "What do we *really* need to do to make sure Kurt is OK?" And I'm not talking about "OK" as in feels good, and everything is the way he wants it so he can keep touring and earning money. What are they doing to try to get his head cleared so he can think a straight thought? What are they doing to keep him alive? They danced around the real issue, and got focused on these tiny, stupid, ego-trippy things. It was just fucking horrible. And Krist and Dave seemed bummed the whole time, but they weren't talking — no one really talked to each other. Alex McLeod is another example of someone I can't believe Nirvana hired. We met him a couple of years before in the U.K., and he was kind of a jerk. A mean guy. He also seemed to think the glory of Nirvana's ascendancy somehow reflected upon him. Why would they hire this mean dude, and why would they keep him once he starts power tripping because he's a tour manager? Why would you want someone like that anywhere near you?

CRAIG MONTGOMERY: I don't know if I would agree with that opinion that much. If you're going to play at that level, you have to have management that knows what it's doing at that level — or else you're going to get steamrolled. The impression I had was John Silva was a good guy — honest with the band. If you're going to get in that game, I felt like the people — for the most part — they were surrounded by were as good as you could find. People like Silva. I'm not surprised Mark would have an opinion like that — that's sort of his aesthetic. At the same time, people like that, their interest is in the band as a business, so they want the business to be successful, with all that that entails — as far as keeping the band working. They only make money if the band is working.

MARK ARM: We rode with Nirvana on their bus one night, while our sound guy and tour manager rode in the van by themselves [laughs]. I think it was on the way to Davenport, Iowa. During the trip, Kurt is explaining all these pills he's on to me, and he's going, "God, I would *really* like to stop doing all this shit. How did you do it?" I'd only stopped in July — so it was a couple of months. But I hadn't hung out with Kurt and Courtney since New Year's Eve of '92 going into '93. I had to stop seeing them because I was trying to save myself. I told him that you have to want to quit bad enough [and] that you've got to stay away from your junkie friends, because they're not really your friends — they're just people who share an interest in heroin with you. You've got to leave these people behind and make a clean break. And what I really wish I had said that night was, "*You've also got to ditch your junkie wife.*"

1994 and Beyond

CHAPTER 29

"It felt like the world had gone seriously wrong": Kurt Cobain's Death and 1994

In the world of music, 1994 will forever be known as the year that Kurt Cobain committed suicide, signalling the end of Nirvana, and to many, also the end of the whole grunge movement.

ADAM KASPER: The next session [at Robert Lang Studios] — which was their last session — got "You Know You're Right." I remember Grohl set up a drum set in the studio, and played drums for eight hours a day while we mixed it. Nonstop. Kurt was not really around for most of the day, but would wake up in the evening, come in, and throw down a vocal harmony, or lay down a line or two. We spent about three days a song — really slow-paced. In the end, I think that people were just burnt out as far as remixing the whole thing — they left it the way it was.

Same kind of scenario [as the *In Utero* mixing session]. Kurt coming here and there. But when he did show up, it was pretty solid — he knocked it out pretty quick. Just to get him in to do that much at that point seemed like . . . basically, Krist would pick him up and drive him to the studio, which was fairly close. He worked with me and nobody else, as far as it being just us in the room. It was a tenuous time, as far as saying, "Let's do demos for eighteen songs and go in and record them." It was more like, "Let's just get him in the studio and see what we can get."

I think the idea was that he took some tapes and listened to stuff that Dave and Krist had written. He was opening up to maybe putting vocals on some of the songs that ended up being on that first Foo Fighters record [1995's *Foo Fighters*]. Dave knocked out a batch of those while we were there — I think to present to Kurt, as a possibility for the Nirvana thing. I remember saying to Dave, "Dude, you should do a solo record someday!" Some of the songs might have worked with Kurt — I'm not sure what he actually heard. That was making the band real happy — they wanted to have some input songwriting-wise too. Or more input, I should say. I think he had ["You Know You're Right"] ready, which he had been working on for a while. He played it before in concert. We did a lot of vocal tracks — punching in, doubling up stuff. We spent a good half a day just doing vocals. A couple of takes and there it is . . . *Nirvana.*

KIM WARNICK: It was steering out of control. It was kind of hard to watch that all going on.

KURT DANIELSON: I remember bowling with Dave Grohl in Seattle — and we said, "We'll see you in Stockholm." We figured during Soundgarden's tour [for which Tad opened], we would be in Stockholm the same time Nirvana was during their tour. But this was when Kurt OD'd in Italy. So that "look forward to meeting" never occurred. Sometimes what happens is you've got human beings who are in intensely personal situations, and they're thrust into the spotlight at the very moment when they least need it. To have to stand by and watch that happen to a friend of yours — who has been isolated by this or that chemical dependency — it's a sad and profoundly moving experience.

EDDIE VEDDER: There was that thing in Rome. I went to buy some smokes, and I saw this thing in the paper about Kurt OD'ing in Italy. I got home — I was alone in the house — and I remember all of a sudden shaking with panic. Feeling like that that would be the worst thing — being panicked at the thought of the music world without him. And then when that kind of blew over, I felt like, "Jesus Christ. Fucking Seattle, it's just *fucking crazy.*"

STEVE TURNER: The last time I actually saw him walking down the street, he looked like absolute hell. I knew he wasn't doing well.

MARK ARM: Right before we went on tour with Pearl Jam in March of '94, Bob Whittaker was talking to Krist a lot. Bob kept telling me that Krist was really concerned about Kurt.

KIM THAYIL: We heard rumors from people that had crossed paths with him, or people that were closer to him. And of course, there was stuff that would pop up in the tabloid and the gossip mill. I don't think Kurt himself was tabloid fodder, but there were elements in his life that openly solicit that kind of attention. So every once in a while, you'd hear shit on the news, the radio, or in a magazine. I remember when there was the incident in Rome, they were calling it "a botched suicide attempt." I probably knew what you knew — plus some extra-added scenester gossip. That's hard to give credence to all that we hear. In retrospect, a lot of what we heard was very credible.

SUSAN SILVER: Kurt was invisible to everyone. So the time that they spent in those latter days was around drugs, [rather] than music. Layne had been in and out of rehab, and Layne and Kurt spent a lot of time together. We were all in fear of what could happen. Alice was working with a really wonderful guy from New York, Lou Cox, a doctor who was instrumental in helping Aerosmith through their recovery. I got an emergency, out of the blue call from Courtney, who had no love lost for me. Previously, I had been a target of hers. She was in a very desperate, understandably frightened state. She said, "You have to help me — *Kurt's going to kill himself.* What should I do?" I said, "First thing, you have to make sure you're safe and your daughter's safe. I will connect you to the people to do an intervention — you have to make sure the people that Kurt trusts are there." I hooked the manager up with Lou Cox. They decided to do an intervention, but they decided to use a different interventionist. And not everybody came to the intervention. I wasn't part of it — I was not "inner circle" with them whatsoever. They did the intervention, and it went very poorly.

ROBERT ROTH: There was a percentage of people doing this intervention [who] were strung out themselves, or were basically living off him. And also, it was business people — who in another sense were living off of him. Maybe there were some people in there that had his best interests at heart, but I don't think that he thought that. Tough love — draped in hypocrisy — completely backfired. It seemed to drive him the other way. I had always heard that a lot of his inner conflict came from the fact that his parents were divorced — he came from a broken family, and he dreaded ever doing that to Frances [Bean Cobain, Kurt's daughter].

DUFF McKAGAN: I bought a house in Seattle in '92, and I was flying home a couple of years later. Flew out of LAX, and Kurt was sitting an aisle over from me. That's the first time I ever really talked to him. He'd told me he just left Exodus, was trying to get clean, and didn't know how to. I could relate because I was trying to get clean at that same time. We talked about stuff we had in common — he seemed bummed. We went to baggage claim together when we got to Seattle. A friend of mine came to get me, and him and Kurt went out to have a smoke. My friend came back in, and I said, "Maybe you should have him come to my house — he seems bummed out." He went out to get Kurt — his car had come and picked him up.

SUSAN SILVER: Kurt went to rehab for a couple of days, went AWOL, and the rest is history.

VAN CONNER: I remember him missing, and us going around Seattle trying to find him. Just thinking, "Oh, he probably just took off somewhere." I remember going home, and hearing on the radio that they found his body. I just remember sitting there in shock. Like, "That's got to be bullshit." Then I thought, "Well, he *has* been missing for three days." Then I called Lanegan, and he had just heard about it too. I had taken him over to Kurt's house, dropped him off, and there were already news reporters there. It was like a circus.

MARK IVERSON: It was like the Andrew Wood thing — times a hundred.

KIM WARNICK: It was just such an awful time to remember — it seemed black. It really upset the city.

ART CHANTRY: I remember when they announced that the body was found in his house. We were in my studio, and everybody knew exactly what it was — the moment that we heard it. It was my birthday when they found [Cobain's body]. The whole city came to a grinding halt. The impact of that was like 9/11 — in Seattle. It still affects me to think about it, because it was so profound.

Everybody blames the music industry for killing Kurt. I'm not sure what killed Kurt — you'd have to ask Kurt that. I don't think he had good health advice. I don't think he had good people around him. See, I'm an alcoholic — I've gone through rehab, and I did a lot of research into that to get through it. Part of the symptoms of withdrawal are deep depression. And if you're a depressed person in the first place, this depression is profoundly disabling. That's actually a symptom that's in the textbooks of withdrawal. And that is followed by very long-term, mild- or medium-level depression. I don't think anybody told him that. Because every time he tried to get clean, he couldn't deal with it — it's like he didn't know what was happening to him. So I wonder what kind of health advice, what kind of therapist that guy had. You don't go through a program and not be told these things, and yet he didn't seem to know. Either that, or he was incapable of dealing with it.

ROBERT ROTH: My theory is there are three things that come closest to an artist's soul — their art, the love and the passion for the people in their life, and drugs and/or spirituality. From what I gather, those three things were in disarray for him. He was very isolated. In my opinion, he would have had to break up his band, break up his family, and quit drugs. It was a tall order for him, or *anyone* in his position, to get out of the situation he was in. I'm not surprised it was too much to deal with.

BLAG DAHLIA: I figured he might OD. But dope makes you depressed, so suicide is always a possibility. I was surprised that he did it by essentially wiping out his identity and removing his own head. But there was a lot of self-hatred there, and a very dysfunctional relationship.

ADAM KASPER: [Krist] knew things weren't right, and he was trying to help Kurt get out of whatever. [Kurt] had a suicidal depression — he always talked about it. I guess it wasn't a total surprise. I mean, Krist literally had gone to his house and basically kidnapped him — "Come on, *we're getting out of here!*" And there's a lot of other dark shit from Courtney that Krist has had to deal with — and Kurt did as well.

SCOTT VANDERPOOL: Then there was that fucking memorial thing at the Seattle Center, which I hated. It was just so against all of my punk rock ethics.

GRANT ALDEN: My girlfriend and I had planned to go through Aberdeen-Hoquiam to a beach for the weekend. So I drove through on Saturday morning or Friday afternoon, and came back on Sunday. The thing that struck me is there wasn't a single reader board on any church in Aberdeen-Hoquiam acknowledging that he had died, nor consoling his family — who were residents there. That says everything you've got to know about Kurt Cobain. No wonder the poor guy felt the way he felt — his hometown didn't give two shakes of a rat's tail for him. Dead or alive. I mean, I live in a small town in Eastern Kentucky now — Keith Whitley is from up the road, they have a big statue to Keith Whitley outside his hometown. They have nothing like that in Aberdeen-Hoquiam. *They just don't care.*

TRACY MARANDER: It was a pretty big surprise. I thought if anything, Nirvana would break up and he would go into seclusion, come back, and do something else. Especially because he had his artwork to fall back on — he had another outlet to do creative stuff. Or you figured he might go the way of Pete Doherty — you would think that something like that might happen as opposed to just him committing suicide. Or to some regards, an accidental overdose would have been less surprising than suicide. Having a two-year-old daughter would make you think twice.

MARK ARM: I intended to see Kurt after this Pearl Jam tour because we were leaving in a day or two. A few days later when we're out with Pearl Jam in Washington, D.C., we got the call that Kurt was dead. It was a total shock. Except for that horrible tour six months previous, I'd hardly seen Kurt for over a year, so I didn't know where he was at. I can't say we were ever close — when we did hang out, we were usually high. He was shy, and quiet enough when he wasn't stoned.

JEFF AMENT: It was a dark night. Nobody really said much, and everybody got really drunk. I didn't know Kurt — I think the main thing I felt was feeling bad for Krist, because he was the guy I knew in the band, and Dave, because we had kinda gone through that. And then thinking just how horrible it was the way he did it. *Horrible.* Unless you've been manic-depressive, I don't think you can fully comprehend those sorts of actions.

EDDIE VEDDER: In the end, I'm happy that there were a couple of phone messages, a couple of phone calls, a couple of things that happened in person. I wish we had more time. I wish history could be changed and I could be talking about, "The first couple of years were bumpy, but the last five years were great," or "When our bands toured together." I don't want to say anything to make him roll over in his grave. I was fortunate because I was in D.C. We weren't going to play the show, and then we did play. I got to sleep at Dischord House — Ian MacKaye took care of me, because it felt like the world had gone seriously wrong.

KURT DANIELSON: It was in Europe [while Tad was on tour with Soundgarden]. I heard this rumor that Kurt had killed himself. So I called up Van — who's my brother-in-law, married to my sister. I knew Mark Lanegan was close to Kurt, and I thought Van might know what's going on. Van said, "There is something going on — call me back in two hours." And I did, by that time he had the facts. So it was contingent upon me to get the Soundgarden and Tad guys all in one room, and get all the reporters out of the room, so I can have some private time with my friends, and share some bad news. There was no good way to say it. I don't remember what I said — I just went ahead and announced it after the room was sealed.

KIM THAYIL: I never saw so many big, hairy, temperamental guys sitting around crying.

ROSS HALFIN: I went to shoot [Soundgarden] with Tad the day Cobain killed himself — they very much just wanted to keep to themselves. But they did a great show, and Chris finished the show with an acoustic version of "Like Suicide."

SUSAN SILVER: It put a pallor over everything. It was so shocking. It's one thing to lose someone to an accident, and it's another thing to lose someone to suicide. It scared everybody — and it certainly scared me. At that time — Eddie's first wife and I were very close — it was terrifying to think of those guys out there. They were both on tour. When the tour manager called to say that they had gotten the news, the Soundgarden guys had just gone wild. They started destroying the dressing room — out of not being able to deal with the profoundness of hearing something like that. I just told him, "Let them go — let them do what they need to do."

And then I went into service work at that point — literally, *service work,* [and helped] get the services together at a private church, and also at the Seattle Center. I went to the service with Eddie's wife. At the end of it, I had the same sort of overwhelming compassion for Courtney that I felt to a complete stranger — Yoko Ono — when John Lennon was shot. My heart just broke for her. I wanted to do something — I wanted to say something. After the service in the church, I walked up to her to offer support. About ten feet away, she noticed I was coming towards her, and she turned her back on me and walked away.

CRAIG MONTGOMERY: I flew back to Seattle from the tour I was on, to go to the memorial service and get-together — the private one. A recording was played of Kurt singing the Vaselines song, "Jesus Doesn't Want Me for a Sunbeam." And that was what got me to break down — hearing his voice. Courtney later told me that Kurt was really alone in his last several months — he was so heavy into his drug addiction that he wasn't seeing any of his friends. And the weird thing was he felt like nobody cared about him. She would say things to me like, "Kurt really valued you as a friend, and he valued your opinion." But in the last year and a half, two years, I really didn't feel like it was my place to call him up and say, "Hey, what are you doing?" So at the service, hearing his voice, it really made me feel sad that I hadn't reached out to him. Even if you're a famous rock star with lots of money, you still need your friends, and you still need human connection. He could be intimidating in a way — he could say something really acerbic that would make you feel stupid. I felt sad, and it felt like a real loss. I felt like I lost my friend Kurt a long time before that. So when he died, the sadness just hit me again.

TINUVIEL: I remember a [Melvins] show in New York, right after Kurt had killed himself — it was at the Limelight. It felt like a memorial service — it went on forever and it was really intense, the emotion. The audience [was] absolutely silent and mesmerized. The music took over — it was spiritual.

KRISHA AUGEROT: Many people were just distraught — having to face that reality of drug addiction, especially heroin, in Seattle is just a huge problem. Similar to Xana and Andy, how Courtney Love was really vilified. She became like . . . *she* killed him, or she could have done something. She couldn't have done anything to change his path.

CHAD CHANNING: I wish I had at least one more opportunity to talk to him. Never had that opportunity.

MARK PICKEREL: It affected me on so many different levels, because on one hand, I loved him as a person, and really enjoyed him. And secondly, from a career perspective, I was upset because I thought I was going to play drums on the next Nirvana record. And then also sad to know that we wouldn't hear anymore from Kurt or Nirvana musically. I thought what they were doing was so important — that would have been like losing John Lennon after *Help!* or *Rubber Soul* came out. I felt like Kurt was probably capable of making even better records than the ones he already had.

NANCY LAYNE McCALLUM: I can't interpret what Layne said after Kurt died. I *can* tell you that Layne said, "Kurt was murdered." I'm not naming names. I think it's the murderous conditions of the partnership between the drug community and the entertainment industry. Anyone that supports it at any level is a part of every drug death. I think that's what Layne was talking about. It starts with the guy at the top who's making how many millions of dollars importing it and getting it into the country. I'd like that guy to have to sit across, knee-to-knee with Layne, and explain to him his rationale. I'm not pointing a finger, and saying there was a murder plot, or there was a murderer. I'm saying that it is a murderous, devilish plot that includes pushers, dealers, runners, suppliers, importers, businesses, and governments.

MEGAN JASPER: There was such a deep and profound sadness, because you knew this kid, we worked with this kid, who was so bright, and so irreverent, and fun. A good person who kept to himself. And that this is how it all ended. There's nothing right about it.

CRAIG MONTGOMERY: Oh, that could be a whole book in itself [when Craig tour managed for Hole]! Courtney's album [1994's *Live Through This*] was ready to come out, but then Kurt died. But we went out and did a U.S. and European tour, also Australia and Japan. It was tough — it was a mess. It was stressful on all of us. Courtney could be a great person — warm, engaging, and a friend — or she could be a nightmare, and make you hate your life. I think I lasted about nine months before I said, "I can't do that anymore."

ROBERT ROTH: Definitely, the music industry changed quite a bit after that. I say that to some people and they think it's crazy, and other people know exactly what I mean. There was no more conscience watching — speaking out. In that sense, everything changed, and that was the death knell of the Seattle scene.

SUSIE TENNANT: After that, other people passed away too. It was just one after another.

CHAPTER 30

"Where I go, you go": Kurt Remembered

Since his death, Kurt Cobain has often been put on a pedestal. Friends and members of fellow bands offer their memories of "Kurt the human being" rather than "Kurt the myth."

ROBERT ROTH: Going against the tide, no matter how gracefully, will beat you up after a while — all artists know this. Cliché as it sounds, [Kurt] walked straight into the oncoming artillery from the '90s so-called culture war. Kurt lobbed the first bombs from our side, and was the first major casualty. He was really full of intense, sacrifice-yourself-for-your-art-at-every-step type fuel that burns up really fast. Where most other great artists may burn long and steady — but not as bright.

KURT DANIELSON: Kurt was like a magpie — he would find bright objects everywhere he looked, pick them up, and feather his nest with them. He was the most skillful thief I've ever seen. And that's what it takes to be a good poet, or a good writer. It was T.S. Elliot that said, "A bad poet borrows, a good poet steals."

LIBBY KNUDSON: He reminded me of one of those Keane paintings — kids with the big eyes, always sad, and holding puppies.

CRAIG MONTGOMERY: Most of the time, Kurt was a really nice, smart, funny guy. Really sharp wit, very low tolerance for stuff that is stupid. He had a temper, and if things were difficult, he wouldn't always react well — if we had problems with sound or something, he could get angry. Throw microphones on the ground and break them — break his guitar.

PIC BY MIKE LEACH — BESTROCKPHOTOS.COM

Kurt Donald Cobain: February 20, 1967 – April 5, 1994

SUSIE TENNANT: He was creative in so many ways — in addition to music. He made these really great sculptures, he liked to read a lot.

TINUVIEL: We mostly talked about art and religion — we never talked about music.

ALICE WHEELER: I had studied "the meaning of life" at Evergreen State College. So I was off on a tangent about the meaning of life — I wanted to get to the bottom of it. I think a lot of those ideas rubbed off on Kurt — he was definitely in that mode. Even though he hadn't gone to college, he hung out with a lot of students. I always found myself gravitating towards people that were into ideas — Kurt, Jesse Bernstein, and Kathleen Hanna.

TRACY MARANDER: He was a really good artist. He would draw cartoons with funny sayings. I have this huge picture of this homeless guy, and it's a satirical thing on how homeless people are mentally ill, they're alcoholics, they had messed up childhoods — but they're expected to fend for themselves in a box in the snow. This is on the back of a giant Aerosmith or Led Zeppelin poster. Whenever he'd send postcards or letters when he was on tour, they'd usually have a little picture drawn on them. It gets lost sometimes that he was a good artist. It also gets lost that he smiled a lot.

ROBERT ROTH: I was really amazed with how green he was with music, and how natural and right on his instincts were. I had older brothers turn me onto the Ramones, Elvis Costello, and all that stuff back in the late '70s. I knew about a lot of bands — Kurt really didn't. I remember trying to tell him and Krist about Television, and they were like, "Oh, we thought that was some weird new wave band." One of Kurt's favorite bands was the Smithereens, which really surprised me. But when you listen to those songs, you can really hear it — especially on *Bleach*. That driving, catchy pop. It was amazing that Kurt could be so artistically pure and right on, without having the references. He already had it.

RON HEATHMAN: He *loved* the Beatles. He was way more informed about the Beatles than I was — I was in the Stones camp. He was telling me that "I Want You (She's So Heavy)" was the greatest song ever. The repetitiveness of it, the lick. At that point, I didn't really know what he was talking about. I was like, "The greatest song is 'Sweet Virginia' by the Stones!" It turns out, after getting into the Beatles more, he was right [laughs].

TAD DOYLE: Really spoke highly of Creedence Clearwater Revival. I got to know him on our first tour together — we toured Europe, co-headlining. My impression of him was he was very specially talented for music — he had a vision, and it was his primary focus in life. He was elegant in everything he did musically.

SLIM MOON: He once said to me that only three bands were cool — Devo, Flipper, and the Stooges. I think what he meant by cool was genuine. They just are what they are without any pretension. Kurt never considered that Nirvana could be as cool as those bands. He thought they didn't have that "genuine-ness." Which is funny, because in terms of pop stars, they're probably seen as the most genuine pop stars ever. But still in his mind, they could never be Flipper.

CHARLES PETERSON: I photographed Kurt on New Year's Day for the *Advocate*, in 1993. The photo shoot didn't happen until eleven in the evening. He, Courtney, and Frances were living at the Inn at the Market Hotel — downtown at the time. In their master bedroom, set up some lights and photographed Kurt against the seamless. Talked about traveling and music. I remember him saying that he wanted to, at some point, buy a house in Scotland. And talking about how surreal it was to be a father. Because it had been New Year's Eve the night before, I think we were both a little hungover. He was of course still in his pajamas.

ALICE WHEELER: My friend and I had started publishing books, so Kurt and I were talking about self-publishing — he said he wanted to make a book about what really happened to him. He felt like the press wasn't getting it right.

BEN SHEPHERD: There was always a rumor through our grapevine that we were going to play music together — me, him, and Buzz.

SLIM MOON: He had these side projects and little bands with his friends.

He did a lot of four-track recordings that were much more sort of minimal. He had a whole musical side that never really got expressed, except for covers of Vaselines songs, or stuff like that.

CHAD CHANNING: Definitely kept to himself a lot. He was more open with Krist about things, but once in a while I'd be surprised — we'd talk about things that were more of an intimate kind of subject. I always liked [Kurt].

GARRETT SHAVLIK: He always wanted to be friends with everybody, which was sweet. He was a little brother.

KIM WARNICK: He would stay at our apartment — I lived with Susie Tennant. I think Kurt was homeless at that point, living in a car. They played a show, it always seemed like they'd end up coming over to our house, and we'd have impromptu parties. One of the best memories I have of Kurt is all of us being so wasted, and me and him dancing to the Partridge Family, "Come On Get Happy." We fell down and knocked the stereo over.

DONITA SPARKS: Dee [Plakas] and I dyed Kurt's hair blue one time in England, because he liked the blue in my hair. But because his hair was naturally blond, it wasn't porous at all — it turned out this gunmetal grey color. We dyed his beard too — the beard you can actually see in some pictures.

MARK ARM: Anyone who claims he was a friend of Kurt Cobain's is probably lying. Dylan Carlson might be the only exception to that rule.

VAN CONNER: Dylan Carlson and I used to hang out. So sometimes we'd hang out, all three of us. We'd go drink. At a party across from the Moore Theatre one night, Cobain decided to jump on my back. Little guys, for some reason, always like to jump on my back. I remember him jumping on my back, and me running as fast as I could backwards, into a wall. Crushing him like four times. *A psycho* — he wouldn't let go. Bashed him into this wall until finally, he let go and hit the ground.

DERRICK BOSTROM: I remember he recently had a baby. When Courtney showed up, Kurt was like, "Curt [Kirkwood], what do you do when the baby cries? We're having an argument about it — do you bring the baby into bed with you, or do you just leave it in its own bed even if it keeps crying?" I don't remember what Curt's answer was . . .

JERRY CANTRELL: I think Layne and him hung out quite a bit — at a particular time. I think Layne was really inspired by him.

MARK PICKEREL: Probably the only guy that kissed me on the lips that I didn't smack.

TRACY MARANDER: He was more of a Gemini than a Capricorn. Not that I believe in astrological stuff, but he was totally weary of people trying to pull one over on him. But at the same time, he could fall for that kind of stuff, because he was a nice guy and wanted to think the best of people.

ALLISON WOLFE: I got the impression that his girlfriend, Tracy, wiped his butt — he seemed like he needed a girl to take care of him at that time. She drove him everywhere, cooked for him. That made a big impression on me, as far as thinking of feminism within the punk rock scene, and how can we change these roles so it's not like the girls taking care of the guys who are the big "musical geniuses?" That scenario is not my idea of fun [laughs]. I think the main thing is that he was human — just a normal guy in a lot of ways. He's never been afforded that reality. He was just a guy with flaws who's a musician.

He was great, but to be honest, I don't think the music is that brilliant. I think the guitar playing is great and the performance is great, but when I listen to the lyrics, to me, they're kind of stupid. I also don't feel like it's a music that has necessarily aged that well. But I think he was great at what he did — he was an incredible person and very beautiful. And I don't mean just in the way he looks. You could see sometimes this sort of boyish pureness coming out of him. I think he was a good person, but he wasn't infallible, he wasn't godlike — like the little boy genius that everybody tried to make him out to be. I sometimes wish people would remember those elements — not to tear him down, but just to humanize.

BEN SHEPHERD: They like to say that he had charisma. *Bullshit.* He didn't have any — he was just 'Kurt,' and that was that endearing quality. *He was just Kurt.* I met him in Olympia; I don't even think he'd started Nirvana yet. I met him at a party — we were both sitting on the end of a couch and I go, "You're like me, huh? You always wind up at this spot at the party?" And he says, "Yep." Everyone else is partying, and we're sitting there, being loners on the end of a couch. There was thankfully a guitar, and we'd swap it back and forth. Smoking cigarettes, talking, and kicking back.

TRACY MARANDER: I've read stories where supposedly he'd done some heroin around [the late '80s]. But if he did, I never knew it. There were no symptoms or signs. Ever since I met him, he could fall asleep anywhere easily — he'd be watching TV and fall asleep. Once in a while, he'd smoke pot or drink — but he really didn't smoke pot that much.

ROBERT ROTH: He would tell me about his severe stomach condition — how he couldn't hold down food, and was in a lot of pain. He really didn't understand what was wrong, and apparently no one else did — doctors either. I'm fairly sure this was prior to any heavy drug use. I know that eventually getting high made the pain go away, and allowed him to enjoy eating, and be able to keep down food — and be able to work.

CHAD CHANNING: Sometimes he'd just beat the crap out of himself, out of his chest, like he was trying to dislodge phlegm. Every now and then, he'd talk about it. He'd be like, "I don't know what it is, just sometimes it feels like it's over-congested."

JIM TILLMAN: I'd see Kurt at parties, and you could just tell he was depressed. I'd had friends that were clinically depressed, and turned to drugs. You could just tell — he's sitting on the side of the room, against the wall, watching people, and not interacting. It was obvious that he was suffering internally and mentally — which helped his songwriting abilities. But ultimately, was his demise.

LARRY REID: When he got involved with junk, it was so sad. I remember seeing him at this bar, Linda's, just before he died, and he was nodding out. I was going to say, "Hi, how's it going?" — but it was pretty obvious it wasn't going too well. It was the last time I saw him.

KATHLEEN HANNA: He was a really special person. It makes me sad the way he's been exploited after he's dead. It's upsetting, and I hope rather than people getting into heroin, they investigate that, and that that could be part of the legacy — that people look at drug addiction in a better way. Because *a lot* of people died of heroin in Olympia — it's really awful and sad. And unnecessary.

KURT DANIELSON: Just because he killed himself doesn't mean he wanted to, really. I mean, you can say, "He wanted to, he did it." If he'd have lived another second longer, he may not have done it. [Drugs] isolated him, as chemicals do. I've been through it all myself, and I know for a fact, that there is a time you come to, where if you have access to a gun, *you will use it.* Unfortunately, he had access to one. It's just really terrible luck. Kurt had the best luck and the worst luck — both at the same time. He was the most gifted and cursed. And also the most ferocious, innocent, and nicest. A bundle of extremes and opposites. They either [put Kurt on a pedestal], or they Satanize him. "Oh, but how could anybody who has a child kill themselves?" Well, I'm sorry, but the world is full of horrible things. Sometimes we're only human.

JOHN BIGLEY: I saw him after the last show they did in town [in January 1994]. We spoke, and he said some real flattering things. He was very much into lineage, and how things — musically, especially — got to where they are. He had this huge entourage, walking down this hallway, stopped, and [said], "Oh, John, it's nice to see you. Did you enjoy the show?" Same sweet guy. "I just want to thank you for being part of this, and you're part of me — where I go, you go." Weeks later, I got the phone call. How do you describe that? I had this heartwarming chat in the hallway a few weeks ago . . .

CHAPTER 31

"The demise of the entire scene": Drugs

Heroin addiction proved to be a major contributor to Kurt Cobain committing suicide. But like any city in the world, drug use was a problem for many, and was nothing new to Seattle's music scene.

ART CHANTRY: I don't know if you've ever had to deal with junkies before — particularly ones that have money. Walls are built around them. It's like the people that are inside protect their junkie — especially if the junkie has the earning power of a Kurt Cobain. What you end up with are layers of . . . it's like concentric circles. That's why that Nirvana T-shirt with that diagram of layers of redemption was so perfect, because that's the way that the structure of the Nirvana camp worked. It was very, very difficult for outsiders to work their way through the various layers to get at people that could actually make decisions. It was all designed as protection. And it was true of any junkie — that's the way junkies operate their lives. That's the way the Alice in Chains camp worked, that's the way Lanegan worked. Nobody got inside the Nirvana camp — it was like a compound. It was even hard for the other band members to get through the layers sometimes.

It's like heroin defined the scene. Seattle's always been "a heroin town." It's a port city. Portland has always been a heroin town. But like all culture explosions since World War II, when the German high command started to use methamphetamines, every major cultural scene in Western civilization — and we're talking bikers, beatniks, hippies, glam rock, punk, funk,

Warhol factory, the surfers, hot-rodders, truckers — were all speed freaks. It has a huge impact on our culture. And in Seattle in the early days, it was no different — crystal meth was the drug of choice. For the longest time, cheap crystal meth was where it was at in this town. There were a few people who took heroin, but usually it's because they got exposed to it in other cities. It wasn't until money rolled in — and this is true of every culture explosion you see in these towns — it's followed by heroin, and there's a heroin epidemic. Heroin follows the money. This is the way these things always work — Seattle fell right into it.

TIM BRANOM: Just pot isn't enough — it had to be heroin. It rains all the time, it's so depressing — what can you do? You can go to a movie, you can go to a party, you can go to the Space Needle, or that's it. The climate's changed — see that's the funny thing. When I moved [out of Seattle] in 1990 — maybe it's global warming or whatever — the climate completely changed. But for most of my life there, which was like twenty-some years, it seemed like it rained every single day. I think it is the suicide capital of the world. I'm telling you, if I stayed there, I probably would have killed myself like Kurt Cobain. It just does it to you — the darkness, the cold, and the attitude.

JOE TOUTONGHI: There was a lot of addiction and alcohol abuse involved in the Bopo Boys, Jak's, and the whole punk rock thing in Seattle. For me, it was a heroin thing. By '82 or '83, I was pretty dedicated to being a full-time heroin addict. All the Bopo Boys used — everybody's clean now and pretty much made it through it. There's a couple of guys that OD'd and died, but for the most part, there were no bad car wrecks or anybody died. The drug scene probably killed the underground punk rock club scene — it moved it into houses at one point. It had a huge part with the local music scene — fading from punk rock to grunge. Cheap heroin arrived — when I started using, you couldn't buy a ten dollar bag of heroin. You bought thirty-five dollar bags. In 1980, that was a lot of money for a twenty-year-old. It was obtainable — cocaine, heroin, and alcohol. Pretty much everybody, at some point or another, got involved in it to a pretty extreme level.

JOHN CONTE: I remember going to the IOOF Hall, up on Capitol Hill. The kids wore colors, and everybody was pogoing. By 1981–82, cocaine entered the scene, and everybody ended up wearing black. Once cocaine got involved, and the way these people got involved with it, it was shooting up. They just skipped doing it dry, up the nose. I remember people shooting up, and it was just cocaine. But at some point, that got even darker for people.

LIBBY KNUDSON: I was totally clueless if people were doing drugs. I was a person who didn't do hard drugs, so a lot of time, you're not included in that world. I know in the mid '80s there was a dance club called the Monastery — MDA and MDMA was very popular, as was acid, and living in the great Pacific Northwest, [marijuana] was always around. And mushrooms, that wonderful fall harvest of mushrooms. One guy that was living at our house at one point, it was like, "Where are all our spoons?"

KYLE NIXON: I split from the punk scene and everyone was doing heroin. I mean *everyone* — all my friends. I didn't want anything to do with that. I was offered heroin in '86. It's sad to see all those good guys go down that way. A lot of those guys still struggle with it today. Some have overcome it, some are dead.

ROD MOODY: The combination of smack, major label interest, and the metal influence pretty much put the nail in the coffin of the close-knit scene that was going on in the late '80s. I was living in the closet of a friend's apartment about 1989, and he was a facilitator — while he didn't deal the stuff directly, he knew how to get heroin on a regular basis. There were always people coming around to cop — from scenesters, to prominent musicians, to regular Joe's. I saw a lot of shit go down in that place, and I am truly thankful I never had the nerve to try dope. Otherwise, I would probably be six feet under with all those other poor people.

VAN CONNER: I'm still recovering. There was just so much drugs around — usually free. I mean, at first . . . then they start charging. And since we didn't work nine-to-five jobs, it was easy to get caught up. It became that was the main thing — the partying — and the music thing was just getting you along. Paying for the partying. I know that had a lot to do with the band not going on anymore, and people dying. I don't blame any one person in the band, because I dealt with it by just getting more wasted. We used drugs and alcohol for "stress reduction." It didn't work.

LARRY REID: Drugs eventually led to the demise of the entire scene. It took a lot of the energy and creativity out of it.

ART CHANTRY: Like any punk scene, it's amazing how many people die. When you treat rock'n'roll as salvation and then you get all this money, a lot of these guys — especially if they come from lower socioeconomic backgrounds — they can't handle it, and it kills them. Usually through self-indulgence — not being able to spend their money right.

STEVE MANNING: In some ways, it didn't fit what was going on — at least my perception of what heroin does to you. The way the shows were — the energy that everybody had — the two didn't really jive.

LILLY MILIC: It just spread — to the point where you'd hear one death after another. We became so hardened by it. I remember sitting down at some bar downtown — someone walks in crying, saying so-and-so died. And people that I was with weren't upset with it. It sounds hard and cold, but one guy said, "I'm not going to shed a tear for her. The last time I heard, she was shooting up in her toes."

BEN REW: I took a hiatus for a couple of years, because everyone was getting addicted to heroin. All my friends — Mark, both Kurts. I hated all that stuff. It seemed like you were either in these huge bands, or you weren't getting a break. So me and a couple of my friends had this total "poor me syndrome," which was bullshit. We'd all get loaded — I was addicted to [heroin] for about a year and a half. All of us were hardcore alcoholics — fueled on beer and pot. And then there was a lot of cocaine at the beginning of the scene.

I remember the Butthole Surfers came up and played — it must have been 1988 or '89. It was almost like their sole purpose was picking up mushrooms and weed, because those were the two things you could get in Seattle that were hard to get everywhere else. I had a friend of mine that sold both, and I remember sitting down with Gibby [Haynes] and J.D. [Pinkus]. They're like, "We want a quarter pound of green bud and all the mushrooms you can get." And then they proceeded to eat enough for about forty people. *It was insane.* I'm not kidding — two or three ounces of dried mushrooms. A lot of times, the first thing that bands would do when they knew you were up here, they were like, "Can you get that Seattle green bud?"

ART CHANTRY: Heroin doesn't do any physical damage to your body — if you have enough money, you can take heroin the rest of your life, and not do any physical damage to your body. As long as it's pure. It's all the stuff that cuts it. The people who make the money off the junkies are the ones that kill them, by cutting the thing. And it's the same thing with how they protect junkies.

MARK IVERSON: I remember a rumor that Mark Arm did heroin. I was like, *"No way."*

MARK ARM: I don't go around flaunting my years of blowing my brains out on hard drugs. It's not something that I wear as a badge of cool. I'm not proud of it — in fact, it's an embarrassing cliché. The rest of the band was not into it, and they were very bummed with me. One thing that actually helped me when I decided I wanted to quit was we went on tour a lot. There was no way I was going to be able to do heroin on tour. I used to do it in New York because it was easy to get, but I couldn't just take off looking for drugs everyplace we played. The rest of the guys wouldn't have stood for it. When I came home from tour I would go back into my little fucked-up world, with my fucked-up girlfriend, and a couple of other fucked-up friends. But because we did a lot of little tours, I was well practiced at quitting. Most people who get strung out fear going through withdrawals. I went through withdrawals fairly regularly. I was used to feeling flu-like symptoms for the first couple of days on tour. I finally realized around '92, the whole heroin addiction thing was not going so well. It's really expensive. It wasn't so much fun anymore — in fact, it got pretty fucking boring.

I made moves in late '92 to get away from it, but I didn't fully stop until the summer of '93. I began enjoying heroin as a recreational weekend activity in '87. I rarely took it two days in a row because I didn't want to get strung out. I thought I was smart and strong enough to avoid that trap. When I came home from our nine-week European tour in '89, my girlfriend informed me that she'd been doing it every day. I was just like, *"Holy shit."* I knew what that meant. We were living together so it was an easy trap to fall into. My habit was at its worst from '91 to the fall of '92. When we went on tour again that fall I gained enough clarity to realize that I would have to quit on my own. So I called my girlfriend from Europe — this isn't the same one from '89, but my *second* junkie girlfriend — and told her to move out of the house before

I came back. I've gotta say that Emily saved my ass. When we started going out in the summer of '93, she asked me if I was ever going to do heroin again. I responded with a wishy-washy line like, "Well, you never know what the future holds." She came right out and said that if I ever did it again, she'd be outta here.

BEN REW: I bailed after '91. This sounds so cliché — I went up to a cabin in the mountains, and started bike riding a lot, and got off that stuff. Came back down, and started up an agency — had Tad on my roster.

ART CHANTRY: Rich junkies are as good as dead. Rich junkies don't live.

CHAPTER 32

"Preparing for the worst": Alice in Chains and Layne Staley's Death

Despite scoring two hit releases in the U.S. — *Jar of Flies* and *Alice in Chains* — and the formation of a popular Alice in Chains side-band, Mad Season, drug addiction effectively brought an end to the Layne Staley–led lineup of the group. But most important, it also proved catastrophic to Staley's life.

JERRY CANTRELL: [1994's] *Jar of Flies* was crazy man. We had already done *Sap*, so we had set a precedent. Between *Dirt* to the dog record [aka 1995's *Alice in Chains*], we were going to do another EP. I think it was after we had planned on having a vacation. Before the vacation, the guys were like, "We want it to be more of a band thing — so don't write a bunch of shit to bring in." I'm like, "OK, that's cool — no problem." I went on vacation and didn't play my guitar at all. We booked a week and came in off of vacation. Everybody gets in, and they're like, "OK, *what have you got?*" Walked in with nothing, and walked out seven days later with that record — pretty much from scratch. I think I might have had "Don't Follow" from the *Dirt* tour in Europe, when we were just burned — you can feel that in the lyrics. Everything you hear on that record was written, recorded, and produced in a week. To this day, it's the only EP to reach or debut at number one.

SEAN KINNEY: That was a really big turning point — it made sense, because things were looking pretty bleak. That was a nice pick-me-up. It was

PIC BY YANNI "JOHNNY" BACOLAS — YANNIBACOLAS.COM

Inside Layne and Yanni's apartment (L-R: Layne Staley, John Baker Saunders, Mike McCready)

like, "Cool, we're moving forward and we're moving on. We're still here and shit's getting better."

YANNI "JOHNNY" BACOLAS: Right after they recorded *Jar of Flies*, [Layne] was really hitting a wall. We went camping on one of those weekends in that period — he was trying to kick heroin. He asked me if I would move in with him, and I guess help him out, which ultimately, I just ended up enabling him. Made it a lot easier for him to do what he did. So we lived together in the mid '90s. I was smoking weed — I wasn't doing anything like he was doing. That's why he trusted me, I think.

NANCY LAYNE McCALLUM: Layne bought his own home, a condo, in 1994. He was very proud of that, and thrilled to have his own space. He could stretch out all of his wonderful projects. He didn't stop writing poetry. His drawings were exhibited in a Seattle gallery. He was experimenting with Sculpey Clay, which comes in many colors — including his favorite "glow-in-the-dark." He was doing one-stop shopping at Fred Meyer. He could go there and get his favorite coconut ice cream bars, clothes, arts and crafts supplies. He experimented with the craft kits for stained glass, designed a few faces for clock kits, and did some animated characters and jewelry from clay. He had his kitty, Sadie, and he liked to order out. He had every cleaning supply known to man, on the face of the earth, because he was very conscientious about having his home clean.

MIKE INEZ: There was one poignant moment for me. We were doing rehearsals at the Moore Theatre, and we were getting ready to go out with Metallica on a couple of dates — a stadium tour. It became real apparent that we couldn't do this. It felt like the wrong thing to do. So we pulled the plug on it. I don't want to say what went on in the meeting, but when I was walking away from the Moore Theatre down the alley, it was raining. I turned around, and saw Layne walking down by himself, down the alley. When I look back on it now, it's the moment for me that everything turned around. I went, "Hmm, *we're not healthy*."

NANCY LAYNE McCALLUM: Layne had taken me to the Grammys in 1994, and he was in horribly rough shape. I know that he was praying that would be the year they would win. He would have been so thrilled to have his mom there. They had been nominated five times. He expected this would be the year. I know it was a huge disappointment to lose.

YANNI "JOHNNY" BACOLAS: The Mad Season thing came about when Mike McCready went to Hazelden to get clean and sober. His roommate was a guy named John Baker Saunders. He told Baker, "Come back to Seattle with me — I'll make sure you have a place to stay. We'll start this band, stay busy, and support each other." They came back to Seattle, and McCready started calling our house. Layne didn't answer the phone very often or answer the door, so I would answer the phone and we would talk. I would talk to Layne, and say, "Hey, man, McCready is calling — he's a good guy and he wants to talk to you. He's sober." McCready is one guy that comes to mind that really tried hard to help Layne. He would fly in these counselors from Hazelden — a guy named Lowell, who Layne loved. Layne really listened to and looked up to this guy. McCready would bring this guy in, and kind of give Layne "the surprise attack."

Layne actually went to Hazelden during this process, and bailed midway through, or a couple of days into it. McCready would keep coming over to the house — he would bring Baker over, make a couple pots of coffee, and just hang out. Layne would wake up and talk to them, and the next thing you know, McCready is playing these ideas on a guitar in the house. Dragged Layne down to Bad Animals Studio — that's where they recorded [1995's *Above*]. I would drive him to the sessions every night, because it was only a minute from our house — we lived on Queen Anne. A month and a half, two months later, they finished a record. He would come in the house at four in the morning, turn the stereo on, and hit the speakers which were in my bedroom — just to wake me up so I could hear the new tracks that he had laid down. He always wanted that pat on the back or "Hey, great job" thing. I would come out of my room all sleepy or dreary, listen to it, and say, "Fuck, this sounds killer!" And he would just be on cloud nine. That's what made him happy — creating music.

KRISHA AUGEROT: In the liner notes [of *Above*], he said something about, "I'll always remember that summer," which was the summer — whatever year it was — where we all went to the beach and went to barbeques. That really fresh, youthful time that we all had before it was all about drugs. He mentioned a few names in there — I think he mentions my name, Demri, and another girl named Fabiola, who was really good friends with the two of them. I know that meant a lot to him — that whole time period.

YANNI "JOHNNY" BACOLAS: [Bacolas' band, Second Coming] ended up playing a show with [Mad Season] on New Year's Eve — it was '95 going into '96 at RKCNDY. The first show they did was the Crocodile, the second show was at RKCNDY with us, the third show I believe was the Moore Theatre. And I think they did one more Crocodile show. And that was it — as far as I know. During that time period, he did probably fifteen to twenty shows with [Second Coming] — he was late every single time. It was exciting — for me to share a stage with him again . . . was great. He wouldn't move a whole lot but he dominated that crowd, just by his presence. He did a song called "It's Coming After," which he recorded with us on our first record [1995's *L.O.V.Evil*].

He would come to some of our gigs, because we were doing a cover band as well — to finance Second Coming. He would come out to some of those shows on the outskirts of Seattle, hop onstage, and sing "Would?" or "Man in the Box" with us. He would usually pull up with my dad. My dad was a big Greek guy — looked like Paul Sorvino, like he belonged in the Mafia. He would show up with my dad and another one of my dad's buddies — total mafioso looking guy. They would be in suits like his two security bodyguards. Picture Layne walking with Paul Sorvino and Robert DeNiro into a club. Layne would be in a suit also. The crowd would go crazy.

MARK ARM: Pearl Jam did this satellite radio thing — they did that twice and we played both of them. Mad Season played one, and I remember Layne coming in — he had his hair up in this knob off the top of his head. He was *so thin*, and greenish-grey. I had a hard time looking at him. I didn't even have the guts to go talk to him. The whole thing made me squeamish, and reminded me of my own bad times. Even if I did talk to him, I don't know what I would have said. Seeing him so far down the line on this trajectory that he had set for himself made me queasy. It seemed to me like once he discovered heroin, he decided he was going to fully embrace it. Based on the songs on *Dirt*, he just jumped in. There was no turning back. It was unfortunate and pathetic. That was the myth he made for himself, and he was living it out. The reference to him in "Into Yer Shtik" is about that. Once he created his persona of a wasted rock star, he had to follow it to its ugly conclusion.

KURT BLOCH: When the first Alice in Chains record came out, we were like, "Sellouts! You suck!" But by the time the second Alice in Chains record came out, I was like, "This is pretty cool." Their third album was *great.*

NANCY LAYNE McCALLUM: I was in Mexico when *Alice in Chains* came out in 1995. What were my thoughts? That Layne's life was in jeopardy, and that none of that other stuff really mattered.

SUSAN SILVER: Really painful putting it together. It took eight or nine months — hours and hours of waiting for Layne to come out of the bathroom. Days of waiting for him to show up at the studio. And through all those last years, he and I were really close. I kept telling him, "*You don't have to do this*. You have enough money to go and have a quiet life if that's what you want," with his longtime girlfriend, Demri. "Just go and do what makes you happy — don't do this if this is what's perpetuating your addiction." I didn't understand that it wasn't the music that was making him take drugs, he had a disease, and it was getting worse. But I was always saying, "What do you want to do? We can stop." "I don't want to stop," he'd say. "I want to keep going" — in terms of music, I'm not talking about drugs. He wanted to keep creating and recording. It was a really painful session because it took so long. It was so horrifying to see him in that condition. Yet, when he was cognizant, he was the sweetest, bright-eyed guy you'd ever want to meet. To be in a meeting with him, and have him fall asleep in front of you was gut wrenching. As the timeline will show — we stopped. We stopped many times to say, "This isn't going to work. We can't keep doing this, even if he says he wants to. It's just tearing everybody to shreds."

MIKE INEZ: That was a really dark time. I look at the album cover — it was very grey, and I think that's where we were at. Layne was going through the depths of his heroin addiction. It was really tough watching that, and it permeated into everything we did. Not to throw rocks at glass houses — we were *all* pretty fucked-up at the time, but not in that way though. We weren't that miserable, it seemed. I just really feel bad for the guy. I wish I could change the world for everybody who's in that place. That was definitely one of the hardest records I've ever had to work on. But some great stuff came out of it — "Heaven Beside You," [and] we got a Grammy nomination. We were still touching people.

JERRY CANTRELL: That was another number one record. That record took a long time to make, because we were all at a bad space. Things had really taken a turn for us. I was not in a good space, and Layne wasn't either. Still, I think it's one of the great records that we put out. That's a career move I wouldn't recommend repeating for anybody — stop touring with two number one records back-to-back [laughs].

KRISHA AUGEROT: Unfortunately, he got sucked into the rock star world, and it didn't work out, because Layne was a junkie. It was so sad, because they worked so hard — really unfair. Jerry just couldn't snap out of it — he was doing a lot of drugs as well. I think he's prone to depression. He's a Pisces, like me and Kurt Cobain — he can get really introverted and stay there. I don't know if it's feeling sorry for himself, or what, but I do the same thing — you get where you just want to be alone. He goes to a dark place — I think that a lot of his songs came from there. He moved to Los Angeles, went downhill, and came out of it somehow. I've seen him since then, and he's clean and sober, which is great.

NANCY LAYNE McCALLUM: If you've ever loved an addict that relapses, you trust your love for them, but you *never* trust the power of that drug on their brain chemistry. You *never* trust the treatment center if they don't address relapse. I once asked a treatment center counselor on family day, "What about relapse? What have these patients been taught about it, and what, as a family, should we do?" The counselor looked at me and said, "Oh, our students never relapse." I knew that we had wasted our time and money . . . my heart just sank. I felt so horrible for Layne, because here I was, his logical, practical, upfront mom, who had asked the question that nobody wanted to ask. I felt as though with all the parents, loved ones, and family surrounding these young people, they would give us a phone number or a counselor we could call, in case we were worried. I was so blind and naive. In a way, it was like the drugs had a spokesperson right there in that room, and it was the counselor. It was sickening.

When Layne went to Hazelden, had he stayed longer and spent a couple of years in the recovery lifestyle, and been able to build long-term friends and sponsors, I believe Layne would have had a chance. Kurt Cobain said it would take three years for him to have a solid new start, and I believe he was correct. But Layne became addicted to drugs when he was quite young, and he never really learned mature problem solving. He just didn't have the wisdom you get over a period of years. Some of the people around Layne were wonderful, sweet-hearted, and professional, and truly had his interests at heart. A young person who is drug addicted can't help bumping up against sleazy people in the entertainment industry — not necessarily the professionals, but others on down the line. You can't stay clean and sober without clean and sober people around you, without "a bodyguard mentality." Layne would've had to have been superhuman. Nobody expected him to be that. It takes walking away for a long period of time with the *support* of the music industry — i.e., had he stayed at Hazelden. Layne told me, "Mom, I have a contract I have to fulfill. There are over forty people on the payroll, and they all count on me being out there." That's where he was coming from, that he had a responsibility to the contract and his people. We need a Humane Society for Musicians.

SUSAN SILVER: The very last time they had played, I left the hotel in the morning to fly back to Seattle from Kansas City. The guys were going to the airport on the bus — it was after the KISS shows. I got the call when I landed that they couldn't revive Layne, and he ended up in a hospital in Kansas City.

SEAN KINNEY: They had asked us for a long time to go out and do those things. Me and Jerry especially [wanted to do it] — I was in the KISS Army and they were bringing back the original lineup. Layne kept saying, "I don't want to do it." We gave up on it — we didn't hear about it for a while. They must have asked again, and he said, "I'll do it." We rolled out there, and those were the last shows we played in public. They went great — they were fun. It was nice being out there. It was only five or six shows, and by the end of the shows, the last one, it was cops, ambulances, and "*Get on the plane! Hide the drugs!*" The same shit was going on. It became more apparent that unless things seriously change, we can't go out and play to our potential — at this level. We can't even get through a fucking week and a half without drama and scary shit going on. That's about right when I mentally started preparing, like, "It's done." Same thing with *MTV Unplugged* — they kept asking if we'd do it. Up to the moment, it was just a nail-biter. Barely any rehearsing at all, guys not showing up — the same shit. Rolled out there and everything worked. Right then is when I knew, "OK, if we never do anything again, I'm good with this. I'd rather leave on a high point instead of throwing drug paraphernalia into a garbage can in an airport, while I'm jumping on a plane, hoping to not get arrested." That's when I started to distance myself from it, and just preparing for the worst. Which, it inevitably happened.

JERRY CANTRELL: We kind of broke apart — we had been living together for years, and we started to think about having our own lives. Got girlfriends, moved into houses — shit like that, that regular people do.

MIKE INEZ: We will be brothers for life. I don't think it was ever about saying, "We're going to break up," or "Jerry's going to do a solo record." It just wasn't healthy for us at that time. It wasn't like Alice in Chains was one of those bands that had a big blowup. Nobody was sleeping with another guy's wife. We just realized it wasn't healthy. But we still talked all the time — to this day, I talk to Jerry and Sean almost daily.

SEAN KINNEY: It was never anger/animosity shit, it was just a long, drawn out process. It all sums up real easy — too many drugs.

JERRY CANTRELL: We all drifted apart into our own worlds. We kept in contact, and there was always talk of something that would maybe happen again. There's a tension created of having two number one records and not being able to do anything about it — but that wasn't all Layne's fault either. He's the one that paid the ultimate price for what we were all fucking around with.

KRISHA AUGEROT: No one could help [Layne] — everyone was done trying, and kind of gave up on him. There's nothing anyone could have done — he just went off and hid in his crazy apartment.

MICHELLE AHERN-CRANE: My aunt was "the queen of the metal scene" in the '80s, and Layne had a huge walk-in closet — [it] was his rental room at her place. [Alice in Chains] were total rockers then — I was really into the punk scene, and thought they were sort of ridiculous. She was always trying to put me and Layne together, and I remember thinking it was cheesy, because he had long golden blond hair, and he wore makeup and spandex. I thought he was just such a fag, y'know?

It was a weird thing — I had a dream about him [one] night, and my phone rang in the morning. My aunt woke me up. She said, "Guess who I saw last night?" And I said, *"Layne."* She's like, "I did, and he thought the girl I was with was you. He came running up, and gave me and my girlfriend a big hug, and then realized it wasn't you." I walked out of my apartment, and he drove past me — he was a passenger in a car. The only thing I recognized was his eyes — he had big blue eyes — because his hair had grown out and was mousey brown. We made eye contact, the car pulled over, and his mom was driving. He got out — he looked terrible. His hands were all wrapped in Ace bandages, with fingerless leather gloves over the bandages. He was holding this little kitten that his mom was helping him take to the vet. He jumped out of the car, and I was taken aback — it was shocking to see him looking like that. He shook his head like, "Come to the other end of the car away from my mom." He's like, "Hey, I was wondering — are you in the program?" He meant AA. I was like, "No, but I know a lot of people who are. I could hook you up with someone." He took my number, and started calling me. It turns out that he only lived a few blocks away.

So I started going over to his house — I was curious, I felt sorry for him. We went and saw a few shows together, and mostly he wanted to hang out, and watch movies — because he was a wreck. The first couple of times I came over, he was like, "One day I would like to have a family — this is what's going on now, but I'm not always going to be like this." A couple of times he disappeared and I was concerned, because we talked every day for a while. One time I didn't get a hold of him for a couple of days, and he called and said he was out in the woods with somebody, calling from a pay phone. He didn't say it, but I could tell he was trying to detox.

JEFF GILBERT: Where it really went off the tracks for Layne was when his girlfriend, Demri, succumbed to heroin [in October 1996]. Those two were supposed to be together. That was a no-brainer for everyone that knew him. She was all he wanted to be with. She was such a small, little gal, and the drugs just shut her down. After that, he was never the same.

NANCY LAYNE McCALLUM: I think they met at a party. She was seventeen and he nineteen — about that. He was very shy, and she was a bright, shining little star flitting about. As time went on, she was part of the family.

KRISHA AUGEROT: [Layne and Demri] — another really cute couple that seemed very happy, but very destructive. Oddly enough, I worked at Espresso Roma in the University District on the Ave, and she was working there as well. I didn't know her, and then later on, I saw her again — I think she went out with Paul Uhlir from Sweet Water first, and then she started dating Layne. Kind of went back and forth between those two guys a couple of times. She was like the sweetest, cutest, tiny hippie chick — just adorable and gorgeous. Never would I have ever imagined what happened to her happening. She started using heroin with Layne, I would guess. That was later on in their relationship, when it got really bad. They were both using, and they were both junkies, essentially. They stopped seeing each other — they went different ways. I know for a fact that she ended up prostituting herself, and doing all kinds of horrible things for drugs. And ended up in the hospital dying — cotton fever, or some kind of complications.

MICHELLE AHERN-CRANE: They were together forever. Finally they had broken up, because he took the attitude that she was worse than he was, but I think she had to do worse things because she didn't have any money. When I would be over there at night watching movies, the doorbell would ring all the time, and he would be like, "Shhh, be quiet — pretend we're not here." Sometimes maybe it was her, and sometimes people coming to party with him. So I asked, "Are you guys totally broken up? What's the deal?" And he said that she was pretty much [a] bottom of the barrel crackhead at that point, and was hanging out and sleeping in bad places — really struggling. I remember going over there in the afternoon once, and there was a note from her. It was like, "I love you — I hope you're doing well." He talked about her, and then when she finally died — even though they weren't together — he was devastated. You'd go to the house, go to the bathroom, and it was scary — blood on the sink and stuff like that. I'd just grab garbage bags and start cleaning up. It was clear that he liked me, but we never fooled around because honestly, I was scared that he might have AIDS. It seemed like he was getting the wrong idea after a couple of months. I just said, "I can't keep coming over here, and pretending everything is cool when it's so *not* cool."

JERRY CANTRELL: The thing about addiction is it's got you well before you ever realize it's got you. You're fucked before you even know it. You can go for years without even knowing it — and everybody else around you knows it. And even if you do, you ain't going to admit it. I've battled with that myself — at some point, you reach a point where you can deal with it, or you don't. In a lot of cases, it deals with you, and you lose people.

MIKE INEZ: He was in a really dark place. It's hard to see it. Kind of inaccessible to all of us. I'd stop by — me and Mark Lanegan would go by and beat on his door. It's hard to get to people if they don't want to be gotten to. I can't really walk in Layne's shoes, because I have not tried that drug. I was always "Mr. Pothead" — smoking the green bud and drinking Coronas. I'd never got into the depths of drug addition that heavy. He definitely wasn't happy.

SEAN KINNEY: It wasn't a mystery. Layne told me straight up, "I'm never coming back. I'm not going to quit doing drugs. I'm going to die like this — *this is it.*" I'm like the co-dependent girlfriend, "*No, no!*" But I knew that was a fact. It was just horrible, it's horrible to do that. I lost a lot of friends, and put myself in a lot of fucked-up situations. I hoped for it and put it out there every day, hoping that I'd get a call — "Hey man, I'm going to go get my shit back, I want to choose to do this." The way he looked at me, and how he said it, I just knew that he had already made up his decision. And you can't change people's minds. People buy a record and read a magazine, and they think that they know you. They come up and give you, "You didn't try to help him — *you could have saved him!*" It's like, "You can't save anybody." And we did everything — we were as supportive as anybody could be. If somebody doesn't want it, they don't want it. He wasn't, like, a bitter guy, and there wasn't any hatred. He just made this decision. A lot of damage had been done. He seemed like he was good with it. I'm not good with it — I'm not good with it today, I never was then. I'll probably never be.

KRISHA AUGEROT: Susan Silver was one of the people who tried to help him most. She was a constant in his life, trying to get him to get clean. Unfortunately, he just never accepted it.

SUSAN SILVER: He wouldn't answer the phone, wouldn't answer the door. Every once in a while he'd let one guy [in] that had been friends with the Alice guys, who ultimately worked in my office. It was one of the only people he would let in to see him, and bring him things from the office. He was very much housebound. He came out for a recording session [a cover of "Another Brick in the Wall Part 2" for 1998's *The Faculty Motion Picture Soundtrack*], and that was the last time I saw him. The session was supposed to start at four in the afternoon. He finally got there at midnight. And that's just the way it was with Layne. You'd go pick him up to take him somewhere, and the next thing you know, four hours have gone by — he could pull you into "the world." Shuffling around, getting something over here, and then getting something over there. Doing something on the Gameboy, and then doing something on the TV. *Days* would go by. He came to that session — I hadn't seen him maybe since I went to his apartment to tell him that his girlfriend died. I wouldn't hardly have recognized him. He looked *different* — he didn't look like himself anymore. But he had the same sparkling wit. Looking at him, thinking, "My God, he's physically changed," and just as sweet, just as funny — quoting lines off silly *Nick at Nite* TV shows.

JERRY CANTRELL: [Two new songs on 1999's *Music Bank* box set] was a really quick affair. We went in and banged it out. It's music that I had, and

Layne put down some lyrics — the songs are a little bit more rambling and open. But it still showed that there was something there — something that would be amazing to be continued. Unfortunately, it wasn't.

MATT FOX: He lived in a condo in the U District, and the District is a pretty pedestrian-oriented place. And you never saw Layne — *ever* — on the street.

DUFF McKAGAN: The apartment he had was not far from my house in Seattle — he lived probably twelve blocks away. Back in 2001 or so, Mark Lanegan and I were going to go up to his apartment and try to talk to him. I think Mark tried, and wanted me to go up. I didn't — it wouldn't have done any good.

JEFF GILBERT: He was a videogame freak, and he would just sit in this condo apartment, with the shades down. Just play videogames dawn to dusk.

NANCY LAYNE McCALLUM: He had a big-screen TV where you could have five different games going with five friends, simultaneously.

YANNI "JOHNNY" BACOLAS: I would always tell him, "Layne, why don't you take off, go to some deserted island, hire the best counselors, and just kick this shit? Go for six months if you have to." And his rebuttal was, "Johnny, I have celebrity status and I have a lot of money. I could fly planes out to deliver me the dope if I wanted to — and that's what I would do. *I can't escape.*"

EDDIE VEDDER: Getting attached to a drug or a drug attaching itself to you, it seems like the insidious part about it is it could happen to anybody. And some people are maybe more vulnerable to it than others. I don't know if that came from him trying to exorcise or desensitize himself from certain things that were going on. Again, you'd hope that the music was enough to do that, or writing songs and being able to isolate that stuff, and put it in its place creates something out of it. It could be just trying something a few times and it's in you.

NANCY LAYNE McCALLUM: I would say that Layne's form of addiction was virulent and aggressive. If it was a cancer, you sure wouldn't say, "Well, you've got two more albums to complete . . . all these people are on your payroll." I use this analogy — some people try recreational drugs and it acts as a single, unbarbed hook. It's in, it slips out, and they walk away. Some people try recreational drugs, and they get hooked . . . it's a single hook with a barb. They're still able to slip free. Some people get hooked with a double-barbed hook, and over time, it does tremendous damage. Some people get hooked with triple double-barbed hooks, and there is no flipping that thing free. And the longer it's in there without some outside help to extricate it, the more inevitable and severe the damage is. That "fish" is going to die. Every disease is like that . . . some people get cancer, they discover it early, the treatment works, and it's rather noninvasive. Depending on the degree of the cancer and the kind of cancer, sometimes it's treatable, sometimes it's not. Sometimes it goes into remission, sometimes it metastasizes.

Drug addiction comes in all different degrees, and in Layne's case, it was a death grip. He needed to be cut loose from his financial responsibilities in order to get the help he required. And it needed to be mandated. Because of the way the laws are written, you can intervene with a meeting, but you can't *make* an addict get help. That law was written so that someone's estate can't be appropriated unless you can prove that they can't tend their business. It's almost impossible to prove, because there are all degrees of sanity — and some of it borders on *"in."* What kept us from helping Layne is the same law that protected his estate. Sadly, one is a human life being treated the same as accumulated goods. These cases need to be handled on an individual basis. We were not able to help our son. When you're using drugs, you're not an adult making adult decisions . . . the drug is thinking for you. Its fangs are a death grip.

MATT FOX: Sean came into the [rehearsal studio], and we jammed for a while — it was a lot of fun. And I said some dumb thing like, "Could you guys get Layne off heroin so I don't have to hear Creed anymore?!"

MICHELLE AHERN-CRANE: He had open sores, and I heard he ended up losing some fingers, or his hand — I don't know exactly what's true. The last time I saw him, I was out for a jog, and this Trans Am with the Firebird painted [on the hood] had crashed into an ambulance. Layne and some white trash guy were fumbling around. Layne always wore this Australian big raincoat towards the end, and he was picking up all this shit that was falling out of the car and out of his pockets. And every time he bent over to pick something up, more paraphernalia would fall out of his pocket.

STEVE TURNER: It's amazing what drugs can do to people, besides just kill you — they can kill you really slowly and completely destroy you, your friends, and your family. That said, drugs are pretty fun — that's the problem. *Therein lies the rub.*

JEFF GILBERT: I ran into him out in the University District. He looked like an eighty-year-old version of himself. His skin was grey, dark circles under his eyes. He had already lost a finger or two from his veins collapsing and not getting enough circulation into his hands. He started losing teeth. I remember seeing him from a distance, and I thought, "That's the oldest punk rocker I've ever seen." He had Doc Martens on, pegged black jeans, black leather jacket. Stunk — *oh my God he stunk.* Barely recognized me, even though I'd known him for years. It was probably the last year of his life.

MATT FOX: I must have seen him in the U District, and he just looked really, really bad. He was all hunched over — he was usually taller than me, and he wasn't really [anymore].

YANNI "JOHNNY" BACOLAS: There was such a cloud of depression over that house — because of the heroin. If you were to live with any heroin addict, you're going to eventually . . . "enough is enough" type thing. What he would do is write me letters and put them on the base of my bed. I would wake up in the morning, and I would have a four to six page letter, handwritten, and he would explain everything that we talked about that prior night — regarding his life, how unhappy he was, and what was going on with him. He didn't really speak about Alice in Chains. As a matter of fact, I wasn't even allowed to listen to Alice in Chains when I lived with him. There were two rules — no interventions, and no listening to Alice in Chains music.

He wasn't getting any better — I felt like by me keeping the house clean, doing the laundry, and getting the groceries, I was making it real easy for him to be an addict. After talking to his mom and his stepfather Jim — even his sisters at the time — I came to the realization that I was enabling him more than I was helping him. And now, it was taking a personal toll on me, because coming home every night, it was not a happy household. He tried, and he wanted it to be — he gave it his all — but with the heroin in the calculus there, it just wasn't going to be a happy household. I had to make a decision for myself to get out of that environment.

The depression came from the cycle of heroin. The lifestyle you lead, the diet — all he really ate was sugar day and night. So I don't think he was getting a lot of nutrients. He wasn't exercising at all. What I've learned from my experience is that it's the lifestyle that kills you more than the heroin. The lifestyle is what causes the ultimate depression, and being chained to this horrible drug. Eventually, they turn on you, and now, you're depressed — you may not know a way to get out of it. I had probably two phone calls [to Layne] in the last couple of years of his life. They were pretty short. There's a time to talk to Layne, and there's a time not to talk to Layne during that point. If someone's using, that's not the time to dive into stuff with them. You wanted to catch him at the perfect opportunity.

NANCY LAYNE McCALLUM: I didn't believe that I would be doing much good poking away at him — "Layne, you've got to do this and you've got to do that." I was trying to be extremely . . . almost like I had my arm linked in his, trying to stay really close in my thoughts and conversations with him. I didn't want Layne to ever feel ashamed. All of us know that there are miracles around recovery. In Alaska, I was attending twelve-step meetings at an Al-Anon — for the family, friends, employers, employees, and concerned others of alcoholics and addicts. I was learning a lot — I probably read 200 books on the effects and studies of alcohol, addiction, and families.

I was trying to discover the key. I wanted to be a voice for that one little phrase that would be the "*A-ha*" for Layne. If it wasn't me, I wanted somebody to find those magic words that would bring Layne back to himself. I never lost hope that I — or someone — would be able to do that. I educated myself about the disease so I could talk with Layne and understand. But a non-addict can never understand — they can only accept and believe that the addict is telling his truth. An addict and a non-addict don't think the same — their brains are wired completely differently. Only an addict can help another addict through recovery.

SEAN KINNEY: I quit answering the phone for five or six years. I didn't want that phone call. Let it ring and let the machine get it. That still even sticks with me to this day — slight phone phobia. It's like, "Shit, bad news!"

Just hoping that it's never going to happen — knowing that chances are, that's going to be "the call" coming in one of these days. Ironically, tomorrow is the day it all went down for everybody — April 5. When they found Layne, and the same day Kurt [eight years earlier] . . . just bizarre timing on that. By then, I had started going away from lots of drugs, and just started drinking — like that's any better.

SUSAN SILVER: It was a call that we all feared for years. No one had heard from him, and the people that we were in touch with to let us know that he was still OK hadn't heard from him. His little odd weekly habits had stopped. Sean got a call from one of those people, and said, "I'm going over there, and I'm going to kick down the door. I have this sick feeling in my gut." I said, "Sean, we need to get the family involved." His step dad and his mom. When he didn't answer the door or respond in any way, the police opened the door, and the rest is history.

NANCY LAYNE McCALLUM: Demri's mom and I take solace in knowing that our children experienced great love from one another, and that they are no longer suffering.

MIKE INEZ: For me, I was run through the ringer, because my best friend, Randy Castillo — he was my drummer in the Ozzy band — caught smoking cancer. He ended up passing away, and this was right before Layne passed away. So we had just took Randy and his body back to Albuquerque, New Mexico. I came back to Big Bear, California, where I have a house. I was sitting in my kitchen, the phone rings, and it was Sean Kinney. He says, "Hey — sit down. *Layne's gone.*" I mean literally, it was the same day, or the day after I got back from New Mexico. I just couldn't believe it.

NANCY LAYNE McCALLUM: In order for Layne to have lived, he should have been released from his contract — with great love, acceptance, and respect. And yes, there was a contract, and yes, there was a commitment, but I don't think that a person has to . . . he didn't sign up to go to Iraq, for God's sake. He signed up for fun and hard work, and he gave his heart and soul . . . and life. At some point, it was real obvious that he couldn't go on, and that he needed freedom from the commitments. Maybe after several years of true recovery — not just cleaning up, going back out, cleaning up, going back

PIC BY YANNI "JOHNNY" BACOLAS — YANNIBACOLAS.COM

Layne Thomas Staley: August 22, 1967 – April 5, 2002

out — maybe the band could have done what the band is doing now . . . with Layne still at the helm.

JERRY CANTRELL: All I can say about it is this, really — at this particular time, years have passed now, and the longer you end up sticking around, the more friends you lose one way or another. It's a part of life. It's unfortunate when it's that type of an exit — because there's a lot of life left to live. But I learned a lot from that guy — I owe a lot to him. Many fond memories and a lot of music to listen to that we created together. I've got a lifetime of memories about him that no one else really will have.

YANNI "JOHNNY" BACOLAS: The guy was one of the nicest, most humble, sincere people that you'll ever meet. I'll give you an example of how humble he was. One night we were watching that movie *Cocktail.* He's watching Tom Cruise — he's spinning all these bottles, and there's all these girls lined up at the bar. Tom Cruise is just a stud in this movie, right? Layne's watching, he looks up — he's got a cigarette in his hand, and of course the ash is about two inches long, that's how he always smoked — and goes, *"Think of all the women he can get."* I'm just like, "Dude, come on! You're a singer in one of the biggest bands in the world!" He wasn't this arrogant, cocky, have-three-chicks-in-the-hot-tub-topless guy. He was just a pure artist, and didn't really think of all that stuff.

NANCY LAYNE McCALLUM: If you're in a situation where everything you do is under the microscope, everything about your life is being planned and managed by somebody else, and that life includes dealers putting pure free drugs in your pocket to keep you coming back — it's a hell on earth. Then people watch and wait for you to die, because they're going to sell all that stuff they stole out of your storage unit. They're going to see to it that it gets to an auction house specializing in sports and rock memorabilia, where it gets sold. Then your parents are going to have to buy it back with your hard-earned money. It's very disgusting, that tangled web they weave. Maybe a person that's involved in that whole web of destruction thinks it's a funny, challenging game. I'd love for that person to have to sit down and talk to my son. "They parted his garments and cast lots." *Ghouls.*

EDDIE VEDDER: Jim Morrison or some historical landmark in rock 'n' roll, you picture Jim Morrison waking up and taking ten or fifteen tabs of acid. That was breakfast, and then he went from there. You just know these are human beings behind this. That was how Layne was when he played music, and it was also a part of his music. In a way, it was what allowed his real personality to be kind and innocent. There was a place where you could exorcise some of the darker things that were going on. Apparently, there were more than we even knew.

NANCY LAYNE McCALLUM: I think Layne knew he was dying, but he didn't plan on it. He had just gotten his driver's license renewed, and he was in the middle of art projects. I really expected that Layne would survive this ordeal. Nobody should die like that. I wish the dealers could have seen what I saw. And truly, may they rot in hell.

MIKE INEZ: Ann Wilson put it great — she spoke at his funeral, and Ann and Nancy sang a song called "Sand" [from Heart's sideband, the Lovemongers' 1997 release, *Whirlygig*]. One of Ann's best friends and employees died from AIDS, and she wrote the song about him. It's just this beautiful acoustic piece. She said, "Layne was too fragile for this earth."

JERRY CANTRELL: It's something I miss. But at the same time, I can't be bummed about it — I'm really thankful for what we had, and what we did. And something that still lasts. I still hear his voice every day on the radio — and if I don't hear him personally, I hear him through some other kid emulating him. And that's great. I was lucky enough to have the experience to be in a band like I was, and be in a band with the type of guys that I was, and still am.

I think he is remembered — as a great singer. A very unique style, and those who knew him personally, was a beautiful person. I can't really ever think of a moment I ever saw him that he was super-pissed about anything. I'm sure he had his moments once or twice, but he was always the guy that was a peacemaker. He cared about people, what he did, and the type of music he played.

KRISHA AUGEROT: What I remember about Layne was this awesome voice, in such a little guy. Just incredible. He was one of my favorite people to watch — I loved watching Alice in Chains.

SUSAN SILVER: Layne was the most atypical lead singer I had ever met or heard about. He had no ill will towards anyone. He had this sweet disposition, and a really tender heart. And a *wicked* sense of humor — just hilarious. He was so witty, so funny, so quick. But no sign of egotism or "LSD" — "Lead Singer Disease." Such a dear person.

MICHELLE AHERN-CRANE: It's weird; I will often awake in the middle of the night with thoughts of Layne. I remember a sad or sweet look he gave me, and even though I know it's stupid — you know, "Never trust a junkie" — I find myself riddled with guilt for not being more sensitive, open, or even helpful. He would often imply that he was looking for a reason to get clean, and I replay those moments over and over again. These flashes in time sometimes keep me awake for hours and make my heart hurt. I know I hurt his feelings and that haunts me. I wish I had been more sensitive because I know, most people know, how capable he was of loving someone — look at his love for Demri. But intellectually, I guess I did the right thing for me — not trusting a junkie.

SEAN KINNEY: I'm just honored to have that time with him in my life. To really know him and have been through the experiences that we had. He still makes a difference and people are still into it. It wasn't just like, "Cool . . . *and next.*" It wasn't for nothing. But still to me, I would give it all back in a second if I would have known what would've happened to us and to him. *I would have left in '87*. If I had a crystal ball, I would have been like, "Fuck this." It's life. Life's a tough deal.

MIKE INEZ: God bless Layne. He was my favorite vocalist — I've never heard of a vocalist that had that much soul. He was hurt and that pain certainly came through. A lot of people identified with it.

NANCY LAYNE McCALLUM: Lots of fans and family members try to reassure me. People try to find the right words to say the right thing to console and make us feel better — and it's kind and the right thing to do. They say things like, "Now he's in Heaven singing in God's choir," "You still have his music to listen to," or "He'll live on through his music and we'll always hear his voice." I would want young people to understand that you don't have to accomplish anything huge to be loved. If Layne had chosen any other career, I couldn't have loved him more. People say, "Well, you have your daughters to console you." I say, "You don't understand. My daughters lost their brother. It's just as profound for them, but a different loss, and I have to be there for them."

When you strip away all of that, what you have left is loving someone, and Layne knew that. He once wrote on an anniversary card to us, "All we need is love." This should never have happened. Layne was sacrificed. No one should be sacrificed. We should all live long, happy lives. A goal for all of us is to try and make the world a better place. When all is said and done, and all the platitudes are stripped away, and all of the condolences and the gifts and the cards, and everyone shares their thoughts, my child has died.

I think the most important thing to remember is that no human being should be seen or treated as a commodity. People should remember him in their own way. He's a human being first. He may have represented other things, but he is a real person, who needed to live, and wanted to live, and should never, never have suffered this horrible death. How should Layne be remembered? He didn't want to be remembered as a drug addict. He wanted to be remembered for what he created and gave to the world. Sadly, the addiction took him too soon, or he would have been able to share more of himself with us. But for me, I feel as though I'm attached to Layne, and that he's with me every minute. How I would want others to remember him I can't say, but I do know how I remember him, and that is *every moment.*

JERRY CANTRELL: I'd say the same thing about Layne that I'd say about Kurt — it's too bad that we lost them, because they were amazing people and amazing artists.

CHAPTER 33

"The final magic": Soundgarden's Breakup

Soundgarden scored their big commercial breakthrough with *Superunknown,* and nearly replicated its success with the follow-up, *Down on the Upside.* But inner band tensions proved impossible to overcome.

ADAM KASPER: Soundgarden was ready to explode right then.

MARK IVERSON: I made my first trip to Europe in '94. You mentioned you were from Seattle, and everybody there was asking you all questions. *"Do you know Kim Thayil?"*

DAWN ANDERSON: They'd staunchly deny that they were stars. Finally, after *Superunknown,* I interviewed Kim, and I said, "You know you're a rock star now, don't you?" And he said, "Well, we outsold the Rolling Stones on this album . . . so I guess we're rock stars, yeah" [laughs].

KIM THAYIL: I think [*Superunknown*] did enter at number one, but its sales were never the meteoric rise of Nirvana or Pearl Jam. It sold a lot of records — but over a steady period of time. That year that *Superunknown* came out, all four of the big Seattle bands had number one records. I did an interview with some guy — he said, "Now Seattle is the greatest rock region in history. You surpassed Liverpool. You had four bands that have had number one records from your city in one year. That's never been done before."

SUSAN SILVER: ["Black Hole Sun"] — you couldn't help but find the toe tapping and find it stuck in your head in the middle of the night. But I felt that way about "Fell on Black Days." You have to remember; I heard so many Chris songs along the way that were equally as beautiful, and as absorbing and memorable. A lot of beautiful, quirky songs, that no one's ever heard to this day. It wasn't a stretch to hear him write a song like that.

KIM THAYIL: I certainly liked "Let Me Drown," "Spoonman." "Black Hole Sun" — when we heard the original demo that Chris had done, we thought, "There's some singles there." I mean, when Hiro heard the ["Black Hole Sun"] demo, he said, "*There's your hit*" — just like Ben said when he heard "Smells Like Teen Spirit." I was at a Metallica gig after *Badmotorfinger* had come out, and [Cliff] Bernstein had shown me some numbers of bands that had grown in a similar way — including Metallica. He said, "You guys are following a similar pattern. The next record, you make 'the record of your life,' and it's through the roof."

MATT CAMERON: The *Superunknown* tour was our first headlining tour. We had production, a sound system, and lighting — and played all over the fucking place. For the most part, it was pretty fun. Then towards the end of that tour, Kurt died, [and] I think the whole fabric of our group was starting to unravel a little bit.

KIM THAYIL: It started off strong — I don't know if the fabric of the band was coming undone. I don't think there was any interpersonal tensions — I think there were stresses from being on the road. I don't think anybody was having problems with anybody else. That might have come to play more after the next album. Our last show was at Memorial Stadium in Seattle — a really bad show. Chris's voice was having a really fucked-up time. When the show was over, he just walked offstage, got in a car, and took off.

MATT CAMERON: We took a little break, then we started to try and get some songs going for [1996's] *Down on the Upside*. It was my idea to record it at Studio Litho with Adam Kasper, because I felt our last situation was intense — all these big named producer guys involved. It just wasn't our scene at all. We just went back to the homemade method of making records with our buddy, Adam. It was good, but we weren't all on the same page. I was certainly trying to keep everyone motivated and just try to get it off the ground, but if people don't want to do things, it's hard to get them going. We weren't enjoying the process as much as we had been.

KIM THAYIL: It was broken up — it seemed to not be very cohesive. We did a little bit of what I thought was just demoing — preproduction. Then we went on tour [in Europe during the summer of 1995].

STEVE TURNER: We did some big festivals with Soundgarden in '95. It was just the worst. The Soundgarden guys — none of them [were] really talking to each other, everyone angry. It was no fun. It was one of those things that we immediately knew we shouldn't have done. I judge a lot on what our drummer, Dan, thinks about things. And that, to this day, is his least favorite trip he's ever been on. So that says a lot to me. They were acting miserable, like they were having the worst time of their lives. Well, then fucking don't do it! The same thing with Nirvana — if you hate it so much, *don't fucking do it.* Either deal with the situation that you created, or don't. Don't continue doing it and acting like a little spoiled child — with really nasty parents [laughs].

KIM THAYIL: Came back, Chris was in the studio doing some demos, and then I went into a studio trying to do some demos. At some point, what I thought was preproduction ended up being *production.* What were demos and preproduction ended up kind of "the thing" — everything was in gear. It was like, "*Wait a minute.*" There was a huge miscommunication in the recording process of *Down on the Upside* — just in terms of pacing and tempo. Stuff was at this one tempo, and then all of sudden, the pace really sped up. The next thing I know it's like, "We need your guitars . . . *now!*"

ADAM KASPER: It was a long six months. Basically the same approach to *Superunknown.* We had so many songs since all the guys were writers. This is before Pro Tools — you were limited and it was a whole different way of recording. Nowadays, you can keep everything and never make a decision until the last day. It was the last sort of analog era — and we did it all analog. If you listen to that record, it's got tons of stuff on it. The band seemed pretty good — they were all fairly independent at that time, as far as writing their songs. Particularly Cornell.

KIM THAYIL: I ended up just writing and completing "Never the Machine Forever." I did it on my own, there wasn't an iota of collaboration with that. There was a lot more collaboration with the band on all the previous records. Collaborations were getting fewer and further between. My participation was diminishing.

BEN SHEPHERD: For me, it was more painful. Because my honey was leaving me the whole time that was going on. But the music, it was way more us. We actually recorded with Randy Johnson [then-pitcher for the Seattle Mariners], after he'd won his first Cy Young. He came to the studio — he played drums, and me and Kim played guitar. We actually made a song and recorded it. Chris was going to sing on it, but never did.

ADAM KASPER: I don't remember much about the song. Let me just say he's a better pitcher than a drummer.

KIM THAYIL: Overall, I don't see it as a pleasant experience. It fucked up the momentum of band personnel dynamics and creative dynamics. To the point that I was not satisfied, and I don't think Chris was satisfied either. And that's something that we carried on the tour. Maybe if I was more frank, sat down, and bitched with the band, things would have worked out.

ADAM KASPER: I think [Kim] felt that during *Superunknown* things were getting commercial-oriented and radio friendly. So that struggle started back then. And the more Chris had hit songs, Soundgarden turned into "a hit radio band." They never were before that — they were heavy, disturbed. That was Kim's leaning. *Down on the Upside*, it was even more evident. Kim was more on one end and Chris the other.

SUSAN SILVER: There was a certain lack of cohesion at that point. I think Chris was really starting to suffer from untreated depression — the way he wasn't focused on what he needed to be focused on, in terms of making the record. And stopped participating in a way that was productive for everybody. Chris would come home and literally be on the floor in a ball, crying, in the middle of the night. He was inconsolable. They weren't communicating — try as I may to get them to sit down and have meetings, and go talk to some kind of a group counselor. I had a book I had given them at one point, that Aerosmith's manager had told me about — something that Aerosmith had read collectively, and helped them a lot — called *The Paradox of Success*. They laughed at me when I gave it to them [laughs]. They were not group therapy candidates. So eventually, everybody retreated into their own corners and stopped communicating. The key to everything, and any relationship that's going to survive is communicating. We watched Pearl Jam go through it and come out the other side, because as difficult as it is at times for anybody to sit down and talk when they're not feeling good about each other or themselves, it's the only way to get to the other side. And Soundgarden wasn't willing to do that.

MATT CAMERON: The sessions were certainly strained. And once we started touring, the shows were increasingly bad. Just horrible. A lot of drinking, bad vibes, rock star bullshit. I was actually thinking about bailing at that point. Ben couldn't really get through an entire show without having some kind of temper tantrum. It was so *not* about music.

SUSAN SILVER: As far as Ben smashing stuff up, it was not an unusual occurrence by then. He had a lot of unseated anger that he didn't deal with in his own life. It became almost like a stage antic, to exhibit all this tension and discontent onstage. And it became an issue. I'd say the same thing over and over: "Ben, *you're giving up your power*. There were 3,000 people there tonight — 2,999 of them got ripped off, because you focused on one guy." It became like a circus act, where everybody's focused on "Why is the bass player so mad, and who is it that he's threatening to beat up?" So we talked about it, and I'd send him magazine articles about different things — how to not give away your power, basically. And other public figures that had gone through that frustration of that catch-22 — of wanting to be in front of an audience, and resenting it at the same time.

JEFF GILBERT: [Ben] was horribly lonely, depressed, and heartbroken. I felt so bad for him, because nobody wanted to be on the road at that point. You know where it started? When they were on the road and got the news of Kurt. They were so far away from home, and they weren't around their support system — their friends, their family. Kim told me, "It wasn't fair. We didn't get to grieve, and be around our family during that period. We were supposed to be on the road. And that's when it began to suck." People dying out of the Seattle music scene simply was not supposed to happen.

MATT CAMERON: We'd done the Lollapalooza tour with Metallica around that time, and that was a total nightmare. We weren't playing good — sounded bad, really bad shows. Kind of embarrassing.

ROSS HALFIN: I was in Paris, and I saw them do a great show — this was the beginning of *Down on the Upside*. Afterwards, I remember being in a room with [Chris] drinking, having a good time. And Chris ended the night by throwing a lamp through a window. What's the point of drinking if you can't enjoy yourself with it? Maybe it's the Irish in him — just wants to start fighting and being stupid. There's no point in being like that if you can't fight.

KIM THAYIL: On tour, Chris did the best job of anyone in trying to communicate. He was grossly inadequate in that department in previous situations — but I think he really took a leadership role on our last tour. In terms of communicating, and trying to get the band on the same page. And I applaud him for that. It might have been too little, too late. I didn't see the band as breaking up — I just saw myself and Ben as being unhappy. Matt was also unhappy. Probably why Chris took a leadership role in trying to direct communication and bring the band together — I think he saw that there was a lot of dissatisfaction. He was definitely ballsy and courageous in trying. But like I said — *too little, too late.*

ROSS HALFIN: The bass player kept walking offstage halfway through the last few shows — you got an idea they weren't getting on! You'd be in Australia, and they'd be holed up all day — Chris would just stay in his room, you never saw him. The Hordern Pavilion in Sydney — when the band was falling apart — Ben Shepherd got fed up, threw his bass down, and walked off. I remember they did five songs without him, and they sounded like the Doors. The last song of the set they played was a song called "We're Better Without You," which was just Cornell chanting it over the PA. This was the end of the road for them — everybody was just not enjoying each other.

BEN SHEPHERD: That last show we played in Hawaii was the night that I found out it was our last show. Because our bass tech, I'd gotten him out of

PIC BY VIKKI ANSELMO

Second to last ever Soundgarden show, February 8, 1997, in Hawaii

rehab, which is another harsh thing about our family that was going on. I got him over to Hawaii, because they were the last shows we were going to do [on the tour]. I thought we'd do "the Beatles thing" — take it easy for a while. *Not fucking break up.* So we played our last show, and he called a band meeting. He's the only guy besides one of us that can call a band meeting, because he had seniority — he was on tours before I was in the band. He goes, "What's this shit I hear — this is your last show and you're breaking up?" Everyone didn't rebut that, they just sat there. I was like, "*What the fuck?*" And of course, my equipment died that night. The opening band had already left, so there was no other equipment in the building. I got pissed and smashed my bass. I was totally out of my head — angry and pissed off. Drunk. And I was lividly sad, because that was the end of the tour after my honey had left me. And that was it, the last show of the tour that she should have been with me on. The last tour was the most creative and destructive music that I'd ever heard or been part of. The final magic.

MATT CAMERON: I think we'd done about nine or ten months of touring for *Down on the Upside.* So we took a little break after. At the time, I was trying to get some songs going for the next one. One morning, I took my dog out for a walk, came back, and Chris's truck was in my driveway. I was like, "Cool, Chris *never* comes to visit — we'll play songs together, work on some stuff. What a great opportunity!" So I go into the house, and my girlfriend at the time, April — who's now my wife — goes, "Chris is in the basement." I go down there, and he just *reeked* of alcohol. I think he'd been up all night drinking, and he looked a little odd. We started talking. We never really hung out that much, so I was like, "OK, why is he here?" [Laughs.] And then he was like, "Well . . . I'm here because I'm leaving the band."

BEN SHEPHERD: Chris Cornell shows up — he's got a bottle of, I think, Canadian Club. We're all standing in my living room, and my friend goes, "Today's the day the Beatles broke up." And Chris goes, "*Here man*," and hands me the bottle. I take a swig, we go down to my car, and he says, "I'm quitting. I'm breaking up the band. How do you feel about that?" I looked down at the ground, spit on the ground, and went, "Alright." That's how I joined the band — when they asked me "Do you want to join the band?" I looked down at the ground, spit, looked up, and said, "*Fuck yeah!*" It was kind of fitting for me.

KIM THAYIL: One of the first things I told [Chris] was I felt relieved. And he was really surprised — he said that was the same thing Matt said. I think Ben took it the hardest. It bummed me out, but I *did not* shed a tear. Ultimately, we were a band for thirteen years — that survives most relationships or most people's employment periods.

SUSAN SILVER: Chris kept it away from me — for reasons of protection, and what he thought would be legality. He consulted with someone else — got another lawyer, and was very thorough about making sure everybody would be safe and protected. Once he got all that in line, [he] let me know what he was intending to do, and then did it a couple of days later. Came home absolutely distraught. There wasn't any overt hatred between them — it was that dysfunctional relationship, where they're figuratively living together and not talking to each other. Which literally is the way Chris became as a husband. Here we are living together — not in this period, but later years — but he's not talking. That became the seat of dysfunctionality. There are these guys that have a career that could continue to grow, they can make it on their own terms. They're unhappy with things about each other, but nobody's saying what they are, or talking to each other about what they are. So it decayed from within. And Chris just kept getting more depressed.

JEFF GILBERT: I asked [Kim], "Twelve years, is that it?" And he said, "We did everything — we took Soundgarden as far as it could go." He felt that Matt and Chris were getting frustrated, because they seemed trapped in "the Soundgarden sound," and wanted to do other stuff. I thought they could have easily gone the Zeppelin route, like with *Physical Graffiti*, and just do *everything*.

CATHY FAULKNER: They were stepping out on top. A lot of bands continue going on and on, and the public knows that they need a break farther ahead than the band knows themselves.

MATT CAMERON: I was hoping that we'd go on for another twenty years. We're all on good terms. It's not like we're bitter about it. I consider the time I had in Soundgarden as being incredibly fortunate. I feel really lucky to have been in that band.

SUSAN SILVER: Once Soundgarden broke up, [Cornell] went off to start a solo career. Not having partners to . . . not necessarily to write with, but to bounce ideas off of, he started to waver in his confidence about what he was doing. The beauty of having the creative tension between band members had helped him solidify his belief in his own songs. When he didn't have that, he started to become unconfident about his own creations. He started to become more depressed, and at that point, he started to self-medicate. Unbeknownst to me, he started using pills, and became addicted — which led to a deeper drug addiction, and ultimately, our parting.

JEFF AMENT: I don't think anyone in Seattle has heard from Chris in a long time. I do think he's the best songwriter to come out of Seattle since Hendrix.

ADAM KASPER: I'd gone on their last tour to record a lot of their live stuff — there's a whole great album's worth of live Soundgarden stuff that's just been sitting. Cool covers like "Helter Skelter." There's a couple of [studio] songs that we did that haven't come out that are killer. There's one, "Christi," from the last record — incredible. Real dirgey, slow — tuned to C. Long, maybe eight minutes long. The "Black Hole Sun" demo is super cool — things like that.

JACK ENDINO: As far as Soundgarden, there are enough rarities and outtakes that they could do a very nice box set. They've just never gotten around to doing it. They did [1997's] *A Sides*, and they were going to do a record called *B Sides*. They have a million B-sides, tons of stuff that never got released, demos. There's enough for two or three CDs of just weird shit.

BEN SHEPHERD: I'd feel like a total fucking idiot [if Soundgarden reunited], because I've dissed that stuff for so long. If that situation ever happened, that philosophy of everybody getting to hear Soundgarden again — that philosophy would have to be in on the decision. But right now, I would say no, because I'd be too damn embarrassed. Definitely I think we could rock out, but I would tell them to go find Hiro [laughs]. I think we could fall back right to where we were, actually.

MATT CAMERON: I don't know, I'd feel it out first. It would have to be the right thing.

KIM THAYIL: I don't see it. I'd imagine it could, it's perfectly within the realm of possibilities — everyone's still alive [laughs]. But I don't see it happening.

MATT CAMERON: Ultimately, we took our music real seriously, but we weren't humorless fucks like most people think the whole grunge scene was. Kim and Chris are two of the funniest guys I've ever met in my life.

ROSS HALFIN: Soundgarden were probably my favorite band of the '90s — they were the most original out of all of them. I like them better than Nirvana. They wrote doomy love songs with a heavy edge. Soundgarden albums improve as they go, where, like, Metallica albums *don't*. *Kill 'Em All* is probably their best album . . . then it goes all downhill from there.

CHAPTER 34

"There was definitely a big Seattle backlash": Mudhoney, Tad, Screaming Trees, Melvins, Truly

Many predicted that Mudhoney, Tad, the Screaming Trees, the Melvins, and Truly would all follow Nirvana and Pearl Jam up the ladder of commercial success. But several things prevented this from happening — and resulted in the dissolution of three of these bands.

GRANT ALDEN: Mudhoney didn't take the money early enough to have the shot at being as big as some of the other bands. Maybe what they did wasn't as catchy, as poppy. That seemed to me like a band if you saw them, you were going to be knocked over. But . . . I'm the patron critic of lost causes.

MARK ARM: After recording [1995's] *My Brother the Cow*, we went down to the label to meet before the record came out. By this time, Lenny Waronker was gone — replaced by Danny Goldberg. Mr. Goldberg had been the head of Gold Mountain Management, which managed Nirvana, and his wife, Rosemary Carroll, was the lawyer who represented Courtney Love. We had a song on *My Brother the Cow* called "Into Yer Shtik," which takes pointed jabs at out of control egos, their pathetic behavior, and the sycophants who make it all possible. The examples I used in the song come straight from people in the Nirvana camp, as well as Layne Staley. There's a line in the song that goes, "Why don't you blow your brains out too?" which a lot of people take as being specifically aimed at Courtney. That line wasn't strictly aimed at her — the attack of the song is more scattershot, but she definitely falls into the group of people that it would fit. Anyway, Danny Goldberg was not very happy with that song, and refused to meet with us. It's really weird to go to your record company and have the president refuse to meet you because of a song. Danny Goldberg didn't stay there very long, he was there maybe a year — but the label had definitely shifted.

STEVE TURNER: In '95, we did *My Brother the Cow* — we hooked back up with Jack Endino. We made a record we liked a lot better — there's some really great stuff on it. It was right after the "new punk" hit really big — Green Day and Offspring. So the kids were moving to that. I argue that nothing ever changed — we started out as a punk band and continued. We were touring the States, we did two European tours in '95, and then everything changed there — we couldn't really go over there. Even Germany would say, "Everything is dance clubs now."

MARK ARM: Reprise had hired David Kahne to be head of A&R. He had produced the breakthrough Sugar Ray album, which was a hit that year [1997's *Floored*]. He wasn't hired as head of A&R because he had any experience in A&R, but because he had produced a record by a band that had a hit. [Kahne] wanted to clean house. But the thing was, our contract was for two albums firm, so even if Warner Bros. wanted to drop us after the first record, they theoretically couldn't. And the third record was an option. Reprise barely released [1998's] *Tomorrow Hit Today*. They just put it out, but didn't do any promotion whatsoever. That record feels virtually unreleased. We were on tour and people would come up to us saying they couldn't find it. It's on a major label for Christ's sake, the whole point of being on a major label is that your record is supposed to get everywhere! Steve released the LP version of *Tomorrow Hit Today* on his label, Superelectro. Vinyl was at its lowest point in '98 — *he sold more copies of it than Reprise did.*

STEVE TURNER: That might have been what made Matt realize he was over it. He just wasn't that involved in the process. Then we went on tour, and that tour was pretty shitty. We toured America, and it was smaller shows than we'd played in years. Which isn't a bad thing, necessarily. I think Matt figured he could make more money being a carpenter, having a better time, than slogging it on the road. Mark had been really frustrated by [Matt's disinterest] . . . he wouldn't bring anything to practice.

PIC BY BOOTSY HOLLER — BOOTSYHOLLER.COM

Mark Arm live at KEXP, 2006

We thankfully got dropped from Warner — as we knew we would — right after that record. Then we took a break after touring and Matt saying he was done. We shut down camp and said, "We're not going to say we're done, we're just not going to do *anything*." The one thing we did — to make everyone think that we broke up — was to do a "best of" [laughs]. Slowly started pondering the idea of doing Mudhoney again, when we had to do one song for a compilation. Wayne Kramer was doing a compilation of bands, and he ended up playing bass on a song.

The idea at first was, "Why don't we try to make a record — the three of us — and get some friends, like Guy [Maddison], to help on bass?" The other guy that we were thinking was Steve Dukich who was in Steel Wool — we got him to fill in when we went to Brazil. But he had no interest in being in a full-time band or a part-time band like us. Once that was over, we realized if we were going to do anything, we had to have an actual bass player. And the only other guy on the list was Guy — he was excited about doing it. Since then, he's really helped keep our energy up and excitement. Having a fourth member actively into it again is great. We went back to Sub Pop for the "best of" [2000's *March to Fuzz*], and stayed there.

MARK ARM: We went back [to England] in '98 and played one show in London at the Garage. The kids were *rabid.* We didn't go back again until 2002, and it was crazy. The people were really into it. We've gone back a couple of times, and it's just been great. The shows are getting bigger each time we return. I wonder how long that'll last?

LILLY MILIC: I thought about doing a Mudhoney documentary. All of the guys are really nice — there's no drama there! They all get along, they're all sweet. We were laughing — after I watched the documentary *Dig*, I'm like, "I can't do a documentary; there's no drama!" I always feel like Mudhoney will be that band that kids will be going to and discovering. They'll be like us and the Stooges, like, "Oh my God, here's this band that makes your ears bleed!"

EDDIE VEDDER: Chuck Klosterman said something that was really good, about how I always wished Mudhoney had more success. But if I'm saying that, at the same time, I'm saying I held success in complete disdain and accused it of ruining certain parts of life. So it's right, I did wish that upon Mark! [Laughs.] Even just to see how they would have handled it. I think they weren't really going to try, but they deserved it anyways. Their shows were as exciting as anybody's — as a Fugazi show, just in a different way. I remember Dead Moon and Mudhoney on New Year's Eve in a smaller venue — it was, like, *earth-shattering*. I'll never forget it. You thought if nothing else, they should at least share in the record sales. At least then we *had* record sales.

TAD DOYLE: We spent a good amount of time [on 1995's *Infrared Riding Hood*]. We had a blast doing it, and recorded it in this studio that was buried in the side of a hill, underneath this guy's house in a residential neighborhood. It was bizarre to come in at noon and out at five in the morning, and never see sunlight for five months. As a three-piece, I was really excited about that. I was able to step out, and just be the guy that had the vision for the guitar alone. Just the things that I heard in my head, to actually put it out on tape the way I really wanted it.

KURT DANIELSON: Finally, what we did was return to working with Jack. That's a record that never got enough attention, because the label dropped the band right away. It didn't get much promotion, not a lot of people knew it existed — not even our friends. To this day I don't think it's a well-known record. That marked the last record we did with Josh on drums — we played a little longer with a new drummer, Mike Mongrain. We did a session — some of that came out in single form, and a lot of those songs are yet to be released, and will be released as the last Tad album. Whenever that time comes.

TAD DOYLE: There were a lot of personal things going on with everybody. We all seemed to be going in a different direction with our lives. [Breaking up] seemed like the right thing to do. The last thing I wanted to be was one of those bands that overstayed their welcome. We had a good jaunt, and it was fun as hell. We got to do a lot of things that a lot people dream of, so I'm very blessed. I got a lot a pictures, and a lot of memories. And a lot of good music.

KURT DANIELSON: I hesitate to say [if Tad could reunite]. I wouldn't rule it out — let's put it that way. But there's no plans. I would like to hope that it's possible, but that's just me.

BEN REW: Tad was really like the "chunk chunk, chunk chunk" kind of thing. I saw tons of bands say, "Soundgarden's a big influence, and Faith No More," and it's *Tad riffs* — straight ripped off.

BEN LONDON: I think that Tad could have been bigger. In some ways, they epitomized grunge more than anybody. But it wasn't as pretty as it could have been [laughs].

VAN CONNER: [1996's *Dust*] is probably my favorite record. I'd always wanted to make more than just [a] one-dimensional rock album. And having Benmont Tench [the keyboardist from Tom Petty and the Heartbreakers] play on it made a big difference. Although it was the worst album ever to make in the songwriting end — we wrote hundreds of songs for that record, and we only put ten on. And it took forever to record — we recorded it twice. The band was going through a lot of turmoil with substance abuse. [Lollapalooza '96] was actually a lot of fun . . . *I think* [laughs]. That was crazed. Burning hot summer. It was like being free all of a sudden — we finally finished that damn record that took us like four years. At that point, I just went, *"I'm going to do whatever I want, all the time."* That was my "living to excess tour." Living the stupid "Keith Moon lifestyle." Like Spinal Tap said, "Toured the world and elsewhere" [laughs].

Josh [Homme, touring guitarist, and later leader of Queens of the Stone Age] was a great guy to tour with, and a really great friend. He made everything a lot more fun. We wanted to have a second guitar — he was in school, so we talked him into going on Lollapalooza. The coolest thing was him and Lee playing together — I wish I had some tapes of the shows, because halfway through the tour, they clicked. Started doing crazy solo jams. Josh was definitely a highlight of the last part of the Trees — he gave us some new energy. I wish we got to record an album with him as part of the songwriting team. We started to plan [an album], but it fell apart. We were going to do another tour, and the drug and alcohol thing just got to be too much. People went to institutions and stuff [laughs].

We actually didn't break up until three years later. In 2000, we played the opening of the EMP [Experience Music Project] in Seattle. Lanegan — on the spur of the moment — said, "We quit," to the press. And he told us right before we played. Before that though, the thing that stopped us was a combination of drugs and just beating our head against the wall for so long. And all of us wanting it our own way — we struggled with each other. I don't know what it was — we always held back on committing all the way. We could never commit to being a real commercial rock band. At every turn, when it came time to kiss somebody's ass to get the money from the label, somebody would tell *them* to kiss their ass. Couldn't tame the Screaming Trees beast.

MEGAN JASPER: Not that they're forgotten, but it amazes me that they never saw a level of success that they were so deserving of. They did well, but those guys should have been full on, worldwide *rock stars.*

MARK PICKEREL: I would love for [a reunion] to happen — even if it was on a temporary basis. Like, to rehearse our existing catalog and do a tour — possibly record another record, tour, and go back to our lives after a year — would be amazing. Oh *hell yes* — I would be so thrilled with that.

VAN CONNER: I don't see any reason to. Unless it was like the Cream reunion, when we're all, like, eighty years old. I guess it would have to be, "What's it for?" and "What is it now?" A month ago, I would say, "No way, it would never happen." But I don't know . . . *probably* not [laughs].

DALE CROVER: Once we got off Atlantic, we recorded *Honky*, that came out in '97. We had that record in the can and ready to go before we got dropped. We'd done three records with Atlantic and we were surprised we'd done that many. We put that record out on Amphetamine Reptile — recorded and mixed in six days, just like the good old days. In fact, I didn't even know what to think of that record until a few years ago when I listened back. I really like that one a lot. Then we signed with Ipecac. We had this idea that we wanted to do a trilogy of records — they were into the idea. We recorded [1999's *The Maggot* and *The Bootlicker*, and 2000's *The Crybaby*] at pretty much the same time, but they all sound different. It worked great. Been doing records with those guys ever since — they are into all of our stupid ideas.

TINUVIEL: They've got the best drummer in the world. They have their own vision that they're following. They don't worry about whatever anyone else is doing.

REGAN HAGAR: I think the world of the Melvins, and I respect them for sticking to their guns for two decades.

ROBERT ROTH: Atlantic Records wanted to sign [Truly] in '91, and we met with them. It was the typical guy in the cowboy boots and shiny jacket, and it scared everybody. We just said, "Nah." Around '93, I said, "I want to do this — this is what I've wanted to do since I was a kid. There's no guilt and shame in wanting to do this." I remember Kurt having said that he was going to put in "a good word" to Gary Gersh [who subsequently signed Truly to Capitol]. That was really exciting, because we were in a position at Capitol where we were getting to make all the decisions. We had freedom that we didn't even have at Sub Pop, as far as artistic control.

The one that's my favorite is [1995's] *Fast Stories . . . from Kid Coma*. I really feel that it's *an album,* in the sense that we weren't just putting together a collection of songs. In our heads, it was like a movie we were making. By the time we made that record, they said things like, "Push the envelope — do what you want to do," and "Don't worry about singles, don't worry about hits until the third or fourth record. We want you to be an album band like Pink Floyd or Zeppelin." We're like, *"Are you sure?"*

HIRO YAMAMOTO: Some of the songs and lyrics [on *Fast Stories*] still put a chill down my spine when I hear them. Certain parts of songs just have this feel, and to me, that's the reason why I always played music — to make that kind of sound.

ROBERT ROTH: When Kurt died, the industry changed quite a bit. There was definitely a big Seattle backlash, and the industry wanted one hit wonders. Our record was getting rave reviews, and Everclear's reviews were horrible. But the head of the A&R department was their A&R guy. We started to break out in England. We were getting huge press there, and when we got back from England, they sent a memo to everybody at the company, saying, "All projects except Foo Fighters, Everclear, Beatles, and Radiohead are on hold." EMI was potentially going to be up for sale.

So they basically told us, "We're sorry we didn't have our shit together when your record came out. We were very confused and disorganized. Rather than stick more money into this album, why don't we just start working on a new one?" At that point, KROQ was playing "Blue Flame Ford." I went there and edited a single version — they were ready to break it as a single. The guy at the radio department said, "We have to get permission. Releasing a single costs $100,000." I'm like, "Why does it cost $100,000 if they're already playing it, and we've already edited it?" And he basically said, "*It's payola* — you have to pay this money." So they sent us back to the studio to make our next record, instead of paying up that 100 grand and continuing to promote the record.

HIRO YAMAMOTO: [1997's] *Feeling You Up* CD was way more pop songs, and we made a decision to do that. I remember saying to Robert, "Let's not try to be 'the psychedelic hippie dream band' — let's make something more concise. No more six or ten minute songs." That's our strength — being able to let it loose and let all that stuff fly. There's a lot of soul and emotion in them.

ROBERT ROTH: Our attorney, Rosemary Carroll, and manager were encouraging us to leave the label, and were going to be shopping us around to other labels. Rosemary had a falling out with our manager, so Rosemary didn't shop us around to anybody. Zak Einstein from Thick Records wanted to put out a Truly *something*, and I said, "We have enough songs for an album, if you can just give us a little bit of money to finish up a few, we can put that out."

And that's what we did. But at that point, I felt like we were going to have to get on a bigger label to have any kind of major success. We went out and toured the States on that tour, and Mark had some personal things going on at home, and we had to cancel the tour halfway through. Apparently, waiting at Spaceland were a bunch of label reps waiting to see us. The band broke up at that point. But to our credit, I think we took the Seattle music thing a lot further — adding Mellotron and keyboards. I know for a fact we were an influence on Radiohead, who at the time, had done *The Bends*, and their next record [1997's *OK Computer*] was full of Mellotron, piano, and crazy guitar sounds. At that point, we were a lot hipper band at Capitol than Radiohead was. They had been signed by the previous regime. So I knew we had an influence.

HIRO YAMAMOTO: We just got together about a month ago and started playing again, and it was like we never stopped playing. It was right back. There is some kind of electricity to the way we play — we hear each other really well and have a great way of playing together.

MARK PICKEREL: I think we made great records. In the last year or so, I've been getting fan mail because of those records, and people showing a real interest in those records again.

CHAPTER 35

"Standing up for something they believed in": Pearl Jam

Along with Mudhoney and the Melvins, Pearl Jam was one of the few grunge bands left standing from the mid '90s onward. But it wasn't easy, as they navigated the tricky waters of success — along with a noble battle against Ticketmaster.

ADAM KASPER: Abbruzzese — I never really saw him. Towards the end of [1994's *Vitalogy*], he was out, as far as Eddie was concerned. He overplayed a lot — it didn't fit the band. But he did a great job on those records — he propelled the band in a good way.

JEFF AMENT: We recorded *Vitalogy* at a bunch of different places — Seattle, New Orleans, and Atlanta. If there was a logical point for us to break up, that was probably it. There were a lot of weird power struggles going on in the band — nobody was communicating. I was ready to just build a cabin in the hills and call it a day. Somehow, we got through that whole process. I'm not really sure how or why. Rightly so, I think a lot of it was Ed taking the reins. Up to that point, in a lot of regards, Stone and I made a lot of the decisions. We got the band together, and Stone had always been the primary songwriter, and I'd always been the artist and his collaborator. It was a natural thing, but there were growing pains with it all the way around. We didn't understand what was changing, and I'm sure in some regard, Ed didn't either.

We certainly didn't know how to talk about it. Dave getting fired probably was what saved the band, and Jack [Irons] joining — that gave Ed an ally. And it made a lot of sense from our standpoint — we wanted him in the band in the first place. I think every lineup change the band's had, there's been a lot of logic behind it — including Matt [Cameron], who played on the first demos that we recorded. All the drummer changes have felt pretty natural — even with "the Spinal Tap element."

EDDIE VEDDER: That's funny — for me, [*Vitalogy*] probably felt better. I think I was doing a little more writing music on that one — bringing in more songs as far as complete. I found it to be liberating, enjoyable, and creatively fulfilling [laughs]. No wonder everyone felt contested and wanted to quit. There was more bizarre experimentation going on, and you'd have a couple well put-together songs. I liked the interesting segues — years later, if I got a new record player and I wanted to hear what our records sounded like on it, I would pick one of those bizarro segues. I found it interesting to listen to and some of the favorite stuff we'd done up to that point. For me, it was grasping what it was like to record — finally feeling ahead of the wave a bit, and not stuck in the whitewash of confusion and intimidation of being in a studio. Also seeing the studio and a reel of blank tape as being silence, and that silence being a blank canvas. And painting on it more than just writing chords and a chorus.

JOHN LEIGHTON BEEZER: They were arguably the biggest band in the world for quite a while, and they could have exploited that to a much greater extent. But when they had their battle with Ticketmaster, that was the absolute wrong career move to make — they should have been selling out stadiums, and building the kind of fanbase that was going to buy album after album for decades. They were basically sidelined.

CATHY FAULKNER: The Pearl Jam/Ticketmaster thing I think was very indicative of the philosophy of the band. If they believed in something, they stood up — no matter how hard it was. And they have always not only fought for themselves and the music that they felt passionately for, but they've always stood up for their fans. Not since the Grateful Dead have I seen a band go above and beyond to include their fans every step of the way. They felt the fans were treated poorly with inconsistent practices with Ticketmaster, and felt somebody needed to stand up. I have all the respect for them for standing up for something they believed in.

KRISHA AUGEROT: It was like a worst nightmare for a manager, but at the same time, he was really excited about it. He was into fighting the corporations and trying to win. He wanted to make a statement, and if it cost Pearl Jam, at least they would be paving the way for other bands in the future. It was a big deal for them — I remember Stone and Jeff going to court and testifying.

COLLEEN COMBS: I had to go to a Department of Justice meeting and explain [the situation] to these people. It was exactly as you would imagine it — very straight white men in suits, having no concept. Where you wanted to go, "Were you ever young? Did you ever go see a live show? Do you know what a venue is?" Trying to explain that to a person who has no idea at all. The kind of person that probably thinks, "How do those rock 'n' roll bands make money?"

I'm not sure who to give credit to for this. In my mind, it started out small. These fees vary from city to city. What is that money for? Where does it go? You start looking into it — something that most people don't question. There's a lot of things that happen that unless someone decides to question it, it just goes along. So Kelly noticed, maybe our production manager — they started looking into it. As soon as Kelly questioned it, it got huge. You realized that something was going on, because you couldn't really get an accounting of where the fees went to, or why they varied. It was very suspicious. So once it got questioned, once it seemed like, "That doesn't make any sense. What can we do about it? We'll do *this*." Seemed small, seemed simple. Suddenly, it snowballed, and there was all this stuff to do. It seemed like a small question that turned into a huge thing.

EDDIE VEDDER: It was at a time when we were accomplishing a lot. The fact that we were able to list a concert date and have it sell out within twenty minutes — that was something valuable, which was *ours*. I'm trying to avoid using the word "power" [laughs]. There was power in that, and there was the power to say, "No," and there was the power to say, "We wanted cheaper ticket prices," and there was the power to say, "We wanted the venues or promoters to

Heeere's Eddie!

take a lesser percent of T-shirt money, so we could sell them at a lesser price." We'd say, "We want T-shirt prices to be . . . at the time, they were twenty dollars. When we went to concerts they were ten dollars." They wanted them to be twenty-five dollars, and we wanted them to be eighteen dollars or something. They're saying, "You can sell them for ten dollars or eighteen dollars, that's fine — but we're still taking our bigger cut." And we're saying, "No — if *we're* taking a smaller cut, then *you* have to take a smaller cut." And the same happened with tickets. If we're taking a smaller cut — if you're charging a four dollar service charge on a twenty-two dollar ticket, and our ticket is going to be seventeen, then it can't be four dollars. You have to lessen it the way we're lessening it. And they weren't having it. So we were accomplishing a lot with these kind of issues. And we were convincing people, "Look, there's enough meat on the pig to go around — let's not eat it all at once."

It seemed that when this first came up, it was a no-brainer and no big deal. We were naive to the fact of how much they had to lose if their cut of the pig was to be tampered with. And that it was going to be some ripple effect [that] would cut them off of millions of dollars or something. For us, at one point, we realized if we played two shows, say in Chicago, and we were selling 40,000 tickets in half an hour, and the band got paid a certain amount for playing these two shows, and that if the ticket surcharge was five dollars on every ticket, they didn't have to do any advertising or any anything because there was a high demand. It was just bizarre to think that that ticket company, without getting off their ass, was making more money than the band was, after we showed up and played for 40,000 people. It seemed like there wasn't an equal amount of profit margin per effort. That seemed normal to address.

It entered a whole other thing, where the Justice Department asked us, and there seemed to be a coalition of other artists and their managers that were all coming together. I think what happened was that Ticketmaster then cut deals with a lot of those guys, and they'd get Green Day on their side. It got fairly diabolical, and they spent a lot of money to protect their interests, where I know we spent some money on attorneys. We probably invested forty grand into the fight, which went on for about a year and a half. But they hired PR firms — a number of them — at once. It started to look good for them when they hired, I believe, a law firm that the head of had just stepped down as a Justice Department official. I think that was a move which brought them one step away from victory. After a year and a half — if I remember correctly — it was like a two line release from the Justice Department, which said, "The suit against Ticketmaster has been dropped. No further investigation against Ticketmaster will take place." *Ta da!* That was it — that was "the big ending." And it happened on like a holiday weekend. So we got to learn — up close and personal — what it's like to be stomped on by a huge corporate entity.

COLLEEN COMBS: Because the band wasn't going to play Ticketmaster venues, they essentially had to build from the ground up. We were playing at a lot of places that were fair sites and parks. I don't know if people really understand what a hassle and cost that is. But that was part of who Pearl Jam was — they would forfeit a certain percentage of profits to do what they thought was the right thing to do. Or hand make tickets, so you had a great memento from a show. They would have artists in Seattle design tickets. We were trying to put together a ticketing system of our own. Really way too much for them — or any of us — to try and do.

They were such a conscientious, great bunch of guys — always trying to make a difference and be good to their fans. Always trying to press vinyl, have a fan club single, have a special show — or now, they do all the bootlegging stuff. They were always clear on who they were as people, so they were good at combating against stuff they didn't really want to do — like during the time of not wanting to do videos. Or trying to go up against Ticketmaster. You don't *have* to do any of that as a band. And I know, especially in that time period, there was a lot of stuff in the press — people expected bands to be political, and role models. And set some sort of example. Which I always thought was way too much to ask of a musician — when you think of where these people usually come from, what causes them to want to be in a band and express themselves artistically. And they're supposed to be a political role model? It seems to be expected of Pearl Jam for some reason — I could never really understand why that was.

DONITA SPARKS: We played quite a few Rock for Choice benefits with Pearl Jam. We were both threatened by the Christian Coalition — physically threatened. There were security issues in Pensacola, Florida, when we went down there for the Rock for Choice show. Threats against our lives slipped under our door in a hotel room.

KURT BLOCH: We got a call to play this radio show they were doing. We go to do this, and listen to the radio on the way over there, and it's Eddie Vedder playing records. Get up there, and there's a satellite broadcasting, and he's got a little mobile home with a DJ thing in it. We got to play, and it's like, "Oh yeah, just play my guitar," it's Stone's awesome '50s Les Paul. We played, chatted, hung out with some people, had a few beers, and then had to go back to my session. Never really thought about it again.

A few months later, the Fastbacks were in Nova Scotia playing some music festival, we're on the way back at the airport, Kim goes to get her messages, and it's like, "Eddie Vedder called and left a message — he wanted to know if we wanted to open a few Pearl Jam shows!" We did three shows with them and it was super fun — we got along with those guys really well, and their crew. They were really nice and went out of their way — you hear all the disasters of arena rock bands not letting the other bands have much stage, or only half the PA. And it wasn't like that at all — we had a great time. Soon after, they were like, "Do you want to do our U.S. tour? Do you want to go to

Europe for five weeks?" So '96 was a pretty great year for the Fastbacks and arena rock — I think we [also] did a bunch of shows with the Presidents of the United States of America that year.

EDDIE VEDDER: One of the things that I wish we could have done more of — things like Monkeywrench Radio. Getting the airwaves for the night, and having Fastbacks or Mudhoney play live. And wanting people to see what real Seattle music [was], as opposed to — not to single out anybody, but a perfect example would be a band like Candlebox, which was doing a pseudo-Seattle sound, and they weren't really from there. A lot of that was going on. The waters were getting polluted.

DAVID MEINERT: It really hit me — '94 or '95 — they were so amazing live. They played for like two and a half hours. Ed was ready to collapse onstage.

KRISHA AUGEROT: Some of the shows I saw in the middle time were great — really more of a connection between the music and Eddie. More connection with the audience on an intimate level than before. Which, I think, is another side of Eddie which is huge.

COLLEEN COMBS: A lot of times when people would complain, it was because they must not understand what the process was — to understand what it really took for them to do what they were doing. There's a time where you might be exhausted or tired — touring is both addictive *and* very hard to do — you turn around and you realize that thirty people depend on you for a living. You can't have a cold and take off a month. Suddenly, if you're having a bad day, it affects this six-month schedule that's been laid out. Pearl Jam had that pressure over and over. Those are the times where you saw things happen — whether they had to cancel dates in Europe, making decisions that they didn't want to do festivals for a while, or when Eddie got sick and the San Francisco show [in 1995] had to be cancelled. Do you have any idea what a nightmare it is?

We got terrible hate mail — people just *complaining*. I'd feel so bad for Eddie. That [San Francisco] show, Neil Young did an entire set, so it wasn't like the people who came to the show got nothing, y'know? Plus, they got their money back. I think that was the nail in the coffin of what we were trying to do with Ticketmaster. After that, there had to be a compromise

— we couldn't do it. Which was interesting — if you look at that historically, it showed that a band that was at the top of their popularity *couldn't* successfully stage a tour without Ticketmaster. And yet, the Justice Department said that Ticketmaster didn't have a monopoly. At the same time, you got all this fallout — I guess as a fan, you only get these scraps of information. Plus, you don't know how this industry really works. But the band got a lot of flak for it, and it was really unfair.

EDDIE VEDDER: All the articles were talking about was, "This is the band that took on Ticketmaster, and this is why they were doing this." They weren't even talking about how we played, or how the crowd was. I think egotistically it was like, "*Fuck.* We're getting pulled apart from why we're doing this — which is to play music." And I think also it was a good time to just focus on making records and making good music — maybe we're getting too caught up in these side-things. And then we went on to make the least commercial records of our lives [laughs].

ROBIN TAYLOR: Eddie Vedder is a saint — what he's done for rock and the city in general.

SUSAN SILVER: It's worth noting that there is one that absolutely made it through and has done such incredible work — publicly, privately, and charitably — and that's Eddie. Really taken his celebrity status and done good with it. He's taken his position as an artist and made great art, and forged a lot of amazing relationships within the music business. People from all generations — he made an effort to pay respect to the people that he was inspired by, and reaches out to young musicians *constantly*. He's been a great example of someone who's in that pressure cooker enjoying their life, as well as doing good work in a quiet way. Pearl Jam does an *unbelievable* amount of charity work under the radar. They do so much good for so many organizations locally, nationally, internationally . . . without having to put out a clothing line.

KURT BLOCH: I just can't imagine any band of their stature being any better than them. Have to hand it to their crew too, for putting up with the Fastbacks in 1996 [laughs].

JOHN LEIGHTON BEEZER: It came full circle for me in the late '90s. I

PIC BY BOOTSY HOLLER — BOOTSYHOLLER.COM

Mike McCready and Jeff Ament, September 2004

planned a trip for Hawaii, and I heard that Mudhoney was going to open for Pearl Jam while I was there. I called Mark and said, "Can I hang out with you guys?" And he said, "Sure." So that got me into the whole "Pearl Jam entourage." I spent a couple of days in Hawaii living "the Pearl Jam life." I walked away from that going, "I'm the world's biggest idiot. How could I laugh at them for setting off on the course that led to this?" They're in really expensive, beachfront, luxury hotels. You stand backstage and you look out at the crowd, and there's just a sea of adoring people. It's a hard life to argue with. They got the last laugh. They've been really gracious to me — I made fun of them at the time, and they probably knew it. And in retrospect, the joke's on me.

DAVE DEDERER: It's pretty cool to have done what they've done. And to come out the other end of it, fifteen years later, go back in, and make another great record [2006's *Pearl Jam*]. To have five of you in a band — just to sustain and manage the relationships for that long is a tremendous life accomplishment. The thing I love about Pearl Jam is that they had the balls to say, "Fuck you, we're not doing any press for ten years. We're not doing any videos, we're not doing any interviews, so don't bother us." It's really cool that Pearl Jam said, *"Fuck you."* Where Pearl Jam is right now, it's a nice, culminating statement on that whole period. They've proved you can do it "the Seattle way."

NILS BERNSTEIN: In a sense, [Pearl Jam] have been the *punkest* band of any of them. When Nirvana was changing "Rape Me" to "Waif Me" to get [*In Utero*] in Kmart, Pearl Jam were trying to take on Ticketmaster, or refusing to make videos because they didn't believe in a lot of MTV's policies. Over time, it's interesting how it's ended up like that. To us at the time, two bands could not be farther apart musically than Pearl Jam and Nirvana. But in talking to people that are in their teens or early twenties now, they think of that as the same music. They don't think that one is more credible than the other — they don't even think that they sound very different.

SCOTT VANDERPOOL: Pretty much the entire radio industry has always been pining for that first Pearl Jam album. They always wanted them to redo that. I thought the band kept getting better — especially after they got Matt Cameron. They're *phenomenal* now.

JEFF AMENT: When we made that record with Neil Young [1995's *Mirror Ball*], he said some things about how if you're in a band long enough — or if you're an artist long enough — sometimes you sell a ton of records, and there's a real ebb and flow to the whole thing. And that includes the creative process. Now I can look back at what he said, and it makes a lot of sense. Some records you really feel that you have a voice creatively, and other records you don't. I think the ones that you don't — if I feel like I don't have some kind of voice — it's hard for me to feel a part of it. During those times, all of us have probably felt like, "This really isn't satiating my creativity." Since then, we've all figured we do our things on our own, and do side projects. If you don't have a bunch of songs on this record, there's a chance that you might on the next.

Whenever somebody hasn't been there 100 percent, somebody else has been there to pick them up, and say, "Come on man, it's going to be alright." That's the beauty of being in the band still. And not just the same person doing that, but having *other* people in the band pick you up. Your connections in the band get stronger with different people at different times — it's a funny family that way. But I feel that I've gotten to know everybody in this band on a pretty intimate level. I really care and love everybody, and I would take a bullet for any of them. I think that only comes over ten or fifteen years of looking back and going, "Oh, OK, *now* I understand why that happened."

EDDIE VEDDER: I'm most grateful that we all survived it as people, and we're still on the planet. But to still be a functioning band that's probably closer than ever — I certainly know people like Stone Gossard so much better than I ever did, and that's gone in leaps and bounds — and stumbles — and leaps and bounds. And small steps too. To think back, it's really . . . I don't know, this planet, it's a huge, massive universe. There was this crazy thing, the big bang, and five billion years. A miracle? I don't know. It's beyond the odds that we exist, and beyond the odds that we've evolved into what we are, and who we are as a race and humans on the planet. I just happened to be around when they learned how to plug in guitars and put voices through speakers big enough so an arena full of people could hear you.

MARK ARM: We just toured with Pearl Jam in South America and Mexico. Someone suggested that we play a Green River song from that first EP during Pearl Jam's encore. We thought that "Come on Down" might be good. Jeff found it online, listened to it, and went, "Nah, *that sucks*" [laughs]. So we ended up doing "Kick Out the Jams" and "Rockin' in the Free World" — which are much better songs [laughs].

KURT BLOCH: I remember at one of the Pearl Jam shows we opened, seeing a couple of punkers right in the front row — one with a Ramones T-shirt, and the other with an AC/DC T-shirt. We were like, "Y'know, that makes me feel so happy to see two people at a show like that." Because in 1981, you would not see a Ramones fan and an AC/DC fan co-mingling. It just wouldn't happen. Everything was so segregated here.

LIBBY KNUDSON: I never knew Eddie until he was one of my clients [through Libby's furniture company, Buffalo Girl], and I did his couch. I was working at his house, and he comes walking through the room with both his hands out, and a bandana in his hand. It had been a headband. He goes, "I don't know what to do with this." He was going through storage and putting stuff in boxes. It was at an in-store or something, he met this girl, and she goes, "My boyfriend loved you guys. He died in a motorcycle crash — here's his bandana." And Eddie's like, "What do I do with this? I can never get rid of this — I can't." And I'm like, *"It goes in good memories."*

EDDIE VEDDER: I'm talking to you staring at the ocean — I'm in Hawaii right now, we just finished a tour here. Because of being in the band, I bought a shack here maybe twelve years ago — out in the middle of nowhere. I'll tell you, it's probably the most incredible life I've ever lived — this one. The ocean — and the waves especially — I could just look at them, ride them, and paint them . . . it's almost as important as music. And sometimes maybe more so, because I feel like I get a lot of music from it. Just to be able to be spending time as a surfer on the beach, and know that it was music that got me there — that you didn't have to hurt anybody, tear up the environment, backstab, sell out, or whatever — it's really provided me with a strong sense of well being. I know that I owe it all to the music, and I owe it all to Seattle. And a lot of it to that one day being in the water.

CHAPTER 36

"Finally — new growth": Post-Grunge

Kurt Cobain's death, the breakup of Soundgarden, and the disappearance of Alice in Chains created a void in the Seattle music scene during the mid–late '90s. But as with the death of any musical movement, there were new bands to emerge in their wake, and ultimately, a rebirth of the local scene.

NILS BERNSTEIN: Kurt's death is a handy end of a certain era. But there was [the] Sub Pop '93 to '97 thing, where it's the Spinanes, Sunny Day Real Estate, the Scud Mountain Boys, and Zumpano — it's basically like all the Sub Pop bands weren't from Seattle anymore. They weren't grunge bands. It seemed natural at the time, but it was also a very decisive move in Seattle — away from that all-for-one grunge scene. As different as Tad, Screaming Trees, and the Fluid are from each other — it's coming from the same thing. Whereas Sunny Day Real Estate, Modest Mouse, and the Murder City Devils aren't necessarily all coming out of the same scene, listening to the same records.

MEGAN JASPER: All of a sudden, great stuff started happening again — that wasn't derivative of grunge. When that started happening, everything started to feel like it was coming to life again. It felt like when you're able to see the first trees and plants that come after a forest fire. Finally — new growth.

LILLY MILIC: All the [grunge] bands were getting dropped by their labels. That was a really odd time — from having that excitement of everybody thinking they could continue their lives as musicians. Which no one expected, but once you have it, and then it's taken away, that was really a hard thing to see. Now everybody has regular jobs again.

LARRY REID: If it weren't for Jon, [Sub Pop] probably wouldn't have got the $20 million from Warner Bros.

STEVE MANNING: It may have been closer to '95 — when Sub Pop's deal with Warner Bros. began. Which in retrospect, I think in Jonathan's opinion, was "the dark days," in that all of the bands had gone through their measure of success. Sub Pop tried to play itself as a major label. Signing bands that they thought could sell records, putting singles out to more mainstream radio, spending outrageous sums in marketing and salaries, and signing bands. And then realizing that outrageous sums for Sub Pop were still nothing compared to what real major labels were doing — those records weren't selling, and things quickly became very difficult at the label. It didn't feel like a family.

KEN STRINGFELLOW: You could follow the fortunes of Sub Pop. Beginning in the mid '90s, they went into decline — spending lots of money and not selling any records. That turned around with Hot Hot Heat, the Shins, the Postal Service. But for a long time, they were in serious decline. I loved Sub Pop's aesthetic very much — they put out a wide variety of really amazing records. In the late '90s, one thing that struck me — they actually put out records that were *bad*. The bands in the early '90s, they all got to a point where they couldn't get much bigger. All those bands had done their victory lap at that point. So things couldn't go anywhere but up from there.

JACK ENDINO: [Jonathan Poneman] is the sole remaining founder of Sub Pop now, because Bruce Pavitt bowed out of the label a few years back.

BRUCE PAVITT: It ceased to become interesting for me. The company itself, because of its success, became very large. And because of its size, it became more corporate, more departmentalized. My business partner and I just had different visions of what the company should look and feel like. I personally would have preferred it to stay more of "a laboratory for creative art." I would have been happy keeping budgets low, selling 25–50,000 copies, and keeping things a little more edgy and interesting. I felt that my business partner was a little more interested in creating something that would ultimately compete with the major labels. That style was a little more conservative. Since then, he's gone on to help keep the label focused, and they've had a lot of commercial success.

STEVE MANNING: In 2000 or late '99, with the dot-com explosion happening in the city, rental space became very valuable. We'd always paid our rent; we'd been a steady tenant in that building. When our lease came up, we got a letter from the management in the building, saying our offices would be better suited in a different building. There were never complaints from other tenants in the building, but the way bands looked, the way the employees looked — physically look — was probably a little off-putting to the management and owners of the building. So we moved to Belltown, which is also in Seattle — just a little bit further north, a quieter neighborhood — to a much smaller and manageable space. At the first office, I had my own office — a desk, a couch, a window. We moved into a space that was all quads — I could literally reach to my left and touch my co-worker, and reach to my right and touch my co-worker. We were really struggling. We weren't selling a lot of records, we were redefining who we were. In 2001, 2002, 2003, business turned around for us — we started to sell a lot of records. We were quickly outgrowing the space we were in, and we moved into the space we're in now, which is Fourth and Virginia — four blocks away from the original space. Now we've got a lot of space. [Sub Pop] felt like a family early on, it feels like a family now — we're all on the same page. We all went to New Zealand together for Christmas this year — the whole staff.

CRAIG MONTGOMERY: There was a second wave of bands that got signed out of Seattle. I don't think very much of some of them [laughs]. There was the Presidents [of the United States of America] phenomenon, which was totally out of left field, but that was because they wrote a great song ["Lump"] and had a huge hit. But now it's gone back to the way it was . . . well, it's not all the way back to the way it was before the explosion. But now you don't have the idea that you're going to get signed to a major and make all this money.

CATHY FAULKNER: With every phenomenon, when it gets overused or to a point where you just can't see anything, you can't rerelease the same old hash. I have ultimate respect again for the bands who are into trying something different.

The Presidents of the United States of America backstage at the Showbox, March 2004 (Dave Dederer on the right)

SUSAN SILVER: In 2006, Alice in Chains decided to take a brave step and go do what they love to do — play Alice in Chains songs. It took four years after Layne's death — and nine years after they had last played — to play again. So they did a benefit for CARE [for the Tsunami victims of Southeast Asia] that raised over $100,000. I said, "Why don't you go do something else?" Into the picture come Ann and Nancy Wilson again, who I really want to stress what incredible guidance they've given musicians in this community. In March '06, Heart was doing a VH1 special, *Decades Live* — usually they take classic rock musicians and bring new musicians to play one of each other's songs. And Ann and Nancy asked if Alice would like to play.

So we all went out there — which for me was significant, because it was five days after I had signed settlement agreements with Chris. Went off to the East Coast — [with] the gracious hosting of Ann and Nancy once again. I realized that it was OK. As much mental anguish as we had gone through — "Is it OK to go on without Layne?" — this mantra kept going through my head as I'm watching these guys rehearse, *"Choose to live, choose to live."* They chose to live and what they love to do — play music. That was really inspiring. It gets to the point where they're going to do an Alice song during Heart's set, which is "Rooster." Ann wanted [William DuVall, Alice in Chains' new singer] to sing. And she did, all these years later, what Chris did for Eddie at the Moore Theatre, when Mookie Blaylock played for Alice in Chains, and gave her blessing to William at that moment during the show. I know that it's really personal for me, but it was also a historic moment. That specific acknowledgment towards how things are now, that there's a history not to be forgotten, and there's a history about to be made.

BEN LONDON: Back in the '80s, if people wanted to further their career, they had to leave Seattle. Now, we're in a place where we have booking agents, managers, two very successful independent record labels, lawyers. You don't have to go to L.A. to get your "team" together the way you once did. Some of the people that were very successful had been very generous with their time — helping to educate younger bands about what to do and what not to do. And how to navigate the system. I know the Pearl Jam guys have given a lot of advice to the Death Cab guys, and Pearl Jam has proven to be a great example of how to run a great business.

CONRAD UNO: It seems to have rebounded. There are lots of people trying to do new stuff or fun stuff, without worrying about it being "product."

ROBIN TAYLOR: Ten years later, here we are, hearing Modest Mouse on the radio. Which is still crazy to me.

CHAPTER 37

"Maybe I'm a geezer": How Will Grunge Be Remembered?

The scene's participants weigh in on how grunge music holds up today, and how it will be remembered in years to come.

STEVE MANNING: Hopefully it will be remembered as one of the most important movements in rock history. Clearly, it changed the music industry — especially in this country. People were not looking outside of L.A. for bands, and then all of a sudden, people realized there was great music everywhere. The Seattle music scene opened everybody's eyes up to that. It was a really vibrant, interesting time in what then was a town. Seattle's a *city* now.

BRUCE PAVITT: It's going to be seen as a very liberating period for rock 'n' roll — records like *Superfuzz Bigmuff* are already seen as classics. Obviously, *Nevermind* is referred to as the most important rock record of the '90s. So much of it was about live shows, and I'm hoping that more documentation of the live events will surface, and people will get a better feel about what was going on. Because you really had to be there. There's no way that the records can translate that energy.

JONATHAN PONEMAN: It's exciting and powerful to me — passionate and inspired. I listen to that music and it still sends a chill up and down my spine.

SUSAN SILVER: Pretty hard-pressed to point to anything that has even come close to it. The heaviest, grooviest sound. For me, being pretty young during the '60s movement, but being alive and cognizant enough of what was going on the radio, and thinking it was pretty cool — it captured a time in history. And that's what I'm most proud of with the music that was made in this area during this time — it captured a time in history. It's the soundtrack for a cultural movement.

MIKE INEZ: Kim Thayil put it great — "I'd just take the money and can the fame" [laughs].

WHITING TENNIS: Kim is like "the Buddha." He shows up at these [local] shows. I said, "How's it going, Kim?" And he goes, "Well, *every day's Sunday*." He's looking more and more like Ravi Shankar.

PIC BY ANITA BLACKMAN

Michelle Ahern-Crane and Scotty Crane

KIM THAYIL: I see a lot of these K-tel-like collections — "Best of the '90s" stuff. And noticeably absent from those collections are Soundgarden, Nirvana, Pearl Jam, and Alice in Chains [laughs]. I thought, "That's how it should be!" Seattle will forever have its place, like San Francisco in the late '60s, Liverpool.

RIKI RACHTMAN: Now more than ever, I hear bands and they should just be writing Alice in Chains royalty checks.

SCOTTY CRANE: Maybe I'm a geezer, but I was talking to my wife the other day [about] how "Hand of God" is one of my favorite Soundgarden songs ever. We had a debate about what was the best line Chris Cornell ever wrote. I said it was *"The hand of God has got a ring about the size of Texas,"* and she said it was *"I'm looking California but feeling Minnesota."* I still go back and listen to early Skin Yard and Soundgarden. The recordings that Endino did with Malfunkshun [on 2005's *Original Remixes*] are amazing— that shows how good the band really was. The Malfunkshun CD [1995's *Return to Olympus*] that was later released was a remix of those recordings — it just doesn't hold a candle to Jack's original mixes.

ADAM KASPER: It was kept honest and raw — that's the thing. You still listen to old Neil Young records and Hendrix — the shit still sounds good today because it was not glossed-over and using trendy effects of the moment. We were very much trying to be authentic. I think that's why it holds up.

DUFF McKAGAN: It's timeless music. And that's the great thing about great music — the bands that didn't stand the test of time, you don't remember their fucking name. If you listen to Warrant or Candlebox — which is kind of two same type of bands — it's not going to sound very good right now. And it didn't sound very good *then.* You hear Soundgarden on the radio, and you're just fucking like, "Yes!" To this day, you turn up your radio.

BLAG DAHLIA: Not well I'm afraid. Too little emphasis on songwriting, too much on achieving a flabby, meandering style. And once the L.A. A&R guys got into the picture it was really laughable. Crybaby metal clowns like Candlebox and Alice in Chains emerged — and the most mediocre band of the era, Pearl Jam — proving once again that there really is gold in the middle of the road. I have good memories of the Seattle shit — it was fun. But I think largely, it's a scene that didn't really yield a lot of great records, it didn't really yield a lot of great bands. There's Nirvana, and there's, like, a bunch of other stuff. The Dwarves of course soldiered on, and we're still the best band of all time. Although it will take most folks a few centuries to figure that one out!

JEFF AMENT: I think it holds up pretty good. I'm always pleasantly surprised when I hear something that I haven't heard in a while. Whether it's Screaming Trees, Green River — even any of the super-old stuff, like demos I have laying around of Bundle of Hiss, Malfunkshun. I think there was a pretty wide variety of music happening, and unfortunately, it all got thrown under the term "grunge." But in some ways, I think grunge means a lot more than just *Superfuzz Bigmuff.* When I think of grunge, I think of Mudhoney, Green River, or the Melvins — *that* was grunge. Nirvana and Pearl Jam kind of introduced it to the rest of the world, but I think the sound and the attitude came from those three early bands.

PIC BY CHAD CHANNING

Chad Channing, 2005

CHAD CHANNING: I think [Nirvana's music] stands up pretty well. It definitely shows a testament to how rapidly a change in music can happen. One kind of music is really popular, and then *bam*, some band comes around, and it's completely changed music. It wouldn't surprise me if Nirvana albums were being bought for years to come. I look at some of the greatest bands around — the Rolling Stones, the Beatles, Zeppelin, Black Sabbath — they're bands that will always sell. To me, it's hard to imagine a day where nobody will ever buy another Rolling Stones album. I think it's possible that Nirvana may end up in a similar thing, where people will always be buying Nirvana records for as long as music is music.

TRACY MARANDER: For some reason, I have an easy time listening to Nirvana music without getting sad — but reading stuff makes me sad.

SUSIE TENNANT: You watch *Rock Star*, and they're doing all Nirvana songs. It's going to be interesting watching [my children] grow up and see if that even registers to them.

TRACY MARANDER: It's hard to say [what Kurt would think of contestants on *Rock Star* singing Nirvana songs]. He might not want to admit it so much, but I think he would think it was secretly funny. I know he was a big fan of Weird Al — he secretly thought it was cool when Weird Al did a parody of them ["Smells Like Nirvana"].

JIM BLANCHARD: And what were we left with? Car commercials with music that sounded like Nirvana wrote it.

TOM NIEMEYER: Alice in Chains' *Dirt* is the one that will remain most memorable for me from that period. It is the sound of our happy, naive little scene being choked to death by greed, power, and the worst elements of this fucking business that ever came to be.

SEAN KINNEY: I don't crank [Alice in Chains albums] up too much. And I hadn't in a long time, for obvious reasons — it's painful, sad, and brings up a lot of shit. Until we started jamming again. It had been long enough, we had dealt with things long enough — for me, it was really therapeutic to go back and go through that. But honestly, I hadn't listened to those records in years.

ROBIN TAYLOR: Looking back, I can see just how special and lucky we all were to be a part of it. Good times, good times.

JIM TILLMAN: When you look at the history of the Northwest, you see that there's representations from every decade, and almost every sort of genre that existed at any time. Starting with the Sonics in the '60s, coming right up to the present.

SCOTT VANDERPOOL: There's a lot of bands — the U-Men, Feast — that were hugely influential on bands like Nirvana and Soundgarden. And no one's ever heard of them.

XANA LA FUENTE: I would like [Mother Love Bone] to be remembered [as] more of an influence than they've gotten credit for in Seattle. They did get the biggest record deal of any band in the country that year, and they did bring a lot of attention to the scene. I think Sony and PolyGram could have done a lot better work getting them more exposure on soundtracks. Anytime I play Mother Love Bone for younger people who haven't heard them, they can't figure out why they don't hear it on the radio just as much as Pearl Jam. I'd like them to be remembered, recognized, and listened to more. I don't think the music is outdated — it's not like "Pour Some Sugar on Me." Maybe a couple of songs, but there are some songs that are just timeless. Of course, I want Andrew to be remembered as a great vocalist and a great writer, and not as an addict. We're all addicts in some form or another.

BEN LONDON: We're on the verge of some major grunge nostalgia. You already see stuff — like a band like the Subways — that has that kind of grunge/Nirvana thing going on. I'm sure we're going to see another resurgence of that.

ART CHANTRY: It was one of those weird little strange things that happened, exploded, and then it was gone. Scarier than hell though — don't ever want to fucking see that again.

TAD DOYLE: I recently saw [the Melvins], and they've still got everything they always had. The passion is there, it's not like watching a Rolling Stones concert — propping up the dead and winding them up. Nothing against the Stones or anything.

GRANT ALDEN: I think it became a fashion, and it got tied up in heroin. It got tied up in all kinds of things, which were neither desirable nor had we anticipated them. The music does fine on its own — it wears better than a lot of the '80s punk it grew from. At the same time, I don't know [if] that's the death of rock 'n' roll — if rock 'n' roll has died. Because I don't know that there's been a similar kind of innovation that's been popular since then. The swagger, the certainty, and the fun of it seems gone. It doesn't sing to me anymore.

SEAN KINNEY: The business has changed so much too. There's *three record companies*, and, like, *two people* run all the radio stations [laughs]. It's getting monopolized — they can put anything on there, and it's like, "You're going to listen to this, we're going to play this video, we're going to play this one song. She doesn't sing, but who gives a shit — she's going to lip-sync and we're going to play it so much that the sheep are going to buy it. *Go buy it, sheep.*" And they're gonna — a lot of people do. But because of that, there's always the flip side — where there's an underground movement of stuff that's blowing up. I think because of MySpace and things like that, bands can get noticed on their own. It seems like it's starting to get back that way. And in the situation that our nation is too — and the world — there's a lot to be angry about if you're growing up. I'd be terrified if I was twenty-one and thought I had to be a millionaire, and have to have a Bentley. Feel like a failure at twenty-five because you're not a CEO, and you don't drive a Bentley and drink Cristal . . . with a bunch of hot chicks on a yacht! It's just a bunch of crap.

PIC BY SCOTTY CRANE — SOUNDHOUSERECORDING.NET

Kim Thayil, Gary King, and Jack Endino at Soundhouse Recording Studios, 2008

What baffles me — we're going to be "classic rock." We probably already are in the Midwest. I'm always taking the piss out of it, but shit, that's a great honor in the big scheme of things. That means you did something right — you're not going away. Just makes you feel old, that's all. The Quad cane and the colostomy bag is probably helping too — with the false teeth and the hair plugs! It's been great, and when I'm in Seattle, I see the dudes from Soundgarden, and you run into the Pearl Jam cats. It's surprising that everybody's really unaffected by it. It was never like "the weird competition thing." When we play, Novoselic's there, Kim Thayil comes up and jams with us. Duff's in town — he comes and jams. Still, you end up in a shitty, goddamn crappy-sounding, musty smelling jam room. And you've got a dude from Soundgarden, a dude from Nirvana, a guy from fucking Queensrÿche, and a guy from Guns N' Roses — and me hacking away at some riff. It hasn't changed much, y'know?

EDDIE VEDDER: I think Mudhoney records will always sound like Mudhoney records, which sound like Stooges records, which will last 'til the end of time. And at the same time, it wasn't like "lo-fi," which means they sound as good on record as they do live. Mudhoney was never overproduced, it was like, *perfect.* If I was in any of those other bands, I certainly would not feel like I had anything to apologize for. Being in my band, I feel like there were a couple of things that I would maybe change, but I'm not ashamed [laughs]. And it mostly comes from what I was doing — it's not a reflection on anybody else in our group.

It took me a while to figure out how to really sing — or not push it. I was a horse being let out of the gate — I was pent up. That first record, it's really "throaty" [laughs]. It didn't mean to be, but it became a vocal style that became co-opted by certain bands that I feel made *really* shitty music. And they weren't making those records until we were on, like, our third record — or even fourth. And what's funny — the bridge would sound like Layne, the verse would sound like me, and the chorus would sound like Kurt. Or they'd look like me and sound like Kurt, or look like Kurt and sound like me [laughs]. All this weird amalgamation stuff.

If you listen to surf music, everybody sounded like the Beach Boys. If you get the Rhino *Cowabunga!* box set, there's all these bands you've never heard of. It all sounded like the Beach Boys, with harmonies, guitars, and "Wipe Out" drum sounds. But it was all kind of *good.* For me what was weird — I was just like, "God, I would never listen to this [grunge-copycat] music. This is not good." And it felt like they were co-opting the angst from whatever

I'd been through. I don't know anything about these people, but I didn't feel like they'd lived through it. It wasn't like they were co-opting what we were doing — it was like, *the first record.* Or those two songs. Still, all those musicians that were part of that time, everyone's still either making music, or part of music in some kind of way — even if their bands aren't the same they used to be. It's still there.

BEN SHEPHERD: Now it's all bloated again. It's because the other industries mock it and market it. Calms it down again. And another genre of art will take over when there's no culture to run with it. It all comes down to music that you're sharing. So just fucking go for it.

MIKE INEZ: We need something like that to happen again — to change the landscape of the face of music. *Right now.*

Cast of Characters

Grant Alden: Journalist for *The Rocket*, later founder of *No Depression* magazine

Jeff Ament: Deranged Diction/Green River/Mother Love Bone/Pearl Jam/Temple of the Dog bassist

Dawn Anderson: Journalist, publisher of the zine *Backlash*, ex-wife of Jack Endino

Mark Arm: Green River and Mudhoney singer/guitarist, the Thrown Ups drummer, husband of Emily Rieman

Jon Auer: The Posies singer/guitarist

Krisha Augerot: Former assistant for Kelly Curtis (Pearl Jam's manager)

Yanni "Johnny" Bacolas: Alice 'N Chains (pre–Alice in Chains)/Second Coming/the Crying Spell bassist, roommate of Layne Staley's in the mid–late '90s

Peter Bagge: Illustrator (*Hate* comic series)

Paul Barker: The Blackouts bassist (later member of Ministry)

John Leighton Beezer: The Thrown Ups bassist

Nils Bernstein: Former Sub Pop publicist

John Bigley: U-Men singer

Jim Blanchard: Concert flyer artist

Kurt Bloch: The Fastbacks guitarist

Jennie Boddy: Former Sub Pop publicist
Derrick Bostrom: Meat Puppets drummer
Tim Branom: Gypsy Rose singer
Matt Cameron: Soundgarden/Temple of the Dog/Pearl Jam drummer
Jerry Cantrell: Alice in Chains guitarist
Dylan Carlson: Earth singer/guitarist, friend of Kurt Cobain
Chad Channing: Nirvana drummer
Art Chantry: Concert poster artist, album cover designer
Colleen Combs: Former assistant for Kelly Curtis (Pearl Jam's manager)
Van Conner: Screaming Trees bassist
John Conte: Concert-goer
Blaine Cook: The Fartz/Ten Minute Warning/The Accüsed singer
Michelle Ahern-Crane: Concert-goer, wife of Scotty Crane
Scotty Crane: Concert-goer, owner of Soundhouse Recording Studio, husband of Michelle Ahern-Crane
Dale Crover: Melvins/Nirvana drummer
Blag Dahlia: Dwarves singer
Kurt Danielson: Tad bassist
Terry Date: Producer (Mother Love Bone, Soundgarden)
Dave Dederer: Presidents of the United States of America guitarist
Matt Dentino: The Shemps guitarist
Tad Doyle: Tad singer/guitarist
Pete Droge: Singer/songwriter
Chuck Dukowski: Black Flag bassist
Jack Endino: Producer/engineer (Soundgarden, Nirvana, Green River, Mudhoney, Tad, Fastbacks, L7, Love Battery), Skin Yard singer/guitarist, ex-husband of Dawn Anderson, Kandi Coded guitarist
Jonathan Evison (aka "Munkeyseeker" and "Johnny Seattle"): March of Crimes singer
Bruce Fairweather: Deranged Diction/Green River/Mother Love Bone guitarist, Love Battery bassist
Cathy Faulkner: KISW DJ
Kathy Fennessy: KCMU music director

Steve Fisk: Producer/engineer (Screaming Trees, Beat Happening, Soundgarden, Girl Trouble, The Gits, Nirvana, Jesse Bernstein)
Ed Fotheringham: The Thrown Ups singer, Mudhoney illustrator
Matt Fox: Bitter End singer
Jeff Gilbert: Journalist for *The Rocket* and *Guitar World*, former employee of Sub Pop Records
Regan Hagar: Malfunkshun/Brad/Satchel drummer
Ross Halfin: Photographer
Stuart Hallerman: Soundgarden's soundman, owner of Avast! Recording Studio
Kathleen Hanna: Bikini Kill singer
Chris Hanzsek: Producer (Green River, the Melvins, the Accüsed, *Deep Six* compilation), Reciprocal Recording Studio founder
Tim Hayes: Concert-goer, worked at (and later owned) Fallout Record Store
Tom Hazelmyer: U-Men bassist, Amphetamine Reptile Records founder
Ron Heathman: Supersuckers guitarist
Daniel House: Skin Yard bassist, C/Z Records founder, former employee of Sub Pop Records
Mike Inez: Alice in Chains bassist
Mark Iverson: KCMU DJ
Megan Jasper: Former Sub Pop Records receptionist, current Sub Pop executive vice president
Calvin Johnson: Beat Happening singer/guitarist, K Records founder
Adam Kasper: Producer/engineer (Soundgarden, Nirvana, Pearl Jam)
Joe Keithley: DOA singer/guitarist
David Kincaid: The Allies singer/guitarist
Sean Kinney: Alice in Chains drummer
Curt Kirkwood: Meat Puppets singer/guitarist
Libby Knudson: Concert-goer, photographer
Xana La Fuente: Andy Wood's girlfriend
Ben London: Alcohol Funnycar singer/guitarist
Steve Mack: The Thrown Ups/That Petrol Emotion singer

Steve Manning: Current Sub Pop publicist
Tracy Marander: Photographer (cover of Nirvana's *Bleach*), girlfriend of Kurt Cobain
Nancy Layne McCallum: Mother of Layne Staley
Duff McKagan: The Vains bassist, Fastbacks drummer, Fartz drummer, Ten Minute Warning guitarist, Guns N' Roses bassist
David Meinert: Concert promoter, manager
Lilly Milic: Owner of the record store Top Hat Records, wife of Garrett Shavlik
Craig Montgomery: Nirvana's soundman
Rod Moody: Deranged Diction singer, Swallow singer/guitarist
Slim Moon: Earth guitarist, Witchy Poo singer/guitarist, solo artist, Kill Rock Stars Records co-founder
Kent Morrill: The Wailers pianist/singer, Etiquette Records co-founder
Joe Newton: Gas Huffer drummer
Tom Niemeyer: The Accüsed/Gruntruck guitarist
Kyle Nixon: Solger singer
Buck Ormsby: The Wailers bassist, Etiquette Records co-founder
Bruce Pavitt: Sub Pop Records co-founder
Charles Peterson: Photographer
Mark Pickerel: Screaming Trees/Truly drummer
Rick Pierce: Ze Fabulous Pickle Sisters/TKO guitarist
Jonathan Plum: Engineer (Pearl Jam, Alice in Chains)
Jonathan Poneman: Sub Pop Records co-founder
Tom Price: U-Men guitarist
Chris Pugh: The Young Pioneers/Swallow guitarist
Riki Rachtman: Host of MTV's *Headbanger's Ball*
Dave Rees: Early Malfunkshun bassist
Larry Reid: U-Men manager, show promoter, owner of art galleries/show venues Rosco Louie and Graven Image
Ben Rew: Tad roadie
Bill Rieflin: The Blackouts drummer (later member of Ministry)
Emily Rieman: Concert-goer, wife of Mark Arm

Johnny Rubato (aka John Rogers): Student Nurse/Red Dress drummer, owner of Rubato Records record store, KRAB DJ
Robert Roth: Truly singer/guitarist
Nick Scott: POPDeFECT drummer
Garrett Shavlik: The Fluid drummer, husband of Lilly Milic
Ben Shepherd: March of Crimes guitarist, Soundgarden bassist, Hater guitarist
Joe Shikany: Big Horn/the Allies guitarist
Susan Silver: Soundgarden/Alice in Chains manager, ex-wife of Chris Cornell
Brad Sinsel: Mojo Hand/Ze Fabulous Pickle Sisters/TKO singer
Mark Smith: The Beakers/Three Swimmers singer/guitarist
Shawn Smith: Brad/Satchel singer/pianist
Jim Sorenson: T-shirt designer
Donita Sparks: L7 singer/guitarist
Ken Stringfellow: The Posies singer/guitarist
Robin Taylor: Concert booking agent
Susie Tennant: DGC Records employee
Whiting Tennis: Concert-goer, painter
Kim Thayil: Soundgarden guitarist
Jim Tillman: U-Men/Love Battery bassist
Tinuviel: Kill Rock Stars Records co-founder
Joe Toutonghi: Concert-goer, skater, member of the Bopo Boys and Jak's Team
Steve Turner: The Thrown Ups/Green River/Mudhoney guitarist
Conrad Uno: Egg Studios owner, Pop Llama Records founder, producer/engineer (Mudhoney, Young Fresh Fellows, Bratmobile, Supersuckers, Love Battery, Presidents of the United States of America)
Kurdt Vanderhoof: The Lewd/Metal Church guitarist
Scott Vanderpool: KCMU/KISW DJ, Room Nine/Young Pioneers drummer
Matt Vaughan: Owner of Easy Street Record Store, Gruntruck manager
Eddie Vedder: Pearl Jam/Temple of the Dog singer
Kim Warnick: The Fastbacks singer/bassist

Alice Wheeler: Photographer
Allison Wolfe: Bratmobile singer
Kevin Wood: Malfunkshun guitarist, brother of Andy Wood
Hiro Yamamoto: Soundgarden/Truly bassist